THE KEY

STUDENT STUDY GUIDE

th 12 Advanced Functions

THE KEY student study guide is designed to help students achieve success in school. The content in each study guide is 100% curriculum aligned and serves as an excellent source of material for review and practice. To create this book, teachers, curriculum specialists, and assessment experts have worked closely to develop the instructional pieces that explain each of the key concepts for the course. The practice questions and sample tests have detailed solutions that show problem-solving methods, highlight concepts that are likely to be tested, and point out potential sources of errors. ***THE KEY*** is a complete guide to be used by students throughout the school year for reviewing and understanding course content, and to prepare for assessments.

Rao, Gautam, 1961 –

THE KEY – Math 12 Advanced Functions (2009 Edition) Ontario

1. Math 12 Advanced Funtions– Juvenile Literature. I. Title

Published by
Castle Rock Research Corp.
2340 Manulife Place
10180 – 101 Street
Edmonton, AB T5J 3S4

1 2 3 FP 10 09 08

Publisher
Gautam Rao

Contributors
Jasmin Benavides
Monica Dhamrait
Bob Frizzell
Jane Gannon
Reg Koslowski
Renee Nutt
Ted Whyte

Dedicated to the memory of Dr. V. S. Rao

THE KEY – MATH 12 ADVANCED FUNCTIONS

THE KEY for Principles of Mathematics 11 is a study guide designed to assist students in preparing for quizzes, unit tests, and final exams. Explanations of curriculum outcomes are included to help students better understand the key concepts in each unit. Questions have been grouped by concepts so students may use the resource throughout the year. While addressing the Principles if Math 11 curriculum, the question have been closely modeled on the format of those that students will experience on the Math 12 provincial exam. The following is an overview of the main sections of ***THE KEY***.

I ***KEY Strategies for School Success*** provides students with examples of study and review strategies. Topics include information on learning styles, study schedules, and developing review notes.

II ***Unit Review*** covers all of the course content. Questions are correlated to the specific outcomes being tested. Questions cover an average to above average level of achievement. Detailed solutions for all questions are provided.

III ***KEY Strategies for Success on Exams*** explores topics such as common exam questions formats and strategies for responding, directing words most commonly used, how to begin the exam, and managing test anxiety.

IV ***Practice Examination*** contains two complete sample final exams. The questions here are distinct from those in the previous section. The practice exam is reflective of what students are likely to encounter as a final test. Students are encouraged to use this exam as a practice simulation of the test-taking environment. Fully developed, step-by-step solutions are provided.

THE KEY *Study Guides* are available for English 11, Biology 11, Chemistry 11, Physics 11, and Principles of Mathematics 11. A complete list of ***THE KEY*** *Study Guides* available for Grades 4 to 12 is included at the back of this book.

For information about any of our resources or services, please call Castle Rock Research at 250.868.8384 or visit our web site at http://www.castlerockresearch.com

At Castle Rock Research, we strive to produce a resource that is error-free. If you should find an error, please contact us so that future editions can be corrected.

CONTENTS

KEY Strategies For School Success

Class Focus

KEY STRATEGIES FOR SUCCESS ON TESTS

PRACTICE TESTS

DATA TABLES

KEY Strategies for School Success

KEY FACTORS CONTRIBUTING TO SCHOOL SUCCESS

In addition to learning the contents of your courses, there are some other things that you can do to help you do your best at school. Some of these strategies are listed below.

- **ATTEND SCHOOL REGULARLY** so you do not miss any classes, notes, or important activities that will help you learn.
- **KEEP A POSITIVE ATTITUDE.** Always reflect on what you can already do and what you already know.
- **BE PREPARED TO LEARN.** Have the necessary materials (pencils, pens, notebooks, and other required materials) with you in class.
- **COMPLETE ALL OF YOUR ASSIGNMENTS.** Do your best to finish all of your assignments. Even if you know the material well, practice will reinforce your knowledge. If an assignment or question is difficult for you, work through it as far as you can so your teacher can see exactly where you are having difficulty.
- **SET SMALL GOALS** for yourself when you are learning new material. For example, when learning formulas, do not try to learn everything in one night. Work on only one formula each study session. When you understand one particular formula and have memorized it, move on to another one. Continue this process until you have learned and memorized all of the required formulas.
- **REVIEW YOUR CLASSROOM WORK** regularly at home to be sure you understand the material you learned in class.
- **ASK YOUR TEACHER FOR HELP** when you do not understand something or when you are having difficulty completing your assignments.
- **GET PLENTY OF REST AND EXERCISE.** Concentrating in class is hard work. It is important to be well-rested and have time to relax and socialize with your friends. This helps you to keep a positive attitude about your school work.
- **EAT HEALTHY MEALS.** A balanced diet keeps you healthy and gives you the energy you need for studying at school and at home.

How to Find Your Learning Style

Every student learns differently. The manner in which you learn best is called your learning style. By knowing your learning style, you can increase your success at school. Most students use a combination of learning styles. Do you know what type of learner you are? Read the following descriptions. Which of these common learning styles do you use most often?

- **Linguistic Learner**: You may learn best by saying, hearing, and seeing words. You are probably really good at memorizing things such as dates, places, names, and facts. You may need **to write and then say out loud** the steps in a process, a formula, or the actions that lead up to a significant event.

- **Spatial Learner**: You may learn best by looking at and working with pictures. You are probably really good at puzzles, imagining things, and reading maps and charts. You may need to use strategies like **mind mapping and webbing** to organize your information and study notes.

- **Kinaesthetic Learner**: You may learn best by touching, moving, and figuring things out using manipulative. You are probably really good at physical activities and learning through movement. You may need to **draw your finger over a diagram** to remember it, **"tap out" the steps** needed to solve a problem, or **"feel" yourself writing** or typing a formula.

SCHEDULING STUDY TIME

You should review your class notes regularly to ensure that you have a clear understanding of all the new material you learned. Reviewing your lessons on a regular basis helps you to learn and remember ideas and concepts. It also reduces the quantity of material that you need to study prior to a test. Establishing a study schedule will help you to make the best use of your time.

Regardless of the type of study schedule you use, you may want to consider the following suggestions to maximize your study time and effort:

- Organize your work so that you begin with the most challenging material first.
- Divide the subject's content into small, manageable chunks.
- Alternate regularly between your different subjects and types of study activities in order to maintain your interest and motivation.
- Make a daily list with headings like "Must Do," "Should Do," and "Could Do."
- Begin each study session by quickly reviewing what you studied the day before.
- Maintain your usual routine of eating, sleeping, and exercising to help you concentrate better for extended periods of time.

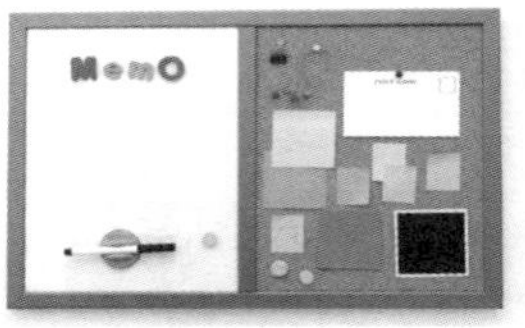

Creating Study Notes

Mind-Mapping or Webbing

- Use the key words, ideas, or concepts from your class notes to create a *mind map* or *mind web*, which is a diagram or visual representation of the given information. A mind map or web is sometimes referred to as a *knowledge map*.
- Write the key word, concept, theory, or formula in the centre of your page.
- Write down related facts, ideas, events, and information and then link them to the central concept.
- The following examples of a Frayer Model illustrate how this technique can be used to study mathematical vocabulary.

Perimeter

Definition – Perimeter is the distance around a polygon	**Characteristics** – Measured in linear units (e.g., metres, centimetres)
Examples – Fence around a yard – Distance around a circle (circumference)	**Non-examples** – Grass covering a yard – Area of rug covering a floor

Cube

Definition A cube is a solid 3-D object that has – 6 square faces, all equal in size – 8 vertices – 12 equal edges	**Visual Presentation** 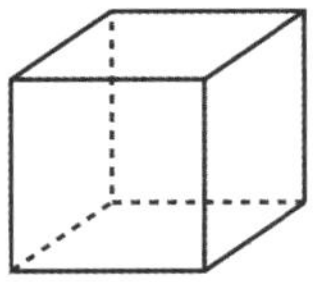
Characteristics or Properties – 6 square faces – 8 vertices – 12 edges – 6 flat faces	**Examples** 

INDEX CARDS

To use index cards while studying, follow these steps:

- Write a key word or question on one side of an index card.
- On the other side, write the definition of the word, answer to the question, or any other important information you want to remember.

What is a prime number?

What is a prime number?

A prime number is a number that has exactly 2 factors. A prime number can be divided evenly only by itself and one. E.g., 2, 3, 5, 7, 17, 19. The number 1 is not a prime number.

SYMBOLS AND STICKY NOTES—IDENTIFYING IMPORTANT INFORMATION

- Use symbols to mark your class notes. For example, an exclamation mark (!) might be used to point out something that must be learned well because it is a very important idea. A question mark (?) may highlight something you are not certain about, and a diamond (◊) or asterisk (*) could mark interesting information you want to remember.
- Use sticky notes to mark a page in a book that contains an important diagram, formula, or explanation.

KEY STRATEGIES FOR REVIEWING

Reviewing textbook material, class notes, and handouts should be an ongoing activity. Spending time reviewing becomes more critical when you are preparing for tests. You may find some of the following review strategies useful when studying during your scheduled study time.

- Before reviewing a unit, note the headings, charts, graphs, and chapter questions.
- Highlight mathematical key concepts, vocabulary, definitions, and formulas.
- Carefully read over each step in a procedure.
- Draw a picture or diagram to help make the concept clearer.

KEY STRATEGIES FOR SUCCESS—A CHECKLIST

Review, review, review: that is a huge part of doing well at school and preparing for tests. Below is a checklist for you to keep track of how many suggested strategies for success you use. Read each question and then put a check mark (✓) in the correct column. Look at the questions for which you have checked the *No* column. Think about how you might try using some of these strategies to help you do your best at school.

***KEY* Strategies for Success**	**Yes**	**No**
Do you attend school regularly?		
Do you know your personal learning style—how you learn best?		
Do you spend 15 to 30 minutes each day reviewing your notes?		
Do you study in a quiet place at home?		
Do you clearly mark the most important ideas in your study notes?		
Do you use sticky notes to mark texts and research books?		
Do you practice answering multiple-choice and written-response questions?		
Do you ask your teacher for help when you need it?		
Do you maintain a healthy diet and sleep routine?		
Do you participate in regular physical activity?		

NOTES

Logarithms and Exponents

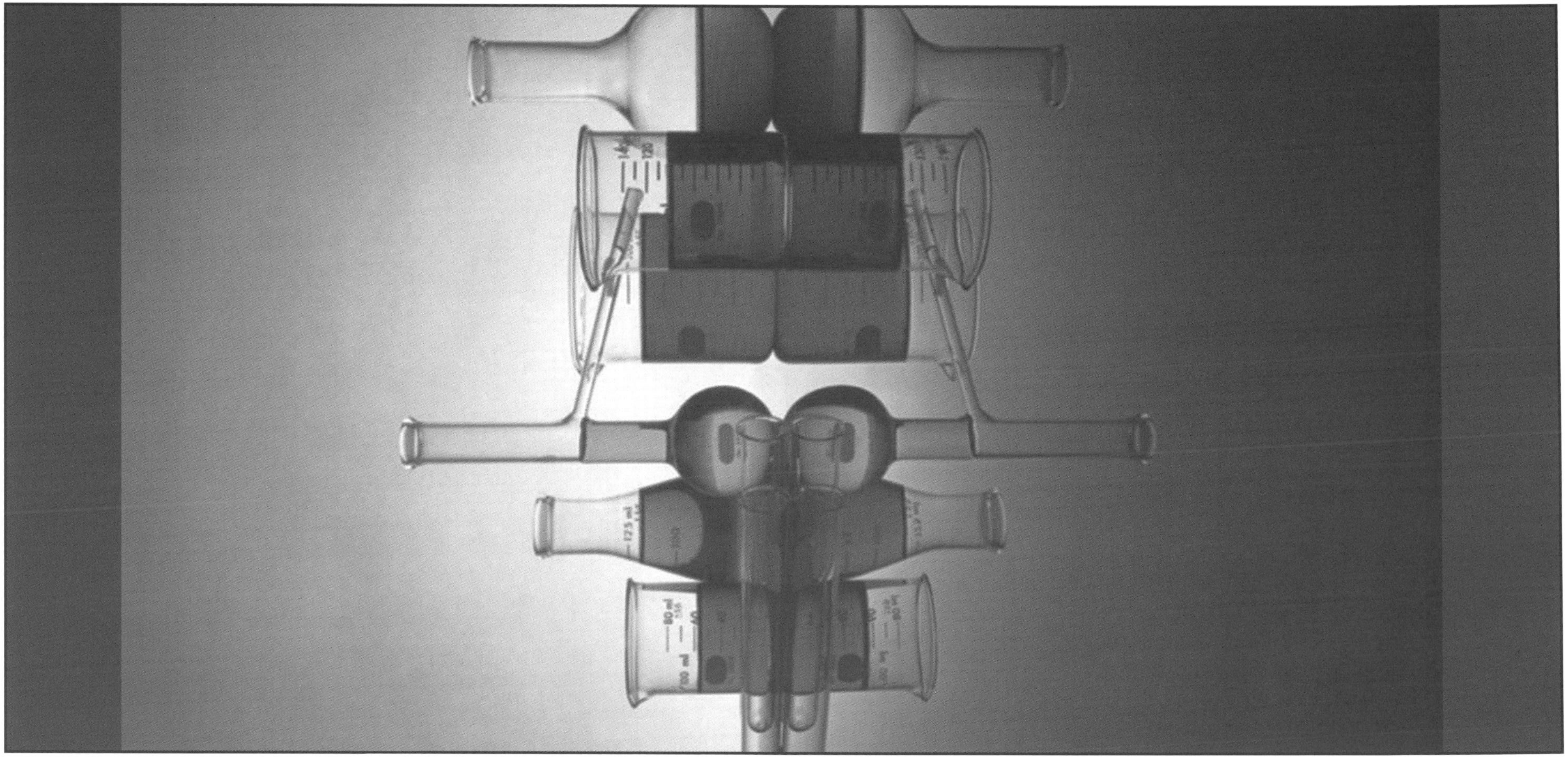

EXPONENTIAL AND LOGARITHMIC FUNCTIONS

Table of Correlations			
	Specific Expectation	**Practice Questions**	**Unit Test Questions**
1.1	*recognize the logarithm of a number to a given base as the exponent to which the base must be raised to get the number, recognize the operation of finding the logarithm to be the inverse operation (i.e., the undoing or reversing) of exponentiation, and evaluate simple logarithmic expressions*	1	1
1.2	*determine, with technology, the approximate logarithm of a number to any base, including base 10*	3	2
1.3	*make connections between related logarithmic and exponential equations, and solve simple exponential equations by rewriting them in logarithmic form*	2	3
1.4	*make connections between the laws of exponents and the laws of logarithms, verify the laws of logarithms with or without technology, and use the laws of logarithms to simplify and evaluate numerical expressions*	4, 5	4, 5
2.1	*determine, through investigation with technology and without technology, key features (i.e., vertical and horizontal asymptotes, domain and range, intercepts, increasing/decreasing behaviour) of the graphs of logarithmic functions of the form* $f(x)=\log_b x, b>0, b\neq 1$, *and make connections between the algebraic and graphical representations of these logarithmic functions*	6, 7	6
2.2	*recognize the relationship between an exponential function and the corresponding logarithmic function to be that of a function and its inverse, deduce that the graph of a logarithmic function is the reflection of the graph of the corresponding exponential function in the line* $y = x$, *and verify the deduction using technology*	8	7
2.3	*determine, through investigation using technology, the roles of the parameters* d *and* c *in functions of the form* $y=\log_{10}(x-d)+c$ *and the roles of the parameters a and k in functions of the form* $y=\text{a}\log_{10}(kx)$ *), and describe these roles in terms of transformations on the graph of* $y=\log_{10}x$. *(i.e., vertical and horizontal translations; reflections in the axes; vertical and horizontal stretches and compressions to and from the x- and* y-*axes)*	9	8
2.4	*pose problems based on real-world applications of exponential and logarithmic functions, and solve these and other such problems by using a given graph or a graph generated with technology from a table of values or from its equation*	10, 11	9, 10
3.1	*recognize equivalent algebraic expressions involving logarithms and exponents, and simplify expressions of these types*	12	11
3.2	*solve exponential equations in one variable by determining a common base and by using logarithms, recognizing that logarithms base 10 are commonly used*	13, 14, NR1, OR1	12, 13, NR1
3.3	*solve simple logarithmic equations in one variable algebraically*	15, 16, NR2	14, 15, NR2, OR1
3.4	*solve problems involving exponential and logarithmic equations algebraically, including problems arising from real-world applications*	17, 18, OR2	16, 17, OR2

EXPONENTIAL AND LOGARITHMIC FUNCTIONS

1.1 *recognize the logarithm of a number to a given base as the exponent to which the base must be raised to get the number, recognize the operation of finding the logarithm to be the inverse operation of exponentiation, and evaluate simple logarithmic expressions.*

1.3 *make connections between related logarithmic and exponential equations and solve simple exponential equations by rewriting them in logarithmic form*

LOGARITHMIC AND EXPONENTIAL EQUATIONS

- An expression of the form *bx* is called a power, where *b* is the base and *x* is the exponent.
- A function of the form $y = b^x$, $b > 0$, $b \neq 1$, is an **exponential function**.
- The inverse of the exponential function (formed by interchanging the variables *x* and *y*) is $x = b^y$. This is a new function, but it is not expressed in the usual way with the equation written in terms of *y*.
- To resolve for *y*, we define a new function, $y = \log_b x$, $b > 0$, $b \neq 1$, called the **logarithmic function**. This function is equivalent to $x = b^y$.
- For every exponential function, there is an equivalent logarithmic function.
- The relationship between $y = \log_b x$, $b > 0$, $b \neq 1$ and its equivalent exponential form $x = b^y$ is fundamental to the understanding of logarithms.
- The function $y = \log_{10} x$ is called the **common** logarithmic function and is often written with the base omitted, that is, as $y = \log x$.
- The function $y = \log_e x$ is called the **natural** logarithmic function and is written as $y = \ln x$.

Example

$y = 2^x$ has the inverse $x = 2^y$, which is equivalent to $y = \log_2 x$.
Likewise, $y = \log_5 x$ is equivalent to $x = 5^y$.
This equivalence between exponentials and logarithms can be extended to numerical expressions.

Example

$6^3 = 216$ is equivalent to $\log_6 216 = 3$ or $\log_6\left(6^3\right) = 3$ and $5^4 = 625$ is equivalent to $\log_5 625 = 4$ or $\log_5\left(5^4\right) = 4$.

From these two examples you can observe that the logarithm of a number in a given base equals the exponent when that number is expressed as a power of that base.

Generally, this is written as $\log_b\left(b^x\right) = x$.

Example

To find the value of $\log_2 32$ solve for *x* so that $2^x = 32$. Since $32 = 2^5$, it follows that $\log_2 32 = 5$.

Likewise, $\log_3 81 = 4$, since $3^4 = 81$.

Example

Determine the value of the following logarithms:

a) $\log_4 64$

b) $\log_2\left(\frac{1}{16}\right)$

c) $\log(-3)$

d) $\log_2 0$

Solution

a) Since $64 = 4^3$, therefore, $\log_4 64 = 3$.

b) Since $\frac{1}{16} = 2^{-4}$, therefore,

$\log_2\left(\frac{1}{16}\right) = -4$.

c) Since the expression does not represent a familiar power, let $\log(-3) = x$, and write the exponential form, which is $10^x = -3$. This is impossible since the base 10 raised to any exponent will not give a negative result.
Therefore, $\log(-3)$ does not exist.

d) Again, let $\log_2 0 = x$, which is equivalent to $2^x = 0$. It is impossible to raise 2 to some exponent and get 0 for an answer, so $\log_2 0$ does not exist.

In all the above situations, when the logarithm does exist, find the value of the logarithm by rewriting a logarithmic equation in the equivalent exponential form.

Exponential equations such as $10^x = 64$ can be solved by rewriting in logarithmic form as $x = \log_{10} 64$, which is usually written as $x = \log 64$.

Example

The solution to the equation $5^x = 20$ is

A. $x = \log_5 20$

B. $x = \log_{20} 5$

C. $x = 5\log 20$

D. $x = 20\log 5$

Solution

A

The equivalent form is $x = \log_5 20$, since x is the exponent (logarithm) for base 5 that gives a result of 20.

Practice Questions

1. The expression $\log_{\frac{1}{a}} 1$, where $a > 1$, is

A. equivalent to $\frac{1}{a}$

B. equivalent to 0

C. equivalent to 1

D. undefined (no solution)

2. The equivalent logarithmic form of $36 = 6^x$ is

A. $x = 6$ **B.** $x = \log_{36} 6$

C. $x = 6\log 36$ **D.** $x = \log_6 36$

1.2 determine with technology, the approximate logarithm of a number to any base, including base 10

The Logarithm of a Number

If you are required to find the approximate value of a logarithm to a specified accuracy (decimal place) by systematic trial, you first need to find the two integers that the logarithm must lie between. The integers can be found by rewriting a logarithmic equation in exponential form.

Example

Determine the two integers that the value of $\log_2 37$ lies between.

Solution

Let $\log_2 37 = x$, which is equivalent to $2^x = 37$. Since $2^5 = 32$ and $2^6 = 64$, the value of $\log_2 37$ must lie between 5 and 6.

For further accuracy, once the two integers are located you observe which integer is likely closest to the required value, and estimate the first decimal place. Check using a calculator, and revise as necessary. Once the first decimal place is determined, the process can be repeated to find the second decimal place, and further if required.

Example

Determine the value of $\log_2 37$ to the nearest hundredth using systematic trial.

Solution

You know that $\log_2 37$ lies between 5 and 6, and since 37 is closer to 32 than 64, the logarithm must be closer to 5. Try 5.2 and 5.3 to start.

$2^{5.2}$ is about 36.758, whereas $2^{5.3}$ is about 39.397. So, 5.2 is closer but is just a bit small, so try 5.21 and maybe 5.22.

$2^{5.21}$ is about 37.014, which is just slightly higher than 37, so there is no need to check 5.22. Expressed to two decimal places the value of $\log_2 37$ is 5.21.

Example

Determine the value of $\log_8 470$ to the nearest hundredth, by using systematic trial.

Solution

You need to find a value of x so that $8^x = 470$. Since $8^2 = 64$, and $8^3 = 512$, our answer lies between 2 and 3 and is closer to 3. Checking values close to 3 you get $8^{2.7} \approx 274.374$, $8^{2.8} \approx 337.794$, and $8^{2.9} \approx 415.873$, so the value lies between 2.9 and 3.

Now try 2.95: $8^{2.95} \approx 461.440$.

Now try 2.96: $8^{2.96} \approx 471.136$.

Thus, to the nearest hundredth, $\log_8 470 = 2.96$.

PRACTICE QUESTION

3. The two integers that the value of $\log_2 100$ lies between are

A. 4 and 5 **B.** 5 and 6

C. 6 and 7 **D.** 7 and 8

1.4 make connections between the laws of exponents and the laws of logarithms, verify the laws of logarithms with or without technology and use the laws of logarithms to simplify and evaluate numerical expressions.

THE LAWS OF EXPONENTS AND LOGARITHMS

The following laws of exponents have been developed in previous courses.

Product of powers: $b^m b^n = b^{m+n}$

Quotient of powers: $b^m \div b^n = b^{m-n}$

Power of a power: $\left(b^m\right)^n = b^{mn}$

Since logarithms are exponents, these laws extend to them as well.

You can determine a relationship between addition of logarithms and multiplication of numbers.

Since $2^2 = 4$ and $2^3 = 8$, rewrite these in logarithmic form as $\log_2 4 = 2$ and $\log_2 8 = 3$. The product of powers law can be applied as $\left(2^2\right)\left(2^3\right) = 2^{2+3} = 2^5 = 32$. The last part of the equation, $2^5 = 32$, is equivalent to $\log_2 32 = 5$. Notice that the exponents are added as $2+3=5$. The equivalent expression to $2+3=5$ with logarithms is $\log_2 4 + \log_2 8 = \log_2 32$, and since $4 \times 8 = 32$ you can see how the two operations of addition of logarithms and multiplication of numbers are connected.

Now, since $\log_2 4 + \log_2 8 = \log_2 (4 \times 8)$, you would expect that $\log_3 9 + \log_3 81 = \log_3 (9 \times 81) = \log_3 729$, which is true. These and other examples can be generalized to give the following product law for logarithms (for all positive real numbers x and y):

$$\log_b x + \log_b y = \log_b (xy)$$

This law states that the sum of the logarithms of two numbers is equal to the logarithm of the product of those two numbers, in any base, $b > 0,\ b \neq 1$.

Similarly, the quotient law of exponents, $b^m \div b^n = b^{m-n}$, suggests the following quotient law for logarithms (for all positive real numbers x and y):

$$\log_b x - \log_b y = \log_b\left(\frac{x}{y}\right)$$

This law states that the difference of the logarithms of two numbers is equal to the logarithm of the quotient of those two numbers, in any base, $b > 0,\ b \neq 1$.

Example

Verify that $\log_2 32 - \log_2 8 = \log_2\left(\frac{32}{8}\right)$

Solution

$\log_2 32 = \log_2\left(2^5\right) = 5$ and

$\log_2 8 = \log_2\left(2^3\right) = 3$, so the left side becomes $5 - 3 = 2$.

For the right side,

$\log_2\left(\frac{32}{8}\right) = \log_2(4) = \log_2\left(2^2\right) = 2$.

Since both sides are equal to 2, we have verified the equation.

The third law of exponents, $\left(b^m\right)^n = b^{mn}$, leads to the following power law for logarithms (for all positive real numbers x).

$$\log_b\left(x^n\right) = n\log_b x$$

This law states that the logarithm of a power is equal to the product of the exponent of that power and the logarithm of the base of that power, for any base b, $b > 0,\ b \neq 1$.

Example

Verify that $\log_3 9^4 = 4\log_3(9)$.

Solution

For the left side,

$\log_3\left(9^4\right) = \log_3\left(\left(3^2\right)^4\right) = \log_3\left(3^8\right) = 8$.

For the right side,

$4\log_3(9) = 4\log_3\left(3^2\right) = 4(2) = 8$.

Since both sides are equal to 8, we have verified the equation.

Examples

Use the laws of logarithms to evaluate the following:

a) $\log_5\left(125^6\right)$

b) $\log_2(512) - \log_2(16)$

c) $\log_5(125 \times 625)$

Solution

a) $\log_5\left(125^6\right)$ $= 6\log_5(125)$	Apply the power law for logarithms
$= 6(3)$	Since $125 = 5^3$, then $\log_5(125) = 3$
$= 18$	
b) $\log_2(512) - \log_2(16)$ $= \log_2\left(\frac{512}{16}\right)$	Apply the quotient law for logarithms
$= \log_2(32)$	Divide
$= 5$	Evaluate (since $32 = 2^5$)
c) $\log_5(125 \times 625)$	Apply the product rule for logarithms
$= \log_5(125) + \log_5(625)$	
$= 3 + 4$	Evaluate (since $125 = 5^3$ and $625 = 5^4$)
$= 7$	Add

A useful relationship that connects logarithmic expressions with different bases is the change of base formula, $\log_b(a) = \frac{\log_c(a)}{\log_c(b)}$.

The proof of this formula is as follows:

Let $\log_b(a) = x$.
Then,

$a = b^x$	Change to exponential form.
$\log_c(a) = \log_c\left(b^x\right)$	Take the logarithm base c of both sides of the equation
$\log_c(a) = x\log_c\left(b^x\right)$	Apply the power law for logarithms
$\frac{\log_c(a)}{\log_c(b)} = x$	Divide both sides of the equation by $\log_c(b)$
$\frac{\log_c(a)}{\log_c(b)} = \log_b(a)$	Substitute, since $\log_b(a) = x$

This formula is often written as $\log_b a = \frac{\log_c a}{\log_c b}$, omitting the parentheses in the expression. Once applied, it allows one to work in base c instead of base b, and in particular if the new base is 10, that is $c = 10$, then this formula becomes $\log_b a = \frac{\log_{10} a}{\log_{10} b}$, more commonly written as $\log_b a = \frac{\log a}{\log b}$.

Since most graphing calculators have only two logarithmic functions, base 10 (log) and base e (ln), you can use the change of base formula to express any logarithm in base 10 or base e and then use the calculator to evaluate the expression.

Example

Determine the value correct to the nearest hundredth of each of the following:

a) $\log_2 1024$

b) $\log_7 28$

Solution

a) $\log_2 1024 = \frac{\log 1024}{\log 2}$	Apply the change of base formula.
$= 10$	Exact answer from the calculator.
b) $\log_7 28 = \frac{\log 28}{\log 7}$	Apply the change of base formula.
≈ 0.71	Approximate answer from the calculator, correct to the nearest hundredth.

Practice Questions

4. The value of $\log_5 35 - \log_5 7 + \log_5 8$ to the nearest hundredth is

A. 1.56

B. 1.60

C. 2.22

D. 2.29

5. When $\log\left(\frac{W^2}{Z\sqrt{Y^3}}\right)$ is written as a sum and difference of logs, the result is

A. $2\log W - \log Z + \frac{3}{2}\log Y$

B. $2\log W - \log Z - \frac{3}{2}\log Y$

C. $2\log W - \log Z + \frac{2}{3}\log Y$

D. $2\log W - \log Z - \frac{2}{3}\log Y$

2.1 *determine, through investigation with technology and without technology, key features of the graphs of logarithmic functions of the form $f(x)=\log_b x$, $b>0$, $b\neq 1$ and make connections between the algebraic and graphical representations of these logarithmic functions.*

THE GRAPHS OF LOGARITHMIC FUNCTIONS

To investigate the graphs of logarithmic functions that are not base 10 or base e logarithms, apply the change of base formula to express the desired function in terms of $y=\log x$ or $y=\ln x$.

Usually base 10 logarithms are used and the required application is $\log_b x=\dfrac{\log x}{\log b}$.

Using a TI-83 calculator, compare the graphs of the functions $f(x)=\log_2 x, g(x)=\log_3 x$, and $h(x)=\log_{10} x$. These functions are all of the type $y=\log_b x$, where $b>1$. Applying the change of base formula, input the following three functions into the Y = editor:
\Y1 = log(*X*)/log(2)
\Y2 = log(*X*)/log(3)
\Y3= log(*X*)

The graphs shown at the right appear in the display when the viewing window is set at:
$X_{min}=-5$ $X_{max}=5$ $X_{scl}=1$ $Y_{min}=-5$
$Y_{max}=5$ $Y_{scl}=1$

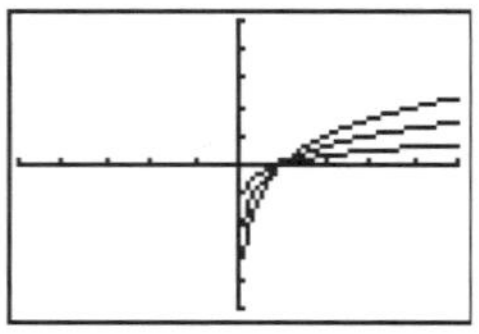

Notice that the graphs do not extend into quadrants 2 and 3. This implies that the domain must be $x>0$ or $x\geq 0$. All three graphs appear to intersect the y-axis, but in fact do not.
The graphing calculator does not always show graphs the way they really should appear.

The graphs shown at the right appear when the viewing window is changed to:
$X_{min}=0$ $X_{max}=2$ $X_{scl}=1$
$Y_{min}=-3$ $Y_{max}=2$ $Y_{scl}=1$

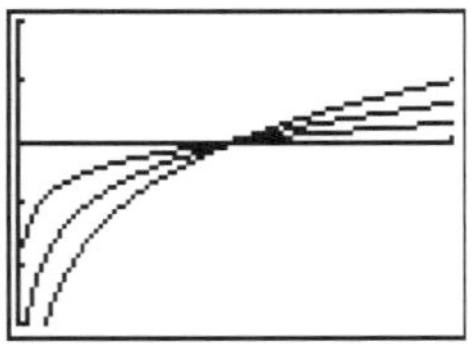

The graph of $h(x)=\log_{10} x$ still appears to intersect the y-axis

The graphs sketched below are not drawn to scale to emphasize the fact that they do not intersect the y-axis.

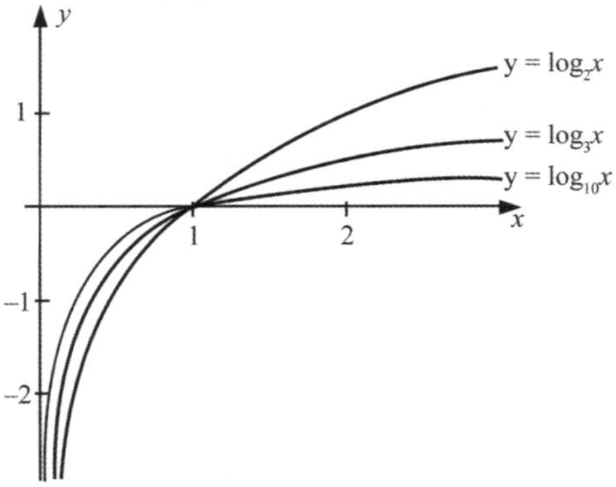

Through this investigation, you can observe the following key features of logarithmic functions and their graphs:

- The y axis is a vertical asymptote, so the domain is $x>0, x\in R$.
- The range is $y\in R$, since the graph extends infinitely upward and downward.
- The x-intercept is 1 for all graphs. This is because $b^0=1$ for all permissible values of b, which is equivalent to $\log_b(1)=0$.
- There is no y-intercept or horizontal asymptote.
- The functions are increasing over the entire domain, since as x increases the corresponding value of y increases and the graph rises. Observe that increasing the value of the base b compresses the graph vertically toward the x-axis.

Graphing $f(x) = \log_{\frac{1}{2}} x$, $g(x) = \log_{\frac{1}{3}} x$ and $h(x) = \log_{\frac{1}{10}} x$, where $0 < b < 1$, on the same axes produces the following three graphs. Note that these graphs are not drawn to scale.

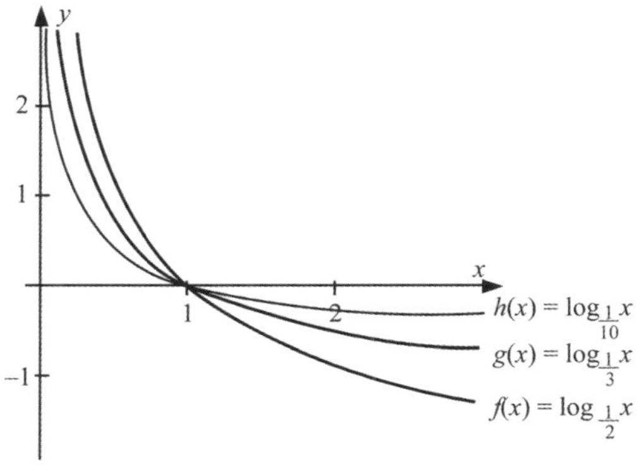

Note that many of the features of the previous graphs (when $b > 1$) apply to these graphs as well. Notice however, that the function values now decrease as the *x*-values increase, and that decreasing the value of *b* compresses the graph toward the *x*-axis.

Key features of the graph of $f(x) = \log_b x$, $b > 0$, $b \neq 1$:

Domain	$x > 0$
Range	$y \in R$
Vertical asymptote	$x = 0$
x-intercept	1
y-intercept	none
Increasing/Decreasing Behavior	decreasing if $0 < b < 1$ increasing if $b > 1$

Example

A student draws the graph of the function $f(x) = \log_5 x$. Then, on the same axes, the student draws the graphs of $g(x) = \log_2 x$ and $h(x) = \log_{\frac{1}{3}} x$.

Describe the similarities and differences of the key features that the student will notice in the three graphs.

Solution

All three graphs have the same domain, $x > 0$, same *x*-intercept, 1, range, $y \in R$, and vertical asymptote, the *y*-axis. If the base is greater than one ($b > 1$) the function increases over the entire domain, so both $f(x) = \log_5 x$ and $g(x) = \log_2 x$ are increasing; however the graph of $f(x) = \log_5 x$ is more compressed toward the *x*-axis than is the graph of $g(x) = \log_2 x$ since it does not increase as rapidly. The function $h(x) = \log_{\frac{1}{3}} x$ decreases as *x* increases because its base is between zero and one $(0 < b < 1)$.

Example

Which of the following changes in the value of the base *b* in the function $f(x) = \log_b x$ will cause the function to change from decreasing to increasing as *x* increases?

A. $b = 2$ to $b = 3$

B. $b = \frac{1}{2}$ to $b = \frac{1}{3}$

C. $b = 2$ to $b = \frac{1}{3}$

D. $b = \frac{1}{2}$ to $b = 3$

Solution

D

The function $f(x) = \log_b x$ is increasing when $b > 1$, and decreasing when $0 < b < 1$, so the change from decreasing to increasing would occur when *b* changes from $\frac{1}{2}$ to 3.

Alternative **D** is correct.

PRACTICE QUESTIONS

Use the following information to answer the next question.

Consider the graphs of the following three functions:

I $f(x) = 6^x$

II $g(x) = \log_6 x$

III $h(x) = 6\log x$

6. Which of the following statements about these graphs is **true**?

A. The graphs of functions **I** and **II** have the same domain.

B. The graphs of functions **I** and **III** have the same y-intercept.

C. The graphs of functions **II** and **III** have the same vertical asymptote.

D. The range for all three graphs is $y \in R$.

7. To the nearest thousandth, the x-intercept of the graph of $f(x) = \log_3(2x) + 4$ is

A. 0.006

B. 0.018

C. 1.008

D. non existent (there is no x-intercept)

2.2 *recognize the relationship between an exponential function and the corresponding logarithmic function to be that of a function and its inverse, deduce that the graph of a logarithmic function is the reflection of the graph of the corresponding exponential function in the line y = x, and verify the deduction using technology*

RELATING LOGARITHMIC AND EXPONENTIAL FUNCTIONS

Recall from Lesson 1 that the inverse of the exponential function $y = b^x$ is the function $x = b^y$ and that the equation $x = b^y$ is equivalent to $y = \log_b x$.

Thus, $y = \log_b x$ is the inverse of the function $y = b^x$.

In a previous math course you likely learned that the line $y = x$ is an axis of symmetry for the graph of every function and its inverse, so to form the graph of the inverse of a function, you can simply reflect the original graph in the line $y = x$.

Example

The partial graph of the function $f(x) = x^2$ is shown. Sketch the graph of the inverse and determine whether or not the inverse is a function.

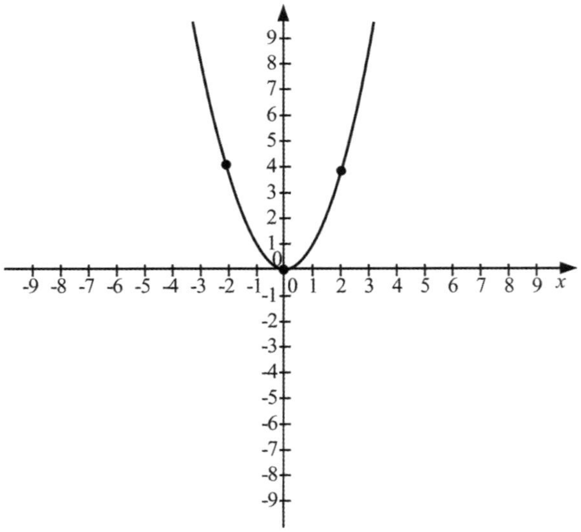

Solution

First, draw in the axis of symmetry $y = x$. You can accurately locate some points on the inverse by interchanging the x- and y-coordinates in the ordered pairs and plotting them. For example, after they are reflected in the line $y = x$, the three points (0, 0), (2, 4), and (–2, 4) are transformed to (0, 0), (4, 2), and (4, –2).

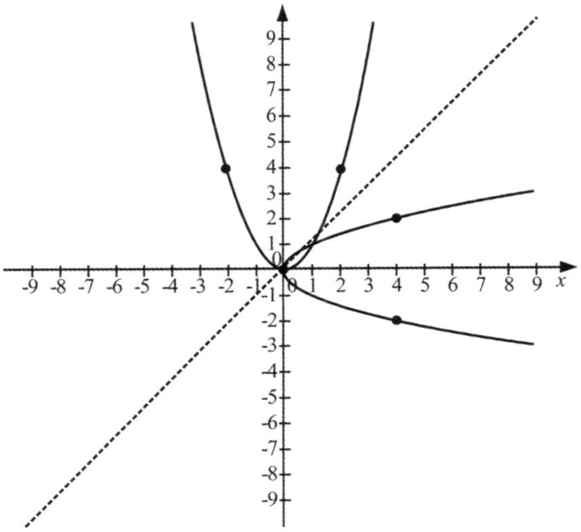

The graph of the original function is a parabola opening upward, while the graph of the inverse is a parabola opening to the right. The inverse is not a function, as can be seen from the two ordered pairs of the inverse (1, 1) and (–1, 1) because these two ordered pairs have different first coordinates but the same second coordinate. As well, it can be observed that the graph does not pass the vertical line test for functions.

The fact that the inverse of $f(x) = x^2$ is not a function can also be explained by analyzing the increasing/decreasing behaviour of $f(x) = x^2$ and its inverse. For $f(x) = x^2$, when $x < 0$ and increasing, $f(x)$ decreases, and when $x > 0$ and increasing, $f(x)$ increases. Since x and y are interchanged to form the inverse, the behaviours of the variables are also interchanged.
This means that in the inverse, when $y < 0$ and increasing, x decreases, and when $y > 0$ and increasing, x increases.

Whenever x changes from increasing to decreasing (or vice versa) as y increases, there will be some overlapping of the x-coordinates and thus the relation is not a function.
Applying this understanding to the original function means that if there is any combination of increasing and decreasing of the function (y-values) as x increases, anywhere on the graph, the inverse will not be a function.
In other words, you can say that a function will have an inverse that is a function if and only if the graph of that function is increasing everywhere on its domain or is decreasing everywhere on its domain.

Now consider an exponential function and its inverse.

Example

The graph of $y = 2^x$ is shown below.

a) Sketch the graph of the inverse.
b) Write the equation of the inverse relation.
c) Using the key features of the graph of $y = 2^x$, explain how you know that the inverse relation is a function.

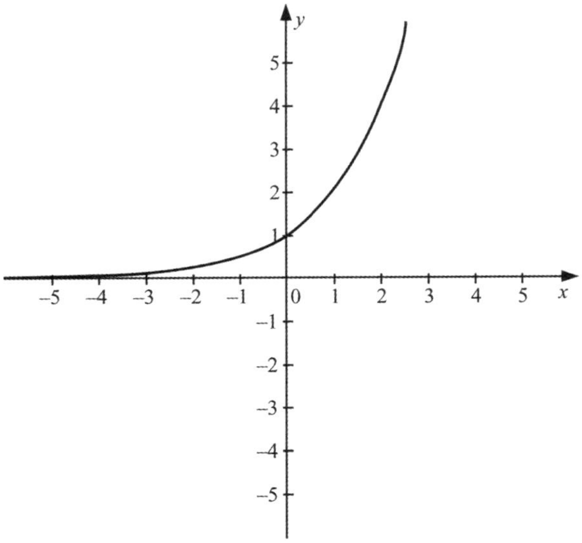

Solution

a) Reflecting the graph in the line $y = x$ gives the graph of the inverse.

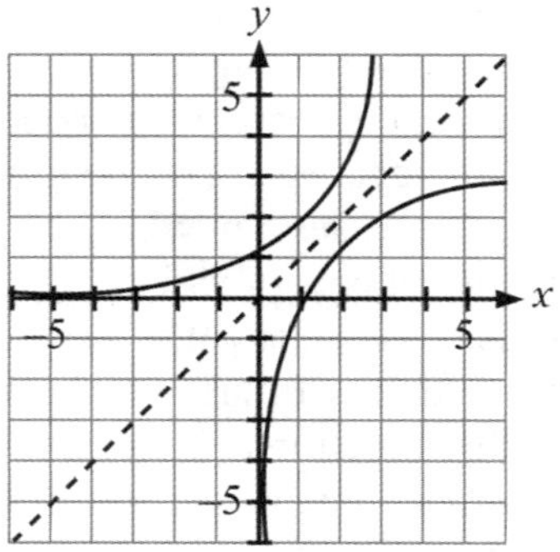

b) The equation of the inverse is $x = 2^y$, which is equivalent to $y = \log_2 x$.

c) Since $y = 2^x$ is increasing over the entire domain, the inverse will be a function. For the graph of $y = 2^x$ every *y*-value is paired with only one *x*-value.
For the graph of the inverse, every *x*-value is paired with only one *y*-value, and therefore the inverse is a function. Observe the characteristic shape of the graph of $y = \log_b x,\ b > 0\ b \neq 1$.

To summarize: every exponential function $y = b^x$ has an inverse function $y = \log_b x$, whose graph is the reflection of the graph of $y = b^x$ in the line $y = x$.

PRACTICE QUESTION

8. The inverse of $f(x) = \log_6(x+2) - 4$ is

A. $g(x) = \dfrac{1}{\log_6(x+2) - 4}$

B. $g(x) = 6^{x+4} - 2$

C. $g(x) = 6^{x+4} + 2$

D. $g(x) = \log_6(x-4)^{-1} + \dfrac{1}{2}$

2.3 determine, through investigation using technology, the roles of the parameters d and c in the functions of the form $y = \log_{10}(x-d) + c$ and the roles of the parameters a and k in the functions of the form $y = a\log_{10}(kx)$, and describe these roles in terms of transformations on the graphs of $y = \log_{10} x$.

TRANSFORMATIONS OF LOGARITHMIC FUNCTIONS

Technology can be used to prove that for all types of functions, the following transformations occur for the corresponding change in the equation of the function.

If the equation $y = f(x)$ is changed to $y = f(x-d)$ by replacing the variable x with $x - d$, then the graph of $f(x)$ will be **translated horizontally** d units left if $d < 0$ and d units right if $d > 0$.

Example

Describe the transformation of $y = \log_{10} x$ that produces the graph of $y = \log_{10}(x+3)$, and sketch the graph. Identify the vertical asymptote and the domain.

Solution

Since $y = \log_{10}(x+3) = \log_{10}(x-(-3))$, parameter $d = -3$. This change causes the graph to be translated horizontally 3 units left. The vertical asymptote is now $x = -3$ and the domain is $x > -3$.

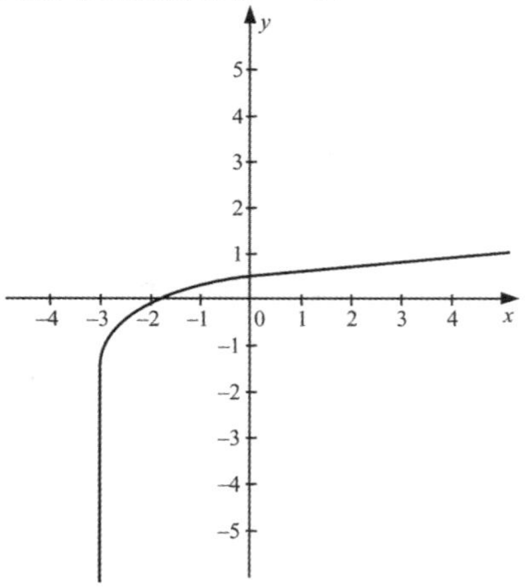

If the equation $y = f(x)$ is changed to $y = f(x) + c$ by adding c to the right side of the equation, then the graph of $f(x)$ will be **translated vertically** c units down if $c < 0$ and c units up if $c > 0$.

Example

Describe the transformation of $y = \log_{10} x$ that produces the graph of $y = \log_{10}(x) + 3$, and sketch the graph. Identify the vertical asymptote and the domain.

Solution

Since 3 is added to $\log_{10} x$, parameter $c = 3$. This change causes the graph to be translated vertically up 3 units. There is no change in the location of the vertical asymptote, $x = 0$, or the domain, $x > 0$.

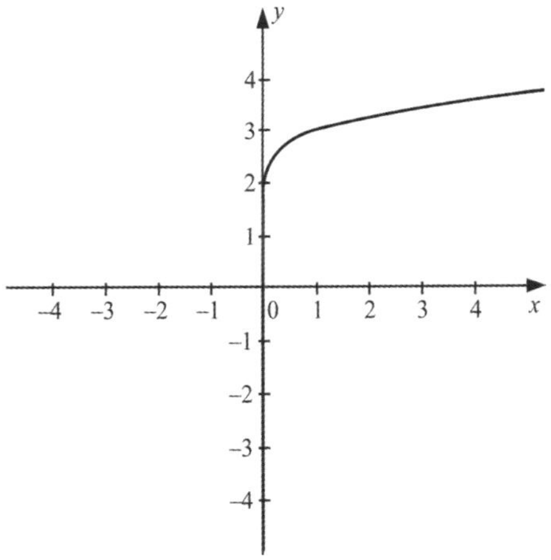

If the equation $y = f(x)$ is changed to $y = af(x)$ by multiplying $f(x)$ on the right side of the equation by a, then the graph of $f(x)$ will be **vertically stretched** from the x-axis if $|a| > 1$ or **vertically compressed** toward the x-axis if $|a| < 1$. The vertical stretch or compression factor is $|a|$. Also if $a < 0$, the graph of $f(x)$ will be reflected in the x-axis.

Example

Describe the transformation of $y = \log_{10} x$ that produces the graph of $y = -2\log_{10}(x)$, and sketch the graph. Identify the vertical asymptote and the domain.

Solution

For the function $y = -2\log_{10}(x)$ parameter $a = -2$. This parameter produces a vertical stretch in the graph by a factor of 2 from the x-axis, as well as a refection of the graph in the x-axis. The transformed graph is sketched below. There is no change in the location of the vertical asymptote, $x = 0$, or the domain $x > 0$.

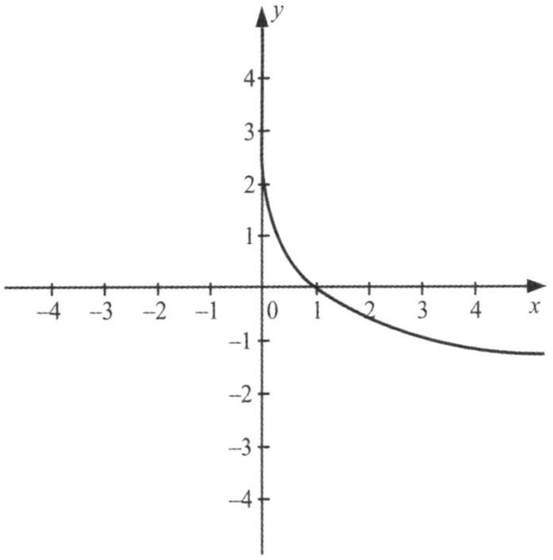

If the equation $y = f(x)$ is changed to $y = f(kx)$ by replacing x with kx, then the graph of $f(x)$ will be **horizontally stretched** from the y-axis if $|k| < 1$ or **horizontally compressed** toward the y-axis if $|k| > 1$. Also if $k < 0$, there will also be a reflection in the y-axis.

Example

Describe the transformation of $y = \log_{10} x$ that produces the graph of $y = \log_{10}(-10x)$, and sketch the graph. Identify the vertical asymptote and the domain.

Solution

For the function $y = \log_{10}(-10x)$, parameter $k = -10$. This parameter produces a horizontal compression of the graph by a factor of $\frac{1}{10}$ to the y-axis, as well as a refection of the graph in the y-axis. The transformed graph is sketched below. There is no change in the location of the vertical asymptote, $x = 0$, but the domain is now $x < 0$.

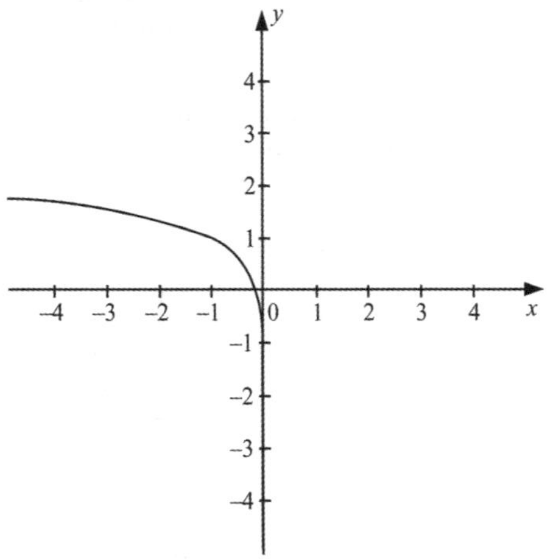

Example

The graph of the function $y = \log_{10}(x)$ is translated horizontally left 4 units and vertically up 3 units. The equation of the transformed function is

A. $y = \log_{10}(x-4)-3$

B. $y = \log_{10}(x+4)-3$

C. $y = \log_{10}(x-4)+3$

D. $y = \log_{10}(x+4)+3$

Solution

D
In order to translate horizontally left 4 units, x must be replaced by $x + 4$, and to vertically translate 3 units up, 3 is added to the right side of the function, so alternative **D** is correct.

Example

The transformations of the graph of the function $y = \log_{10}(x)$ that would produce the graph of $y = 5\log_{10}(-x)$ are a reflection in the

A. y-axis and a vertical stretch away from the x-axis by a factor of 5

B. x-axis and a horizontal stretch away from the y-axis by a factor of 5

C. y-axis and a vertical compression toward the x-axis by a factor of $\frac{1}{5}$

D. x-axis and a horizontal compression toward the y-axis by a factor of $\frac{1}{5}$

Solution

A
Since parameter $a = 5$ and parameter $k = -1$, a vertical stretch by a factor of 5 away from the x-axis, and a reflection in the y-axis are produced.
Thus, alternative **A** is the correct.

Practice Question

9. The graph of the function $y = \log_5 x$ is reflected in the line $y = x$ and then translated 3 units to the left and 6 units down.
The equation that represents the new graph is

A. $y = 5^{x+3} - 6$

B. $x = \log_5 6(y+6) - 3$

C. $y = 5^{x-3} + 6$

D. $y = \dfrac{1}{\log(x-3)} + 6$

2.4 pose problems based on real-world applications of exponential and logarithmic functions and solve these and other such problems by using a given graph or the graph generated with technology from a table of values or from its equation

APPLICATIONS OF EXPONENTIAL AND LOGARITHMIC FUNCTIONS

A quantity is described as experiencing **exponential growth** if it can be modeled by an exponential function of the form $y = ab^x$, where $b > 1$. The growth of bacteria populations is an example of exponential growth. Biologists are concerned with the doubling time of a population, which is the length of time it takes the population to double in size. Because of the doubling effect, the equation for bacterial growth is often written with a base of 2 and expressed in a form such as $A(t) = A_0(2)^{\frac{t}{d}}$, where A_0 is the initial population, d is the doubling time period, and $A(t)$ is the population after t units of time have passed.

Example

a) Write the function that predicts the population for a bacteria culture that has an initial population of 50 and doubles every 4.5 hours.

b) Use technology and the function from part **a)**, to determine, to the nearest tenth, the number of hours it will take this population of bacteria to reach 3 300.

Solution

a) Using $A(t) = A_0(2)^{\frac{t}{d}}$, you can write the function as $A(t) = 50(2)^{\frac{t}{4.5}}$.

b) To solve the second part graph the two functions $y = 50(2)^{\frac{x}{4.5}}$ and $y = 3\,300$ on the same set of axes and determine the x-coordinate of the point of intersection. Using a TI-83 calculator, the functions are entered as $Y_1 = 50(2)^\wedge(x/4.5)$ and $Y_2 = 3\,300$. Appropriate window settings and the graph are shown.

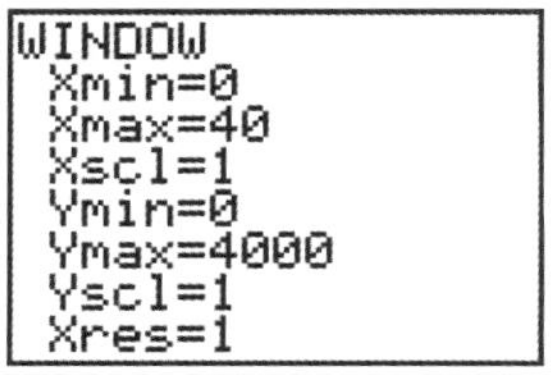

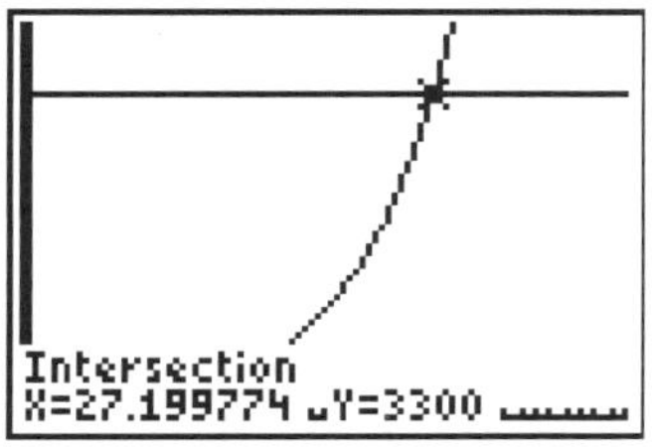

Using [2nd] [CALC] [5:intersect] gives an x-value of approximately 27.2. Thus, it will take approximately 27.2 hours for the population to reach 3 300.

A quantity is described as experiencing **exponential decay** if it can be modeled by an exponential functions of the form $y = ab^x$, where $0 < b < 1$. Radioactive decay is an example of exponential decay. Physicists are concerned with the half-life of an element, which is the length of time it takes the element to decay so that only half of the original element remains. Because of the halving effect, the equation for radioactive decay is often written with a base of $\frac{1}{2}$, and expressed in a form such as $A(t) = A_0\left(\frac{1}{2}\right)^{\frac{t}{h}}$, where A_0 is the initial mass or activity of the element, h is the half-life, and $A(t)$ is the mass or activity after t units of time have passed.

Example

An isotope of Radon has a half-life of 3.82 days. Use a graph to determine the length of time to the nearest day that it takes a sample of 80.0 g to decay to a mass of 9.0 g.

Solution

Using the equation $A(t)=A_0\left(\frac{1}{2}\right)^{\frac{t}{h}}$,

write the function $A(t)=80.0\left(\frac{1}{2}\right)^{\frac{t}{3.82}}$.

Enter this function into a graphing calculator as $Y_1=80.0(0.5)^\wedge(x/3.82)$.

Also graph $Y_2=9$. Using appropriate window settings such as indicated gives the graph shown.

```
WINDOW
 Xmin=0
 Xmax=20
 Xscl=1
 Ymin=0
 Ymax=90
 Yscl=1
 Xres=1
```

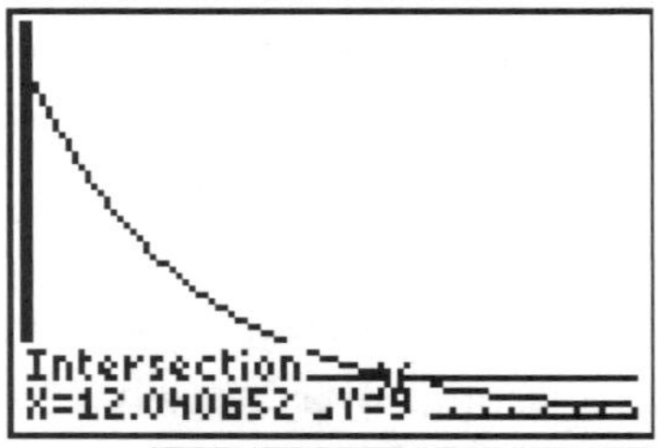

Using [2nd] [CALC] [5:intersect] gives an x-value of approximately 12. Thus, the mass will decay to 9.0 g in approximately 12 days.

The **Richter Scale** is used to compare the intensities of earthquakes. During an earthquake a tremendous amount of energy is transmitted through the earth in waves. The **intensity** is a measure of this energy, and since energy is a relative quantity, the amount of energy transferred by an earthquake is compared to a reference amount. The Richter scale magnitude, *M*, of an earthquake, is defined by the equation

$M=\log_{10}\left(\frac{I}{I_0}\right)$, where I is the intensity of the earthquake, and I_0 is the intensity of the reference earthquake.

Example

Determine the magnitude of the reference earthquake, and an earthquake whose intensity is 1 000 times greater than the reference intensity.

Solution

If you set $I=I_0$ and substitute into the defining equation you get

$M=\log_{10}\left(\frac{I_0}{I_0}\right)=\log_{10}(1)=0$ for the magnitude of the reference earthquake.

For the second earthquake set $I=1000I_0$ and substitute to get

$M=\log_{10}\left(\frac{1000I_0}{I_0}\right)=\log_{10}(1000)=3.$

Because the magnitude is defined in terms of logarithms with a base of 10, every ten-fold increase in the amount of energy transmitted causes an increase of 1 in the magnitude.

Chemists use the pH scale to rate the strength of acids and bases, according to the equation $\text{pH}=-\log C$, where C is the concentration of $[H^+]$ ions in multiples of M = 1 mol/L.

Example

Model the relation $\text{pH}=-\log C$ by graphing the function $y=-\log x$ to find, to the nearest tenth, the pH of an acid whose concentration is 4.00×10^{-5} mol/L.

Solution

Using a graphing calculator with an appropriate window, graph $Y_1=-\log x$ and then determine the y-value when $x=4.00\times10^{-5}$. A possible window and the graph are shown below.

```
WINDOW
 Xmin=0
 Xmax=.01
 Xscl=1
 Ymin=0
 Ymax=10
 Yscl=1
 Xres=1
```

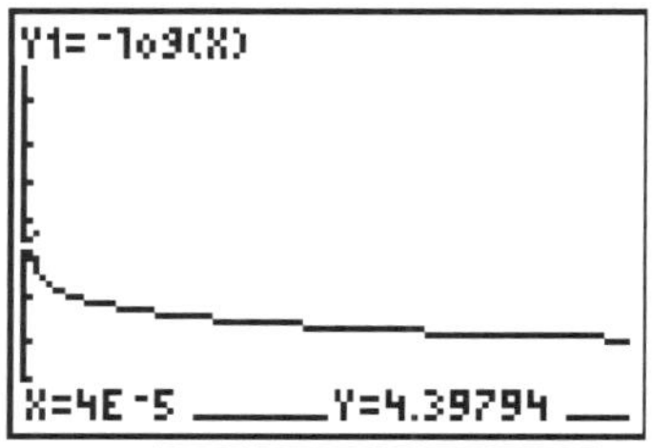

Using [2nd] [CALC] [1:value] 4×10^(−5) gives an x-value of approximately 4.4. Thus, the pH of the acid is approximately 4.4.

PRACTICE QUESTIONS

10. Graph the function for Richter scale magnitude as $M = \log(x)$, where $x = \dfrac{I_e}{I_r}$, with I_e representing the intensity of an earthquake and I_r representing the intensity of the reference earthquake.
Use appropriate window settings.
According to this, the Richter scale magnitude, to the nearest tenth, of an earthquake that is 245 000 times stronger than the reference earthquake is

A. 2.5 **B.** 4.4
C. 5.0 **D.** 5.4

11. The compound interest formula is $A = P(1+i)^n$, where A is the compound amount, P is the principal (initial amount) invested, i is the rate of interest per compounding period, and n is the number of compounding periods. Graph a function of the form $y = 100\left(1+\dfrac{x}{2}\right)^{20}$ and graph $y = 300$ to determine, to the nearest tenth of a percentage, the annual interest rate that will produce a \$300 compound amount from a \$100 initial investment in a period of 10 years. The required rate is

A. 1.1%
B. 5.7%
C. 11.3%
D. 22.6%

3.1 recognize equivalent algebraic expressions involving logarithms and exponents, and simplify expressions of these types

SIMPLIFYING EXPONENTIAL AND LOGARITHMIC EXPRESSIONS

By applying the laws of logarithms and/or using the inverse relationship between logarithms and exponents one is able to simplify complicated expressions and express them in an equivalent form.

Example

Sketch the graphs of $f(x) = \log_2(8x)$ and $g(x) = 3 + \log_2 x$.
Then compare the graphs and explain your findings algebraically.

Solution

Using a TI-83 calculator to graph both $f(x)$ and $g(x)$ on the same axes yields only the one graph shown below.
Use $Y_1 = \log(8x)/\log(2)$ and
$Y_2 = 3 + \log(x)/\log(2)$

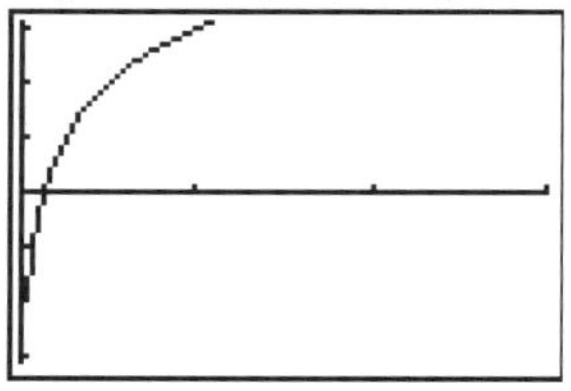

Both graphs have an x-intercept of 0.125 and both pass through the point (1, 3).
It appears from the graphs that the functions are equivalent. The fact that they are equivalent can be verified algebraically by applying the product law for logarithms, $\log_b(mn) = \log_b m + \log_b n$.

$$\begin{aligned} f(x) &= \log_2(8x) \\ &= \log_2(8) + \log_2 x \\ &= \log_2\left(2^3\right) + \log_2 x \\ &= 3\log_2(2) + \log_2 x \\ &= 3 + \log_2 x \\ &= g(x) \end{aligned}$$

This algebraic verification demonstrates that a horizontal compression of the graph of $y = \log_2 x$ by a factor of $\frac{1}{8}$ about the y-axis, which transforms $y = \log_2 x$ into $f(x) = \log_2(8x)$, is equivalent to the transformation of $y = \log_2 x$ into $g(x) = 3 + \log_2 x$, which is a vertical translation, 3 units up, of the graph of $y = \log_2 x$.

Example

Express $3\log_2 x - \frac{1}{2}\log_2 y + 2\log_2 z$ as a single logarithm.

Solution

Apply the power law for logarithms $\log_b(x^n) = n\log_b x$.

$$3\log_2 x - \frac{1}{2}\log_2 y + 2\log_2 z$$

$$= \log_2(x^3) - \log_2\left(y^{\frac{1}{2}}\right) + \log_2(z^2)$$

Apply the quotient law for logarithms $\log_b\left(\frac{x}{y}\right) = \log_b x - \log_b y$.

$$= \log_2\left(\frac{x^3}{y^{\frac{1}{2}}}\right) + \log_2(z^2)$$

Apply the product law for logarithms $\log_b(xy) = \log_b x + \log_b y$.

$$= \log_2\left(\frac{x^3 z^2}{y^{\frac{1}{2}}}\right)$$

PRACTICE QUESTION

12. An expression equivalent to $\log_{\frac{1}{2}}(32x^2)$ is

A. $2\log_{\frac{1}{2}} x + \frac{1}{5}$ **B.** $2\log_{\frac{1}{2}} x - \frac{1}{5}$

C. $2\log_{\frac{1}{2}} x + 5$ **D.** $2\log_{\frac{1}{2}} x - 5$

3.2 *solve exponential equations in one variable by determining a common base and by using logarithms recognizing that logarithms base 10 are commonly used*

SOLVING EXPONENTIAL EQUATIONS

Whenever all the bases in an exponential equation are powers of a common base, solving the equation is straightforward.

Example

Solve $4^x = 8^{x+3}$ by expressing each side as a power of 2.

Solution

$4^x = 8^{x+3}$	
$(2^2)^x = (2^3)^{x+3}$	Substitute $4 = 2^2$ and $8 = 2^3$
$2^{2x} = 2^{3x+9}$	Apply the power of a power law for exponents: $(x^m)^n = x^{mn}$
$\log_2(2^{2x}) = \log_2(2^{3x+9})$	Take the logarithm base 2 of each side
$2x = 3x + 9$	Apply the identity $\log_b(b^x) = x$
$-x = 9$	Subtract $3x$ from each side
$x = -9$	Multiply each side by -1

The procedure shown can be used whenever all the bases are powers of a common base.

You should be able to recognize some of the powers when the bases are small whole numbers such as 2, 3, 4, 5, 6 and 10 because recognizing powers will allow you to rewrite the expressions with a common base.

Example

Solve $25(125)^{x+2} = 625^{1-x}$

Solution

Use base 5 because
$25 = 5^2$, $125 = 5^3$ and $625 = 5^4$.

$5^2\left(5^3\right)^{x+2} = \left(5^4\right)^{1-x}$	Substitute the powers
$5^2\left(5^{3x+6}\right) = 5^{4-4x}$	Apply the power of a power law for exponents: $\left(x^m\right)^n = x^{mn}$
$5^{3x+8} = 5^{4-4x}$	Apply the power of a product law for exponents: $\left(b^m\right)\left(b^n\right) = b^{m+n}$
$\log_5\left(5^{3x+8}\right) = \log_5\left(5^{4-4x}\right)$	Take the logarithm base 5 of each side
$3x + 8 = 4 - 4x$	Apply the identity, $\log_b\left(b^x\right) = x$
$7x = -4$	Subtract 8 from and add $4x$ to each side
$x = -\dfrac{4}{7}$	Divide each side by 7

If the exponential equation cannot be rewritten with powers of the same base then an approximate solution can be obtained by taking the logarithm of each side of the equation in a common base. Base 10 logarithms are commonly used for this purpose.

Example

Solve $3^x = 7$, algebraically, to nearest hundredth.

Solution

Since 3 and 7 are not powers of a common base, start by taking $\log_{10}$ of each side.

$\log\left(3^x\right) = \log 7$	Take the common logarithm of both sides
$x \log 3 = \log 7$	Apply the power law for logarithms: $\log_b\left(x^n\right) = n \log_b x$
$x = \dfrac{\log 7}{\log 3}$	Divide each side by log 3: this is the exact solution.
$x \approx 1.77$	Determine the approximate solution correct to the nearest hundredth by using a calculator

Example

Solve $15\left(5^{x-2}\right)=8^{2x+1}$, algebraically, to nearest hundredth.

Solution

$\log\left[15\left(5^{x-2}\right)\right]$ $=\log\left[8^{2x+1}\right]$	Take the common logarithm of each side
$\log 15+\log\left(5^{x-2}\right)$ $=\log\left(8^{2x+1}\right)$	Apply the product law for logarithms: $\log_b(xy)=$ $\log_b x+\log_b y$
$\log 15+(x-2\log 5)$ $=(2x+1)\log 8$	Apply the power law for logarithms: $\log_b\left(x^n\right)=n\log_b x$
$\log 15+x\log 5-2\log 5$ $=2x\log 8+\log 8$	Apply the distributive property
$\log 15-2\log 5-\log 8$ $=2x\log 8-x\log 5$	Subtract $\log 8$ and $x\log 5$ from each side
$\log 15-2\log 5-\log 8$ $=x[2\log 8-\log 5]$	Factor out the common factor of x on the right side
$\dfrac{\log 15-2\log 5-\log 8}{2\log 8-\log 5}$ $=x$	Divide each side by 2log8 –log5
$-1.02\approx x$	Determine the solution, correct to the nearest hundredth, using a calculator

Note: The expression $\dfrac{\log 15-2\log 5-\log 8}{2\log 8-\log 5}$ must be entered into the calculator with brackets around both the numerator and the denominator. It can be shown using the laws of logarithms that this expression is equivalent to $\dfrac{\log\left(\dfrac{15}{25\times 8}\right)}{\log\left(\dfrac{64}{5}\right)}$ which is much simpler to evaluate.

Example

Solve $300(1.05)^n=600$, algebraically, to nearest hundredth.

Solution

In order to get a simpler, exponential equation start by dividing each side by 300 to get $(1.05)^n=2$

$\log(1.05)^n=\log 2$	Take the common logarithm of each side
$n\log 1.05=\log 2$	Apply the power law for logarithms: $\log_b\left(x^n\right)=n\log_b(x)$
$n=\dfrac{\log 2}{\log 1.05}$	Divide each side by $\log 1.05$
$n\approx 14.21$	Approximate solution from a calculator

If an exponential equation involves the operations of addition and subtraction of terms, it cannot be solved using logarithms immediately. Sometimes it can be rewritten by factoring to create multiplication of terms that results in an equation with powers that have the same base. The following example illustrates this procedure.

Example

Solve $2^{x+2} - 2^x = 12$

Solution

Since the left hand side of the equation involves subtraction factor out a common factor which is 2^x since $2^{x+2} = (2^x)(2^2)$.

$2^{x+2} - 2^x = 12$	
$(2^x)(2^2) - 2^x = 12$	Rewrite 2^{x+2} as $(2^x)(2^2)$
$2^x(2^2 - 1) = 12$	Factor out the common factor of 2^x
$2^x(3) = 12$	Apply $2^2 - 1 = 3$
$2^x = 4$	Divide both sides by 3
$x = 2$	Evaluate ($2^2 = 4$)

PRACTICE QUESTIONS

13. The solution to $16^{2x+5} = 2^{4x}$ is

A. $x = \frac{5}{3}$ **B.** $x = \frac{5}{2}$

C. $x = -5$ **D.** $x = 5$

14. If $3^{5x-2} = 4$ then $x =$

A. $\frac{5\log 4}{\log 3} + 0.4$

B. $\frac{0.2\log 4}{\log 3} + 0.4$

C. $\frac{0.2\log 3}{\log 4} + 0.4$

D. $\frac{5\log 3}{\log 4} + 0.4$

Numerical Response

NR1. The solution to $(4^{2x-3})(16) = 64^{x-5}$ is $x =$ __________.

Open Response

OR1. Solve $3^{x+3} + 3^{x+4} = 56$, correct to the nearest hundredth.

3.3 solve simple logarithmic equations in one variable algebraically

SOLVING LOGARITHMIC EQUATIONS

The steps for solving logarithmic equations are:

1. Write all expressions that involve logarithms on one side of the equation.
2. If necessary, use the laws of logarithms to combine logarithmic expressions into one logarithmic expression.
3. Rewrite the logarithmic equation as an exponential equation by using the definition, $\log_B A = x \rightarrow B^x = A$.
4. Solve the exponential equation.
5. Check for extraneous roots by substituting solution values into the original equation to verify that the left-hand side = the right-hand side (LHS = RHS). Eliminate any solution values that result in the log of a number that is less than or equal to 0.
6. State the solution.

Example

Solve: $\log_3(5x+6)=2$

Solution

Since the left side is a single logarithm and the right side is a single number, the logarithmic equation can be written as an exponential equation (Step 3 in the procedure outlined above).

$3^2 = 5x+6$

$9 = 5x+6$

$3 = 5x$

$\frac{3}{5} = x$

Check: Substitute $x=\frac{3}{5}$ into the original equation.

$\text{LHS} = \log_3\left(5\left(\frac{3}{5}\right)+6\right)$

$\log_3(3+6) = \log_3(9) = 2 = \text{RHS}$

Since LHS = RHS, the solution $x=\frac{3}{5}$ is verified.

Example

Solve: $\log_2(x+5)+\log_2(x-1)=4$

Solution

First, apply the product law for logarithms on the left side of the equation (Step 2 from above)

$\log_2[(x+5)(x-1)] = 4$	$\log_b(x)+\log_b(y) = \log_b(xy)$
$\log 2\left[x^2+4x-5\right]=4$	Multiply $(x+5)(x-1)$
$2^4 = x^2+4x-5$	Rewrite in exponential form
$16 = x^2+4x-5$	
$0 = x^2+4x-21$	Subtract 16 from both sides
$0=(x+7)(x-3)$	Factor
$x+7=0$ or $x-3=0$	Set each factor equal to zero

$x=-7$ or $x=3$

Check: $x=-7$ by substituting -7 into the left-hand side of the equation.

LHS: $\log_2(-7+5)+\log_2(-7-1)$

$= \log_2(-2)+\log_2(-8)$

Since you can only take the logarithm of a positive number, $x=-7$ is extraneous.

Check: $x=3$ by substituting 3 into the left-hand side of the equation.

LHS: $\log_2(3+5)+\log_2(3-1)$

$=\log_2(8)+\log_2(2)$

$=3+1$

$=4=$ RHS

Since LHS = RHS, the solution $x=3$ is verified.

Practice Questions

15. When $\log_2(x-3)+\log_2(x-1)=3$ is solved, the sum of all the solution values is

A. less than 1

B. between 1 and 4 inclusive

C. exactly 5

D. more than 5

Use the following information to answer the next question.

Rebecca carried out the following steps in solving $\log_3(3x-7)=3$.

Step 1: $3x-7=3^3$
Step 2: $3x-7=9$
Step 3: $3x=16$
Step 4: $x=\frac{16}{3}$

16. Which of the following statements regarding Rebecca's procedure is **true**?

A. Rebecca made her first mistake in Step 1.

B. Rebecca made her first mistake in Step 2.

C. Rebecca made her first mistake in Step 3.

D. Rebecca did not make a mistake in solving the equation.

Numerical Response

NR2. The solution to $\log_{0.4}(3x-5)=2$ is $x=$ ____________.

3.4 solve problems involving exponential and logarithmic equations algebraically, including problems arising from real-world applications

Exponential and Logarithmic Equation Problems

Example

The pH or acidity of a liquid is measured in pH, where pH is given by the equation $\text{pH}=-\log C$, with C being the concentration of $[H^+]$ ions in multiples of $M = 1$ mol/L. Suppose you are given a solution of hydrochloric acid with a pH of 1.7 and asked to increase the pH of the solution by 1.4. Determine by how much you must dilute the solution. Does your answer differ if you start with a pH of 2.2?

Solution

Let C_1 be the concentration of acid with a pH of 1.7, and C_2 be the concentration of acid with a pH of $1.4+1.7=3.1$ (since the pH is to be increased by 1.4).
Write the following two equations:
$1.7=-\log C_1$ and $3.1=-\log C_2$
Multiplying both sides of the equations by -1 gives $-1.7=\log C_1$ and $-3.1=\log C_2$
In exponential form these equations are
$C_1=10^{-1.7}$ and $C_2=10^{-3.1}$
The ratio of the concentrations of the two acids is

$\frac{C_2}{C_1}=\frac{10^{-3.1}}{10^{-1.7}}=10^{-3.1-(-1.7)}=10^{-1.4}$, which is approximately 0.0398.
The concentration of [H+] ions must be diluted to $\frac{1}{10^{1.4}}$ or approximately 0.0398 of the original concentration.
The concentration of [H+] ions changes from $10^{-1.7}\approx 0.01995$ mol/L to $10^{-3.1}\approx 7.94\times10^{-4}$ mol/L.
If the original pH is x, and you increase the pH by 1.4, the new pH is $x+1.4$.

Therefore $\frac{C_2}{C_1}=\frac{10^{-(x+1.4)}}{10^{-x}}=10^{-1.4}$.

Thus, it does not matter what the original pH is, if you want to increase the pH by 1.4, then you need to change the concentration of [H+] ions by a factor of $10^{-1.4}$.
Because pH is a negative log base 10 scale, every increase of 1 unit in the pH decreases the concentration of [H+] ions by a factor of $\frac{1}{10}$.

Example

A sample of Radium-224 decays from 450 g to 146 g over a 60-day period. Determine the half-life of Radium-224 to the nearest day.

Solution

You can use the exponential function $A(t)=A_0\left(\frac{1}{2}\right)^{\frac{t}{h}}$, where A_0 is the initial amount, $A(t)$ is the amount remaining after t days have passed, and h is the half-life.
Substituting the values from the question gives the exponential equation

$$146=450\left(\frac{1}{2}\right)^{\frac{60}{h}}.$$

To solve, first divide both sides of the equation by 450, and then take the log base 10 of both sides.

$$\frac{146}{450}=\left(\frac{1}{2}\right)^{\frac{60}{h}}$$

$$\log\left(\frac{146}{450}\right)=\log\left(\frac{1}{2}\right)^{\frac{60}{h}}$$

$$\log\left(\frac{146}{450}\right)=\frac{60}{h}\log\left(\frac{1}{2}\right)$$

Apply the logarithm of a power law, $\log_b\left(x^n\right)=n\log_b(x)$.

$$h=\frac{60\log\left(\frac{1}{2}\right)}{\log\left(\frac{146}{450}\right)}$$

Multiply both sides by h and divide by $\log\left(\frac{146}{459}\right)$.

$h=37$ days, to the nearest day.

Evaluate using a calculator

PRACTICE QUESTIONS

17. An earthquake along the San Andreas Fault in California was measured at magnitude 7.0 on the Richter scale. This was followed by an aftershock that measured 5.3. How many times more intense, to the nearest tenth, was the earthquake than its aftershock?

A. 1.7
B. 2.0
C. 20.9
D. 50.1

18. How many times more acidic is lemonade, which has a pH of 3.0, than ammonia, which has a pH of 11.8?

A. 3.93
B. $10^{3.93}$
C. $10^{8.8}$
D. 8 511

Open Response

OR2. A bacteria culture triples every 5 minutes. At 4:27 P.M. the population is 50 000. Determine what the population was 27 minutes earlier, at 4:00 P.M.

ANSWERS AND SOLUTIONS—EXPONENTIAL AND LOGARITHMIC FUNCTIONS

1. B	**7. A**	**13. C**	**NR2. 1.72**
2 D	**8. B**	**14. B**	**17. D**
3. C	**9. A**	**NR1. 14**	**18. C**
4. D	**10. D**	**OR1. See Solution**	**OR2. See Solution**
5. B	**11. C**	**15. C**	
6. C	**12. D**	**16. B**	

1. **B**

Let $\log_{\frac{1}{a}} 1 = x.$

In exponential form, this equation is

$\left(\frac{1}{a}\right)^x = 1.$

Since $a > 1$, $\frac{1}{a}$ is a positive number.

The exponent on a positive base that gives a result of 1 is 0 because by definition $b^0 = 1$, $b > 0$.

Therefore, $x = 0$.

2. **D**

The equivalent logarithmic form of $36 = 6^x$ is $x = \log_6 36$ since x is the exponent (logarithm) for base 6 that gives a result of 36. The numerical result is 2, but this is not given as an alternative.

3. **C**

Since $2^6 = 64$ and $2^7 = 128$, it is clear that $\log_2 100$ is between 6 and 7.

4. **D**

Applying the product and quotient laws for logarithms to the expression gives:

$$\begin{aligned}\log_5 35 - \log_5 7 + \log_5 8 &= \log_5\left(\frac{35}{7}\right) + \log_5 8\\ &= \log_5\left(\frac{35}{7}\times 8\right)\\ &= \log_5(40)\end{aligned}$$

Applying the change of base formula and evaluating gives

$$\begin{aligned}\log_5 40 &= \frac{\log 40}{\log 5}\\ &\approx 2.29 \text{ (from the calculator)}\end{aligned}$$

5. **B**

First, note that $\sqrt{Y^3} = Y^{\frac{3}{2}}$.

Applying the product, quotient, and power laws for logarithms gives:

$$\begin{aligned}\log\left(\frac{W^2}{ZY^{\frac{3}{2}}}\right) &= \log W^2 - \log\left(ZY^{\frac{3}{2}}\right)\\ &= \log W^2 - \left(\log Z + \log Y^{\frac{3}{2}}\right)\\ &= \log W^2 - \log Z - \log Y^{\frac{3}{2}}\\ &= 2\log W - \log Z - \frac{3}{2}\log Y\end{aligned}$$

6. **C**

A. This is not correct. The domain for the graph of function (I) is $x \in R$. The domain for the graph of function (II) is $x > 0$.

B. The graph of function (I) intersects the y-axis at (0, 1); the graph of function (III) does not intersect the y-axis.

C. The graphs of both function (II) and function (III) have a vertical asymptote of $x = 0$.
This is the correct answer.

D. The graphs of functions (II) and (III) have the range $y \in R$; however, the range for the graphs of function (I) is limited to $y > 0$.

7. **A**

Using a TI-83 calculator, enter the function as $Y_1 = \log(2x)/\log(3) + 4$.
Using appropriate window setting such as x:[0, 0.1, 1], y:[–3, 5, 1] gives the graph shown below.

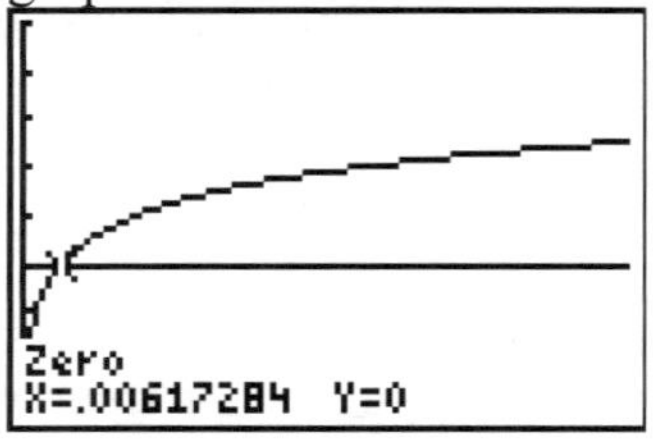

Using the 2nd CALC 2:zero function gives an x-intercept of approximately 0.006, as shown the graph.

8. **B**

The inverse of $f(x) = \log_6(x+2) - 4$ is $x = \log_6(y+2) - 4$.
Resolving for y gives:

$x + 4 = \log_6(y+2)$

$y + 2 = 6^{x+4}$

$y = 6^{x+4} - 2$

If this is written as the function $g(x)$, then $g(x) = 6^{x+4} - 2$.

9. **A**

Since the graph is reflected in the line $y = x$, the new relation is the inverse of $y = \log_5 x$, which is $x = \log_5 y$.
Writing this equation in exponential form gives $y = 5^x$. Translating the graph 3 units to the left and 6 units down changes the equation $y = 5^x$ to $y = 5^{x+3} - 6$.

10. **D**

Graph $y = \log(x)$.
An appropriate window setting and the graph are shown below.

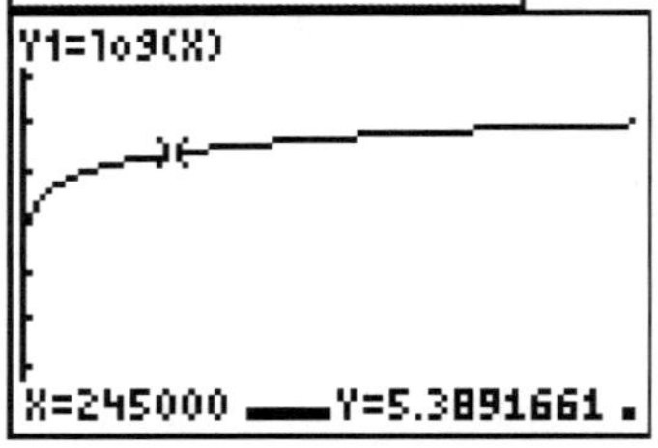

Using 2nd CALC 1:value 245000 shows that the Richter scale magnitude is approximately 5.4.

11. **C**

An appropriate window setting and the graphs are shown below.

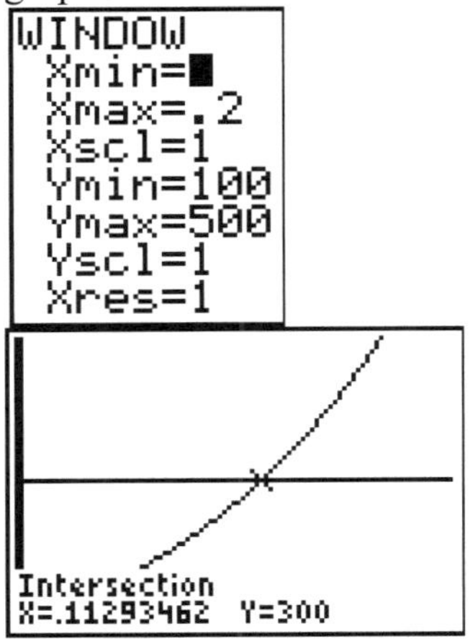

Using [2nd] [CALC] [5:interect] shows that the interest rate is approximately 0.113 or 11.3%.

12. **D**

$$\log_{\frac{1}{2}}\left(32x^2\right) = \log_{\frac{1}{2}}(32) + \log_{\frac{1}{2}}\left(x^2\right)$$

$$= \log_{\frac{1}{2}}\left(2^5\right) + \log_{\frac{1}{2}}\left(x^2\right)$$

$$= \log_{\frac{1}{2}}\left(\left(\frac{1}{2}\right)^{-5}\right) + \log_{\frac{1}{2}}\left(x^2\right)$$

$$= -5 + 2\log_{\frac{1}{2}} x$$

$$= 2\log_{\frac{1}{2}} x - 5$$

13. **C**

$$16^{2x+5} = 2^{4x}$$

$$\left(2^4\right)^{2x+5} = 2^{4x}$$

$$2^{8x+20} = 2^{4x}$$

$$8x + 20 = 4x$$

$$4x = -20$$

$$x = -5$$

14. **B**

$$3^{5x-2} = 4$$

$$\log 3^{5x-2} = \log 4$$

$$(5x-2)\log 3 = \log 4$$

$$5x - 2 = \frac{\log 4}{\log 3}$$

$$5x = \frac{\log 4}{\log 3} + 2$$

$$x = \frac{1}{5}\left(\frac{\log 4}{\log 3} + 2\right)$$

$$x = 0.2\left(\frac{\log 4}{\log 3} + 2\right)$$

$$x = \frac{0.2\log 4}{\log 3} + 0.4$$

NR1. **14**

$$\left(4^{2x-3}\right)(16) = 64^{x-5}$$

$$\left(4^{2x-3}\right)\left(4^2\right) = \left(4^3\right)^{x-5}$$

$$4^{2x-1} = 4^{3x-15}$$

$$2x - 1 = 3x - 15$$

$$14 = x$$

OR1.

$$3^{x+3} + 3^{x+4} = 56$$

$$3^{x+3}(1+3) = 56$$

$$3^{x+3}(4) = 56$$

$$3^{x+3} = 14$$

$$\log 3^{x+3} = \log 14$$

$$(x+3)\log 3 = \log 14$$

$$x + 3 = \frac{\log 14}{\log 3}$$

$$x = \frac{\log 14}{\log 3} - 3$$

$$x \approx -0.60$$

15. **C**

$\log_2(x-3)+\log_2(x-1)=3$

$\log_2((x-3)(x-1))=3$

$\log_2(x^2-4x+3)=3$

$x^2-4x+3=2^3$

$x^2-4x+3=8$

$x^2-4x-5=0$

$(x-5)(x+1)=0$

$x=5$ or $x=-1$

Since $x=-1$ does not satisfy $x>3$, only $x=5$ is a possible answer.
Thus, the sum of all the solution values is exactly 5.

16. **B**

Rebecca made the mistake of writing 3^3 as 9 instead of 27.

NR2. **1.72**

$\log_{0.4}(3x-5)=2$

$3x-5=(0.4)^2$

$3x-5=0.16$

$3x=5.16$

$x=1.72$ (exactly)

17. **D**

For the original earthquake:

$M=\log\left(\frac{I_e}{I_r}\right)=7.0$ and thus the intensity $I_e=I_r(10)^7$. For the aftershock: $M=\log\left(\frac{I_a}{I_r}\right)=5.3$ and thus the intensity $I_a=I_r(10)^{5.3}$.

The ratio of the intensities is

$$\frac{I_r(10)^7}{I_r(10)^{5.3}}=10^{1.7}\approx 50.1.$$

18. **C**

For lemonade: $-\log[H^+]=3.0$ or $\log[H^+]=-3.0$. Thus, $[H^+]=10^{-3}$

For ammonia: $-\log[H^+]=11.8$ or $\log[H^+]=-11.8$. Thus, $[H^+]=10^{-11.8}$

The ratio of acidities $([H^+])$ is

$$\frac{10^{-3.0}}{10^{-11.8}}=10^{-3.0-(-11.8)}=10^{8.8}$$

OR2.

The exponential function has the form $A(t)=A_0(3)^{\frac{t}{5}}$. Since the population after 27 minutes is 50 000, then:

$$50000=A_0(3)^{\frac{27}{5}}$$

$$\frac{50000}{3^{\frac{27}{5}}}=A_0$$

$133\approx A_0$ From the calculator

Thus, the population at 4:00 P.M. was approximately 133.

UNIT TEST—
EXPONENTIAL AND LOGARITHMIC FUNCTIONS

1. Which of the following expressions can be simplified to a numeric value?

A. $\log_b 0, b > 0$

B. $\log_1 a, a > 1$

C. $\log_b 3, b < 0$

D. $\log_b 1, b > 0$

2. The value of $\log_3 2^8$ lies between

A. 3.0 and 3.1

B. 4.0 and 4.1

C. 5.0 and 5.1

D. 7.9 and 8.1

3. The solution of the equation $10^{2x+3} = 4^2$ is

A. $x = \log 8 - \frac{3}{2}$

B. $x = \log 8 - 3$

C. $x = \frac{1}{2}\log 16 - \frac{3}{2}$

D. $x = \log 4 - 3$

4. Given that $\log_2 5 = x$, then an expression for $\log_2 80$ in terms of x is

A. $5x$

B. $16x$

C. $x + 4$

D. $2x + 3$

5. The value of $\dfrac{2\log x^{10} - \log x^7}{\log x^5 + \log x^3}$ is

A. 0.375

B. 0.5

C. 1.375

D. 1.625

6. A student wanted to illustrate that $\log(x-3)^2 = 2\log(x-3)$ by graphing $y = \log(x-3)^2$ and $y = 2\log(x-3)$ using a graphing calculator. If the student correctly graphed the two functions, he would have realized that

A. both functions have the same graph and thus, $\log(x-3)^2 = 2\log(x-3)$

B. the vertical asymptotes of the two graphs are different

C. the domains for the two functions are different

D. the ranges for the two functions are different

7. If the graph of $f(x) = 3^{2x-1} - 6$ is reflected in the line $y = x$ to create a new graph, then the new graph is defined by

A. $h(x) = 2\log_3(x+6) + 2$

B. $h(x) = \log_3(2x-1) + 3$

C. $h(x) = \frac{1}{2}\log_3(x+3)$

D. $h(x) = \frac{1}{2}\log_3(x+6) + \frac{1}{2}$

8. If the graph of $f(x) = \log_4(x+3) - 1$ is translated 1 unit to the right and 2 units up, then the equation of the vertical asymptote of the new graph is

A. $x = 1$

B. $x = -2$

C. $x = -4$

D. $x = -3$

9. A radioactive compound has a half-life of 184 days. Graph a function of the form $y = 50\left(\frac{1}{2}\right)^{\frac{x}{h}}$. Also graph $y = 36$ to determine the length of time it takes 50 g of the compound to decay to 36 g. According to these graphs, the length, of time to the nearest day, required for this compound to decay to 36 g is

A. 36 days

B. 82 days

C. 87 days

D. 184 days

10. The population of grizzly bears in a region of northern Alberta is changing such that it can be modelled by to the formula $P = 1200\left(10^{-0.045x}\right)$, where P is the population of grizzly bears x years after January 1, 1995. Use a graphical approach to determine the year in which the population first fell to 750 bears.

A. 1997

B. 1998

C. 1999

D. 2000

11. If $g(x)$ is the inverse of $f(x) = 5\log k^2 x - 10\log k$, then $g(x)$ is

A. $g(x) = 10^{\frac{x}{5}}$

B. $g(x) = 5^{\frac{5}{x}}$

C. $g(x) = 10^{x-1}$

D. $g(x) = 5^{10-x}$

12. A correct step in the solution of the equation $5(2)^{x+3} = 30$ is

A. $x\log 2 + 3 = \log 6$

B. $x\log 2 + 3\log 2 = \log 6$

C. $x\log 10 + 3 = \log 30$

D. $x\log 10 + 3\log 10 = \log 30$

13. If $(81)(27)^{2x-5} = 9^{3-4a}$, then $x =$

A. $-4a + 5$

B. $-2a + \frac{10}{3}$

C. $-2a + 4$

D. $-\frac{4a}{3} + \frac{17}{6}$

Numerical Response

NR1. The solution to $3^{2x-6} = 100$, to the nearest hundredth, is ____________.

14. The solution to $-2 = \log_2\left(\frac{1}{3}x + 3\right)$ is

A. $x = -\frac{33}{4}$

B. $x = \frac{3}{2}$

C. $x = -\frac{3}{2}$

D. undefined

Use the following information to answer the next question.

Charles carried out the following steps in solving $\log_4 x + \log_{16} x = 6$.

Step 1: $\log_4 x + \dfrac{\log_4 x}{\log_4 16} = 6$

Step 2: $\log_4 x + \dfrac{\log_4 x}{2} = 6$

Step 3: $2\log_4 x + \log_4 x = 12$

Step 4: $3\log_4 x = 12$

15. Which of the following statements is **true**?

A. Charles made his first mistake in Step 1.

B. Charles made his first mistake in Step 2.

C. Charles made his first mistake in Step 3.

D. Charles did not make a mistake in solving the equation.

Numerical Response

NR2. The solution to $\log_{(x-2)}(x^2 - 2x - 5) = 2$ is $x =$ ____________.

Open Response

OR1. Solve $\log_2(x+4) - \log_2(x-1) = 4$.

16. The half-life of a radioactive compound is 180 days. Approximately how many days will it take 200 g of the compound to decay to 65 g?

A. 88 days

B. 292 days

C. 324 days

D. 382 days

17. The Golden Eagle is an endangered species in Ontario. If the population of Golden Eagles in Ontario is changing such that it can be modelled by the formula $P = 1100\left(10^{-0.032x}\right)$, where P is the population of Golden Eagles x years after January 1, 1998, then in which year did the population first fall to 600 Golden Eagles? (Use an algebraic approach to solve this problem).

A. 2003

B. 2004

C. 2005

D. 2006

Open Response

OR2. If a 50 g sample of substance Z decays to 47 g in 11 days, what is the half-life of substance Z? Give your answer to the nearest day.

NOTES

ANSWERS AND SOLUTIONS—UNIT TEST EXPONENTIAL AND LOGARITHMIC FUNCTIONS

1. D	**7. D**	**13. D**	**16. B**
2 C	**8. B**	**NR1. 5.10**	**17. D**
3. C	**9. C**	**14. A**	**OR2. See Solution**
4. C	**10. C**	**15. D**	
5. D	**11. A**	**NR2. 4.5**	
6. C	**12. B**	**OR1. See Solution**	

1. **D**

For A, let $\log_b 0 = x$. Then, $b^x = 0$. There is no value of x that satisfies this equation.

For B, let $\log_1 a = x$. Then, $1^x = a$. The number 1 to any exponent is equal to 1 and, since $a > 1$, there is no value of x that satisfies this equation. Also, by definition, the number 1 is not an allowable base for a logarithmic expression.

For C, the base b is a negative number. By definition, $b > 0, b \neq 1$, so there is no numerical value for this expression.

For **D**, let $\log_b 1 = x$. Then, $b^x = 1$. When $b > 0$, this equation has the solution $x = 0$. Generally, $b^0 = 1, b \neq 0$. Note that 0^0 is undefined.

2. **C**

Since $2^8 = 256$, the exponent for base 3 that gives a power that is close to 256 is required. Since $3^5 = 243$ and $3^{5.1} \approx 271$, it is clear that $\log_3 2^8$ is between 5.0 and 5.1.

3. **C**

Converting $10^{2x+3} = 4^2$ to logarithmic form gives $2x + 3 = \log\left(4^2\right)$, which is equivalent to $2x + 3 = \log 16$.

Solving for x gives:

$2x = \log 16 - 3$ (Subtract 3 from each side)

$x = \frac{1}{2}\log 16 - \frac{3}{2}$ (Divide each side by 2)

4. **C**

Since $\log_2 5 = x$, rewrite $\log_2 80$ so that it includes $\log_2 5$.

$\log_2 80 = \log_2(5\times 16)$ (Rewrite 80 as 5×16)

$= \log_2 5 + \log_2 16$ (Apply the product law)

$= x + 4$ (Replace $\log_2 5$ with x and evaluate $\log_2 16$)

5. **D**

Applying the power law for logarithms first gives:

$$\frac{2\log x^{10} - \log x^7}{\log x^5 + \log x^3} = \frac{20\log x - 7\log x}{5\log x + 3\log x}$$

Collecting like terms results in:

$$\frac{20\log x - 7\log x}{5\log x + 3\log x} = \frac{13\log x}{8\log x}$$

Dividing out the like terms and simplifying gives:

$$\frac{13\cancel{\log x}}{8\cancel{\log x}} = \frac{13}{8} = 1.625$$

6. **C**

The graphs of the two functions are shown below. Note that the function $y = \log(x-3)^2$ must be entered into the calculator as $\mathrm{Y} = \log\left((x-3)^2\right)$.

The total graph shown—including both the thick and thin curves—is the graph of $y = \log(x-3)^2$; the graph of $y = 2\log(x-3)$ is only the thick curve on the right side.

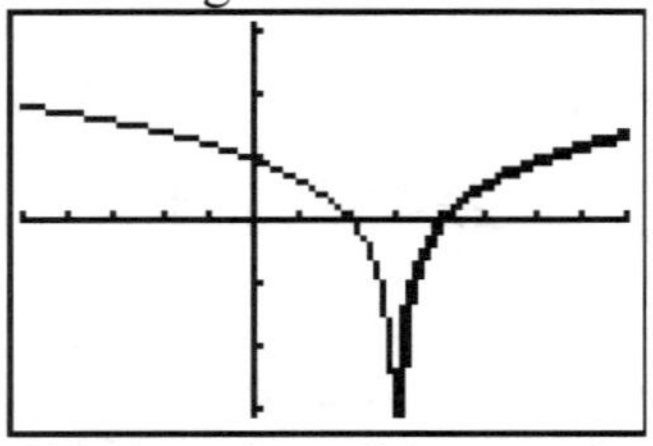

The domains of the two functions are different because $y = \log(x-3)^2$ exists for x-values that are less than 3. This is because $(x-3)^2 > 0$ for $x < 3$.

7. **D**

The inverse of $f(x) = 3^{2x-1} - 6$ is $x = 3^{2y-1} - 6$.

Resolving for y gives:

$$x + 6 = 3^{2y-1}$$
$$2y - 1 = \log_3(x+6)$$
$$2y = \log_3(x+6) + 1$$
$$y = \frac{1}{2}\log_3(x+6) + \frac{1}{2}$$

Defining this function as $h(x)$ gives:

$$h(x) = \frac{1}{2}\log_3(x+6) + \frac{1}{2}$$

8. **B**

The equation of the new function is $y = \log_4(x+2) + 1$.

The vertical asymptote is 2 units left of the asymptote for $y = \log_4 x$, which is $x = 0$. Thus, the equation of the vertical asymptote is $x = -2$.

9. **C**

Graph $y = 50\left(\frac{1}{2}\right)^{\frac{x}{184}}$ and $y = 36$.

An appropriate window setting and the graphs are shown below.

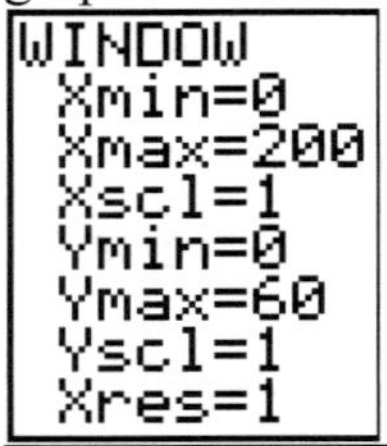

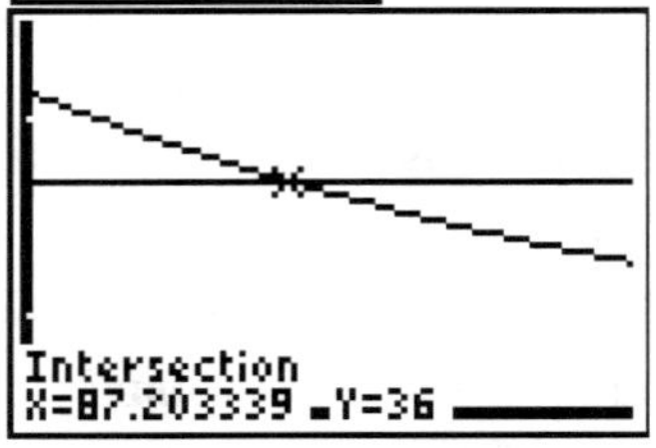

Using [2nd] [CALC] [5:interect] we see that the length of time to the nearest day is 87 days.

10. **C**

Graph $y = 1200\left(10^{-0.045x}\right)$ and $y = 750$.

An appropriate window setting and the graphs are shown below.

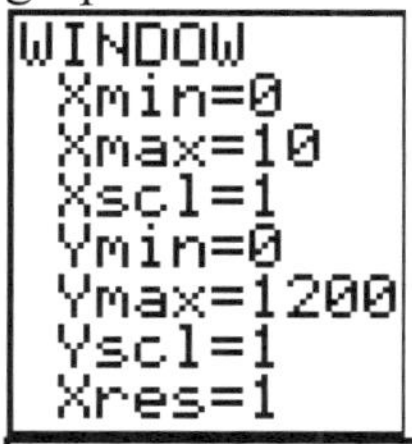

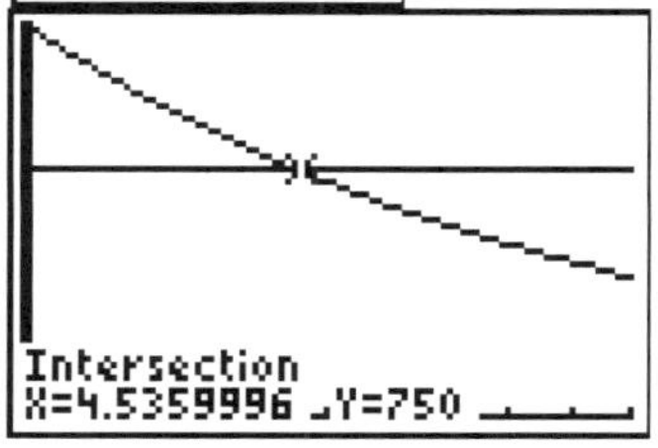

Using [2nd] [CALC] [5:interect] shows that the amount of time after January 1, 1995, is approximately 4.5 years.
This time period would occur in the year 1999.

11. **A**

$f(x) = 5\log k^2 x - 10\log k$

$f(x) = 5\left(\log k^2 x - 2\log k\right)$

$f(x) = 5\left(\log k^2 x - \log k^2\right)$

$f(x) = 5\left(\log \frac{k^2 x}{k^2}\right)$

$f(x) = 5\log x$

The inverse is:

$x = 5\log y$

$\frac{x}{5} = \log y$

$y = 10^{\frac{x}{5}}$ or $g(x) = 10^{\frac{x}{5}}$

12. **B**

$5(2)^{x+3} = 30$

Divide both sides by 5

$(2)^{x+3} = 6$

Take the common logarithm of both sides

$\log(2)^{x+3} = \log 6$

Apply the logarithm of a power law

$(x+3)\log 2 = \log 6$

Distributive property

$x\log 2 + 3\log 2 = \log 6$

13. **D**

$(81)(27)^{2x-5} = 9^{3-4a}$

$\left(3^4\right)\left(3^3\right)^{2x-5} = \left(3^2\right)^{3-4a}$

$\left(3^4\right)\left(3^{6x-15}\right) = \left(3^{6-8a}\right)$

$3^{6x-11} = 3^{6-8a}$

$\log_3\left(3^{6x-11}\right) = \log_3\left(3^{6-8a}\right)$

$6x - 11 = 6 - 8a$

$6x = 17 - 8a$

$x = \frac{17}{6} - \frac{8a}{6}$

$x = -\frac{4a}{3} + \frac{17}{6}$

NR1. **5.10**

$3^{2x-6} = 100$

$\log\left(3^{2x-6}\right) = \log(100)$

$(2x-6)\log 3 = 2$

$2x - 6 = \frac{2}{\log 3}$

$2x = \frac{2}{\log 3} + 6$

$x = \frac{1}{\log 3} + 3$

$x \approx 5.10$

14. **A**

$$-2=\log_2\left(\frac{1}{3}x+3\right)$$

$$\frac{1}{3}x+3=2^{-2}$$

$$\frac{1}{3}x+3=\frac{1}{4}$$

$$\frac{1}{3}x=\frac{1}{4}-3$$

$$x=3\left(\frac{1}{4}-3\right)$$

$$x=\frac{3}{4}-9$$

$$x=\frac{3}{4}-\frac{36}{4}=-\frac{33}{4}$$

We must verify that this solution is valid, as we cannot take the logarithm of a negative number.

$$\frac{1}{3}\left(-\frac{33}{4}\right)+3=-\frac{11}{4}+\frac{12}{4}=\frac{1}{4}$$

$$\log_2\left(\frac{1}{4}\right)=-2$$

so $-\frac{33}{4}$ is the solution

15. **D**

The steps are correct.

NR2. **4.5**

$$\log_{(x-2)}\left(x^2-2x-5\right)=2$$

$$x^2-2x-5=(x-2)^2$$

$$\cancel{x^2}-2x-5=\cancel{x^2}-4x+4$$

$$2x=9$$

$$x=\frac{9}{2}$$

$$x=4.5$$

OR1. $\frac{4}{3}$

$$\log_2(x+4)-\log_2(x-1)=4$$

$$\log_2\left(\frac{x+4}{x-1}\right)=4$$

$$\frac{x+4}{x-1}=2^4$$

$$\frac{x+4}{x-1}=16$$

$$x+4=16x-16$$

$$-15x=-20$$

$$x=\frac{20}{15}=\frac{4}{3}$$

16. **B**

Using the equation $A(t)=A_0\left(\frac{1}{2}\right)^{\frac{t}{h}}$,

where $A(t)=65,\ A_0=200$ and $h=180$ gives:

$$65=200\left(\frac{1}{2}\right)^{\frac{t}{180}}$$

First, divide each side by 200:

$$\frac{65}{200}=\left(\frac{1}{2}\right)^{\frac{t}{280}}$$

Use logarithms to solve for t.

$$\log\left(\frac{65}{200}\right)=\log\left(\frac{1}{2}\right)^{\frac{t}{180}}$$

$$\log\left(\frac{65}{200}\right)=\frac{t}{180}\log\left(\frac{1}{2}\right)$$

$$180\log\left(\frac{65}{200}\right)=t\log\left(\frac{1}{2}\right)$$

$$\frac{180\log\left(\frac{65}{200}\right)}{\log\left(\frac{1}{2}\right)}=t$$

$$t\approx 291.87$$

17. D

Substitute $P = 600$ into the equation $P = 1100\left(10^{-0.032y}\right)$

This gives:

$600 = 1100\left(10^{-0.032y}\right)$

Divide each side by 1100:

$$\frac{600}{1100} = \left(10^{-0.032y}\right)$$

Convert to logarithmic form and solve for y:

$$-0.032y = \log\left(\frac{600}{1100}\right)$$

$$y = \frac{\log\left(\frac{600}{1100}\right)}{-0.032}$$

$$y \approx 8.2$$

A time of 8.2 years after Jan. 1, 1998, would occur in the year 2006.

OR2.

The exponential function has the form where $A(11) = 47$, $A_0 = 50$, and $t = 11$

Thus, $47 = 50\left(\frac{1}{2}\right)^{\frac{11}{h}}$

Divide each side by 50 and use logarithms to solve for h.

$$\frac{47}{50} = \left(\frac{1}{2}\right)^{\frac{11}{h}}$$

$$\log\left(\frac{47}{50}\right) = \log\left(\left(\frac{1}{2}\right)^{\frac{11}{h}}\right)$$

$$\log\left(\frac{47}{50}\right) = \frac{11}{h}\log\left(\frac{1}{2}\right)$$

$$h\log\left(\frac{47}{50}\right) = 11\log\left(\frac{1}{2}\right)$$

$$h = \frac{11\log\left(\frac{1}{2}\right)}{\log\left(\frac{47}{50}\right)}$$

$h \approx 123$ Using the calculator

To the nearest day, the half-life of substance Z is 123 days.

NOTES

Trigonometric Functions

TRIGONOMETRIC FUNCTIONS

Table of Correlations			
	Specific Expectation	**Practice Questions**	**Unit Test Questions**
1.1	*recognize the radian as an alternative unit to the degree for angle measurement, define the radian measure of an angle as the length of the arc that subtends this angle at the centre of a unit circle, and develop and apply the relationship between radian and degree measure*	1, NR1	1,
1.2	*represent radian measure in terms of π and as a rational number*	2	2
1.3	*determine, with technology, the primary trigonometric ratios (i.e., sine, cosine, tangent) and the reciprocal trigonometric ratios (i.e., cosecant, secant, cotangent) of angles expressed in radian measure*	3	3
1.4	*determine, without technology, the exact values of the primary trigonometric ratios and the reciprocal trigonometric ratios for the special angles 0[fractions missing] and their multiples less than or equal to 2π*	4	4, 5
2.1	*sketch the graphs of f(x) = sin x and f(x) = cos x for angle measures expressed in radians, and determine and describe some key properties in terms of radians*	5	6
2.2	*make connections between the tangent ratio and the tangent function by using technology to graph the relationship between angles in radians and their tangent ratios and defining this relationship as the function f(x) = tan x, and describe key properties of the tangent function*	6	7
2.3	*graph, with technology and using the primary trigonometric functions, the reciprocal trigonometric functions (i.e., cosecant, secant, cotangent) for angle measures expressed in radians, determine and describe key properties of the reciprocal functions, and recognize notations used to represent the reciprocal functions*	7, 8	8, 9, NR1
2.4	*determine the amplitude, period, and phase shift of sinusoidal functions whose equations are given in the form f(x) = a sin (k(x – d)) + c or f(x) = a cos(k(x – d)) + c, with angles expressed in radians*	9, 10, NR2	10, 11, NR2
2.5	*sketch graphs of y = a sin (k(x – d)) + c and y = a cos(k(x – d)) + c by applying transformations to the graphs of f(x) = sin x and f(x) = cos x with angles expressed in radians, and state the period, amplitude, and phase shift of the transformed functions*	11, OR1	12
2.6	*represent a sinusoidal function with an equation, given its graph or its properties, with angles expressed in radians*	12, 13	13
2.7	*pose problems based on applications involving a trigonometric function with domain expressed in radians, and solve these and other such problems by using a given graph or a graph generated with or without technology from a table of values or from its equation*	14, 15	14, 15, OR1
3.1	*recognize equivalent trigonometric expressions, and verify equivalence using graphing technology*	16	16
3.2	*explore the algebraic development of the compound angle formulas, and use the formulas to determine exact values of trigonometric ratios*	17, 18	17, 18
3.3	*recognize that trigonometric identities are equations that are true for every value in the domain (i.e., a counter-example can be used to show that an equation is not an identity), prove trigonometric identities through the application of reasoning skills, using a variety of relationships, and verify identities using technology*	19, 20, OR2	19, 20
3.4	*solve linear and quadratic trigonometric equations, with and without graphing technology, for the domain of real values from 0 to 2π, and solve related problems*	21, 22, NR3	21, 22, NR3, OR2

TRIGONOMETRIC FUNCTIONS

1.1. recognize the radian as an alternative unit to the degree for angle measurement, define the radian measure of an angle as the length of the arc that subtends this angle at the centre of a unit circle, and develop and apply the relationship between radian and degree measure.

RADIAN MEASURE

Angle measures can be expressed in degrees for some situations, but for many other situations it is preferable or necessary to express angle measures in radians.

One radian is defined as the measure of a central angle in a circle that is subtended by an arc equal in length to the radius of that circle.

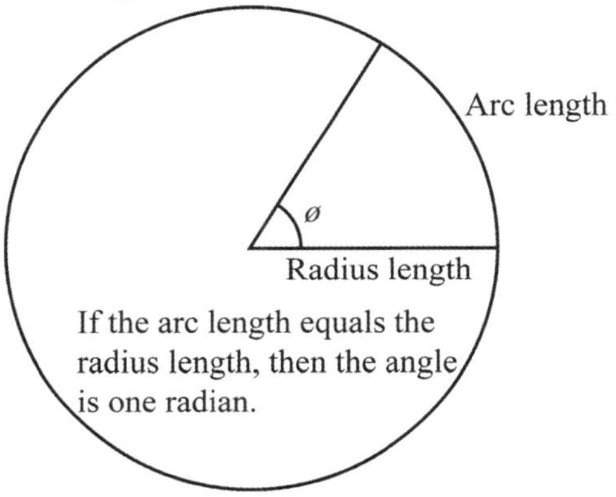

For a circle of radius r there is a direct relationship between the arc length, a, and the angle measure, θ, expressed in radians.

For example, if the arc length is twice the radius **length** then the angle measure is two radians. If the arc length is triple the radius length, the angle measure is three radians. The equation $\theta = \frac{a}{r}$ represents this relationship between arc length, radius, and angle measure in radians.

Example

What is the measure in radians of a central angle in a circle of radius 20 cm subtended by an arc of length 45 cm.

Solution

$\theta = \frac{a}{r} = \frac{45}{20} = 2.25$ rad (The abbreviation for radians is "rad".)

This result of 2.25 rad means that the length of the arc that subtends the angle is 2.25 times the length of the radius.

Also, note that with a **unit circle**, which has a radius of 1 unit,

the equation becomes $\theta = \frac{a}{r} = \frac{a}{1} = a$, so that the angle measure and the radius are equal in value. Consider any circle of radius r. The circumference, C, is given by the equation $C = 2\pi r$.

If a section is drawn on a diameter of this circle in order to create a semicircle, the central angle would be 180° and the arc length will be $a = \frac{1}{2}(2\pi r) = \pi r$.

In radians the measure of this central angle will be $\theta = \frac{a}{r} = \frac{\pi r}{r} = \pi$.

Thus, π rad = 180°

Dividing both sides of this equation by π yields 1 rad = $\frac{180^\circ}{\pi} \approx 57.3^\circ$.

This ratio $\frac{180}{\pi}$ is used to convert radians into degrees.

Example

Perform each of the following conversions:

a) 5.32 rad into degrees, expressed to the nearest degree.

b) $\frac{2\pi}{3}$ rad into degrees.

Solution

a) $5.32 \times \frac{180}{\pi} \approx 305^\circ$

b) $\frac{2\pi}{3} \times \frac{180}{\pi} = 120^\circ$

The reciprocal factor, $\frac{\pi}{180}$, is used to convert degrees into radians.

Example

Convert 45° into radians, giving both an exact answer and an approximate answer rounded to the nearest hundredth.

Solution

$$45\times\frac{\pi}{180}=\frac{\pi}{4}\text{rad (exactly)} \approx 0.79 \text{ rad}$$

PRACTICE QUESTIONS

1. An angle of $\frac{11\pi}{45}$ rad, expressed in degrees, is

A. 0.004°

B. 26°

C. 44°

D. 88°

Numerical Response

NR1. An arc of a circle with a radius of 42 cm subtends a central angle of 1.6 rad. The length of the arc, correct to the nearest tenth of a centimetre, is ____________ cm.

1.2 represent radian measure in terms of π and as a rational number

ANGLES IN RADIAN MEASURE

Angles in radian measure are sometimes expressed as an exact value and sometimes as an approximate number rounded to a specified number of decimal places.

Since π rad = 180°, use the ratio $\frac{\pi}{180}$ to convert any angle that is in degree measure to its equivalent radian measure.

Example

For example, $30° = 30\times\frac{\pi}{180}=\frac{\pi}{6}$ rad.
This is the exact value. If you use a calculator to divide π by 6 you get 0.5236 rad as an approximate answer correct to four decimal places.
All multiples of 30° can be expressed in the form $\frac{n\pi}{6}$ rad, $n\in I$. So 150° which is $5\times 30°$ is equivalent to $\frac{5\pi}{6}$ rad exactly, or approximately 2.62 rad, to the nearest hundredth.
Three other common angles and their conversion into radian measure are:

$45° = \frac{\pi}{4}$ rad ≈ 0.785 rad.

Multiples are of the form $\frac{n\pi}{4}$ rad, $n\in I$.

$60° = \frac{\pi}{3}$ rad $\doteq 1.05$ rad

Multiples are of the form $\frac{n\pi}{3}$ rad, $n\in I$.

$90° = \frac{\pi}{2}$ rad $\doteq 1.57$ rad

Multiples are of the form $\frac{n\pi}{2}$ rad, $n\in I$.

Example

When 480° is converted to radian measure, its exact value is

A. $\frac{7\pi}{6}$ rad **B.** $\frac{8\pi}{6}$ rad

C. $\frac{7\pi}{3}$ rad **D.** $\frac{8\pi}{3}$ rad

Solution

$$480° = 480 \times \frac{\pi}{180°} = \frac{480\pi}{180} = \frac{8\pi}{3}\text{ rad}$$

so alternative **D** is the correct answer.

Example

Which of the following statements about an angle whose measure is 5.85 rad is **true**?

A. It is larger than an angle whose measure is 2π rad.

B. It is smaller than an angle whose measure is π rad.

C. It is between an angle whose measure is π rad and an angle whose measure is $\frac{3\pi}{2}$ rad.

D. It is between an angle whose measure is $\frac{3\pi}{2}$ rad and an angle whose measure is 2π rad.

Solution

Since $\pi \approx 3.14$, $\frac{3\pi}{2} \approx 4.71$, and $2\pi \approx 6.28$, an angle whose measure is 5.85 rad lies between an angle whose measure is $\frac{3\pi}{2}$ rad and angle whose measure is 2π, so alternative **D** is correct.

PRACTICE QUESTION

2. When 645° is converted to radian measure, its exact value is

A. $\frac{7\pi}{2}$ rad

B. $3.58\overline{3}$ rad

C. 11.257 rad

D. $\frac{43\pi}{12}$ rad

1.3 determine, with technology, the primary trigonometric ratios (i.e., sine, cosine, tangent) and the reciprocal trigonometric ratios (i.e., cosecant, secant, cotangent) of angles expressed in radian measure.

THE PRIMARY AND RECIPROCAL TRIGONOMETRIC RATIOS

In order to use a calculator to determine the values of the trigonometric ratios of angles expressed in radian measure, the calculator must be in radian mode.

Using a TI-83 Plus calculator, press [MODE], and observe the third row. If the word *Radian* is shaded, then the calculator is in the correct mode. If the word *Degree* is shaded, scroll down to the third row and press [ENTER] while the cursor is flashing on *Radian*, and the calculator will be in radian mode.

To determine the sine, cosine and/or tangent of any angle in radian measure, press, in order, the appropriate function, the angle in radians, and [ENTER].

Example

Find, to the nearest thousandth:

a) $\sin\left(\frac{4\pi}{3}\right)$

b) $\tan(2.07)$

Solution

Since there is no degree symbol, you know that the angles are in radians.

a) In radian mode, input $\sin(4\pi/3)$ and press ENTER. The display shows -0.8660254038 so, to the nearest thousandth, $\sin\left(\frac{4\pi}{3}\right) = -0.866$

b) Input tan(2.07) and press ENTER. The display shows -1.833957347 so, to the nearest thousandth, $\tan(2.07) = -1.834$

The three reciprocal trigonometric ratios are defined as follows.
The reciprocal of the sine ratio is the cosecant ratio, abbreviated as csc.

Thus, $\csc\theta = \frac{1}{\sin\theta}$, $\sin\theta \neq 0$.

The reciprocal of the cosine ratio is the secant ratio, abbreviated as sec.

Thus, $\sec\theta = \frac{1}{\cos\theta}$, $\cos\theta \neq 0$.

The reciprocal of the tangent ratio is the cotangent ratio, abbreviated as cot.

Therefore, $\cot\theta = \frac{1}{\tan\theta}$, $\tan\theta \neq 0$.

To calculate the reciprocal ratios using your calculator, input 1/(primary ratio).
For example,
to calculate the cosecant of any angle, θ, input $1/\sin(\theta)$

Example

Determine the value of $\cot\left(\frac{5\pi}{6}\right)$ to the nearest thousandth.

Solution

In radian mode, input $1/\tan(5\pi/6)$ and press ENTER. The display shows -1.732050808 so, to the nearest thousandth, $\cot\left(\frac{5\pi}{6}\right) = -1.732$.

Example

The correct calculator input in radian mode to determine the value of $\sec\left(\frac{3\pi}{5}\right)$ is

A. $\cos^{-1}(3\pi/5)$

B. $\cos(5/3\pi)$

C. $1/\cos(3\pi/5)$

D. $1/\cos(5/3\pi)$

Solution

The secant is the reciprocal of the cosine ratio, not the cosine of the reciprocal of the angle, which is incorrectly shown in both choice **B** and **D**. Choice **A** is finding the inverse cosine, not the reciprocal. Alternative **C** is correct.

Example

The value of $\csc(0.55)$ to the nearest thousandth is

A. 0.582

B. 1.913

C. 33.367

D. 104.176

Solution

Since cosecant is the reciprocal of sine, the correct input in radian mode is $1/\sin(0.55)$, which gives the value 1.913, to the nearest thousandth. Alternative **B** is correct.

Practice Question

3. The value of $\sec\left(\frac{11\pi}{8}\right)$, to the nearest thousandth, is

A. -2.613

B. -1.527

C. 0.146

D. 0.997

1.4 determine, without technology, the exact value of the primary trigonometric ratios and the reciprocal trigonometric ratios for the special angles $0, \frac{\pi}{6}, \frac{\pi}{4}, \frac{\pi}{3}, \frac{\pi}{2}$, and their multiples less than or equal to 2π.

THE EXACT VALUE OF TRIGONOMETRIC RATIOS

An angle that is on a Cartesian plane and that has its vertex at the origin and one arm along the x-axis is said to be in *standard position*.
If the angle is formed by rotating the *terminal* arm in a counter clockwise direction from the *initial arm* along the x-axis, then the angle is a *positive* angle. If the rotation is clockwise, then the angle is a *negative* angle.

Angles in Standard Position

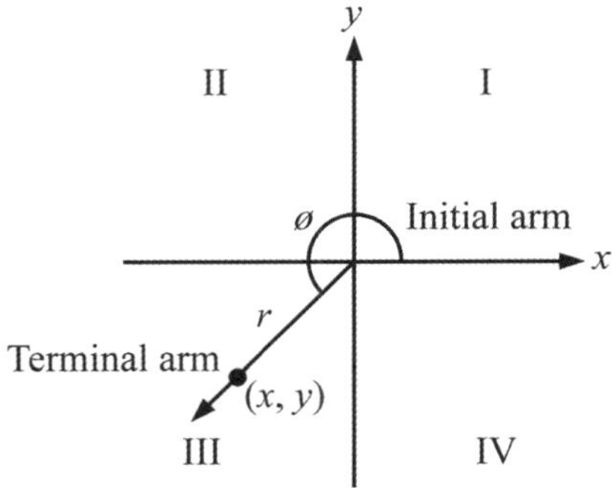

The definitions of the trigonometric ratios for an angle, θ, in standard position with (x, y) on the terminal arm are:

$\sin\theta = \frac{y}{r}$ $\quad$ $\csc\theta = \frac{r}{y}$

$\cos\theta = \frac{x}{r}$ $\quad$ $\sec\theta = \frac{r}{x}$

$\tan\theta = \frac{y}{x}$ $\quad$ $\cot\theta = \frac{x}{y}$

where $r = \sqrt{x^2 + y^2}$

In order to determine the exact value of particular trigonometric ratios begin by drawing triangles with angles 45°, –45°, –90°, and 30°, –60°, –90°, each with hypotenuse of length 1 unit as shown.

Missing side lengths are determined from the Pythagorean theorem.
Draw a square with a diagonal of length 1 unit and determine the dimensions of the sides.

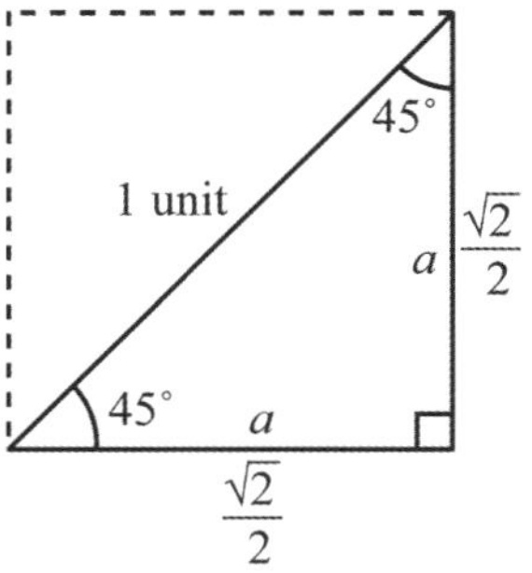

$$a^2 + a^2 = 1$$
$$2a^2 = 1$$
$$a^2 = \frac{1}{2}$$
$$a = \frac{1}{\sqrt{2}} = \frac{\sqrt{2}}{2}$$

Draw an equilateral triangle with sides of length 1 unit and then draw a line from a vertex to the midpoint of the opposite side.

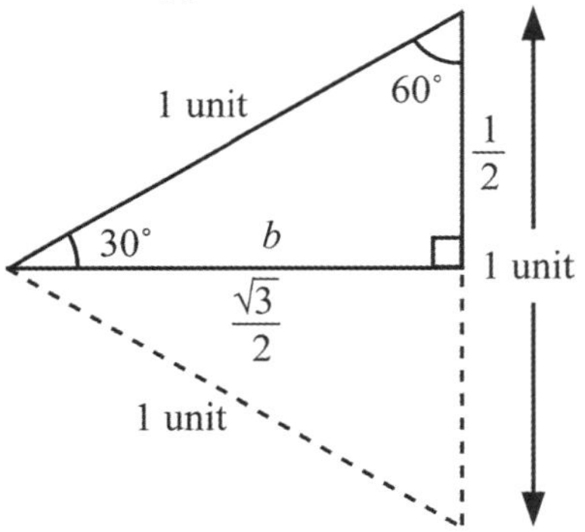

$$b^2 + \left(\frac{1}{2}\right)^2 = 1$$
$$b^2 + \frac{1}{4} = 1$$
$$b^2 = \frac{3}{4}$$
$$b = \frac{\sqrt{3}}{2}$$

These triangles can be inscribed in the unit circle in any of the four quadrants.

Recall that $30° = \frac{\pi}{6}$ rad, $45° = \frac{\pi}{4}$ rad, and $60° = \frac{\pi}{3}$ rad.

The triangles with theses three angles in standard position are drawn below.

An angle of $\frac{\pi}{6}$:

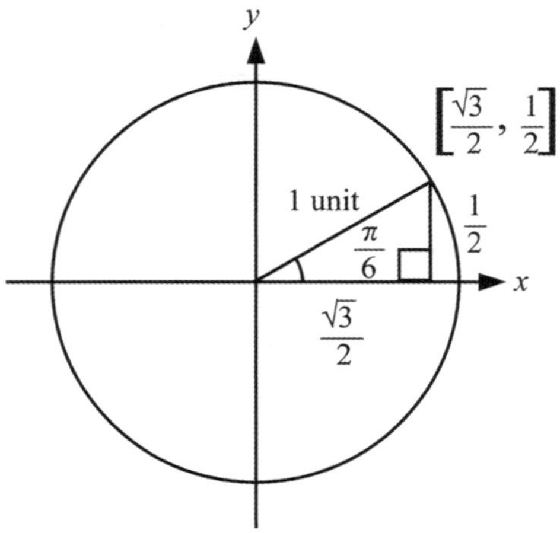

An angle of $\frac{\pi}{4}$:

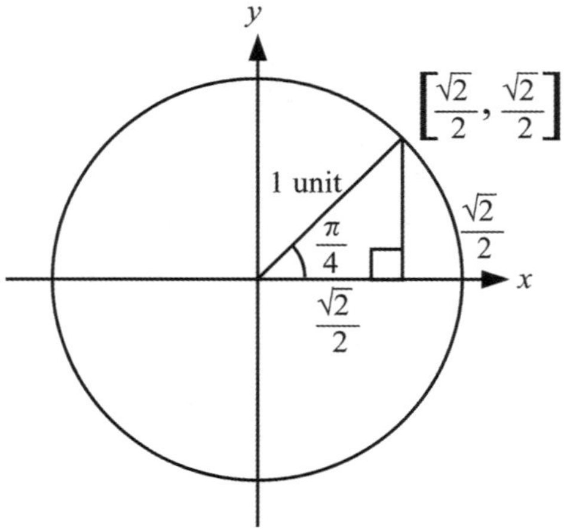

An angle of $\frac{\pi}{3}$:

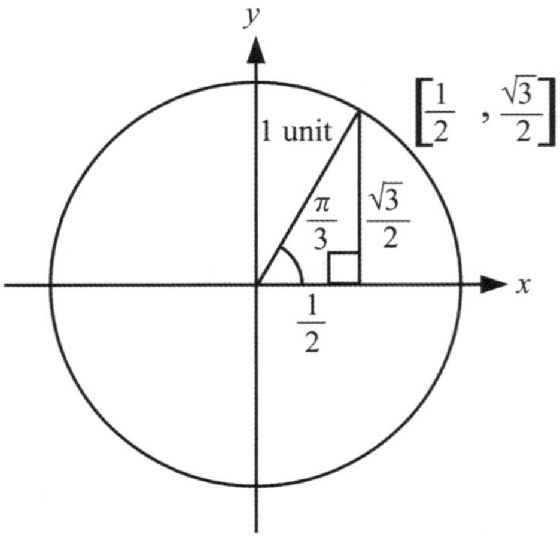

From these diagrams and the definitions it is possible to determine the exact values of the trigonometric ratios for the three angles.

For example, $\sin\left(\frac{\pi}{3}\right) = \frac{y}{r} = \frac{\frac{\sqrt{3}}{2}}{1} = \frac{\sqrt{3}}{2}$.

When the angle is not between 0 and $\frac{\pi}{2}$ rad (not between 0° and 90°) a reference angle can be used to determine the trig ratio. The reference angle is the positive angle between the terminal arm and the x-axis. The following example illustrates the technique.

Example

Determine the exact value of $\cos\left(\frac{5\pi}{6}\right)$.

Solution

Begin by sketching a unit circle and an angle of approximately $\frac{5\pi}{6}$ rad.

Recall that a complete revolution is equivalent to 2π rad so half a revolution is equal to π rad.

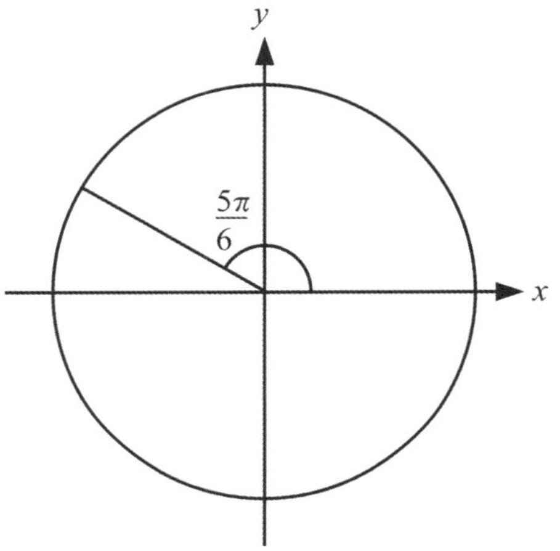

The reference angle is $\pi - \frac{5\pi}{6} = \frac{\pi}{6}$.

Since $\frac{\pi}{6} = 30°$, the 30-60-90 triangle can be drawn with one side on the x-axis. The side lengths can be labeled with the correct lengths. Note that the bottom side length is negative because x is negative in quadrant II.

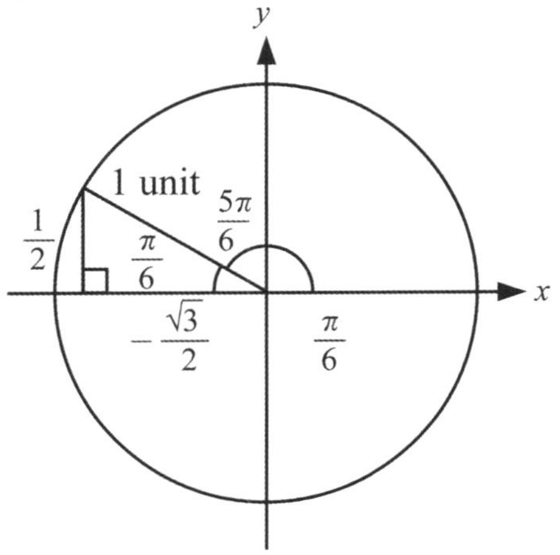

Now, it is clear that

$$\cos\left(\frac{5\pi}{6}\right) = \frac{x}{r} = \frac{x}{1} = x = -\frac{\sqrt{3}}{2}$$

An alternative method to sketching the approximate angle and using the reference angle is to draw all the possible locations of the special angles in the unit circle and refer to this when the trig ratio of a special angle is required. The unit circle with the special angles and endpoint coordinates is shown below.

Unit Circle

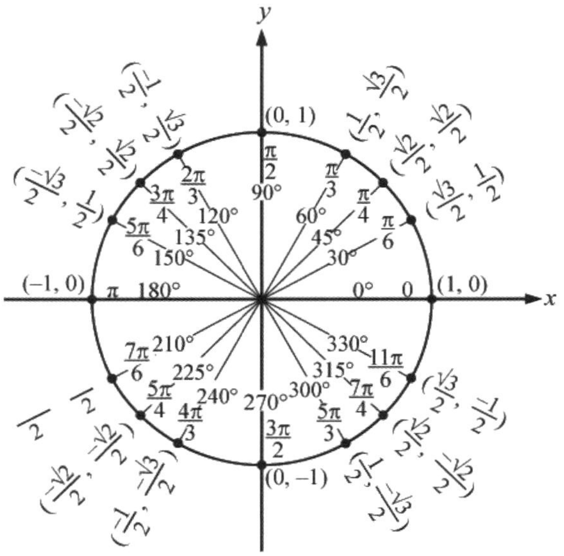

You can memorize the unit circle by memorizing the values in the first quadrant and using reflections to get the values in the other quadrants.

The radius of the unit circle is 1 and therefore, for rotation angles, $\cos\theta = \frac{x}{r} = \frac{x}{1} = x$ and $\sin\theta = \frac{y}{r} = \frac{y}{1} = y$. Furthermore, every x-coordinate on the unit circle is the cosine of the angle that terminates in that location when the angle is drawn in standard position. Likewise, the y-coordinate is the sine of that angle.

Example

Use the unit circle to determine the exact values of

$\sin\left(\frac{5\pi}{4}\right)$, $\cos(\pi)$, and $\tan\left(\frac{3\pi}{2}\right)$.

Solutions

$\sin\left(\frac{5\pi}{4}\right) = -\frac{\sqrt{2}}{2}$ because this is the y-coordinate of the corresponding point on the terminal arm.

$\cos(\pi) = -1$ because this is the x-coordinate of the terminal point on the circle.

$\tan\left(\frac{3\pi}{2}\right)$ is undefined because $\tan\theta = \frac{y}{x}$, and the x-coordinate of the corresponding point on the circle is 0.

PRACTICE QUESTION

4. Which of the following procedures would be **most appropriate** to determine the exact value of $\sin\left(\frac{4\pi}{3}\right)$?

   A. Sketch an angle with a reference angle of $\frac{\pi}{6}$ in quadrant II.

   B. Sketch an angle with a reference angle of $\frac{\pi}{6}$ in quadrant III.

   C. Sketch an angle with a reference angle of $\frac{\pi}{3}$ in quadrant III.

   D. Sketch an angle with a reference angle of $\frac{\pi}{4}$ in quadrant III.

2.1 *sketch the graphs of $f(x) = \sin x$ and $f(x) = \cos x$ for angle measures expressed in radians, and determine and describe some key properties in terms of radians.*

THE GRAPHS OF THE FUNCTIONS SINE AND COSINE

A partial graph of the function $f(x) = \sin x$ is shown below.

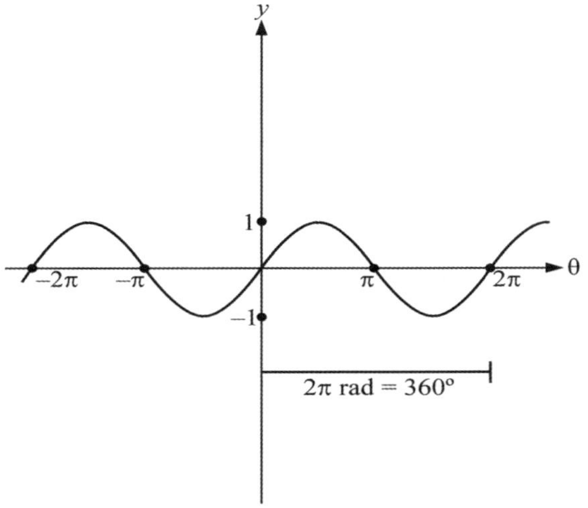

The domain of $f(x) = \sin x$ is $x \in R$, and its range is $-1 \leq y \leq 1$. This function is also periodic since the function values (y-coordinates) repeat every 2π rad change in the x-coordinates. The period is 2π.

The vertical distance between the centre of the graph and its maximum value (or its minimum value) is called the amplitude.

The amplitude of $f(x) = \sin x$ is 1.

The amplitude can be determined by using the equation $\text{amplitude} = \frac{\max - \min}{2}$.

Here, $\text{amplitude} = \frac{1-(-1)}{2} = 1$.

A partial graph of $f(x) = \cos x$ is shown below.

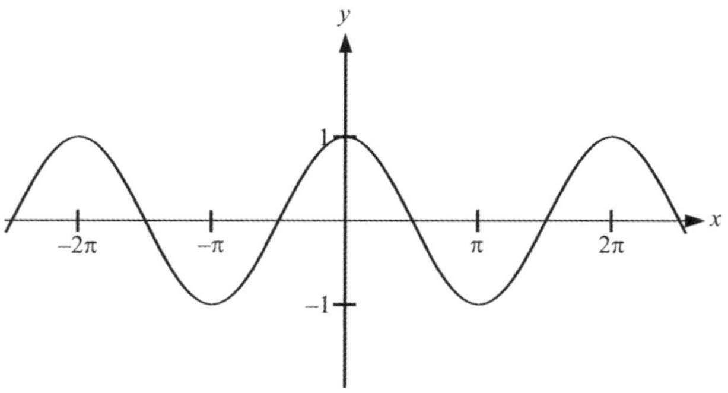

The domain of $f(x)=\cos x$ is $x\in R$, and its range is $-1\le y\le 1$. The period of this graph is 2π, and the amplitude is 1.

PRACTICE QUESTION

5. The amplitude of $y=\cos x$ is
   - **A.** 1
   - **B.** 2
   - **C.** π
   - **D.** 2π

2.2 make connections between the tangent ratio and the tangent function by using technology to graph the relationship between angles in radians and their tangent ratios and defining this relationship as the function $f(x)=\tan x$, and describe key properties of the tangent function.

THE TANGENT RATIO AND FUNCTION

The tangent function is defined for any rotation angle θ as $\tan\theta=\frac{y}{x}, x\neq 0$, where x and y are the coordinates of any point on the terminal arm of θ drawn in standard position.

Using the unit circle, the following tangent ratios are easily determined.

$\tan 0=0$, $\tan\frac{\pi}{6}=\frac{1}{\sqrt{3}}$, $\tan\frac{\pi}{4}=1$,

$\tan\frac{\pi}{3}=\sqrt{3}$ and $\tan\frac{\pi}{2}$ is undefined.

Using technology to graph the function $f(x)=\tan x$, on the domain $-\frac{5\pi}{2}\le x\le\frac{5\pi}{2}$, produces the following graph:

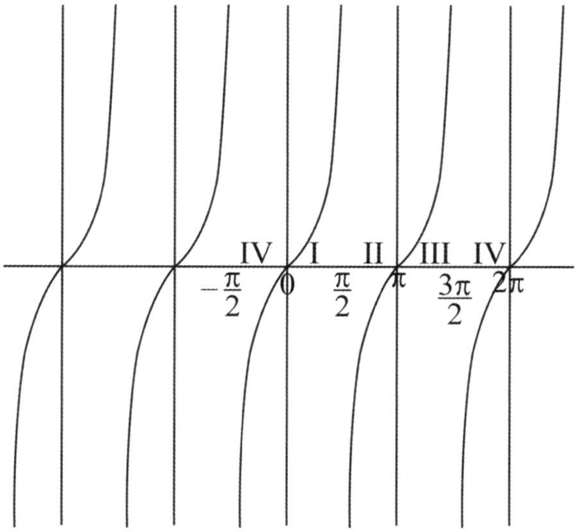

There are vertical asymptotes at $x=\pm\frac{\pi}{2},\ \pm\frac{3\pi}{2},\ \pm\frac{5\pi}{2},\ \ldots$, which can be more conveniently written as $x=\frac{\pi}{2}+n\pi,\ n\in I$.

Thus, the domain of $f(x)=\tan x$ is

$x\neq\frac{\pi}{2}+n\pi,\ n\in I$.

The range is $y\in R$. The period is π and there is no amplitude for this function.

PRACTICE QUESTION

6. The domain of $f(\theta)=\tan\theta$ is
   - **A.** $\theta\in R$
   - **B.** $\theta\neq n\pi,\ n\in I$
   - **C.** $\theta\neq n\frac{\pi}{2},\ n\in I$
   - **D.** $\theta\neq\frac{\pi}{2}+n\pi,\ n\in I$

2.3 graph, with technology and using the primary trigonometric functions, the reciprocal trigonometric functions for angle measures expressed in radians, determine and describe key properties of the reciprocal functions, and recognize notations used to represent the reciprocal functions

THE GRAPHS OF THE RECIPROCAL TRIGONOMETRIC FUNCTIONS

Recall that the definition of the cosecant of angle θ is the ratio $\frac{r}{y}$ for a point on the terminal arm of θ. Since $\frac{r}{y}=\frac{1}{\frac{y}{r}}$,

then $\csc\theta=\frac{1}{\sin\theta}$. If x represents the angle measure, then csc x is the reciprocal of $\sin x$, which is $\csc x=\frac{1}{\sin x}$. In order to graph the function $y=\csc x$ using a TI-83 calculator, input $Y_1=1/\sin(x)$. The graph of $y=\csc x$ using the viewing window $x:\left[-2\pi,2\pi,\frac{\pi}{2}\right]$ and $y:[-4,4,1]$ yields the graph shown below.

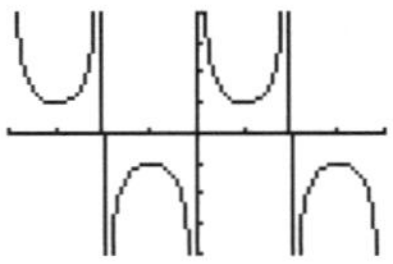

Since $y=\csc x=\frac{1}{\sin x}$ is not defined when $\sin x=0$, the graph does not exist when $x=\pm\pi$ or in fact for all multiples of π.

There are asymptotes at all multiples of π because as x approaches a multiple of π $\sin x$ approaches 0 and $\frac{1}{\sin x}$ approaches $-\infty$ when $(\sin x)<0$. and $+\infty$ when $(\sin x)>0$

Thus, the domain of $y=\csc x$ is $x\neq n\pi,\ n\in I$.

By examining the graph and the values of the function you can see that the range of $y=\csc x$ is $y\geq 1$ or $y\leq -1$, which can be written as $|y|\geq 1$.

The period of $y=\csc x$ is 2π and amplitude does not apply.

Note: Although it appears that the calculator has drawn the vertical asymptotes at $x=\pm\pi$,it actually has not. In the normal draw mode the calculator draws curves by connecting points with straight lines. The calculator is actually connecting two points, one on one side of the asymptote to one on the other side. If you look closely you can see that the lines are not quite vertical. Although they are not drawn by the calculator, the asymptotes do exist.

The definition of the secant of angle θ is the ratio $\frac{r}{x}$ for a point on the terminal arm of θ. Since $\frac{r}{x}=\frac{1}{\frac{x}{r}}$, then $\sec\theta=\frac{1}{\cos\theta}$.

If x represents the angle measure, then sec x is the reciprocal of $\cos x$, which is $\sec x=\frac{1}{\cos x}$.

In order to graph the function $y=\sec x$, input $Y_1=1/\cos(x)$. Use the same window settings as for the previous graph. The resulting graph is shown below.

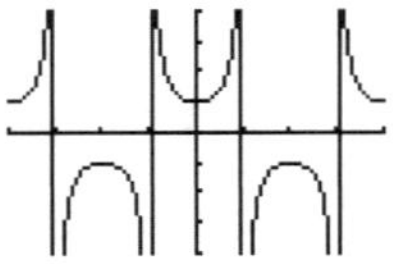

Again, the lines that appear to be asymptotes are not really asymptotes but asymptotes do exist. A similar analysis as for $y=\csc x$, reveals the following properties for $y=\sec x$.

The domain of $y=\sec x$, is $x\neq\frac{\pi}{2}+n\pi,\ n\in I$.

The range of $y=\sec x$ is $y\geq 1$ or $y\leq -1$, which can be written as $|y|\geq 1$.

The period of $y=\sec x$ is 2π and amplitude does not apply.

The definition of the cotangent of angle θ is the ratio $\frac{x}{y}$ for a point on the terminal arm of θ

Since $\frac{x}{y}=\frac{1}{\frac{y}{x}}$, then $\cot\theta=\frac{1}{\tan\theta}$. If x represents the angle measure, then $\cot x$ is the reciprocal of $\tan x$, which is $\cot\theta=\frac{1}{\tan\theta}$. In order to graph the function $y=\cot x$, input $Y_1=1/\tan(x)$. Use the same window settings as for the previous graphs. The resulting graph is as shown below.

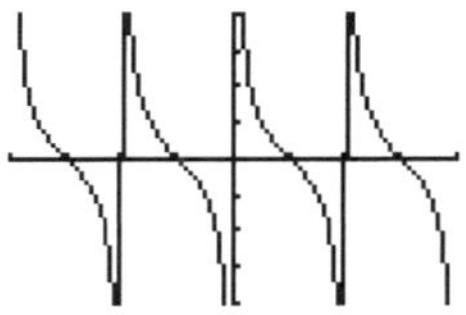

Again, the lines that appear to be asymptotes are not really asymptotes but asymptotes do exist. A similar analysis as for the previous two functions reveals the following properties for $y=\cot x$.

The domain of $y=\cot x$ is $x\neq n\pi,\ n\in I$.

The range of $y=\cot x$ is $y\in R$.

The period of $y=\cot x$ is π and amplitude does not apply.

Note that when the notation $f^{-1}(x)$ is used, it represents the inverse of the function, not the reciprocal. It is true that when an exponent of -1 is written for a number or a variable it does indicate the reciprocal of that number or variable, which is $x^{-1}=\frac{1}{x},\ x\neq 0$, or $5^{-1}=\frac{1}{5}$. However, when the notation is used on a function it represents the inverse function.

So, for example, $\sin^{-1}x\neq\frac{1}{\sin x}$ and $\sec x\neq\cos^{-1}x$.

Practice Questions

7. The functions $y=\csc x$ and $y=\sec x$ have the same

A. range

B. domain

C. y-intercept

D. reciprocal function

8. The graphs of the functions $y=\csc x$ and $y=\cot x$ are graphed on the same set of axes. Which of the following statements about these graphs is **true**?

A. Neither graph has asymptotes.

B. Both graphs have the same asymptotes.

C. Both graphs have the same x-intercepts.

D. Both functions are always decreasing functions (as x increases).

2.4 determine the amplitude, period, and phase shift of sinusoidal functions whose equations are given in the form $f(x)=a\sin(k(x-d))+c$ or $f(x)=a\cos(k(x-d))+c$ with angles expressed in radians.

Transformations of Sinusoidal Functions

Sinusoidal functions are functions whose graphs are transformations of the wave-shaped graph of $y=\sin x$ (or $y=\cos x$, since $y=\cos x$ is the same shape as $y=\sin x$).

When the function $y=f(x)$ is changed into $y=af(k(x-d))+c$, the graph of $f(x)$ is affected by each parameter in the following way.

- Parameter a causes a vertical stretch $(|a|>1)$ or compression $(0<|a|<1)$ about the x-axis. Each y-coordinate is multiplied by a.
  If $a<0$, there is also a reflection in the x-axis. Since the amplitude is expressed as a positive number, amplitude $=|a|$.

- Parameter k causes a horizontal stretch $(0<k<1)$ or compression $(k>1)$ about the y-axis. Since the period of a function of the form $y=f(x)$ is measured in terms of x, parameter k will affect the period.

  The stretch factor is $\frac{1}{k}$ so the period for the sinusoidal functions $y=\sin kx$ or $y=\cos kx$ is $2\pi\times\frac{1}{k}=\frac{2\pi}{k}$, since both $y=\sin x$ and $y=\cos x$ have a period of 2π.
- Parameter d causes a horizontal translation, which for sinusoidal functions is referred to as a phase shift of d units. The phase shift is to the right if $d>0$, and to the left if $d<0$.
- Parameter c causes a vertical translation, which for sinusoidal functions is sometimes called a vertical displacement. The displacement is up if $c>0$, and down if $c<0$.
- Combining the vertical stretch (compression) with the vertical displacement allows the range to be determined as $c-|a|\le f(x)\le c+|a|$.

Example 1

Determine the amplitude, period phase shift, and range of the sinusoidal function $f(x)=-3\cos\left(2x+\frac{\pi}{2}\right)-4$.

Solution

Before you analyze the function it must be changed into the form $f(x)=-3\cos\left(2\left(x+\frac{\pi}{4}\right)\right)-4$ by factoring 2 from each term inside the parentheses.

The parameter values are $a=-3,\ k=2,\ d=-\frac{\pi}{4}$, and $c=-4$.

The amplitude is $|a|=|-3|=3$. The period is $\frac{2\pi}{k}=\frac{2\pi}{2}=\pi$. The phase shift is $\frac{\pi}{4}$ left. (Note: for sinusoidal functions the units for the period and phase shift are radians unless otherwise indicated).

The range is $-4-3\le f(x)\le -4+3$, or $-7\le f(x)\le -1$.

PRACTICE QUESTIONS

9. If $y=\sin x$ is transformed to $y=3\sin\left(4x-\frac{\pi}{2}\right)$, the period and phase shift are, respectively,

A. $\frac{\pi}{2}$ and $\frac{\pi}{8}$ to the right

B. $\frac{\pi}{2}$ and $\frac{\pi}{8}$ to the left

C. $\frac{\pi}{2}$ and $\frac{\pi}{2}$ to the right

D. $\frac{\pi}{2}$ and 2π to the right

10. The amplitude of $f(\theta)=-7\cos\left(2\theta+\frac{\pi}{3}\right)+4$ is

A. 4

B. 7

C. 11

D. 14

Numerical Response

NR2. The period of the graph of $y=-2\cos\left(\frac{2\theta}{5}\right)+6$ is ____________.

2.5 sketch graphs of $y = a\sin(k(x-d))+c$ and $y = a\cos(k(x-d))+c$ by applying transformations to the graphs of $f(x)=\sin x$ or, $f(x)=\cos x$ with angles expressed in radians, and state the period, amplitude, and phase shift of the transformed functions

SKETCHING THE GRAPHS OF SINUSOIDAL FUNCTIONS

Example

The graph of $y=\sin\theta$ is shown below. The steps required to transform the graph of $y=\sin\theta$ into the graph of $y=2\sin\left(2\left(\theta-\frac{\pi}{2}\right)\right)$ follow.

Partial graph of $y=\sin\theta$

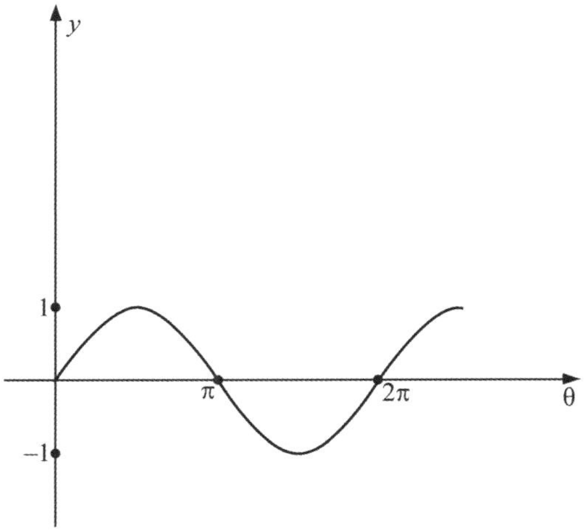

Parameter $a=2$ so there is a vertical stretch by a factor of 2 about the x-axis, and the amplitude $|a|=2$.

Partial graph of $y=2\sin\theta$

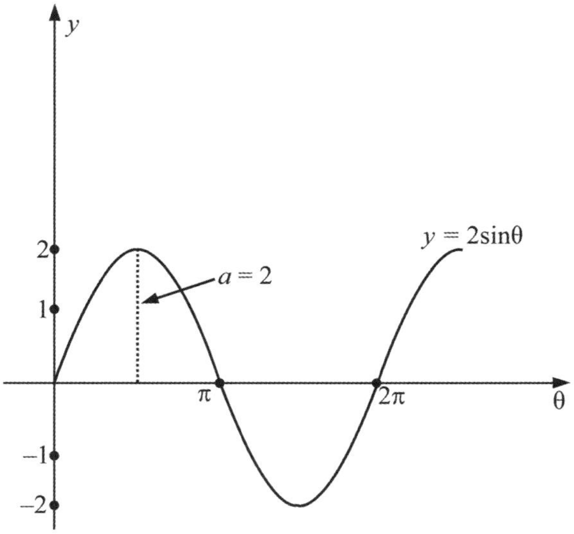

Parameter $k=2$, so the new period is $\frac{2\pi}{2}=\pi$. This causes a horizontal compression about the y-axis by a factor of $\frac{1}{2}$.

Partial graph of $y=2\sin 2\theta$

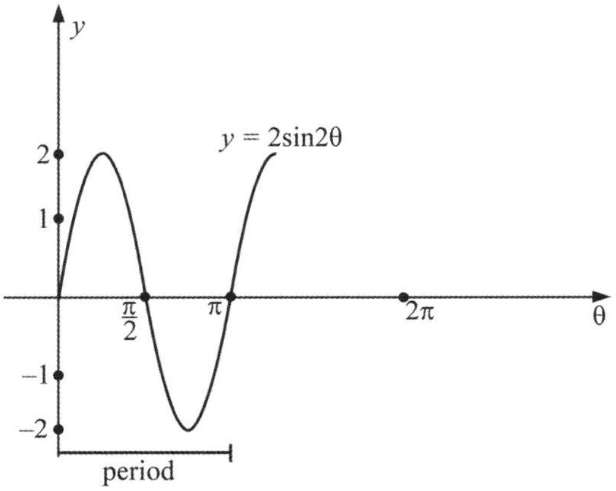

Parameter $d=\frac{\pi}{2}$, so there is a phase shift of $\frac{\pi}{2}$ units to the right.

Partial graph of $y = 2\sin\left(2\left(\theta - \frac{\pi}{2}\right)\right)$

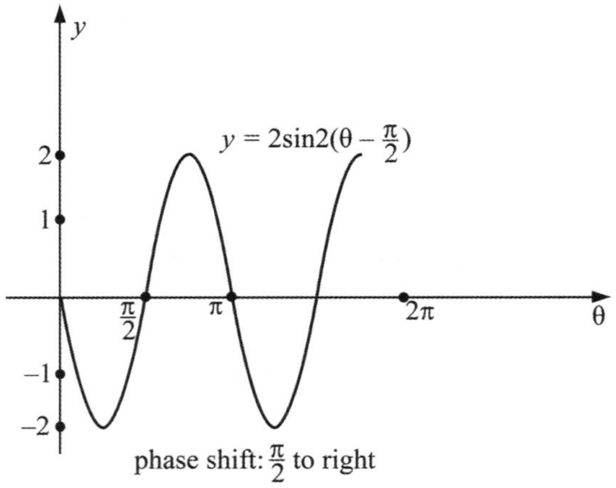

PRACTICE QUESTIONS

11. The graph of $y = 3\cos\left(\theta + \frac{1}{3}\right) + 2$ is the graph of $y = 3\cos\theta$ translated

A. $\frac{1}{3}$ radian right and 2 units up

B. $\frac{1}{3}$ radian left and 2 units up

C. $\frac{\pi}{3}$ radians right and 2 units up

D. $\frac{\pi}{3}$ radians left and 2 units down

Open Response

OR1.

a) Given $y = \frac{1}{2}\cos\left(\frac{1}{2}x\right) + 4$, describe the transformations that must be applied to the graph of $y = \cos x$ to obtain the graph of $y = \frac{1}{2}\cos\left(\frac{1}{2}x\right) + 4$,

Use the transformations from part a) to sketch the graph of $y = \frac{1}{2}\cos\left(\frac{1}{2}x\right) + 4$, on the grid provided.

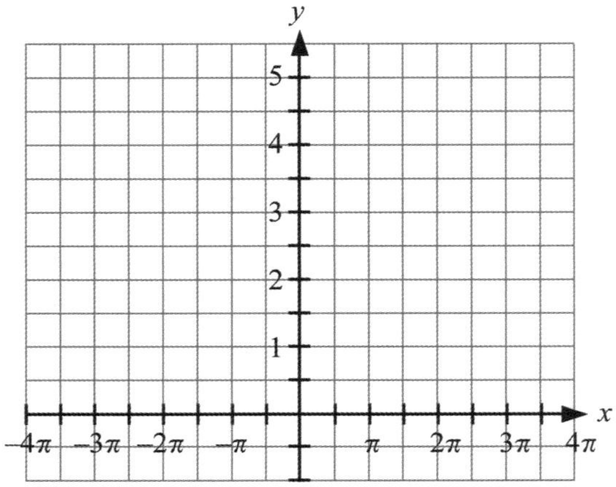

b) Relative to the graph of $y = \cos x$, what are the amplitude, period, phase shift, and vertical displacement for the graph of $y = \frac{1}{2}\cos\left(\frac{1}{2}x\right) + 4$,

2.6 *represent a sinusoidal function with an equation, given its graph or its properties, with angles expressed in radians.*

THE EQUATION OF A SINUSOIDAL FUNCTION

Example

For the sinusoidal function whose graph is shown below, represent the equation of the function in each of the following ways:

a) As a cosine function with the least possible phase shift and with $a > 0$

b) As a cosine function with no phase shift.

c) As a sine function with the least possible phase shift and with $a > 0$

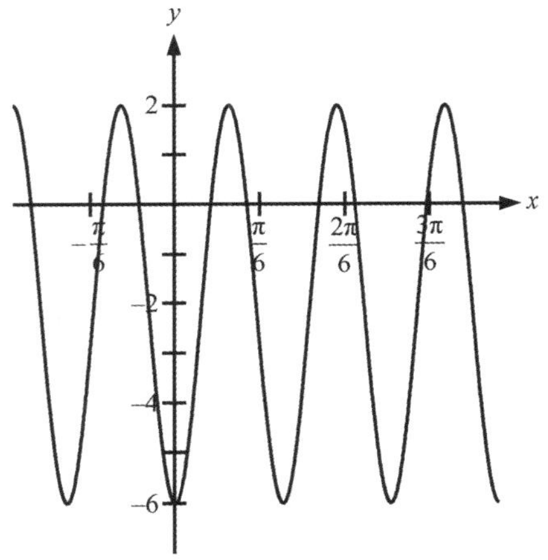

Solution

The maximum value is 2 and the minimum is –6, therefore

amplitude $= \frac{2-(-6)}{2} = 4$.

If $a > 0$, $a = 4$ and if $a < 0$, $a = -4$.

The vertical displacement, c, can be calculated from

$c = \frac{\max + \min}{2} = \frac{2+(-6)}{2} = -2$.

There is a minimum for the function at $x = 0$ and also at $x = \frac{4\pi}{6}$. Thus, the period is $\frac{4\pi}{6} = \frac{2\pi}{3}$. Since period $= \frac{2\pi}{k}$, then $k = \frac{2\pi}{\text{period}} = \frac{2\pi}{\frac{2\pi}{3}} = 2\pi \times \frac{3}{2\pi} = 3$.

a) For a cosine function, the maximum value occurs on the y-axis if there is no phase shift. For this function the maximum has been shifted either right or left of the vertical axis to $\frac{\pi}{3}$ (right) or to $-\frac{\pi}{3}$ (left).

So, $d = \frac{\pi}{3}$ or $d = -\frac{\pi}{3}$. Thus, possible equations are $y = 4\cos\left(3\left(x - \frac{\pi}{3}\right)\right) - 2$ or $y = 4\cos\left(3\left(x + \frac{\pi}{3}\right)\right) - 2$.

b) Since the minimum occurs on the y-axis, this graph could also be defined by a cosine function reflected about the horizontal axis with no phases shift. Here, $a = -4$, so the equation is $y = -4\cos(3x) - 2$.

To express this function in terms of sine determine where the graph is increasing and intersects the horizontal line, $y = -2$. This intersection occurs at $x = \frac{\pi}{6}$ so, as a sine function, there would be a phase shift of $\frac{\pi}{6}$ units right. Thus, the function can be expressed as $y = 4\sin\left(3\left(x - \frac{\pi}{6}\right)\right) - 2$.

All these equations can be verified on the calculator.

Practice Questions

Use the following graph to answer the next question.

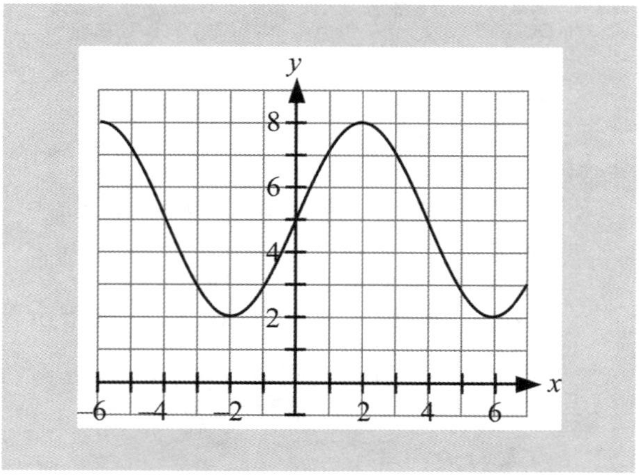

12. Which of the following equations of a sine function defines the given graph?

A. $y = 5\sin\left(\dfrac{x}{4}\right) + 3$

B. $y = 3\sin(4x) + 5$

C. $y = 3\sin\left(\dfrac{\pi x}{4}\right) + 5$

D. $y = 3\sin(4\pi x) + 5$

13. If the graph of $y = \cos x$ is stretched vertically about the x-axis by a factor of $\dfrac{1}{2}$, reflected in the x-axis, and then translate horizontally $\dfrac{\pi}{4}$ radians right, its equation is

A. $y = -2\cos\left(\dfrac{x}{4} - \pi\right)$

B. $y = -2\cos\left(x - \dfrac{\pi}{4}\right)$

C. $y = \dfrac{1}{2}\cos\left(-\dfrac{1}{4}(4x + \pi)\right)$

D. $y = -\dfrac{1}{2}\cos\left(\dfrac{1}{4}(4x - \pi)\right)$

2.7 pose problems based on applications involving a trigonometric function with domain expressed in radians, and solve these and other such problems by using a given graph or a graph generated with or without technology from a table of values or from its equation.

Applications of Trigonometric Functions

Example

On a particular day the height of the tide, relative to a pier in the Bay of Fundy, varies from a low of 3.5 m at 02:08 to a high of 16.3 m at 08:21 (time measured by a 24-hour clock).

a) Assume that the height of the tide can be modelled as a sinusoidal function of the time of day, and then determine an equation in the form $h(t) = a\cos(k(t-d)) + c$, where $h(t)$ is the height of the tides at the pier, in metres, and t is the time of day in hours. (Round all parameter values to the nearest hundredth.)

b) Determine the height of the tide relative to the pier at 11:30. Give your answer to the nearest 0.1 m.

c) A boat needs a depth of at least 10.0 m to dock at the pier. Use a graphical approach to determine when the boat is able to dock and when it must leave.

Solution

a) The parameters can be determined as follows:

$$a = \frac{\max - \min}{2} = \frac{16.3 - 3.5}{2} = 6.4 \text{ m}$$

$$c = \frac{\max + \min}{2} = \frac{16.3 + 3.5}{2} = 9.9 \text{ m}$$

The time interval between low tide and high tide, 08:21 – 02:08 = 06:13, is equal to half of the period. The period is $2 \times 06:13 = 12:26$, which is

$12 + \dfrac{26}{60} \approx 12.43$ h. The value of

parameter k is $\dfrac{2\pi}{12.43}$.

Parameter d is the phase shift.
When there is no phase shift, the cosine function has its maximum value on the vertical axis. The new maximum value occurs at $8:21 = 8 + \frac{21}{60} = 8.35$ h.
Since this phase shift is to the right, the value of c is -8.35. Therefore, the equation is

$$h(t) = 6.4\cos\left(\frac{2\pi}{12.43}(t - 8.35)\right) + 9.9.$$

b) Since 11:30 = 11.5 h, to find the height at this time evaluate $h(11.5)$.
Entering this information into the calculator in radian mode results in

$$h(11.5) = 6.4\cos\left(\frac{2\pi}{12.43}(11.5 - 8.35)\right) + 9.9$$

≈ 9.8 m

c) To find when the height of the tide relative to the pier is 10.0 m, we can graph

$$h(t) = 6.4\cos\left(\frac{2\pi}{12.43}(t - 8.35)\right) + 9.9$$

and $h(t) = 10$ and than find their points of intersection.

Using a TI-83 calculator with an appropriate viewing window such as $x:[0,12.43,1]$, $y:[0,16.5,2]$, input $Y_1 = 6.4\cos(2\pi/12.43(X - 8.35)) + 9.9$ and $Y_2 = 10$ into the Y= menu.

The resulting graphs are shown below.

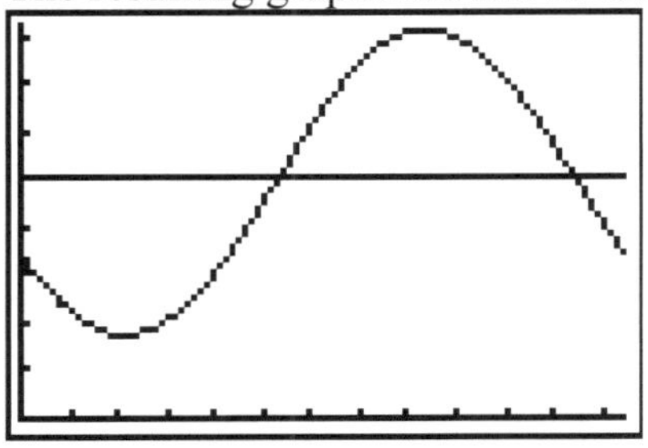

Applying the intersect feature, shows that the tide first rises above 10.0 m at approximately 5.273 hours, which is at time 5 + .2734 × 60 = 05:16, and falls below 10.0 m at approximately 11.4266 hours, which is at time 11 + .4266 × 60 = 11:26 The boat is safe to dock from about 5:17 until 11:25.

Practice Questions

Use the following information to answer the next 2 question.

The height of a person above the ground on a Ferris wheel is given by the function $h(t) = 9\sin\left(\frac{\pi}{20}\left(t - \frac{\pi}{2}\right)\right) + 12$ where $h(t)$ is the height in metres of the person t seconds after getting on.

14. How long does it take the Ferris wheel to make one complete revolution?

A. 10 s

B. 20 s

C. 40 s

D. 60 s

15. How long, to the nearest second, after the rider gets on the Ferris wheel does the rider first reach a height of 18 m? (**Hint**: use a graphical approach to determine the answer)

A. 15 s

B. 20 s

C. 25 s

D. 28 s

3.1 recognize equivalent trigonometric expressions, and verify equivalence using graphing technology.

EQUIVALENT TRIGONOMETRIC EXPRESSIONS

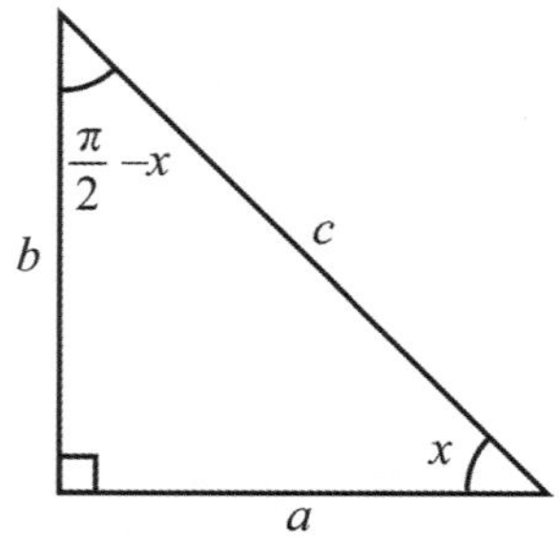

Since $90° = \frac{\pi}{2}$ rad, in a right triangle in which one of the acute angles has a measure of x rad, the other acute angle would have a measure of $\frac{\pi}{2} - x$ rad as shown in the triangle above.

The sides of the triangle are designated as a, b, and c as indicated in the diagram.

From the triangle,

$$\sin x = \frac{\text{side opposite angle } x}{\text{hypotenuse}} = \frac{b}{c} \text{ and}$$

$$\cos\left(\frac{\pi}{2} - x\right) = \frac{\text{side adjacent angle }\left(\frac{\pi}{2} - x\right)}{\text{hypotenuse}} = \frac{b}{c}.$$

Thus, $\sin x = \cos\left(\frac{\pi}{2} - x\right)$

Consider the function $y = \cos\left(x + \frac{\pi}{2}\right)$.

This is a horizontal translation of the graph of $y = \cos x$ to the left $\frac{\pi}{2}$ units. The graph of $y = \cos x$ is grey, and the graph of $y = \cos\left(x + \frac{\pi}{2}\right)$ is black in the diagram.

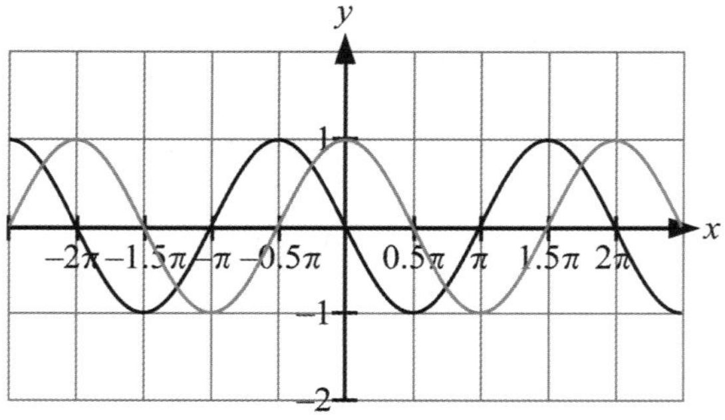

The graph of $y = -\sin x$ is shown below.

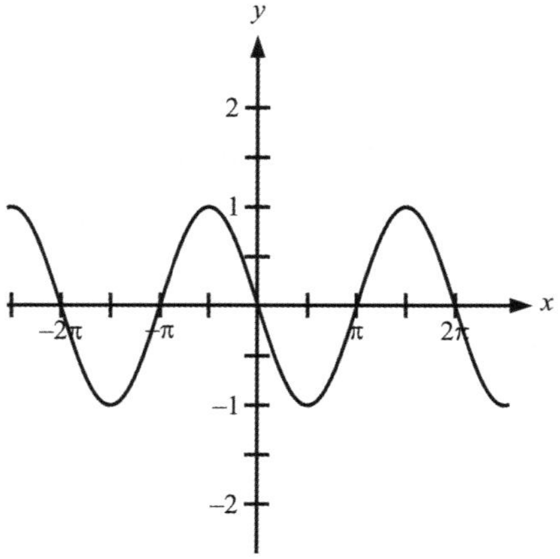

The function $y = -\sin x$ is a reflection of the graph of $y = \sin x$ in the x-axis. The result of translating $y = \cos x$ to the left $\frac{\pi}{2}$ units is equivalent to a reflection of the graph of $y = \sin x$ in the x-axis. The preceding two graphs illustrate that $\cos\left(x + \frac{\pi}{2}\right) = -\sin x$.

Example

Verify that $\sin\left(x - \frac{\pi}{2}\right) = -\cos x$ with a graphing calculator by graphing two different functions.

Solution

Graph $Y_1 = \sin(x - \frac{\pi}{2})$ and $Y_2 = -\cos(x)$ with appropriate window settings such as $x:[-2\pi, 2\pi, \pi]$, $y:[-2, 2, 1]$. The graphs are shown.

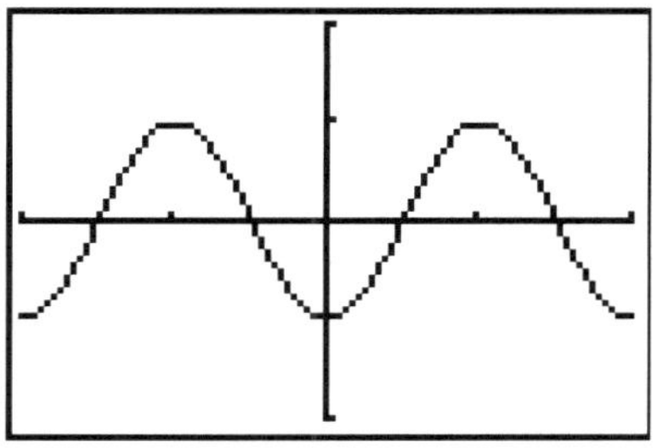

The fact that both graphs are the same verifies that $\sin\left(x-\frac{\pi}{2}\right)=-\cos x$

Practice Question

16. The expression $\cos x$ is equivalent to

A. $\cos\left(\frac{\pi}{2}-x\right)$

B. $-\sin x$

C. $\sin\left(\frac{\pi}{2}-x\right)$

D. $\sin\left(x-\frac{\pi}{2}\right)$

3.2 explore the algebraic development of the compound angle formulas and use the formulas to determine exact values of trigonometric ratios.

The Compound Angle Formulas

The following six formulas are referred to as the compound angle formulas.

$$\sin(x+y)=\sin x\cos y+\cos x\sin y$$

$$\sin(x-y)=\sin x\cos y-\cos x\sin y$$

$$\cos(x+y)=\cos x\cos y-\sin x\sin y$$

$$\cos(x-y)=\cos x\cos y+\sin x\sin y$$

$$\tan(x+y)=\frac{\tan x+\tan y}{1-\tan x\tan y}$$

$$\tan(x-y)=\frac{\tan x-\tan y}{1+\tan x\tan y}$$

Example

Using exact value, verify the formula $\sin(x+y)=\sin x\cos y+\cos x\sin y$ for $x=\frac{\pi}{3}$ and $y=\frac{5\pi}{6}$.

Solution

Recall the following exact values:

$\sin\left(\frac{\pi}{3}\right)=\frac{\sqrt{3}}{2}, \cos\left(\frac{\pi}{3}\right)=\frac{1}{2},$

$\sin\left(\frac{5\pi}{6}\right)=\frac{1}{2},$ and $\cos\left(\frac{5\pi}{6}\right)=-\frac{1}{2}.$

Substituting into the left side (L.S.) and the right (R.S.) separately gives

$$\text{L.S.}=\sin\left(\frac{\pi}{3}+\frac{5\pi}{6}\right)=\sin\left(\frac{2\pi}{6}+\frac{5\pi}{6}\right)$$

$$=\sin\left(\frac{7\pi}{6}\right)$$

$$=-\frac{1}{2}$$

$$\text{R.S.}=\sin\left(\frac{\pi}{3}\right)\cos\left(\frac{5\pi}{6}\right)+\cos\left(\frac{\pi}{3}\right)\sin\left(\frac{5\pi}{6}\right)$$

$$=\frac{\sqrt{3}}{2}\times\left(-\frac{\sqrt{3}}{2}\right)+\frac{1}{2}\times\frac{1}{2}=-\frac{3}{4}+\frac{1}{4}$$

$$=-\frac{1}{2}$$

L.S. = R.S

Example

Determine the exact value of $\cos\left(\frac{7\pi}{12}\right)$.

Solution

$$\cos\left(\frac{7\pi}{12}\right)=\cos\left(\frac{\pi}{4}+\frac{\pi}{3}\right)$$

$$=\cos\left(\frac{\pi}{4}\right)\cos\left(\frac{\pi}{3}\right)-\sin\left(\frac{\pi}{4}\right)\sin\left(\frac{\pi}{3}\right)$$

$$= \frac{\sqrt{2}}{2} \times \frac{1}{2} - \frac{\sqrt{2}}{2} \times \frac{\sqrt{3}}{2}$$
$$= \frac{\sqrt{2}}{4} - \frac{\sqrt{6}}{4}$$
$$= \frac{\sqrt{2} - \sqrt{6}}{4}$$

Practice Question

17. The exact value of $\sin\left(\frac{\pi}{12}\right)$ can be determined by calculating

A. $\sin\left(\frac{\pi}{3}\right)\cos\left(\frac{\pi}{4}\right) + \cos\left(\frac{\pi}{3}\right)\sin\left(\frac{\pi}{4}\right)$

B. $\cos\left(\frac{\pi}{3}\right)\cos\left(\frac{\pi}{4}\right) - \sin\left(\frac{\pi}{3}\right)\sin\left(\frac{\pi}{4}\right)$

C $\sin\left(\frac{3\pi}{4}\right)\cos\left(\frac{2\pi}{3}\right) + \cos\left(\frac{3\pi}{4}\right)\sin\left(\frac{2\pi}{3}\right)$

D. $\sin\left(\frac{3\pi}{4}\right)\cos\left(\frac{2\pi}{3}\right) - \cos\left(\frac{3\pi}{4}\right)\sin\left(\frac{2\pi}{3}\right)$

18. When $\cos\left(\theta + \frac{\pi}{4}\right) + \cos\left(\theta - \frac{\pi}{4}\right)$ is simplified, it is equal to

A. $2\cos\theta$

B. $\sqrt{2}\cos\theta$

C. $\frac{\sqrt{2}}{2}\cos\theta$

D. 0

3.3 *recognize that trigonometric identities are equations that are true for every value in the domain, prove trigonometric identities through the application of reasoning skills, using a variety of relationships, and verify identities using technology*

Trigonometric Identities

An **identity** is a statement of equality that is true for all permissible values of the variable(s).

An example of an identity is $\frac{x}{x} = 1,\ x \neq 0.$

Example

Determine the values for which the identity $\frac{\cos^2 x}{\cos x} = \cos x$ is true in the interval $0 \leq x \leq 2\pi,$

Solution

This identity is undefined if $\cos x = 0$. In the interval $0 \leq x \leq 2\pi,$ this occurs when $x = \frac{\pi}{2}$ or $\frac{3\pi}{2}$. As long as $x \neq \frac{\pi}{2}$ or $\frac{3\pi}{2}$, $\frac{\cos^2 x}{\cos x}$ can be replaced by $\cos x$.

To prove that identities are true for all permissible values, each side is simplified independent of the other until each side is shown to be equal to a common result.

The processes used in the simplification are:

1) Replacing one part of a given identity with its equal
2) Performing operations, $+, -, \times, \div$ sometimes with fractional expressions
3) Factoring and reducing

Example

Prove the identity

$$\frac{1+\cos x}{\sin x} + \frac{\sin x}{1+\cos x} = 2\csc x$$

Solution

L.S. =

Obtain a common denominator

$$\left(\frac{1+\cos x}{\sin x}\right)\left(\frac{1+\cos x}{1+\cos x}\right)+\left(\frac{\sin x}{1+\cos x}\right)\left(\frac{\sin x}{\sin x}\right)$$

Multiplication

$$=\frac{1+2\cos x+\cos^2 x}{(\sin x)(1+\cos x)}+\frac{\sin^2 x}{(\sin x)(1+\cos x)}$$

Addition

$$=\frac{1+2\cos x+\cos^2 x+\sin^2 x}{(\sin x)(1+\cos x)}$$

Since $\cos^2 x+\sin^2 x=1$

$$=\frac{1+2\cos x+1}{(\sin x)(1+\cos x)}$$

Addition

$$=\frac{2+2\cos x}{(\sin x)(1+\cos x)}$$

Remove common factor

$$=\frac{2(1+\cos x)}{(\sin x)(1+\cos x)}$$

Cancel common factor

$$=\frac{2}{\sin x}$$

R.S. =

Since $\csc x=\dfrac{1}{\sin x}$

$$2\times\frac{1}{\sin x}$$

$$=\frac{2}{\sin x}$$

Thus, **L.S.** = **R.S**.

The double angle formulas are:

a) $\sin 2x=2\sin x\cos x$

b) $\cos 2x=\cos^2 x-\sin^2 x$

$=1-2\sin^2 x$

$=2\cos^2 x-1$

c) $\tan 2x=\dfrac{2\tan x}{1-\tan^2 x}$

These double angle formulas (identities) can be proven by using the compound angle formulas.

Example

Prove that $\cos 2x=1-2\sin^2 x$.

Solution

L.S. $=\cos 2x$

$=\cos(x+x)$

Using $\cos(x+y)=\cos x\cos y-\sin x\sin y$ and substituting x for y.

$=\cos x\cos x-\sin x\sin x$

$=\cos^2 x-\sin^2 x$

Substituting $1-\sin^2 x$ for $\cos^2 x$

$=\left(1-\sin^2 x\right)-\sin^2 x$

$=1-\sin^2 x-\sin^2 x$

$=1-2\sin^2 x$

R.S. = $1-2\sin^2 x$

Thus, **L.S.** = **R.S**.

PRACTICE QUESTIONS

19. Which of the following sets lists **all** undefined values for the expression $\dfrac{\sin\theta-\sin^3\theta}{1-\sin^2\theta}$ in the interval $0\le\theta\le 2\pi$?

A. $\left\{\frac{3\pi}{2}\right\}$

B. $\left\{\frac{\pi}{2}\right\}$

C. $\left\{\frac{\pi}{2},\frac{3\pi}{2}\right\}$

D. $\{\ \}$ (the expression is defined for all values of θ)

20. For all permissible values of x, $\frac{\sec x}{\sin x} - \frac{\sin x}{\cos x}$ is equivalent to

A. $\sec x$

B. $\cot x$

C. $\tan x$

D. $\frac{1}{\tan x - 1}$

Open Response

OR2. Given the identity $\frac{\sin^2 x}{1+\cos x} = 1 - \cos x$,

a) Verify the identity for $x = \frac{\pi}{2}$

b) Verify the identity graphically over the interval by using technology

c) Prove the identity algebraically

3.4 solve linear and quadratic trigonometric equations, with and without graphing technology, for the domain of real values from 0 to 2π, and solve related problems

SOLVING TRIGONOMETRIC EQUATIONS

There you will work with an example of a linear trigonometric equation.

Example

Determine the exact solutions of $2\sin x + 1 = 0,\ 0 \le x \le 2\pi.$

Solution

First isolate the trig expression.

$$2\sin x + 1 = 0$$
$$2\sin x = -1$$
$$\sin x = -\frac{1}{2}$$

Next, use the unit circle to determine where the sine function equals $-\frac{1}{2}$.

This occurs when $x = \frac{7\pi}{6}$ or $\frac{11\pi}{6}$, so these are the two values for x that satisfy the equation $2\sin x + 1 = 0$ in the internal $0 \le x \le 2\pi$.

To verify the answers $\frac{7\pi}{6}$ and $\frac{11\pi}{6}$ graphically using a TI-83 calculator (in radian mode), input $Y1 = 2\sin(X)+1$ with a window setting such as $x:\left[0, 2\pi, \frac{\pi}{6}\right]$ and $y:[-3,3,1]$.

The solutions are the x-intercepts, which occur at the 7th and 11th units on the x-axis of the graph as shown below.

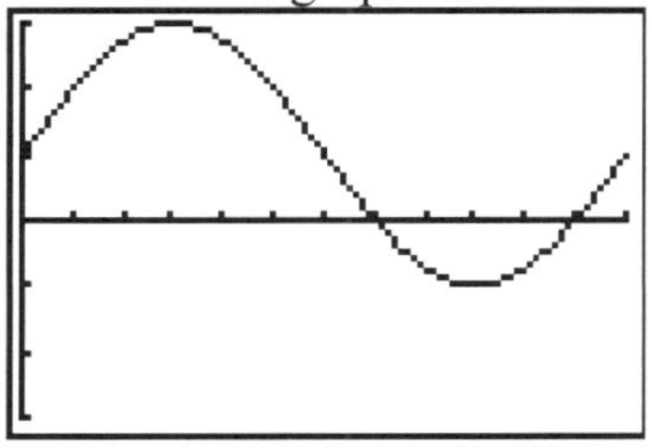

The next two examples are quadratic trigonometric equations.

Example

Solve $4\cos^2 x - 3 = 0$, $0 \le x \le 2\pi$, giving exact solutions.

Solution

Solve by isolating $\cos^2 x$ and then taking the square root of each side.

$$4\cos^2 x - 3 = 0$$

$$4\cos^2 x = 3$$

$$\cos^2 x = \frac{3}{4}$$

$$\cos x = \pm\sqrt{\frac{3}{4}} = \pm\frac{\sqrt{3}}{2}$$

Using the unit circle, the solutions are $x = \frac{\pi}{6}, \frac{5\pi}{6}, \frac{7\pi}{6}, \frac{11\pi}{6}$.

Example

Solve $4\cos^2 x - \cos x - 3 = 0$, $0 \le x \le 2\pi$, giving exact solutions.

Solution

Begin by writing the left side of the equation in factored form.

$$4\cos^2 x - 4\cos x - 3 = 0$$

$$(2\cos x - 3)(2\cos x + 1) = 0$$

$$2\cos x - 3 = 0 \text{ or } 2\cos x + 1 = 0$$

$$\cos x = \frac{3}{2} \text{ or } \cos x = -\frac{1}{2}$$

The equation $\cos x = \frac{3}{2}$ has no solutions since the range of $\cos x$ is $-1 \le \cos x \le 1$.

The solutions of $\cos x = -\frac{1}{2}$ are $x = \frac{2\pi}{3}, \frac{4\pi}{3}$.

The solution to some equations require the use of an identity.

Example

Solve $\sin 2x = \cos x$, $0 \le x \le 2\pi$, giving exact solutions.

Solution

$\sin 2x = \cos x$

Replace $\sin 2x$ by its equivalent form $2\sin x \cos x$.

$2\sin x \cos x = \cos x$

Get one side equal to zero since the equation is quadratic.

$2\sin x \cos x - \cos x = 0$

Remove common factor of $\cos x$.

$\cos x(2\sin x - 1) = 0$

Set the factors equal to zero

$\cos x = 0$ or $2\sin x - 1 = 0$

$$2\sin x = 1$$

$$\sin x = \frac{1}{2}$$

Now, find the solutions from the unit circle.

Thus the solutions are $x = \frac{\pi}{6}, \frac{\pi}{2}, \frac{5\pi}{6}, \frac{3\pi}{2}$.

Example

Solve $\sin 2x = \frac{\sqrt{2}}{2}$, $0 \le x \le 2\pi$, giving exact solutions.

Solution

This is not the same type of question as the previous one because there is only one trigonometric expression in the equation. You could try replacing $\sin 2x$ with $2\sin x \cos x$ as in the previous example, but you would find that doing so would not create an equation that is easily solvable. As well, you need a technique for expressions involving other multi-angles such as $\sin 3x$ or $\cos\left(\frac{1}{2}x\right)$.

The following procedure works for equations of this type.
First, adjust the given domain so that you can solve for $2x$ first. Do this by multiplying the given domain, $0 \le x \le 2\pi$, by 2 to get $0 \le 2x \le 4\pi$.
This indicates that the solutions for $2x$ exist in two rotations of the unit circle. From the unit circle it is clear that the cosine ratio equals $\frac{\sqrt{2}}{2}$ at $\frac{\pi}{4}$ and $\frac{3\pi}{4}$.
These are solutions less than 2π. To find the solutions from 2π to 4π, we add 2π. to each of these solutions.

Therefore $2x = \frac{\pi}{4}, \frac{3\pi}{4}, \frac{\pi}{4} + 2\pi, \frac{3\pi}{4} + 2\pi$

$$2x = \frac{\pi}{4}, \frac{3\pi}{4}, \frac{9\pi}{4}, \frac{11\pi}{4}$$

To solve for x, divide each of these solution values by 2.

$$x = \frac{\pi}{8}, \frac{3\pi}{8}, \frac{9\pi}{8}, \frac{11\pi}{8}$$

Practice Questions

Use the following information to answer the next questions.

In solving the trigonometric equation $\sin^3 \theta = \sin \theta$, a student performed the following first four steps.

$\sin^3 \theta = \sin \theta$

Step 1 $\sin^2 \theta = 1$ Divide each side by $\sin \theta$

Step 2 $\sin^2 \theta - 1 = 0$ Subtract 1 from each side

Step 3 $(\sin \theta - 1)(\sin \theta + 1) = 0$ Factor

Step 4 $\sin \theta = \pm 1$ Solve for $\sin \theta$

21. Which of the following statements about the student's work is correct?

- **A.** The student's first error was made in Step 1.
- **B.** The student's first error was made in Step 3.
- **C.** The student's first error was made in Step 4.
- **D.** The student did not make an error.

22. The complete solution set for the equation $\frac{2\sin^2 x - \sin x}{1 - \cos x} = 0$, $0 \le x \le 2\pi$ is

- **A.** $\left\{0, \frac{1}{2}\right\}$
- **B.** $\left\{0, \frac{\pi}{6}\right\}$
- **C.** $\left\{\frac{\pi}{6}, \frac{5\pi}{6}, \pi\right\}$
- **D.** $\left\{0, \pi, \frac{\pi}{6}, \frac{5\pi}{6}, 2\pi\right\}$

Numerical Response

NR3. The number of solutions to the equation $a\sin 4x = 0$, $0 \le x \le 2\pi$ is ___________.

NOTES

ANSWERS AND SOLUTIONS—TRIGONOMETRIC FUNCTIONS

1. C	**7. A**	**12. C**	**19. C**
NR1. 67.2	**8. B**	**13. D**	**20. B**
2. D	**9. A**	**14. C**	**OR2. See Solution**
3. A	**10. B**	**15. A**	**21. A**
4. C	**NR2. 15.7**	**16 C**	**22. C**
5. A	**11. B**	**17. D**	**NR3. 9**
6. D	**OR1. See Solution**	**18. B**	

1. **C**

Since π rad = 180 °, an angle of $\frac{11\pi}{45}$ rad , expressed in degrees, is

$$\frac{11\pi}{45}\text{rad} = \frac{11\pi}{45}\left(\frac{180}{\pi}\right) = 44°$$

NR1. **67.2**

An arc of a circle with a radius of 42 cm subtends a central angle of 1.6 rad. Find the length of the arc by using the formula

$\theta = \frac{a}{r}$, where $\theta =$ central angle in radians, a = arc length, and r = radius. Substituting $\theta = 1.6$ and $r = 42$ gives:

$$1.6 = \frac{a}{42}$$

$$a = 42(1.6) = 67.2 \text{ cm}$$

2. **D**

$$645° = 645 \times \frac{\pi}{180} = \frac{645\pi}{180} = \frac{43\pi}{12} \text{ rad}$$

3. **A**

In radian mode, input $1/\cos(11\pi/8)$ and press ENTER. The display shows -2.61312593, so, to the nearest thousandth, $\sec\left(\frac{11\pi}{8}\right) = -2.613$.

4. **C**

An angle of $\frac{4\pi}{3}$ rad terminates in quadrant III and has a reference angle of $\frac{\pi}{3}$.

5. **A**

The amplitude is determined by $\frac{\text{max} - \text{min}}{2}$. For $y = \cos x$, this is $\frac{1-(-1)}{2} = 1$.

6. **D**

Since the function $f(\theta) = \tan\theta$ is defined as $\tan\theta = \frac{y}{x}$, where x and y are coordinates on the terminal arm of the angle θ in standard position, it is not defined when $x = 0$

This occurs when $\theta = \frac{\pi}{2} + n\pi,\ n \in I$ and thus, $\theta \neq \frac{\pi}{2} + n\pi,\ n \in I$.

7. **A**

The range of both $y = \csc x$ and $y = \sec x$ is $|y| \geq 1$.

8. **B**

The asymptotes for both graphs are given by equations of the form $x = n\pi,\ n \in I$. Notice that the definitions $\csc\theta = \frac{r}{y}$ and $\cot\theta = \frac{x}{y}$ are both undefined when $y = 0$, which is when $x = n\pi,\ n \in I$.

9. **A**

First, factor the 4 out of the part in parentheses so that the function fits the form $y = a\sin\left(k\left(x-d\right)\right)+c$.

$y = 3\sin\left(4x - \frac{\pi}{2}\right)$

$y = 3\sin\left(4\left(x - \frac{\pi}{8}\right)\right)$

The period is $\frac{2\pi}{k} = \frac{2\pi}{4} = \frac{\pi}{2}$.

The phase shift is $\frac{\pi}{8}$ to the right.

10. **B**

The amplitude of $f\left(\theta\right) = a\cos\left(k\left(\theta - d\right)\right)+c$ is $|a|$, which in this case is $|-7| = 7$.

NR2. **15.7**

In the given equation, the value of k (the coefficient of θ) is $\frac{2}{5}$.

The period is $\frac{2\pi}{k}$ which is

$$\frac{2\pi}{\frac{2}{5}} = 2\pi \times \frac{5}{2} \approx 15.7$$

11. **B**

In relation to the standard form of the function $f(x) - a\cos(k(x-d)) + c$ parameter d is $-\frac{1}{3}$ and parameter c is +2. The parameters result translation of $-\frac{1}{3}$ rad left and 2 units up.

0R1.

a) When $y = \frac{1}{2}\cos\left(\frac{1}{2}x\right)+4$ is compared with $y = a\cos(k(x-d)+c$ the parameters are $a = \frac{1}{2},\ k = \frac{1}{2}$, and $c = 4$. These parameters indicate transformations of: a vertical compression about the x-axis by a factor of $\frac{1}{2}$, a horizontal stretch about the y-axis by a factor 2, and a translation of 4 units up.

b)

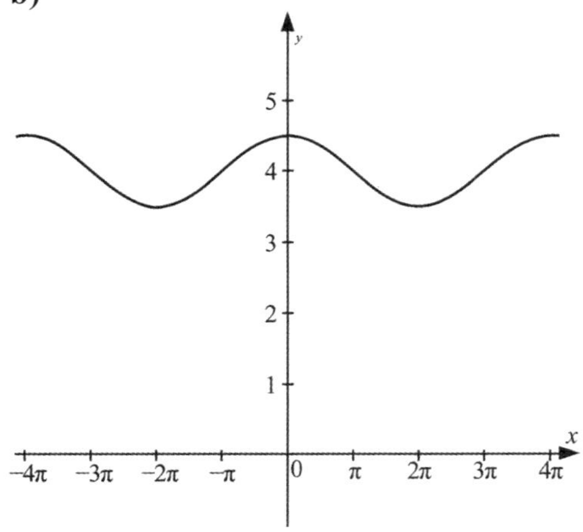

c) Amplitude = $\frac{1}{2}$, the period = 4π, there is no phase shift, and the vertical displacement is 4 units up.

12. C

Fit the equation into the form $y = a\sin(k(x-d)) + c$. Examine the graph to determine that the amplitude is 3 and note that the sine function is not reflected in a horizontal axis, so a is positive. Thus, $a = +3$. Since the function is translated up 5 units, $c = 5$. There is no phase shift, so $d = 0$. Examination of the graph also shows that the period is 8, so $\frac{2\pi}{k} = 8$, which gives $k = \frac{\pi}{4}$. Thus, the equation is

$$y = 3\sin\left(\frac{\pi}{4}(x-0)\right) + 5 \text{ or}$$

$$y = 3\sin\left(\frac{\pi x}{4}\right) + 5.$$

13. D

Given the standard form of the function, $y = a\cos(k(x-d)) + c$, the parameters are a is $-\frac{1}{2}$, k is 1, d is $\frac{\pi}{4}$, and c is 0. When these parameters are entered, the function is

$$y = -\frac{1}{2}\cos\left(1\left(x - \frac{\pi}{4}\right)\right) + 0, \text{ which is}$$

equivalent to $y = -\frac{1}{2}\cos\left(\frac{1}{4}(4x - \pi)\right)$.

14. C

The time it takes the Ferris wheel to make one revolution is equal to the period of the function. First, change

$$h(t) = 9\sin\left(\frac{\pi}{20}t - \frac{\pi}{2}\right) + 12 \text{ to}$$

$$h(t) = 9\sin\left(\frac{\pi}{20}(t-10)\right) + 12 \text{ by}$$

factoring the expression in parentheses.

The period is $\dfrac{2\pi}{\frac{\pi}{20}} = 2\pi \times \frac{20}{\pi} = 40$ s.

15. A

Using a TI-83 calculator with an appropriate viewing window such as $x:[0, 60, 1]$, $y:[0, 25, 1]$ input $Y_1 = 9\sin(\pi/20(X-2) + 12$ and $Y_2 = 18$ into the Y= menu.

The graphs are shown below.

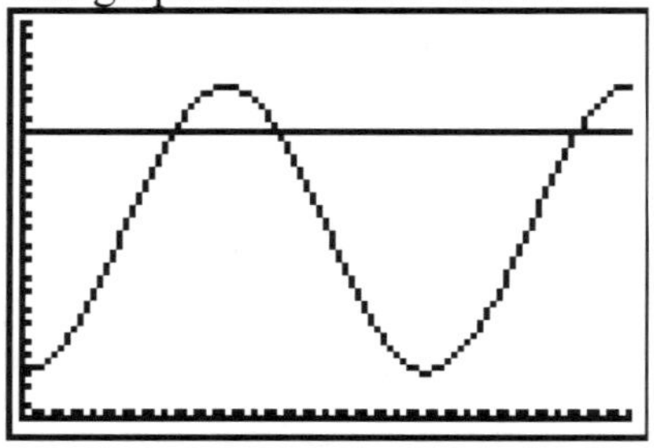

Applying the intersect feature shows that the ferris wheel reaches 18 m first after approximately 15 s.

16 C

Given a right triangle, as shown below, $\cos x = \frac{a}{c}$ and $\sin\left(\frac{\pi}{2} - x\right) = \frac{a}{c}$.

Therefore, $\cos x = \sin\left(\frac{\pi}{2} - x\right)$.

The expressions can also be shown to be equivalent by graphing $y = \cos x$ and $y = \sin\left(\frac{\pi}{2} - \pi\right)$.

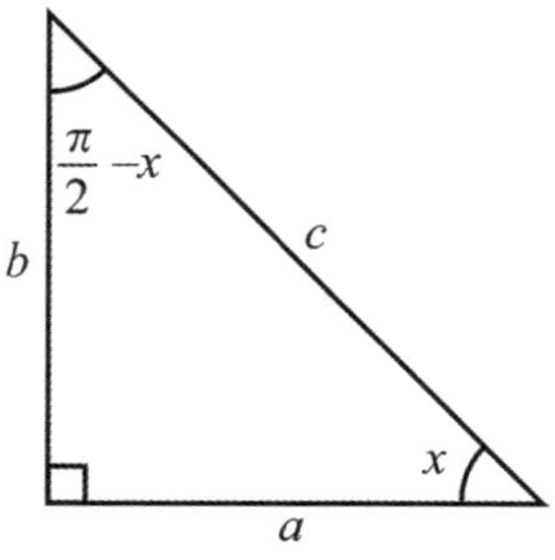

17. **D**

The exact value of $\sin\left(\frac{\pi}{12}\right)$ is determined by using a compound angle formula with two special angles that have a sum or difference of $\frac{\pi}{12}$.

From the alternatives that are given:

$\frac{\pi}{3}-\frac{\pi}{4}=\frac{4\pi}{12}-\frac{3\pi}{12}=\frac{\pi}{12}$ or

$\frac{3\pi}{4}-\frac{2\pi}{3}=\frac{9\pi}{12}-\frac{8\pi}{12}=\frac{\pi}{12}$. Since the formula for the sine of a difference is

$$\sin(x-y)=(\sin x)(\cos y)-(\cos x)(\sin y)$$

the expression that fits this pattern is required. The expression that fits is

$$\sin\left(\frac{3\pi}{4}\right)\cos\left(\frac{2\pi}{3}\right)-\cos\left(\frac{3\pi}{4}\right)\sin\left(\frac{2\pi}{3}\right).$$

18. **B**

Use the formulas

$\cos(x+y)=\cos x\cos y-\sin x\sin y$

and

$\cos(x-y)=\cos x\cos y+\sin x\sin y$.

$$\cos\left(\theta+\frac{\pi}{4}\right)+\cos\left(\theta-\frac{\pi}{4}\right)$$

$$=\cos\theta\cos\left(\frac{\pi}{4}\right)-\sin\theta\sin\left(\frac{\pi}{4}\right)+\cos\theta\cos\left(\frac{\pi}{4}\right)+\sin\theta\sin\left(\frac{\pi}{4}\right)$$

$$=2\cos\theta\cos\left(\frac{\pi}{4}\right)$$

$$=(2\cos\theta)\left(\frac{\sqrt{2}}{2}\right)$$

$$=\sqrt{2}\cos\theta$$

19. **C**

The expression $\frac{\sin\theta-\sin^3\theta}{1-\sin^2\theta}$ is undefined when $1-\sin^2\theta=0$ which is when $\sin\theta=\pm1$. In the interval $0\le\theta\le2\pi$, $\sin\theta=1$ when $\theta=\frac{\pi}{2}$ and $\sin\theta=-1$ when $\theta=\frac{3\pi}{2}$. Note that

$$\frac{\sin\theta-\sin^3\theta}{1-\sin^2\theta}=\frac{\sin\theta\left(1-\sin^2\theta\right)}{1-\sin^2\theta}=\sin\theta$$

only if $1-\sin^2\theta\neq1$

20. **B**

$$\frac{\sec x}{\sin x}-\frac{\sin x}{\cos x}$$

Write with a common denominator

$$=\frac{\sec x\cos x-\sin^2 x}{\sin x\cos x}$$

Since $\sec x=\frac{1}{\cos x}$

$$=\frac{\left(\frac{1}{\cos x}\right)\cos x-\sin^2 x}{\sin x\cos x}$$

Cancel $(\cos x)$

$$=\frac{1-\sin^2 x}{\sin x\cos x}$$

Since $1-\sin^2 x=\cos^2 x$

$$=\frac{\cos^2 x}{\sin x\cos x}$$

Cancel $(\cos x)$

$$=\frac{\cos x}{\sin x}$$

Since $\frac{\cos x}{\sin x}=\cot x$

$$=\cot x$$

0R2.

a) Substituting $x=\frac{\pi}{2}$ into each side of the equation gives:

$$\textbf{L.S.}=\frac{\sin^2\left(\frac{\pi}{2}\right)}{1+\cos\left(\frac{\pi}{2}\right)}$$

$$=\frac{(1)^2}{1+(0)}$$

$$=1$$

$$\textbf{R.S.}=1-\cos\left(\frac{\pi}{2}\right)$$

$$=1-0$$

$$=1$$

Since **L.S.** = **R.S.**, the identity is verified for $x=\frac{\pi}{2}$.

b) One method of verifying the identity graphically is to graph the two functions $y=\frac{\sin^2 x}{1+\cos x}$ and $y=1-\cos x$, and observe that they appear to be the same graph. Using a TI-83 calculator and appropriate window settings such as $x:[-2\pi,2\pi,\pi]$, $y:[-3,3,1]$, graph $Y_1=(\sin(X))^2/(1+\cos(X))$ and $Y_2=1-\cos(X)$. The graphs are shown below with the second function graphed with a thicker line in order to illustrate that the second function graphs on top of the first.

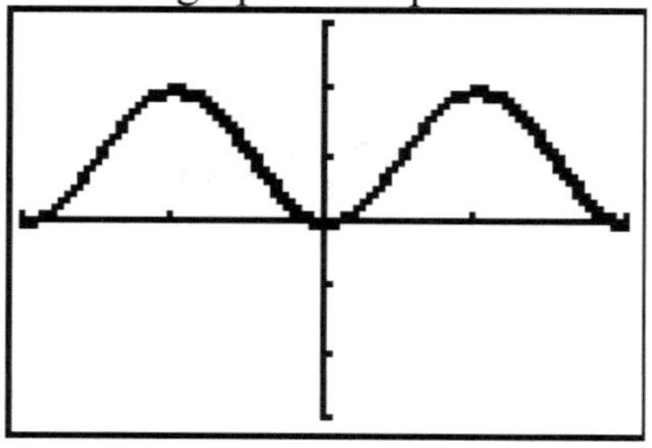

c)

$$\textbf{L.S.}=\frac{\sin^2 x}{1+\cos x}$$

Since $\sin^2 x=1-\cos^2 x$

$$=\frac{1-\cos^2 x}{1+\cos x}$$

Factor

$$=\frac{(1-\cos x)(1+\cos x)}{1+\cos x}$$

Cancel $(1+\cos x)$

$$=1-\cos x$$

R.S. = $1-\cos x$

Since **L.S.** = **R.S.**, the identity is verified.

21. A

Dividing each side of the equation by $\sin\theta$ results in an equation that is not equivalent to the original because it does not include the solutions when $\sin\theta=0$ The student should have subtracted $\sin\theta$ from both sides and then proceeded to factor the expression on the left side.

22. C

First, notice that $1-\cos x\neq 0$ and thus, $\cos x\neq 1$, which means that $x\neq 0,\text{or } 2\pi$

Solving gives:

$$\frac{2\sin^2 x-\sin x}{1-\cos x}=0$$

Multiply each side by $1-\cos x$

$$2\sin^2 x-\sin x=0$$

Factor

$$\sin x(2\sin x-1)=0$$

$$\sin x=0 \text{ or } 2\sin x-1=0$$

$$\sin x=\frac{1}{2}$$

$$x=0,\pi,2\pi \text{ or } x=\frac{\pi}{6},\frac{5\pi}{6}$$

But, recall that $x\neq 0 \text{ or } 2\pi$ Therefore, the solution set is $\left\{\frac{\pi}{6},\frac{5\pi}{6},\pi\right\}$.

NR3. 9

Since $0 \leq x \leq 2\pi$ then $0 \leq 4x \leq 8\pi$
The solutions for $4x$ are $0, \pi$, and 2π.
The solutions for x are 0, $\frac{\pi}{4}$, and $\frac{\pi}{2}$,
plus 6 more solutions, for a total of 9.

UNIT TEST — TRIGONOMETRIC FUNCTIONS

1. An angle of $125°$ expressed in radians to the nearest tenth, is

A. 2.2 rad

B. 4.4 rad

C. 8.8 rad

D. 7162.0 rad

2. Which of the following radian measures is a multiple of $30°$?

A. $\frac{9\pi}{8}$ rad

B. $\frac{17\pi}{3}$ rad

C. $\frac{7\pi}{12}$ rad

D. 240 rad

3. The correct calculator input in radian mode to determine the value of $\cot\left(\frac{7\pi}{3}\right)$ is

A. $\tan(3/(7\pi))$

B. $1/\tan((7\pi)/3)$

C. $1/\tan(7\pi)/3$

D. $\tan^{-1}\left(\frac{7\pi}{3}\right)$

4. The exact value of $\cot\left(\frac{5\pi}{3}\right)$ is

A. $\frac{1}{\sqrt{3}}$

B. $-\frac{\sqrt{3}}{3}$

C. $-\sqrt{3}$

D. $\sqrt{3}$

5. If θ is an angle in standard position with $\sec\theta = -\frac{2\sqrt{3}}{3}$ and $\tan\theta > 0$, then the measure of θ, in radians, is

A. $\frac{2\pi}{3}$ rad

B. $\frac{4\pi}{3}$ rad

C. $\frac{5\pi}{3}$ rad

D. $\frac{7\pi}{6}$ rad

6. Which of the following statements about the graphs of the functions $y = \sin x$ and $y = \cos x$ is **false**?

A. They have the same range

B. They have the same period.

C. They have the same domain.

D. They have the same y-intercept.

7. The range of $y = \tan x$ is

A. $y \in R$

B. $y \neq 0,\ y \in R$

C. $y \geq 1$ or $y \leq -1$

D. $y \neq \frac{\pi}{2} + n\pi,\ n \in I$

8. Which of the following functions is not a representation of the reciprocal of $f(x) = \tan x$?

A. $y = \cot x$

B. $y = \frac{1}{\tan x}$

C. $y = \frac{1}{f(x)}$

D. $y = \tan^{-1}(x)$

9. Which of the following statements about the periods of reciprocal functions is true?

A. Each one has the same period as its corresponding primary function.

B. The reciprocals of $y = \sin x$ and $y = \cos x$ have the same period as their corresponding primary functions but the reciprocal of $y = \tan x$ does not.

C. The reciprocal of $y = \tan x$ has the same period as its corresponding primary function but the reciprocals of $y = \sin x$ and $y = \cos x$ do not.

D. No reciprocal has the same period as its corresponding primary function.

Numerical Response

NR1. The number of times that $y = \csc\theta$, where $0 \le \theta \le 10\pi$, has a value of 1 is ____________.

10. If $y = \sin\theta$ is transformed to $y = 4\sin(k\theta + 4) - 2$ such that the phase shift is π left, then the value of k is

A. 4

B. 4π

C. $-\frac{4}{\pi}$

D. $\frac{4}{\pi}$

11. Given the trigonometric function $g(\theta) = a\cos(2\theta - \pi) - 3$, where $a > 0$, an expression that defines the range of this function is

A. $-3a \le g(\theta) \le 3a$

B. $-3 - a \le g(\theta) \le -3 + a$

C. $3 - a \le g(\theta) \le 3 + a$

D. $|3 - a| \le g(\theta) \le |3 + a|$

Numerical Response

NR2. If the range of $y = -6\cos(2\theta - \pi) + c$ is $-2.5 \le y \le m$, then the value of m is ____________.

12. Which of the following transformations could be applied to the graph of $y = \sin\theta$ to obtain the graph of $y = \sin(3\theta + \pi) - 1$?

A. A horizontal stretch about the y-axis by a factor of 3 followed by translations of $\frac{\pi}{3}$ radians right and 1 unit down

B. A horizontal stretch about the y-axis by a factor of 3 followed by translations of $\frac{\pi}{3}$ radians left and 1 unit down

C. A horizontal stretch about the y-axis by a factor of 3 followed by translations of π radians right and 1 unit down

D. A horizontal stretch about the y-axis by a factor of 3 followed by translations of π radians left and 1 unit down

13. The graph of $y = -4\cos(2\theta)$ is translated $\frac{\pi}{4}$ units to the right. The equation of the transformed graph is

A. $y = -4\cos\left(2\theta + \frac{\pi}{4}\right)$

B. $y = -4\cos\left(2\theta - \frac{\pi}{4}\right)$

C. $y = -4\cos\left(2\theta + \frac{\pi}{8}\right)$

D. $y = -4\cos\left(2\theta - \frac{\pi}{2}\right)$

Use the following information to answer the next question.

At a small port in Nova Scotia at a certain time of year the water has a maximum depth of 21 m at 7:00 A.M. and a minimum depth of 9 m 6 hours later

14. At a port, the depth of the water, $h(t)$, at any time of day, t, based on a 24-hour clock, is defined by an equation of the form $h(t) = a\cos(k(t-d)) + c$, where a and d are positive numbers. The equation that models this situation is

A. $h(t) = 6\cos(6\pi(t-7)) + 10$

B. $h(t) = 6\cos\left(\frac{\pi}{6}(t-7)\right) + 10$

C. $h(t) = 10\cos\left(\frac{\pi}{6}(t-7)\right) + 6$

D. $h(t) = 6\cos\left(\frac{\pi}{12}(t-7)\right) + 10$

15. The population size, P, of foxes (predators) in a certain region of Ontario over a 3-year period can be modelled by the function $P(t) = 1200 + 80\sin\left(\frac{\pi t}{36}\right)$, where t represents the time in months beginning January 1, 2000. The population size, p, of rabbits (prey) in the same region over the same period is given by $p(t) = 13000 + 200\cos\left(\frac{\pi t}{36}\right)$. In which month and year after January 1, 2000, were the populations of foxes and rabbits the same? (Hint: use a graphical approach).

A. June 2001

B. July 2001

C. August 2001

D. September 2001

Open Response

OR1.

Use the following information to answer the next question

The number of hours of daylight is a function of the time of year. At a town in Ontario the least daylight occurs on December 21 when there is 8 hours of daylight. The day of the year with the most daylight has 16 hours of daylight. Assume that the year is a leap year (366 days) and that the number of hours of daylight $N(t)$, for each day can be modelled by one period of a sine function of the form $N(t) = a\cos(k(t+10)) + c$ where t is the number of the day of the year with January 1st considered as day 1 and $a < 0$.

a) Determine the equation of the sine function that represents the number of hours of daylight related to the day of the year.

b) Determine, to the nearest tenth of an hour, the number of hours of daylight on February 28.

c) Use a graphical approach to determine the date of the day of the year that should have the most hours of daylight.

d) How can the answer to part **c)** be obtained from knowing the period of this function?

16. The expression $\sin\left(x + \frac{3\pi}{2}\right)$ is equivalent to

A. $-\sin x$

B. $\cos x$

C. $\sin\left(\frac{\pi}{2} - x\right)$

D. $-\cos x$

17. The expression $\cos\left(\frac{\pi}{6}\right)\cos(A) - \sin(A)\sin\left(\frac{\pi}{6}\right)$ is equivalent to

A. $\sin\left(\frac{\pi}{6} + A\right)$

B. $\sin\left(\frac{\pi}{6} - A\right)$

C. $\cos\left(\frac{\pi}{6} + A\right)$

D. $\cos\left(\frac{\pi}{6} - A\right)$

18. The exact value of $\cos\left(\frac{7\pi}{12}\right)$ can be determined by calculating

A. $\cos\left(\frac{2\pi}{3}\right)\cos\left(\frac{5\pi}{4}\right) + \sin\left(\frac{2\pi}{3}\right)\sin\left(\frac{5\pi}{4}\right)$

B. $\cos\left(\frac{2\pi}{3}\right)\cos\left(\frac{5\pi}{4}\right) - \sin\left(\frac{2\pi}{3}\right)\sin\left(\frac{5\pi}{4}\right)$

C. $\cos\left(\frac{\pi}{3}\right)\cos\left(\frac{\pi}{4}\right) + \sin\left(\frac{\pi}{3}\right)\sin\left(\frac{\pi}{4}\right)$

D. $\cos\left(\frac{3\pi}{4}\right)\cos\left(\frac{\pi}{6}\right) + \sin\left(\frac{3\pi}{4}\right)\sin\left(\frac{\pi}{6}\right)$

19. For all permissible values of x, $\dfrac{\sin x}{\sin(2x)}$ is equivalent to

A. $\dfrac{\sec x}{2}$

B. $\sec x$

C. $\dfrac{\csc x}{2}$

D. $\csc x$

20. For all permissible values of x, $\dfrac{\sin^3 x}{\cos^3 x - \cos x}$ is equivalent to

A. $\tan x$

B. $-\tan x$

C. $\cot x$

D. $-\cot x$

21. If $2\cos^2\theta + 5\cos\theta - 3 = 0$, then part of the solution is derived from

A. $\cos\theta = \dfrac{1}{3}$

B. $\cos\theta = 1$

C. $\cos\theta = -1$

D. $\cos\theta = \dfrac{1}{2}$

Use the following information to answer the next question.

In solving the trigonometric equation $\sin x = \cos 2x$, a student performed the following first four steps.

$\sin x = \cos 2x$

Step 1: $\sin x = \cos^2 x - \sin^2 x$.
Replace $\cos 2x$ with $\cos^2 x - \sin^2 x$

Step 2: $\sin x = 1 - \sin^2 x - \sin^2 x$
Replace $\cos^2 x$ with $1 - \sin^2 x$

Step 3: $2\sin^2 x + \sin x - 1 = 0$
Make = 0

Step 4: $(2\sin x + 1)(\sin x - 1) = 0$
Factor

22. Which of the following statements about the student's work is correct?

A. The student's first error was made in Step 1.

B. The student's first error was made in Step 2.

C. The student's first error was made in Step 4.

D. The student did not make an error.

Numerical Response

NR3. The number of solutions to the equation $\sin 2\theta + \cos 3\theta = 0,\ 0 \le \theta \le 2\pi$ is ____________.

Open Response

OR2. Determine the exact solutions to
$2\cos^2 x = 3\cos x + 2,\ 0 \le x \le 2\pi$.

ANSWERS AND SOLUTIONS—UNIT TEST TRIGONOMETRIC FUNCTIONS

1. A	**8. D**	**13. D**	**19. A**
2 B	**9. A**	**14. B**	**20. B**
3. B	**NR1. 5**	**15. C**	**21. D**
4. B	**10. D**	**OR1. See Solution**	**22. C**
5. D	**11. B**	**16 D**	**NR3. 4**
6. D	**NR2. 9.5**	**17. C**	**OR2. See Solution**
7. A	**12. B**	**18. D**	

1. A

Since $180° = \pi$ radians, an angle of $125°$ in radians is

$125° = 125\left(\frac{\pi}{180}\right) \approx 2.2$ rad

2. B

Since $30° = \frac{\pi}{6}$ rad, the answer must be an integral multiple of $\frac{\pi}{6}$. Divide each of the alternatives by $\frac{\pi}{6}$ to find the one that gives a quotient that is an integer.

For **A**: $\frac{9\pi}{8} \div \frac{\pi}{6} = \frac{9\not{\pi}}{\not{8}4} \times \frac{\not{6}3}{\not{\pi}} = \frac{27}{2}$, which is not an integer

For **B**: $\frac{17\pi}{3} \div \frac{\pi}{6} = \frac{17\not{\pi}}{\not{3}1} \times \frac{\not{6}2}{\not{\pi}} = 34$, which is an integer

For **C**: $\frac{7\pi}{12} \div \frac{\pi}{6} = \frac{7\not{\pi}}{\not{12}2} \times \frac{\not{6}1}{\not{\pi}} = \frac{7}{2}$, which is not an integer

For **D**: $240 \div \frac{\pi}{6} = 240 \times \frac{6}{\pi} = \frac{1440}{\pi}$, which is not an integer

3. B

The cotangent is the reciprocal of the tangent ratio, not the tangent of the reciprocal of the angle, which is incorrectly shown in alternative A. Alternative C is incorrect because it is entered incorrectly. The angle is $(7\pi)/3$, so this complete expression must be included in the parentheses. The expression shown in alternative **B** is correct.

4. B

The cotangent ratio is defined as $\cot\theta = \frac{x}{y}$.

From the unit circle, the coordinates of the endpoint on the terminal side of an angle of $\frac{5\pi}{3}$ rad are $\left(\frac{1}{2}, -\frac{\sqrt{3}}{2}\right)$.

Thus, $\cot\left(\frac{5\pi}{3}\right) = \frac{\frac{1}{2}}{\frac{-\sqrt{3}}{2}} = -\frac{1}{\sqrt{3}} = -\frac{\sqrt{3}}{3}$

5. **D**

Since $\sec\theta = -\frac{2\sqrt{3}}{3}$, $\cos\theta = -\frac{3}{2\sqrt{3}}$.
Rationalizing the denominator gives
$\cos\theta = -\frac{3}{2\sqrt{3}} \times \frac{\sqrt{3}}{\sqrt{3}} = -\frac{3\sqrt{3}}{6} = -\frac{\sqrt{3}}{2}$.
Since $\cos\theta < 0$ and $\tan\theta > 0$, the angle is in quadrant III. From the unit circle, the angle has a measure of $\frac{7\pi}{6}$ rad.

6. **D**

The y-intercept of $y = \sin x$ is 0, and for $y = \cos x$ it is 1; therefore, the graphs of these functions do not have the same y-intercept.

7. **A**

The function $f(\theta) = \tan\theta$ is defined as $\tan\theta = \frac{y}{x}$, where x and y are coordinates on the terminal arm of the angle θ in standard position. The ratio of these coordinates can be any real number, including 0.

8. **D**

The function $y = \tan^{-1}(x)$ represents the inverse function, not the reciprocal. All of the other alternatives represent the reciprocal of $f(x) = \tan x$.

9. **A**

The functions $y = \csc x$ and $y = \sec x$ have periods of 2π, which is the same as for $y = \sin x$ and $y = \cos x$. The period of $y = \cot x$ is π, the same as for $y = \tan x$.

NR1. **5**

The function $y = \csc\theta$, which is $y = \frac{1}{\sin\theta}$, has a value of 1 when $\sin\theta = 1$. This occurs when $\theta = \frac{\pi}{2} + 2n\pi,\ n \in I$. For $0 \le \theta \le 10\pi$, the values of θ where $\theta = \frac{\pi}{2} + 2n\pi,\ n \in I$ are $\frac{\pi}{2}, \frac{5\pi}{2}, \frac{9\pi}{2}, \frac{13\pi}{2}$, and $\frac{17\pi}{2}$.
Alternatively, you can graph $Y_1 = 1/\sin(x)$ in the domain $0 \le x \le 10\pi$ and count the number of times that $y = 1$. There are 5 occurrences.

10. **D**

First, factor the k out of the part in parentheses so that the function fits the form $y = a\sin(k(\theta - d)) + c$.

$y = 4\sin(k\theta + 4) - 2$

$y = 4\sin\left(k\left(\theta - \frac{-4}{k}\right)\right) - 2$

Now, $\frac{-4}{k} = -\pi$ and thus, $k = \frac{4}{\pi}$.

11 **B**

The range of $f(x) = a\cos(k(x-d)) + c$ is $c - |a| \le f(x) \le c + |a|$. In the given function, a is positive, so $|a| = a$ and c is –3. Thus, the range is $-3 - a \le g(\theta) \le -3 + a$.

NR2. **9.5**

Since the amplitude is $|-6| = 6$, then the value of m is $-2.5 + 2(6) = 9.5$.

12. **B**

First, factor the 3 out of the parentheses.

$y = \sin(3\theta + \pi) - 1 \rightarrow$

$y = \sin\left(3\left(\theta + \frac{\pi}{3}\right)\right) - 1$

From this form, it is clear that the horizontal stretch factor is 3 and the translations are $\frac{\pi}{3}$ radians left and 1 unit down.

13. **D**

When the graph is translated $\frac{\pi}{4}$ units to the right, θ is replaced by $\left(\theta - \frac{\pi}{4}\right)$ in the equation. Thus, the equation is $y = -4\cos\left(2\left(\theta - \frac{\pi}{4}\right)\right)$, which is equivalent to $y = -4\cos\left(2\theta - \frac{\pi}{2}\right)$.

The answer is **D.**

14. **B**

The value of $|a|$ is

$\frac{\text{max} - \text{min}}{2} = \frac{21 - 9}{2} = 6$.

Since the minimum occurs 6 hours after the maximum, the period is $2 \times 6 = 12$ hours. Thus, $\frac{2\pi}{k} = 12$, which gives $k = \frac{\pi}{6}$. Since the maximum depth occurs at 7:00 A.M., the value of d is 7. The value of c is

$\frac{\text{max} + \text{min}}{2} = \frac{21 + 9}{2} = 10$. Therefore, the equation is $h(t) = 6\cos\left(\frac{\pi}{6}(t-7)\right) + 10$.

15. **C**

Using a TI-83 calculator and appropriate window settings such as $x:[0,36,1]$, $y:[1000,1500,1]$, graph $\text{Y}_1 = 1200 + 80\sin(\pi X / 36)$ and $\text{Y}_2 = 1300 + 200\cos(\pi X / 36)$.

The resulting graphs are shown below.

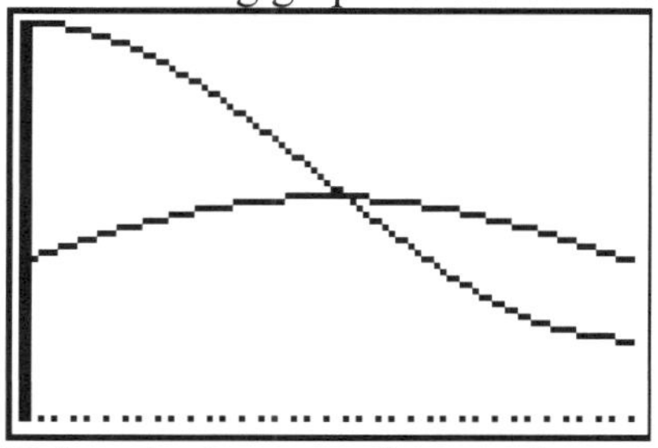

Using the intersect feature shows that the populations are the same after approximately 19.2 months. This would be the 7.2 months into 2001, which is the 8th month, or August 2001.

OR1.

a) Parameter $a = -|a| = -\dfrac{\text{max} - \text{min}}{2}$

$$= -\frac{16-8}{2} = -4.$$

Since the period is 366 days, $\dfrac{2\pi}{k} = 366$, and thus, $k = \dfrac{\pi}{183}$.

Parameter $c = \dfrac{\text{max} + \text{min}}{2} = \dfrac{16+8}{2} = 12.$

The equation is $N(t)$

$$= -4\cos\left(\frac{\pi}{183}(t+10)\right) + 12.$$

b) February 28 is day number 59.
The number of hours of daylight is $N(59)$

$$= -4\cos\left(\frac{\pi}{183}(59+10)\right) + 12 \approx 10.5$$

c) Using a TI-83 calculator with an appropriate viewing window such as $x:[0,366,1]$, $y:[0,30,1]$, input $\text{Y}_1 = -4\cos(\pi / 183(X+10)) + 12$ into the Y= menu.

The resulting graph is shown below.

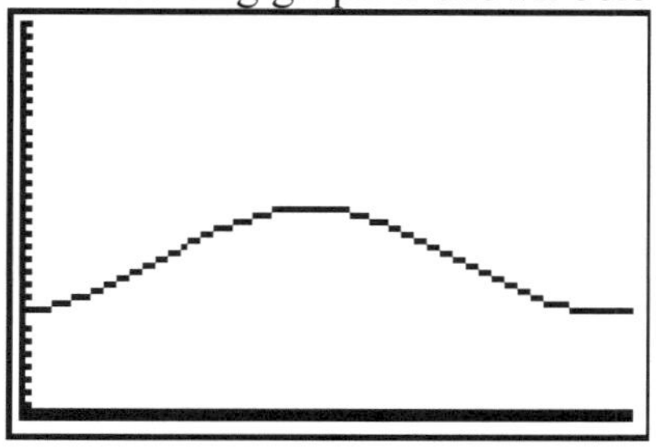

Using the [2nd] [CALC] 4:maximum feature shows that the maximum temperature occurs on day 173, which equates to June 22.

d) Since the period is 366 days, half the period is 183 days.
The maximum should occur 183 days after the minimum on December 21. This is 173 days into the New Year.

16. **D**

On a TI-83 calculator, graph $y = \sin\left(x + \dfrac{3\pi}{2}\right)$ as $\text{Y}_1 = \sin(X + (3\pi)/2)$ to get the graph shown below.

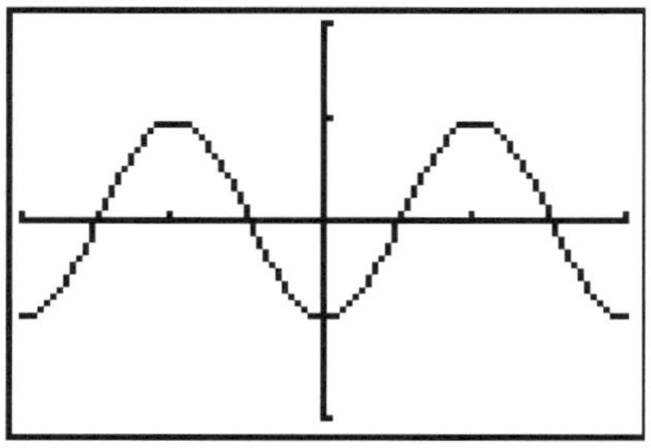

This is the graph of $y = -\cos x$, which can be verified by graphing $\text{Y}_1 = -\cos(X)$.

17. **C**

The expression

$\cos\left(\frac{\pi}{6}\right)\cos(A)-\sin(A)\sin\left(\frac{\pi}{6}\right)$ is the same as the expression

$\cos\left(\frac{\pi}{6}\right)\cos(A)-\sin\left(\frac{\pi}{6}\right)\sin(A)$, which has the form of $\cos(x+y)$.

Thus, $\cos\left(\frac{\pi}{6}\right)\cos(A)-\sin\left(\frac{\pi}{6}\right)\sin(A)$

$$=\cos\left(\frac{\pi}{6}+A\right).$$

18. **D**

The exact value of $\cos\left(\frac{7\pi}{12}\right)$ is determined by using a compound angle formula with two special angles that have a sum or difference of $\frac{7\pi}{12}$.

The angles in alternatives A and D do not have a sum or difference of $\frac{7\pi}{12}$.

In alternative C,

$\frac{\pi}{3}+\frac{\pi}{4}=\frac{4\pi}{12}+\frac{3\pi}{12}=\frac{7\pi}{12}$, the expression is incorrect for the cosine of a sum.

It would need to be

$\cos\left(\frac{\pi}{3}\right)\cos\left(\frac{\pi}{4}\right)-\sin\left(\frac{\pi}{3}\right)\sin\left(\frac{\pi}{4}\right)$.

In alternative D,

$\frac{3\pi}{4}-\frac{\pi}{6}=\frac{9\pi}{12}-\frac{2\pi}{12}=\frac{7\pi}{12}$, the expression has the correct form for the cosine of a difference:

$\cos(x-y)=\cos x\cos y+\sin x\sin y$.

19. **A**

Since $\sin(2x)=2\sin x\cos x$

$$\frac{\sin x}{\sin(2x)}=\frac{\sin x}{2\sin x\cos x}$$

Cancel ($\sin x$)

$$=\frac{1}{2\cos x}$$

Since $\frac{1}{\cos x}=\sec x$

$$=\frac{\sec x}{2}$$

20. **B**

Factor

$$\frac{\sin^3 x}{\cos^3 x-\cos x}=\frac{\sin x\left(\sin^2 x\right)}{\cos x\left(\cos^2 x-1\right)}$$

Factor (-1) $=\frac{\sin x\left(\sin^2 x\right)}{-\cos x\left(1-\cos^2 x\right)}$

Since $1-\cos^2 x=\sin^2 x$

$$=\frac{\sin x\left(\sin^2 x\right)}{-\cos x\left(\sin^2 x\right)}$$

Cancel ($\sin^2 x$) $=\frac{\sin x}{-\cos x}$

Since $\frac{\sin x}{\cos x}=\tan x$

$$=-\tan x$$

21. **D**

Solving $2\cos^2\theta+5\cos\theta-3=0$ gives:

$(2\cos\theta-1)(\cos\theta+3)=0$

Factor

$2\cos\theta-1=0$ or $\cos\theta=-3$

(No solution to this part)

$\cos\theta=\frac{1}{2}$

22. **C**

The factoring is incorrect in Step 4.
It should be $(2\sin x - 1)(\sin x + 1) = 0$.

NR3. **4**

Graphing $Y_1 = \sin(2X) + \cos(3X)$ with appropriate window settings such as $x: \left[0, 2\pi, \frac{\pi}{6}\right]$, $y: [-3, 3, 1]$ and counting the number of x-intercepts, shows that the number of solutions is 4.

OR2.

$2\cos^2 x - 3\cos x - 2 = 0$ Make = 0

$(2\cos x + 1)(\cos x - 2) = 0$ Factor

$2\cos x + 1 = 0$ or $\cos x - 2 = 0$

$\cos x = -\frac{1}{2}$ or $\cos x = 2$ (no solution)

$x = \frac{2\pi}{3}$ or $\frac{4\pi}{3}$

NOTES

Polynomial & Rational Functions

POLYNOMIAL AND RATIONAL FUNCTIONS

Table of Correlations

Specific Expectation	Practice Questions	Unit Test Questions
1.1 *recognize a polynomial expression (i.e., a series of terms where each term is the product of a constant and a power of x with a nonnegative integral exponent, such as x – 5x + 2x – 1); recognize the equation of a polynomial function, give reasons why it is a function, and identify linear and quadratic functions as examples of polynomial functions*	1	1
1.2 *compare, through investigation using graphing technology, the numeric, graphical, and algebraic representations of polynomial (i.e., linear, quadratic, cubic, quartic) functions (e.g., compare finite differences in tables of values; investigate the effect of the degree of a polynomial function on the shape of its graph and the maximum number of x-intercepts; investigate the effect of varying the sign of the leading coefficient on the end behaviour of the function for very large positive or negative x-values)*	2, 3	2, 3
1.3 *describe key features of the graphs of polynomial functions*	4, 5	4,
1.4 *distinguish polynomial functions from sinusoidal and exponential functions, and compare and contrast the graphs of various polynomial functions with the graphs of other types of functions*	6	5
1.5 *make connections, through investigation using graphing technology, between a polynomial function given in factored form and the x-intercepts of its graph, and sketch the graph of a polynomial function given in factored form using its key features*	7, 8	6, 7
1.6 *determine, through investigation using technology, the roles of the parameters a, k, d, and c in functions of the form y = a f (k(x – d)) + c, and describe these roles in terms of transformations on the graphs of* $f(x)=x^3$ *and* $f(x)=x^4$ *(i.e., vertical and horizontal translations; reflections in the axes; vertical and horizontal stretches and compressions to and from the x- and y-axes)*	9, 10	8
1.7 *determine an equation of a polynomial function that satisfies a given set of conditions using methods appropriate to the situation, and recognize that there may be more than one polynomial function that can satisfy a given set of conditions*	11, 12, NR1, OR1	9, 10
1.8 *determine the equation of the family of polynomial functions with a given set of zeros and of the member of the family that passes through another given point*	13, 14	11, NR1
1.9 *determine, through investigation, and compare the properties of even and odd polynomial functions, and determine whether a given polynomial function is even, odd, or neither*	15	12
2.1 *determine, through investigation with and without technology, key features (i.e., vertical and horizontal asymptotes, domain and range, intercepts, positive/negative intervals, increasing/decreasing intervals) of the graphs of rational functions that are the reciprocals of linear and quadratic functions, and make connections between the algebraic and graphical representations of these rational functions*	16, 17	13, 14, NR2

2.2 *determine, through investigation with and without technology, key features (i.e., vertical and horizontal asymptotes, domain and range, intercepts, positive/negative intervals, increasing/decreasing intervals) of the graphs of rational functions that have linear expressions in the numerator and denominator, and make connections between the algebraic and graphical representations of these rational functions*	18, 19, NR2, OR2	15, 16, OR1
2.3 *sketch the graph of a simple rational function using its key features, given the algebraic representation of the function*	20	17
3.1 *make connections, through investigation using technology, between the polynomial function f(x), the divisor x – a, the remainder from the division [fraction missing] and f(a) to verify the remainder theorem and the factor theorem*	21	18, 19
3.2 *factor polynomial expressions in one variable, of degree no higher than four, by selecting and applying strategies (i.e., common factoring, difference of squares, trinomial factoring, factoring by grouping, remainder theorem, factor theorem)*	22, 23, 24	20, 21, NR3
3.3 *determine, through investigation using technology, the connection between the real roots of a polynomial equation and the x-intercepts of the graph of the corresponding polynomial function, and describe this connection*	25, 26	22
3.4 *solve polynomial equations in one variable, of degree no higher than four, by selecting and applying strategies (i.e., common factoring, difference of squares, trinomial factoring, factoring by grouping, remainder theorem, factor theorem), and verify solutions using technology*	27, 28, NR3, NR4	23, 24
3.5 *determine, through investigation using technology, the connection between the real roots of a rational equation and the x-intercepts of the graph of the corresponding rational function, and describe this connection*	29, 30	25
3.6 *solve simple rational equations in one variable algebraically, and verify solutions using technology*	31, 32, NR5	26, NR4, OR2
3.7 *solve problems involving applications of polynomial and simple rational functions and equations*	33, 34	27, 28
4.1 *explain, for polynomial and simple rational functions, the difference between the solution to an equation in one variable and the solution to an inequality in one variable, and demonstrate that given solutions satisfy an inequality*	35, 36	29
4.2 *determine solutions to polynomial inequalities in one variable and to simple rational inequalities in one variable by graphing the corresponding functions, using graphing technology, and identifying intervals for which x satisfies the inequalities*	37	30
4.3 *solve linear inequalities and factorable polynomial inequalities in one variable in a variety of ways, and represent the solutions on a number line or algebraically*	38, 39, 40	31, 32

POLYNOMIAL AND RATIONAL FUNCTIONS

1.1 recognize a polynomial expression, recognize the equation of a polynomial function, give reasons why it is a function, and identify linear and quadratic functions as examples of polynomial functions.

POLYNOMIAL FUNCTIONS

Here are some important definitions related to polynomials and polynomial functions.

A **polynomial expression** in one variable has the form

$a_n x^n + a_{n-1}x^{n-1} + a_{n-2}x^{n-2} + \ldots + a_1 x^1 + a_0$,

where $a_0, a_1, a_2, \ldots, a_n \in R$, and $n \in W$.

Any equation of the form

$P(x) = a_n x^n + a_{n-1}x^{n-1} + a_{n-2}x^{n-2} + \ldots + a_1 x^1 + a_0$

represents a **polynomial function**.

In a polynomial, the constants $a_0, a_1, a_2, \ldots, a_n$ are called the **coefficients** of the terms and they represent real numbers.

The exponents $n, n-1, n-2, \ldots$ must be whole numbers.

The highest exponent, *n*, is called the **degree** of the polynomial. The coefficient of the term of highest degree, a_n, is called the **leading coefficient.**

Example

The expression $2x^3 - 5x^2 + 3x - 7$ is a polynomial of degree 3. The expression $2x^5 - 5x^{-2} + 3x - 7$ is not a polynomial because the exponent –2 is not a whole number.

Any function of the form $y = c$, where *c* is a constant, has a degree of zero and is called a **constant function**. The degree of a constant function is zero because it could be written as $y = cx^0$. The graph of such a function is a horizontal line. For example, $y = 3$ is a constant function.

Any function of the form $y = mx + b,\ m \neq 0$ has a degree of one and is called a **linear function;** for example, $y = 3x - 2$ and $f(x) = -\frac{1}{2}x$ are linear functions.

Any functions of the form $y = ax^2 + bx + c$, $a \neq 0$ is a function of degree two and is called a **quadratic function**.

Two examples are

$y = -2x^2 + 6x - 7$ and $f(x) = \frac{5}{4}(x-8)^2 + 3$.

A third-degree polynomial function such as $g(x) = 2x^3 - 4x + 1$ is called a **cubic** polynomial function, a fourth-degree polynomial function is called **quartic**, and a fifth-degree polynomial is **quintic.**

Example

Which of the following functions are polynomial functions? For those that are, give their degree, and for those that are not, explain how you know they are not.

a) $y = 4x^2 + \frac{6}{x} - 7$

b) $g(x) = -5x^4 + 3x^3 - 8x^2 - 4x + 5$

c) $y = 5(2)^x$

d) $h(x) = 2\sqrt{x} + 3x^2$

Solution

a) This function is not a polynomial function because the term $\frac{6}{x}$ is equivalent to $6x^{-1}$, and –1 is not a whole number.

b) This function is a polynomial function of degree four.

c) This function is not a polynomial function. It is an exponential function because the exponent is a variable, not a whole number.

d) This function is not a polynomial function since the term $2\sqrt{x}$ is equivalent to $2x^{\frac{1}{2}}$, and $\frac{1}{2}$ is not a whole number.

Example

The degree and leading coefficient of the polynomial function $P(x)=6x^2-5x^4+4x-18+3x^3$ are, respectively,

A. 4 and 6 **B.** 2 and 6

C. 4 and 5 **D.** 4 and –5

Solution

D

When the function is expressed with the terms in descending order of degree, it is $P(x)=-5x^4+3x^3+6x^2+4x-18$. The highest degree term is $-5x^4$, so the degree of the function is 4 and the leading coefficient is –5. Therefore, alternative **D** is the correct answer.

PRACTICE QUESTION

1. Which of the following is **not** a polynomial function?

A. $f(x)=3x^3+2x^2+x$

B. $h(x)=-\sqrt{17}x^4+47$

C. $g(x)=4x^{-4}-3x^{-1}+5x^2+67$

D. $m(x)=\frac{39}{11}-\frac{x}{5}$

1.2 compare, through investigation using graphing technology, the numeric, graphical, and algebraic representations of polynomial functions.

REPRESENTATIONS OF POLYNOMIAL FUNCTIONS

The domain of every polynomial function is $x \in R$. The degree of the polynomial determines the shape of the graph.

- Graphs of constant functions (degree zero) are horizontal lines.
- Every linear polynomial function (degree one) has an oblique line as its graph.
- The graph of every quadratic polynomial function (degree two) is a parabola.
- The shapes of the graphs of higher degree polynomial functions vary depending on the individual terms present.

One property of the graph of a polynomial function is that the degree of the polynomial is equal to the maximum number of x-intercepts.

Example

What is the maximum number of x-intercepts of $P(x)=5x^3-3x^2+10x^4$?

A. 1 **B.** 3

C. 4 **D.** 9

Solution

C

The degree of this polynomial function is 4, so alternative **C** is correct.

The term of the highest degree becomes the dominant term for extreme values of x (negative or positive). You can determine the end behaviour of a polynomial function by determining what type of number (positive or negative) results when an extreme negative or positive number is substituted into the polynomial.

Example

Consider the function $P(x) = 5x^5 - 3x^2 + 5x - 12$. The highest degree term is $5x^5$. If x is replaced by an extreme negative number (such as –100), the result is negative.

This means that the graph of $P(x)$, for extreme negative numbers, will be in quadrant III where $y < 0$, and will be increasing (rising up towards the x-axis). Likewise replacing $5x^5$ with an extreme positive number (such as +100) will result in a positive value, so for such values, the graph of $P(x)$ will be in quadrant I and will be increasing.

If the sign of the leading coefficient is reversed, the end behaviour is also reversed. If $5x^5$ is changed to $-5x^5$ in the previous example, then for extreme negative values, the graph would be in quadrant II and decreasing, and for extreme positive numbers, the graph would be in quadrant IV and decreasing.

Example

Which of the following polynomial functions has the left and right ends of its graph, respectively, in quadrants II and I?

A. $P(x) = -3x^3 + x^2 + 5x - 1$

B. $Q(x) = 6x^4 - 3x^3 + 7x - 18$

C. $R(x) = 4x^3 + 6x^2 - 5x + 2$

D. $S(x) = -x^6 - 3x^4 + 5x^2 + 6$

Solution

B

You need a function whose highest degree term results in a positive value for both extreme negative number replacements and extreme positive number replacements. This is $Q(x)$ with the highest degree term of $6x^4$, so alternative **B** is correct.

If you are given a table of values for a polynomial function with the x-coordinates increasing in a uniform manner, then you can find the first finite differences by subtracting the consecutive y-coordinates. If you subtract the new values consecutively, you get the second finite differences.

Repeating this a third time yields the third finite differences. If you get to a stage where all the differences are equal to the same constant, then the number of that stage is equal to the degree of the polynomial function.

Example

A polynomial function is described by the table of values below.

x	3	2	1	0	1	2	3
y	138	58	14	0	10	38	78

Determine the degree of this polynomial function.

Solution

Since the values of x are increasing uniformly by 1, find the finite differences to determine the degree.

y	1st Difference	2nd Difference	3rd Difference
138			
58	58 – 138 = –80		
14	14 – 58 = –44	–44 – (–80) = 36	
0	0 – 14 = –14	–14 – (–44) = 30	30 – 36 = –6
10	10 – 0 = 10	10 – (–14) = 24	24 – 30 = –6
38	38 – 10 = 28	28 – 10 = 18	18 – 24 = –6
78	78 – 38 = 40	40 – 28 = 12	12 – 18 = –6

Since the third differences have a constant value of –6, the degree of the polynomial is three.

PRACTICE QUESTIONS

Use the following information to answer the next question.

The graph of a particular polynomial function is given below.

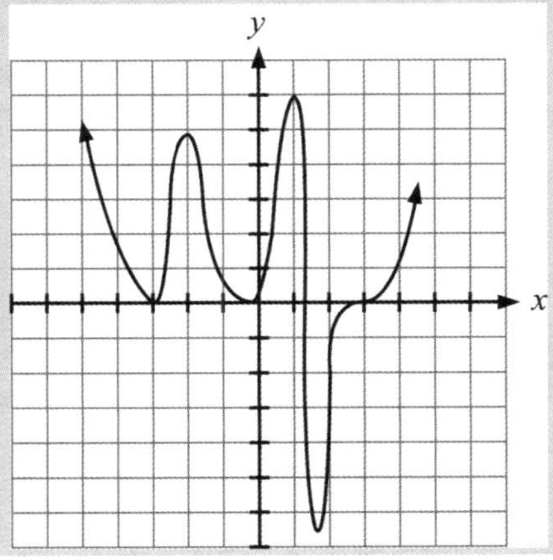

2. If all the x-intercepts of the graph are shown, then the minimum possible degree of the polynomial function is
   A. 4
   B. 6
   C. 7
   D. 8

3. The maximum number of x-intercepts for the graph of the polynomial function $P(x) = Ax^4 + Bx^2 + 7$, where A and B represent real numbers, is
   A. 3
   B. 4
   C. 6
   D. 7

1.3 describe key features of the graphs of polynomial functions.

THE GRAPHS OF POLYNOMIAL FUNCTIONS

The domain of all polynomial functions is $x \in R$.
If the degree of a polynomial function is an odd number, such as 1, 3, or 5, the range will be $y \in R$. For example, consider a polynomial function whose highest degree term is $6x^3$. Examining the behaviour of the left end of the graph of this function shows that as $x \to -\infty$, $y \to -\infty$. Thus, for extreme negative values of x, the y-values are also negative and the graph will be in quadrant III and falling to the left.
For the right-end behaviour, as $x \to +\infty$, $y \to +\infty$. Thus, for extreme positive values of x, the y-values are also positive and the graph will be in quadrant I and rising to the right.
If the leading coefficient is negative, for example $-6x^3$, the effect reverses, so that for any odd-degree polynomial function, the left end is in quadrant II while the right end is in quadrant IV.
If the degree of a polynomial functions is an even number the two ends of the graph are both above or both below, the x-axis. For example, if the highest degree term is $-3x^4$, then $y \to -\infty$ as $x \to \pm\infty$. Thus, the extreme ends of the graph are in quadrants II and IV. The graph would have a maximum y-value somewhere between the extreme values such that the range of the function would be all real numbers less than or equal to that maximum.

Example

If a, b, c, and d are all positive real numbers, then which of the following polynomial functions could have a range of $y \geq 20$?

A. $P(x) = -ax^3 + bx^2 + cx - d$

B. $Q(x) = ax^4 - bx^3 + cx - d$

C. $R(x) = ax^3 + bx^2 - cx + d$

D. $S(x) = -ax^6 - bx^4 + cx^2 + d$

Solution

B

The solution of this problem must be a polynomial function whose degree is even and for which both ends of its graph are in the positive direction.

This would be $Q(x) = ax^4 - bx^3 + cx - d$ since its highest degree term is ax^4, which would result in positive y-values for both extreme positive and extreme negative replacements of x. Since $y \to \infty$ as $x \to \pm\infty$, the function must have a minimum, which could be 20.

The correct answer is **B**.

PRACTICE QUESTIONS

Use the following information to answer the next question.

The graph of a particular polynomial function is shown below.

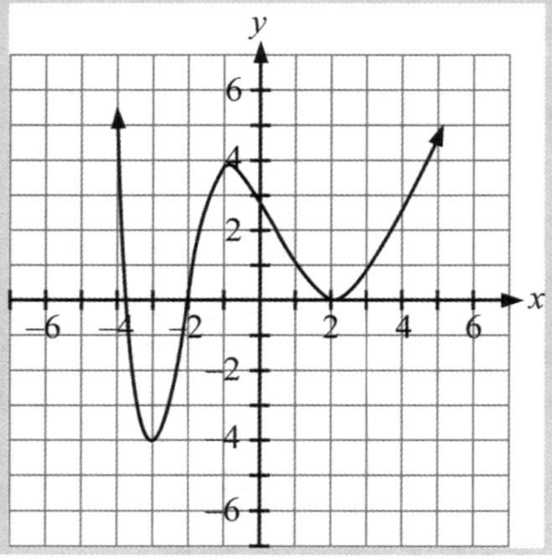

4. The domain and range of the given polynomial function are, respectively,

A. $x \in R$ and $y \in R$

B. $x \in R$ and $y \geq -4$

C. $-4 \leq x \leq 6$ and $y \in R$

D. $-4 \leq x \leq 6$ and $y \geq -4$

5. Which of the following polynomial functions, where A, B, and C are positive real numbers, could have a range of $y \leq 25$?

A. $P(x) = Ax^3 + Bx^2 - Cx + 10$

B. $Q(x) = -Ax^3 + Bx^2 + Cx - 10$

C. $R(x) = Ax^4 - Bx^3 + Cx - 10$

D. $S(x) = -Ax^4 + Bx^3 - Cx + 10$

1.4 distinguish polynomial functions from sinusoidal and exponential functions and compare and contrast the graphs of various polynomial functions with the graphs of other types of functions.

COMPARING THE GRAPHS OF POLYNOMIAL FUNCTIONS AND OTHER TYPES OF FUNCTIONS

Sinusoidal functions have equations of the form $y = a\sin(k(x-d))+c$ or of the form $y = a\cos(k(x-d))+c$. The graphs of these functions are periodic and have a wave-shaped pattern. For each of these functions the domain is $x \in R$, and range is $c-|a| \le y \le c+|a|$. Exponential functions have the form $y = b^x$, $b>0$, $b \ne 1$ or transformations of this form. The domain of $y = b^x$ is $x \in R$, and its range is $y > 0$. The graph of $y = b^x$ has a horizontal asymptote of $y = 0$.

The inverses of exponential functions are logarithmic functions of the form $y = \log_b x$, $b>0$, $b \ne 1$, or a transformation of this form. The domain of $y = \log_b x$ is $x > 0$, and its range is $y \in R$. The graph of $y = \log_b x$ has a vertical asymptote of $x = 0$.

Any equation of the form $P(x) = a_n x^n + a_{n-1}x^{n-1} + a_{n-2}x^{n-2} + \ \ldots\ + a_1 x^1 + a_0$ represents a polynomial function. Of the four types of functions considered here, polynomial functions are the only ones whose graphs have end behaviour of going to positive or negative infinity at both ends. Their domains are $x \in R$, and if they are of odd degree, the range is $y \in R$. If their degree is even and the leading coefficient is negative, the range is $y \le p$, where p is the maximum y-coordinate of the graph.

If they are of even degree and have a positive leading coefficient, the range is $y \ge p$, where p is the minimum y-coordinate of the graph.

Example

Which of the following types of functions could have a range of $-6 \le y \le -3$.

A. Sinusoidal **B.** Exponential
C. Polynomial **D.** Logarithmic

Solution

A

The correct answer is **A** because as sinusoidal functions are the only type of function listed whose range is restricted between two values.

Example

Which of the following types of functions is illustrated by the graph shown?

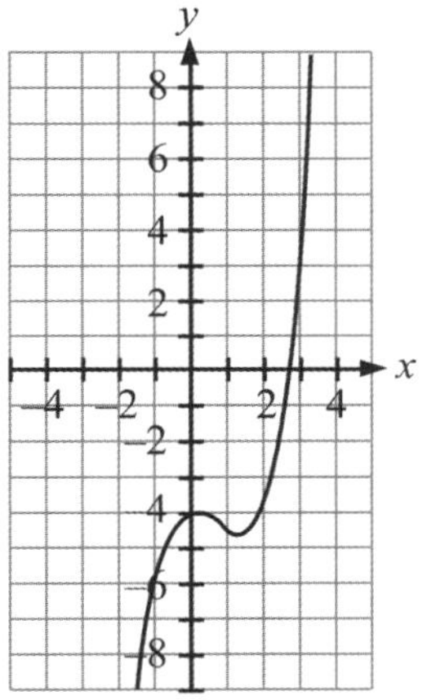

A. Sinusoidal **B.** Exponential
C. Polynomial **D.** Logarithmic

Solution

C

The correct answer is **C** because the graph illustrates the end behaviour typical of an odd-degree polynomial function.

PRACTICE QUESTION

6. Which of the following types of functions could have a range of $y > 0$?

A. Polynomial **B.** Exponential
C. Logarithmic **D.** Sinusoidal

1.5 make connections, through investigation using graphing technology, between a polynomial function given in factored form and the x-intercepts of its graph, and sketch the graph of a polynomial function given in factored form using its key features.

SKETCHING THE GRAPH OF A POLYNOMIAL FUNCTION

When a polynomial function is expressed in its factored form, such as $f(x)=3(x+2)(x-3)(x-5)$, it is easy to identify the zeros of the function from the factors. In this example, they are $x=-2,\ 3,\text{ and }5$.

The zeros are *x*-coordinates whose corresponding *y*-coordinate is zero. These values are also the *x*-intercepts of the graph of the function.

If a factor occurs only once in the factored form of a polynomial function, then the graph of the function will cross the *x*-axis at the corresponding zero.

For $f(x)=3(x+2)(x-3)(x-5)$, the graph will cross the *x*-axis at $x=-2,\ 3,\text{ and }5$, as shown.

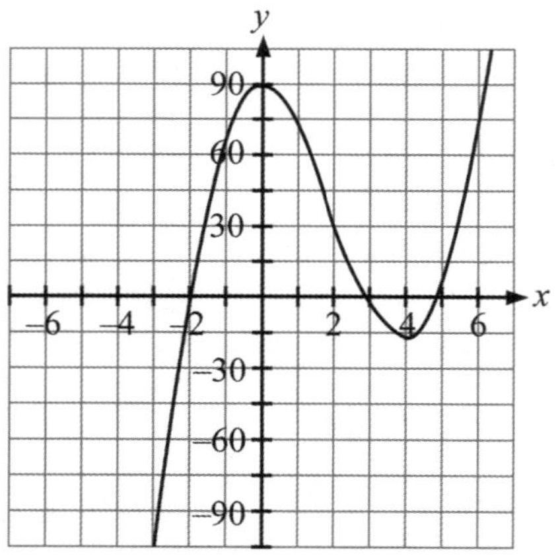

If a factor occurs exactly twice in the factored form of a polynomial function, then the graph of the function will be tangent to the *x*-axis at the corresponding zero.

For the function

$f(x)=-3(x+2)(x+2)(x-5)=-3(x+2)^2(x-5)$

the factor $(x+2)$ occurs twice. There are two zeros: $x=-2$ and 5. At $x=-2$, the graph will approach the *x*-axis, touch, and turn away, as shown below.

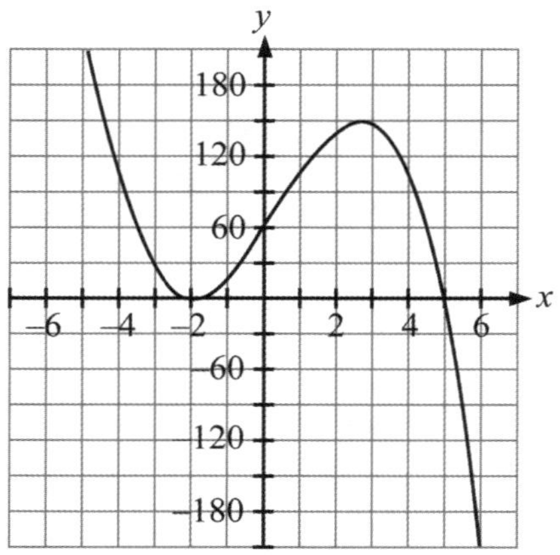

When a factor occurs three times, as in

$$f(x)=2(x-3)(x-3)(x-3)(x+2)$$
$$=2(x-3)^3(x+2)$$

the graph will pass through the *x*-axis with a point of inflection at the corresponding zero, as shown at $x=3$ in the graph below.

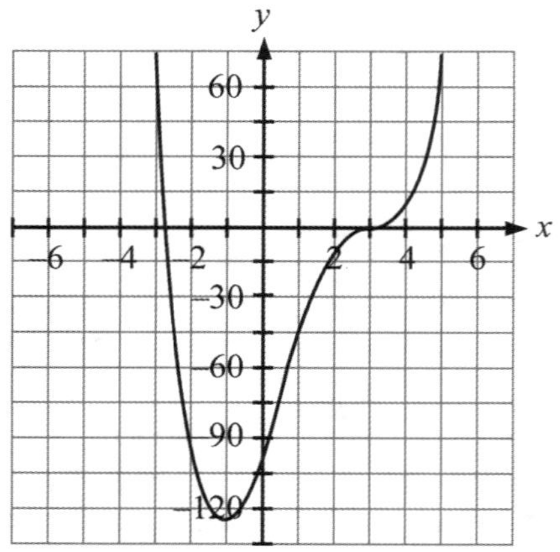

Example

Give the *x*-intercepts, end behaviour and shape of the graph of $f(x)=-2x(x+3)^2(x-4)$, and provide a sketch of the graph.

Solution

The function is a fourth-degree polynomial function with a leading term of $-2x^4$ when expressed in standard form. Substituting either an extreme negative number or positive number into this term produces a negative result. So, the end behaviour is away from the x-axis toward $-\infty$ in both quadrants III and IV.
There are three zeros: $x = -3,\ 0,$ and 4. Since the factor $x + 3$ occurs twice, the graph will be tangent to the x-axis at $x = -3$ and will cross the x-axis at $x = 0$ and 4. From left to right, the graph will rise to the x-axis in quadrant III, touch the x-axis at -3, and turn back into quadrant III. The graph will then turn again and pass through the origin, reach a maximum in quadrant I, turn once more, pass through $x = 4$, and finally head toward $-\infty$ in quadrant IV.

The graph is shown below.

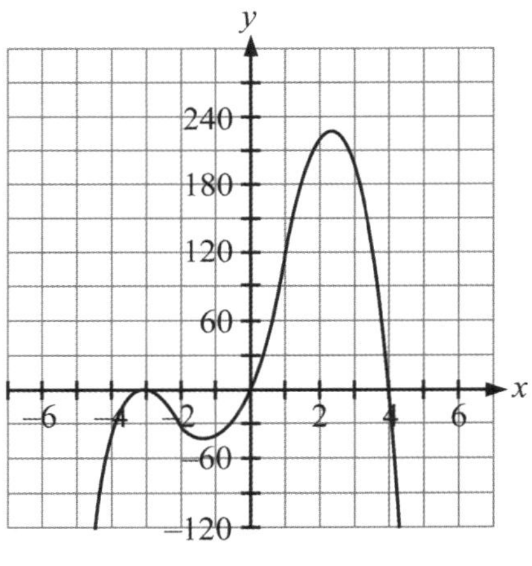

PRACTICE QUESTIONS

Use the following information to answer the next questions

The graph of a particular polynomial function with integral x-intercepts is shown below.

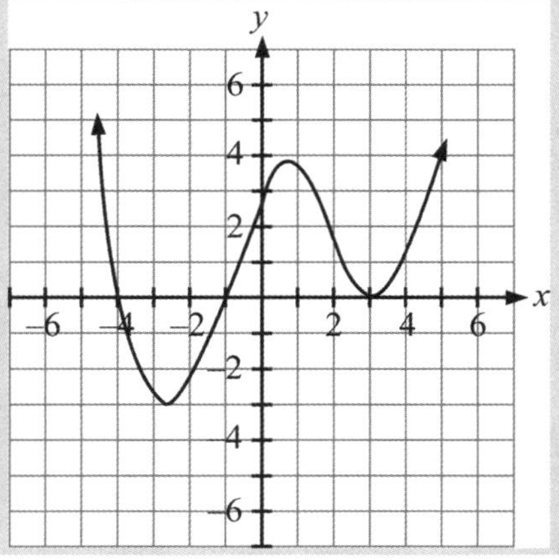

7. Which of the following factors is **not** a factor of the polynomial function whose graph is shown above?

A. $(x+1)$

B. $(x-3)$

C. $(x+4)$

D. $(x-4)$

8. Sarah wants to graph the polynomial function $p(x) = -4(x-2)(x+2)(x-1)$ without the help of technology. She decides to locate positive and negative regions of the graph using test values. Which of the following regions represents the set of test regions that Sarah will need to use?

A. $-2 < x < 1$ and $1 < x < 2$

B. $-2 < x < -1$ and $-1 < x < 2$

C. $x < -2$, $-2 < x < 1$, $1 < x < 2$, and $x > 2$

D. $x < -2$, $-2 < x < 1$, $-1 < x < 2$, and $x > 2$

1.6 determine, through investigation using technology, the roles of the parameters a, k, d, and c in functions of the form $y = af\left(k\left(x-d\right)\right)+c$, and describe these roles in terms of transformations on the graphs of $f\left(x\right)=x^3$ and $f\left(x\right)=x^4$ (i.e., vertical and horizontal translations; reflections in the axes; vertical and horizontal stretches and compressions to and from the x- and y-axes)

TRANSFORMATIONS OF POLYNOMIAL FUNCTIONS

When the function $y = f\left(x\right)$ is transformed into $y = af\left(k\left(x-d\right)\right)+c$, the parameters *a*, *k*, *d*, and *c* perform the following transformations on the graph of the function:

- If $a < 0$, there is a reflection in the *x*-axis.
  If $|a| < 1$, the graph is compressed vertically by a factor of $|a|$ to the *x*-axis.
  If $|a| > 1$, the graph is stretched vertically by a factor of *a* from the *x*-axis.
- If $k < 0$, there is a reflection in the *y*-axis.
  If $|k| < 1$, the graph is stretched horizontally by a factor of $\frac{1}{k}$ about the *y*-axis.
  If $|k| > 1$, the graph is compressed horizontally by a factor of $\frac{1}{k}$ about the *y*-axis.
- If $d < 0$, the graph of $f\left(x\right)$ is translated horizontally *d* units to the left.
  If $d > 0$, the graph of $f\left(x\right)$ is translated horizontally *d* units to the right.
- If $c < 0$, the graph of $f\left(x\right)$ is translated vertically down *c* units.
  If $c > 0$, the graph of $f\left(x\right)$ is translated vertically up *c* units.

Example

If the graph of $f\left(x\right)=x^3$ is stretched vertically by a factor of 3 from the *x*-axis and then translated horizontally 4 units left to produce the function $g\left(x\right)$, then the equation of $g\left(x\right)$ is

A. $g\left(x\right)=\frac{1}{3}x^3+4$ **B.** $g\left(x\right)=\frac{1}{3}x^3-4$

C. $g\left(x\right)=3\left(x+4\right)^3$ **D.** $g\left(x\right)=3\left(x-4\right)^3$

Solution

C

In order to perform a vertical stretch by a factor of 3, parameter $a = 3$. For a horizontal translation of 4 units left, parameter $d = -4$. Thus,

$$g\left(x\right)=3f\left(x-\left(-4\right)\right)^3=3f\left(x+4\right)^3$$
$$=3\left(x+4\right)^3.$$

The correct answer is **C**.

Example

If the function $f\left(x\right)=\left(x+4\right)\left(x-2\right)\left(x-3\right)$ is transformed into $g(x) = -f(2x)$, then the *x*-intercepts of the graph of $g(x)$ are

A. -2, 1, and $\frac{3}{2}$ **B.** 2, -1, and $-\frac{3}{2}$

C. -8, 4, and 6 **D.** 8, -4, and -6

Solution

A

The zeros, and thus the *x*-intercepts, of $f(x)$ are -4, 2, and 3. Since $a = -1$ in $-f(2x)$, the graph of $f(x)$ is reflected in the *x*-axis, which has no effect on the *x*-intercepts. Since parameter $k = 2$ in $-f(2x)$, there is a horizontal compression by a factor of $\frac{1}{2}$ to the *y*-axis, so every *x*-intercept is halved. Thus, the *x*-intercepts of $g(x) = -f(2x)$ are halves of -4, 2, and 3; therefore, they are -2, 1, and $\frac{3}{2}$.

The correct alternative is **A**.

PRACTICE QUESTIONS

9. If the point (–3, 7) lies on the graph of $y = f(x)$, what corresponding point would lie on the graph of the transformed function defined by $y = f(x - 1) - 3$?

A. (–2, 4) **B.** (–2, 10)

C. (–4, 4) **D.** (–4, 10)

10. The function $y = f(x)$ is transformed into the function $y = af\left(k\left(x-d\right)\right)+c$.

If $-1 < k < 0$, then the graph of $y = f(x)$ is stretched horizontally about the y-axis by a factor of

A. k, followed by a reflection in the x-axis

B. $\frac{1}{k}$, followed by a reflection in the x-axis

C. $|k|$, followed by a reflection in the y-axis

D. $\frac{1}{|k|}$, followed by a reflection in the y-axis

1.7 determine an equation of a polynomial function that satisfies a given set of conditions, using methods appropriate to the situation, and recognize that there may be more than one polynomial function that can satisfy a given set of conditions

THE EQUATION OF A POLYNOMIAL FUNCTION

A polynomial function of degree n has at most n first-degree factors however, the factors do not determine a unique polynomial function. When given just the factors or zeros of a polynomial function, it is possible to write an infinite number of functions with those factors or zeros.

Example

The graph of a fourth-degree polynomial function, $P(x)$, has x-intercepts at –3, 1, and 4 only. Determine two possible equations of $P(x)$, and sketch their graphs.

Solution

Since there are zeros at –3, 1, and 4, $P(x)$ must have the factors

$(x+3)$, $(x-1)$, and $(x-4)$.

However, the product of these three factors would give only a third-degree polynomial function. Thus, one of these factors must occur twice. You cannot add a different factor, such as $x - 5$, because then $P(x)$ would have another zero (x-intercept) of 5, and this would contradict the stated conditions.

Two possible equations with their graphs are shown.

$P(x) = (x+3)(x+3)(x-1)(x-4)$

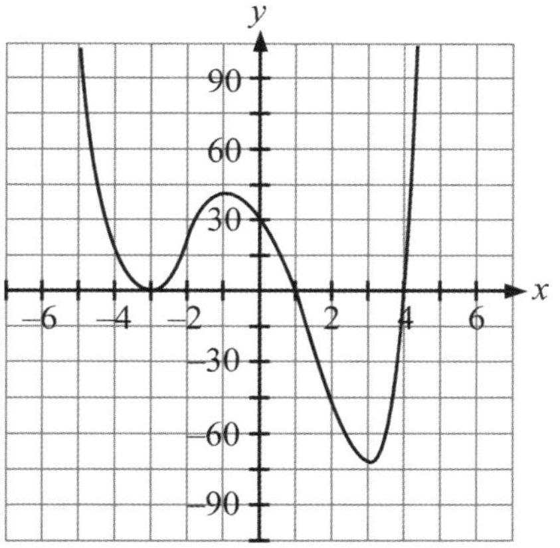

$P(x) = (x+3)(x-1)(x-1)(x-4)$

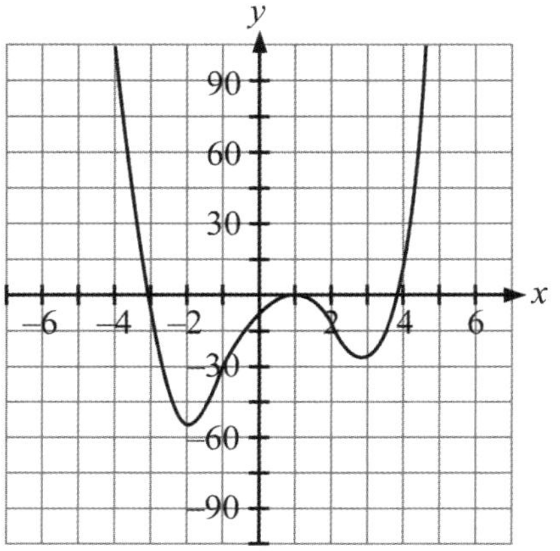

PRACTICE QUESTIONS

11. A third-degree polynomial function is of the form $P(x)=x^3+bx^2+cx+d$, where *b*, *c*, and *d* are real numbers.
If $P(-5)=P(-2)=P(6)=0$, then the value of *c* is

A. –52 **B.** –32

C. 32 **D.** 52

12. A polynomial function is defined by the equation $p(x)=y=2x^3+bx^2+7x-6$, where *b* is a real number. If one *x*-intercept of the graph of this function is at –2, then the value of *b* is

A. –9 **B.** –2

C. 2 **D.** 9

Numerical Response

NR1. A polynomial function of the form $p(x)=ax^4+bx^3+cx^2+dx+e$, where *a*, *b*, *c*, *d*, and *e* are real numbers, has zeros at –2, 1, and 3. If the zero 3 occurs twice and $f(4)=36$, then the value of *e* is __________.

Open Response

OR1. The graph of a fourth-degree polynomial function, *P*(*x*), with *x*-intercepts of –3, 2, and 4 is shown below.

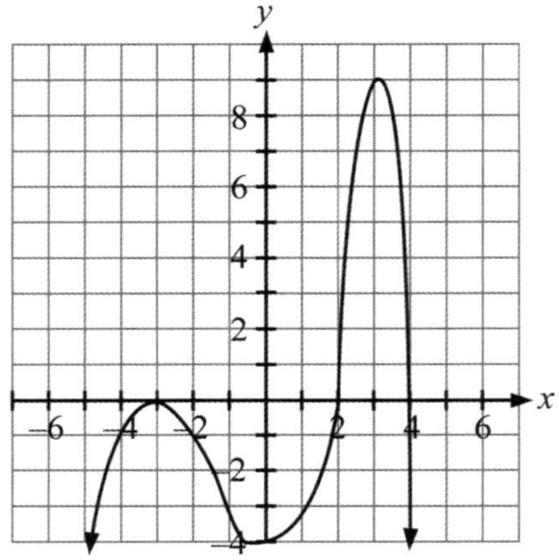

a) Determine the equation of the polynomial function in factored form.

b) What is the *y*-intercept of the graph of the polynomial function $y=P(x)$?

1.8 determine the equation of the family of polynomial functions with a given set of zeros and of the member of the family that passes through another given point.

ZEROS OF A POLYNOMIAL FUNCTION

If all the zeros of a polynomial function are real numbers, then you can express a family of functions having those zeros in the form of $P(x)=k(x-a)(x-b)(x-c)\ldots,$ where $a, b, c, \ldots$ are the zeros of the function and k is a non-zero constant. The parameter k causes a vertical stretch or compression of the function $f(x)=(x-a)(x-b)(x-c)\ldots,$ and also a reflection in the x-axis if $k<0$.

For example, the family of fourth degree polynomial functions that has the four distinct zeros -5, -3, 1, and 2, is represented by $P(x)=k(x+5)(x+3)(x-1)(x-2)$.

If you know one more additional point on the graph of $P(x)$, you can determine the equation of the unique family member meeting the stated conditions.

For example, if you know that $P(x)=k(x+5)(x+3)(x-1)(x-2)$ has a y-intercept of -120 you can determine the value of k by substitution. If the y-intercept is -120, then the point $(0,-120)$ must satisfy the equation and thus, $P(0)=-120$.

Substituting gives:

$$-120=k(0+5)(0+3)(0-1)(0-2)$$
$$-120=30k$$
$$-4=k$$

The equation of the function is $P(x)=-4(x+5)(x+3)(x-1)(x-2)$.

Generally, to obtain the equation of a polynomial function that has real zeros only, you need one additional set of coordinates other than the x-intercepts in order to determine the unique function.

Polynomial functions can be used to approximate other functions on a portion of their domain.

Example

Use a fourth degree polynomial function to approximate the graph of $f(x)=\cos x$ over the interval $0\le x\le 2\pi$.

Solution

The graph of the function $f(x) = \cos x$ is shown below.

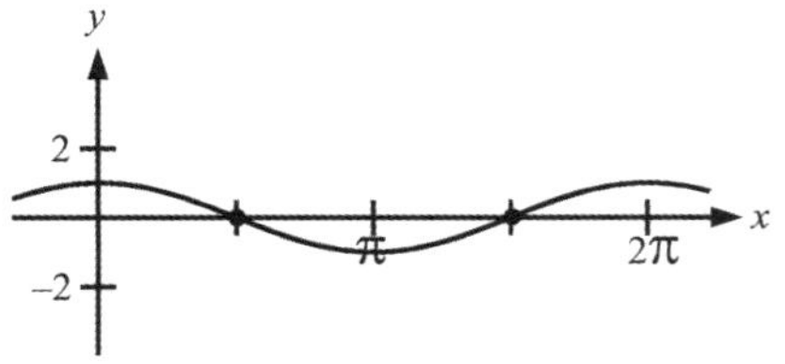

You need to identify at least five points that can be used to approximate $f(x)=\cos x$ as a fourth-degree polynomial function.

Five points that you can use are $(0,1), \left(\frac{\pi}{2},0\right), (\pi,-1), \left(\frac{3\pi}{2},0\right)$, and $(2\pi,1)$.

Clear the lists on a TI-83 calculator. Then, input the x-coordinates into L1 in the Stats menu and the y-coordinates into L2.

Next, press [STAT], scroll right to CALC, and choose option 7, which is QuartReg (Quartic regression). Now press [2nd] [1] [,] [2nd] [2] [,] [Vars], and then scroll right to Y-Vars, and press [Enter] three times.

The calculator display shows the values of the parameters a, b, c, d, and e, which are the coefficients of the fourth-degree function $y=ax^4+bx^3+cx^2+dx+e$.

When these coefficients are rounded to the nearest thousandth, the polynomial function is

$$y=-0.027x^4+0.344x^3-1.148x^2+0.424x+1.$$

If you press GRAPH, the graph will be displayed. If you also graph $y = \cos x$ by entering it as $Y_2 = \cos(x)$, and change the window settings for the domain to $x:[0, 2\pi, 1]$, $y:[-3, 3, 1]$ you can see how closely the polynomial function matches the trigonometric function for the given domain. The graph is shown below.

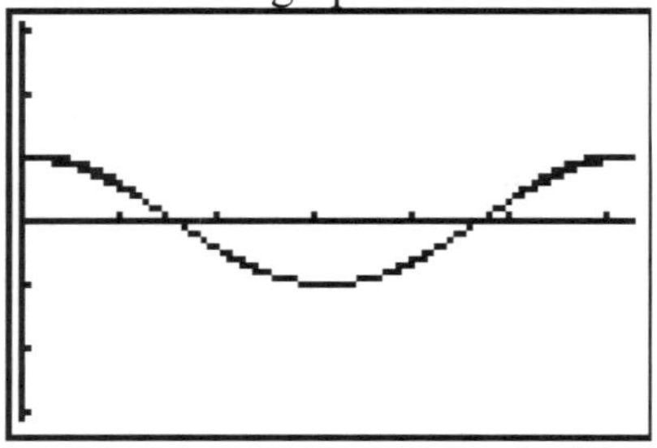

PRACTICE QUESTIONS

13. A polynomial function of the form $y = a(x-m)(x-n)$ has zeros at –5 and 7 and has a y-intercept at 70. In expanded form, the function is

A. $y = 2x^2 - 4x - 70$

B. $y = -2x^2 + 4x + 70$

C. $y = -2x^2 - 4x + 70$

D. $y = 2x^2 + 4x - 70$

Use the following information to answer the next question.

The graph of a polynomial function of the form $f(x) = K(x-a)(x-b)(x-c)$, where a, b, and c are the zeros of the function and K is a non-zero constant is shown below.

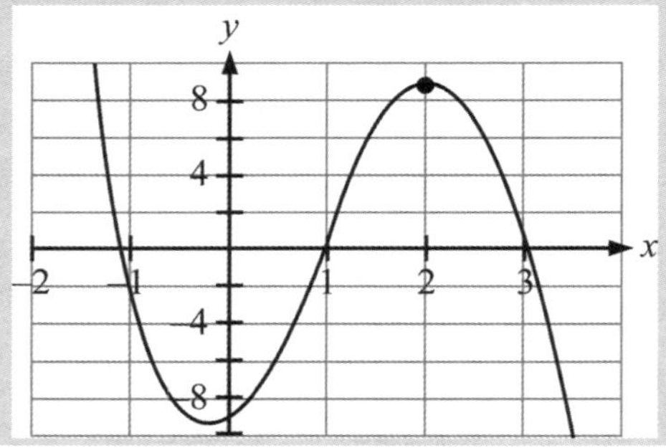

14. The value of K is

A. 9

B. 3

C. –3

D. $\frac{1}{9}$

1.9 determine, through investigation, and compare the properties of even and odd polynomial functions, and determine whether a given polynomial function is even, odd, or neither.

EVEN AND ODD POLYNOMIAL FUNCTIONS

A function $f(x)$ is considered to be **even** if it satisfies the condition that $f(-x)=f(x)$ for all x in its domain. This means that the y-coordinate for any value of x must equal the y-coordinate at $-x$. So, for every point on the right side of the y-axis, a mirror image exists on the left side of the y-axis. An even function is symmetrical about the y-axis.

A function $f(x)$ is considered to be **odd** if it satisfies the condition that $f(-x)=-f(x)$ for all x in its domain. This means that the y-coordinate for any value of x must equal the negative of the y-coordinate at $-x$. Thus, for every point on the graph, there must be another point located directly through the origin, the same distance from the origin as the point itself. An odd function is symmetrical about the origin.

Example

Determine if the polynomial function $f(x)=2x^3-5x$ is odd, even, or neither.

Solution

$$\begin{aligned} f(-x) &= 2(-x)^3-5(-x) \\ &= -2x^3+5x \\ &= -(2x^3-5x) \\ &= -f(x) \end{aligned}$$

Since $f(-x)=-f(x)$, $f(x)$ is an odd function that is symmetrical about the origin.

It can be shown that any polynomial function whose terms consist of only odd-degree monomials is an odd function, and any polynomial function consisting of only even-degree monomials is an even function.

If the polynomial function has any combination of odd-degree and even-degree terms, then the function is neither odd nor even.

So, $f(x)=2x^6-3x^4+5x^2-9$ is even and symmetrical to the y-axis, while the function $g(x)=2x^5-3x^4+5x^3-9$ is neither even nor odd.

PRACTICE QUESTION

15. Which of the following graphs of four different functions of the form $y=f(x)$ illustrates that $f(-x)=-f(x)$??

A.

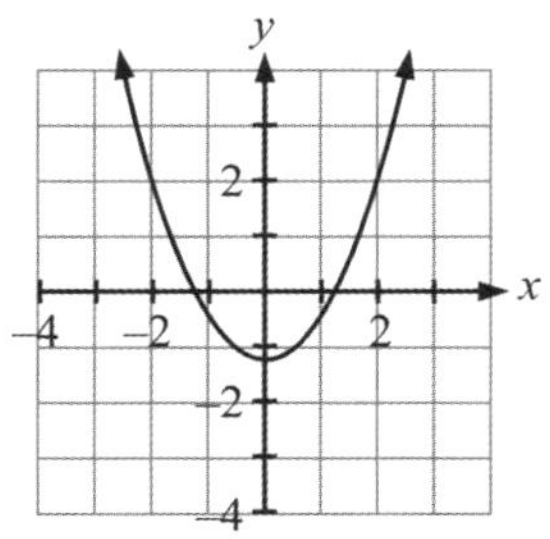

B.

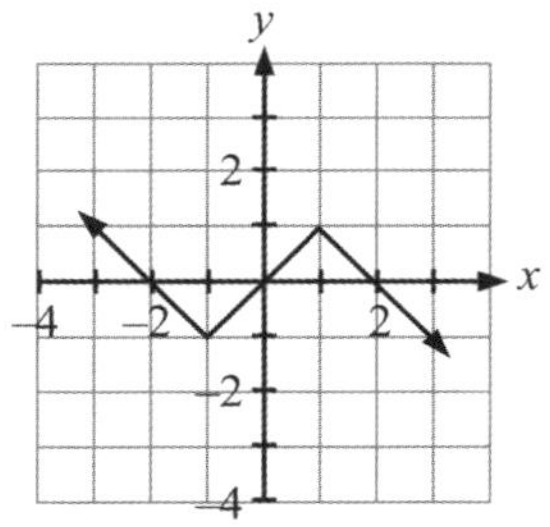

C.

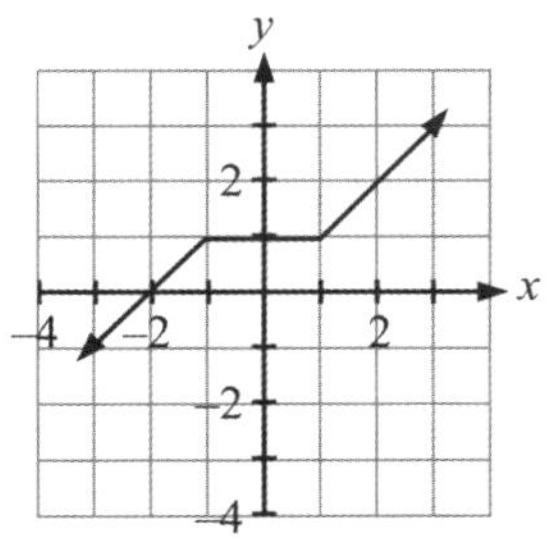

D.

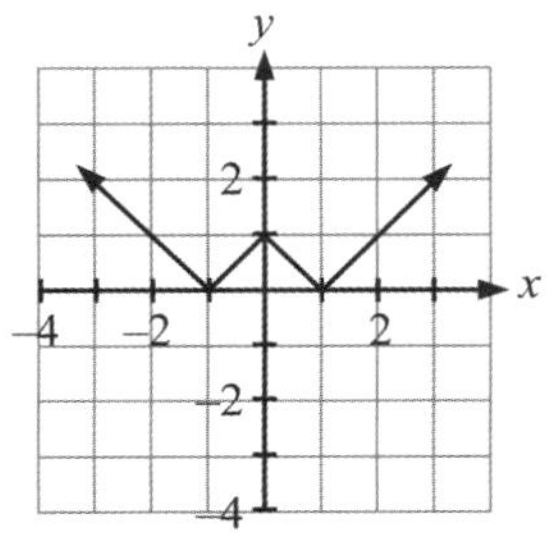

2.1 determine, through investigation with and without technology, key features of the graphs of rational functions that are the reciprocals of linear and quadratic functions, and make connections between the algebraic and graphical representations of these rational functions.

THE GRAPHS OF RATIONAL FUNCTIONS: RECIPROCAL FUNCTIONS

Example

Use the graph of $y = x^2 - 9$ to identify the key features of the graph of its reciprocal function $y = \dfrac{1}{x^2 - 9}$ and to sketch the graph of the reciprocal function.

Solution

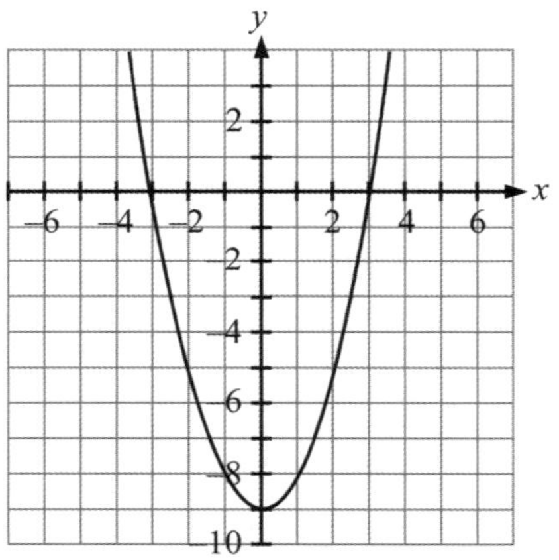

The graph of $y = x^2 - 9$ has two zeros: one at $x = +3$ and one at $x = -3$. Since the reciprocal of zero is undefined, the graph of $y = \dfrac{1}{x^2 - 9}$ will not exist for $x = \pm 3$, but it will have vertical asymptotes at both of these locations. The domain of $y = \dfrac{1}{x^2 - 9}$ is $x \neq \pm 3,\ x \in R$.

Since the reciprocal of 1 is 1 and the reciprocal of –1 is –1, the four points on the graph of $y = x^2 - 9$ where $y = \pm 1$ will remain at those same coordinates for the reciprocal function. These are the points $\left(\pm\sqrt{10}, 1\right)$ and $\left(\pm 2\sqrt{2}, -1\right)$.

On the interval $-3 < x < 3$, the y-coordinates are negative and so are their reciprocals. The minimum value of the function $x^2 - 9$ occurs at $(0, -9)$, so the maximum value of the reciprocal function $y = \dfrac{1}{x^2 - 9}$ on this interval is at $\left(0, -\dfrac{1}{9}\right)$. This value is the y-intercept.

As the graph of $y = x^2 - 9$ approaches the x-axis near both $x = 3$ and $x = -3$, the y-coordinates get closer and closer to zero, so the reciprocals approach $-\infty$ and the graph of $y = \dfrac{1}{x^2 - 9}$ approaches the two asymptotes.

For the intervals $x < -3$ and $x > 3$, the function values are positive, so the reciprocal values are also positive and, therefore, above the x-axis. As $y \to \pm\infty$ in $y = x^2 - 9$, the reciprocal gets close to zero and the graph approaches the x-axis as a horizontal asymptote.

As the graph of $y = x^2 - 9$ approaches $x = 3$ and $x = -3$, the y-coordinates get closer and closer to zero, so the reciprocals approach $+\infty$ and the graph approaches the two vertical asymptotes. This information gives the approximate graph sketched below.

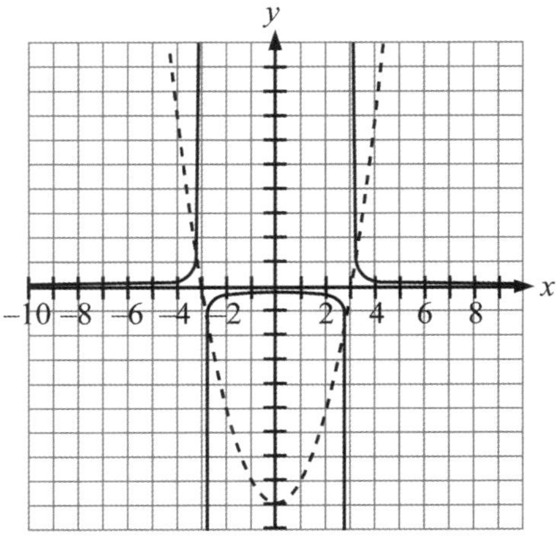

The range of $y = \dfrac{1}{x^2 - 9}$ is

$y \le -\dfrac{1}{9}$ or $y > 0$. Whenever the graph of a function is decreasing, the graph of the reciprocal of the function will be increasing, and vice versa.

Since the graph of $y = x^2 - 9$ is decreasing for $x < 0$ and increasing for $x > 0$, the graph of the function $y = \dfrac{1}{x^2 - 9}$ is increasing for $x < 0$ and decreasing for $x > 0$.

PRACTICE QUESTIONS

16. The lines $y = 1$ and $y = -1$ are significant to the graphs of $y = f(x)$ and $\dfrac{1}{f(x)}$ because

A. they indicate the location of any vertical asymptotes

B. they indicate the location of any horizontal asymptotes

C. the invariant points of the two functions lie only on these two lines

D. the graph of the reciprocal function must lie between these two lines

17. The range of the rational function $f(x) = y = \dfrac{1}{x - 3}$ is

A. $y \in R$

B. $y \ne 3,\ y \in R$

C. $y \ne 0,\ y \in R$

D. $0 < y < 3,\ y \in R$

2.2 determine, through investigation with and without technology, key features of the graphs of rational functions that have linear expressions in the numerator and denominator, and make connections between the algebraic and graphical representations of these rational functions

THE GRAPHS OF RATIONAL FUNCTIONS

The key features of the graphs of the family of rational functions of the form

$f(x)=\dfrac{2x}{nx-4}$ for n = 1, 2, 4, and 8 will now be considered. These key features can then be used to make connections between the equations and the asymptotes.

The graph of every member of the family of rational functions $f(x)=\dfrac{2x}{nx-4}$ has a vertical asymptote when the denominator $nx-4=0$, or $x=\dfrac{4}{n}$. The domain for every member is $x\neq\dfrac{4}{n}$, $x\in R$.

There is a horizontal asymptote at $y=\dfrac{2}{n}$ so that the range of every member function is $y\neq\dfrac{2}{n}$, $y\in R$.

Since $f(0)=0$ for all family members, they all pass through the origin.

All members of this family of functions will be decreasing over the entire domain.
The functions are positive on the intervals $x<0$ or $x>\dfrac{4}{n}$, and negative on $0<x<\dfrac{4}{n}$.

The graph of $f(x)=\dfrac{2x}{x-4}$, where $n=1$ is shown below

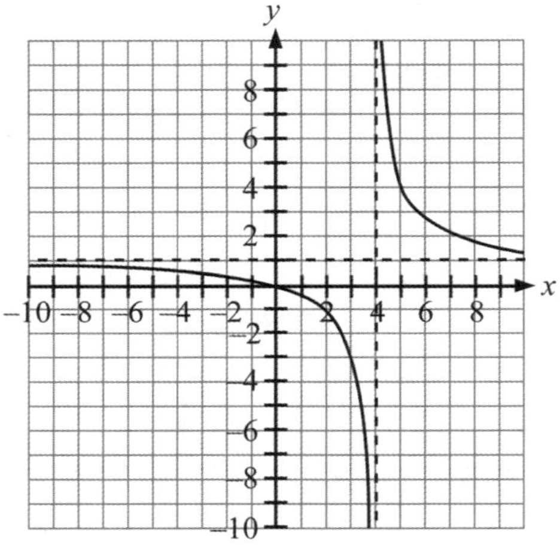

The key features of functions of the form $f(x)=\dfrac{2x}{nx-4}$ with various values of n are illustrated in the following table.

Function	Vertical asymptote	Domain	Horizontal asymptote	Intercepts
$f(x)=\dfrac{2x}{x-4}$	$x=4$	$x\neq 4$	$y=2$	$x=0$ $y=0$
$f(x)=\dfrac{2x}{2x-4}$	$x=2$	$x\neq 2$	$y=1$	$x=0$ $y=0$
$f(x)=\dfrac{2x}{4x-4}$	$x=1$	$x\neq 1$	$y=\dfrac{1}{2}$	$x=0$ $y=0$
$f(x)=\dfrac{2x}{8x-4}$	$x=\dfrac{1}{2}$	$x\neq\dfrac{1}{2}$	$y=\dfrac{1}{4}$	$x=0$ $y=0$

Range	Increasing	Decreasing	Positive	Negative
$y\neq 2$	never	$x\in R$, $x\neq 4$	$x<0$ or $x>4$	$0<x<4$
$y\neq 1$	never	$x\in R$, $x\neq 2$	$x<0$ or $x>2$	$0<x<2$
$y\neq\dfrac{1}{2}$	never	$x\in R$, $x\neq 1$	$x<0$ or $x>1$	$0<x<1$
$y\neq\dfrac{1}{4}$	never	$x\in R$, $x\neq\dfrac{1}{2}$	$x<0$ or $x>\dfrac{1}{2}$	$0<x<\dfrac{1}{2}$

PRACTICE QUESTIONS

Use the following information to answer the next question.

Using technology, Amanda drew the graph of the function $y = \dfrac{3x}{3x-5}$. She then analyzed her graph and come to the following conclusions.

I The domain of the function is $x \neq \dfrac{5}{3}, x \in R$

II $y = 1$ is the equation of a horizontal asymptote

III $x = \dfrac{5}{3}$ is the equation of the only vertical asymptote

IV The range of the function is $y \in R$.

V $x = 0$ is the only x-intercept

18. Which of Amanda's conclusions are correct?

A. I, II, and IV only

B. I, III, and V only

C. II, IV, and V only

D. I, II, III, and V only

Use the following information to answer the next question.

The graph of a rational function is shown below

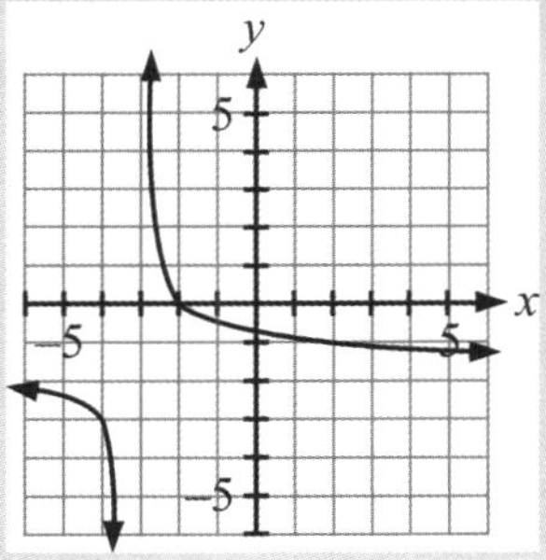

19. The equations of the asymptotes are

A. $x = 3$ and $x = -3$

B. $y = 3$ and $y = -2$

C. $x = -3$ and $x = -2$

D. $x = -3$ and $y = -2$

Numerical Response

NR2. The x-intercept, to the nearest tenth, of the graph of the function $y = \dfrac{2x-5}{x}$ is ___________.

Open Response

OR2.

a) Algebraically, determine the solution to the inequality $x^3 + x^2 - 9x - 9 > 0$.

b) Explain how to determine the solution to the inequality $x^3 + x^2 - 9x - 9 > 0$ by using a graphical approach.

2.3 *sketch the graph of a simple rational function using its key features, given the algebraic representation of the function*

SKETCHING THE GRAPH OF A RATIONAL FUNCTION

Example

Sketch the graph of the rational function $f(x)=\dfrac{-3x}{x+2}$ by identifying key features.

Solution

The graph has a domain of $x \neq -2$ and a vertical asymptote at $x=-2$. There is a horizontal asymptote at $y=-3$ and the range is $y \neq -3$. Since $f(0)=0$, both the x-intercept and the y-intercept are zero. The graph is a hyperbola that is always decreasing and that is only positive on the interval $-2<x<0$. These properties produce the graph that is shown.

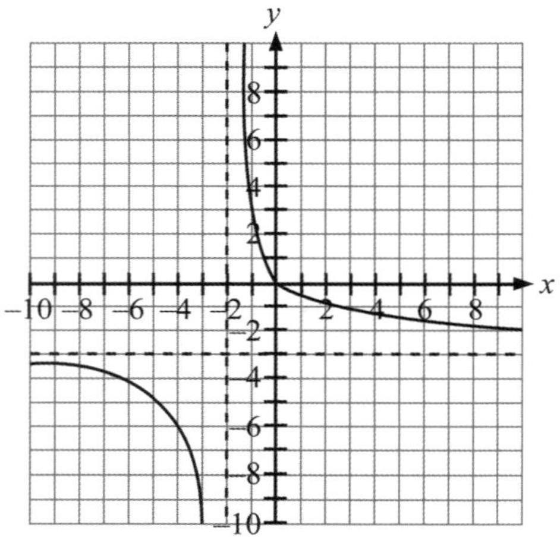

PRACTICE QUESTION

Use the following information to answer the next question.

The following two true statements were made about the graph of a particular function.

I The graph of the function is decreasing on the intervals $0<x<2$ and $x>2$.

II The graph of the function is increasing on the intervals $x<-2$ and $-2<x<0$.

20. Which of the following graphs do these statements pertain to?

A.

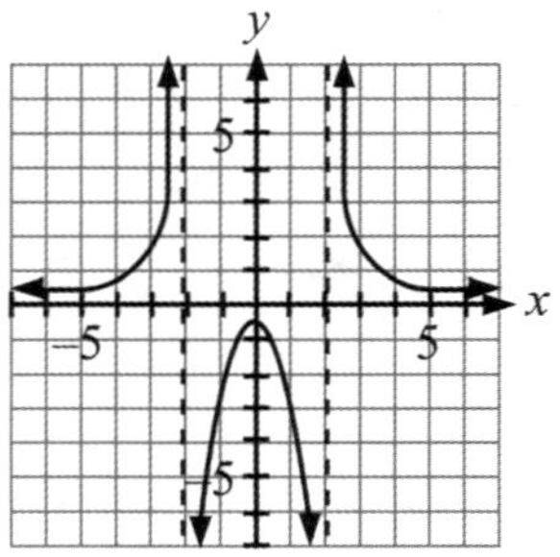

B.

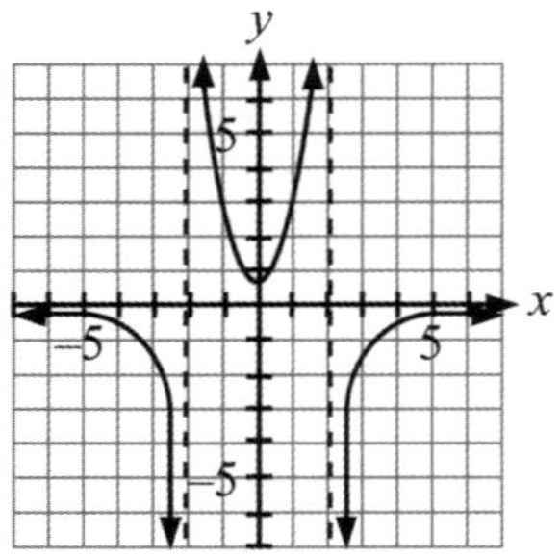

C.

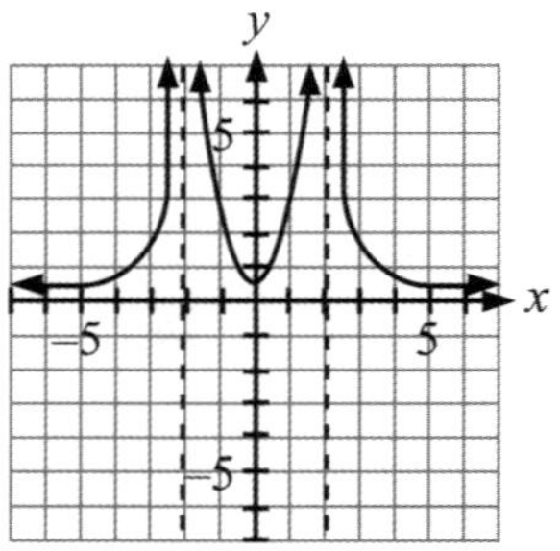

D.

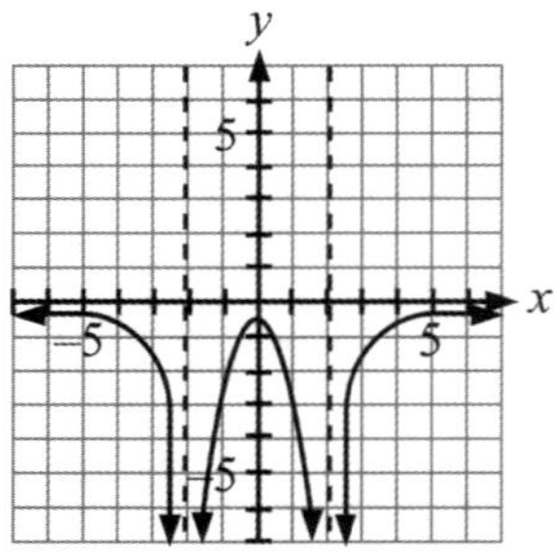

3.1 *By the end of this course, students will make connections, through investigation using technology, between the polynomial function f(x) the divisor x – a, the remainder from the division* $\frac{f(x)}{x-a}$ *and* $f(a)$ *to verify the remainder theorem and the factor theorem.*

3.2 *By the end of this course, students will factor polynomial expressions in one variable, of degree no higher than four, by selecting and applying strategies*

FACTORING POLYNOMIAL EXPRESSIONS

The remainder theorem states that if a polynomial function $f(x)$ is divided by a binomial $x-a$, then the remainder is $R=f(a)$.

Example

Without dividing, find the remainder when $f(x)=x^3-x^2-6x-8$ is divided by $x+2$.

Solution

$$\begin{aligned}R=f(a)=f(-2)&=(-2)^3-(-2)^2-6(-2)-8\\&=-8-4+12-8\\&=-8\end{aligned}$$

The factor theorem states for any polynomial function, $f(x)$, that $f(a)=0$ if and only if $x-a$ is a factor of $f(x)$.

This means two things:

- if $f(a)=0$, then $x-a$ is a factor of $f(x)$
- if $x-a$ is a factor of $f(x)$then $f(a)=0$.

Example

If a polynomial function$f(x)$ is such that $f(3)=0,\ f(-2)=0,$ and $f(0)=5$, then which of the following binomials must be factors of $f(x)$?

A. $(x+3),(x-2)$and$(x+5)$

B. $(x-3),(x+2)$ and$(x-5)$

C. $(x+3)$ and$(x-2)$

D. $(x-3)$and$(x+2)$

Solution

D

You can see that 3 and -2 are zeros of $f(x)$, so according to the factor theorem, $x-3$ and $x+2$ are factors of $f(x)$. The fact that $f(0)=5$ gives the y-intercept of 5 but no factor of $f(x)$ means that alternative **D** is correct.

Example

Factor completely the polynomial $f(x)=2x^3-9x^2+7x+6$.

Solution

Any integral zero of $f(x)$ must be a factor of its constant term 6. The possible integral zeros are $\pm1,\pm2,\pm3,\pm6$.
By substituting, you will find that $f(1)=6, f(-1)=-12,$and $f(2)=0$.
According to the factor theorem, $x-2$ is a factor of $f(x)$. Using synthetic division, you can find the other second-degree factors of $f(x)$.

$$\begin{array}{r|rrrr}-2 & 2 & -9 & 7 & 6\\ & & -4 & 10 & 6\\\hline & 2 & -5 & -3 & 0\end{array}$$

The quotient gives us a factor of $2x^2-5x-3$

$$\begin{aligned}\text{So, } f(x)&=(x-2)(2x^2-5x-3)\\&=(x-2)(2x+1)(x-3)\end{aligned}$$

You can verify that the other factors are correct as $f\left(-\frac{1}{2}\right)=0$ and $f(3)=0$.

PRACTICE QUESTIONS

Use the following information to answer the next question.

Consider the following statements.

I A factor of $2x^{10}-x^7-1$ is $x-1$

II The remainder for $\left(2x^{10}-x^7-1\right)\div(x-1)$ is 0.

III If $p(x)=2x^{10}-x^7-1$, then $p(1)=0$.

21. Which of the preceding statements are **true**?

A. I and II only **B.** I and III only

C. II and III only **D.** I, II, and III

22. If a polynomial $p(x)$ can be expressed as $p(x)=2(x-3)(x-2)^2(x+4)$, then which of the following statements is **true**?

A. $p(3)=p(2)=p(-4)=0$

B. $p(6)=p(4)=p(-8)=0$

C. $p(-3)=p(-2)=p(4)=0$

D. $p(-6)=p(-4)=p(8)=0$

23. Which of the following is a factor of $p(x)=30x^3-x^2-11x+2$?

A. $(3x-2)$ **B.** $(2x-1)$

C. $(5x+1)$ **D.** $(x+2)$

24. The complete factorization of the polynomial $2x^3+3x^2-2x-3$ is

A. $(x+1)(2x+3)^2$

B. $(x+1)(x-1)(2x+3)$

C. $(x+1)(x-1)(2x+3)^2$

D. $(x-1)(2x-3)(2x+3)$

3.3 By the end of this course, students will determine, through investigation using technology, the connection between the real roots of a polynomial equation and the x-intercepts of the graph of the corresponding polynomial function, and describe this connection

3.4 By the end of this course, students will solve polynomial equations in one variable, of degree no higher than four, by selecting and applying strategies, and verify solutions using technology

SOLVING POLYNOMIAL EQUATIONS

Example

Solve the equation $2x^3+5x^2-18x-45=0$, algebraically and verify the roots graphically.

Solution

The polynomial $2x^3+5x^2-18x-45$ can be factored by grouping and the difference of squares. Hence:

$$2x^3+5x^2-18x-45=0$$
$$x^2(2x+5)-9(2x+5)=0$$
$$(2x+5)(x^2-9)=0$$
$$(2x+5)(x-3)(x+3)=0$$
$$2x+5=0 \quad \text{or } x-3=0 \quad \text{or} \quad x+3=0$$
$$x=-\frac{5}{2} \quad \text{or } x=3 \quad\quad x=-3$$

Graphing \$Y_1=2X\wedge 3+5X^2-18X-45$ on a viewing window $x:[-5,5,1]$ $y:[-100,100,10]$ gives us the graph below.

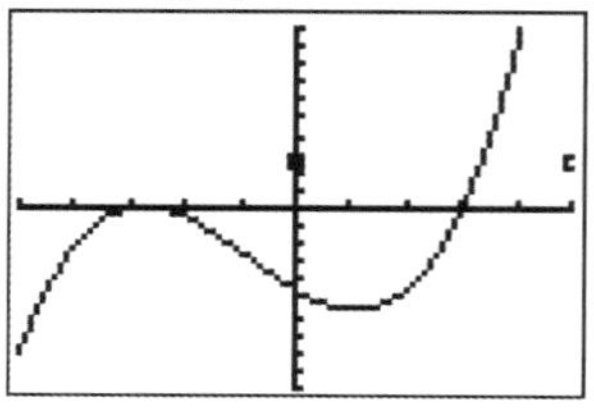

However the two x-intercepts –3 and $-\frac{5}{2}$ are very close together and not obvious on this window.

If we change the viewing window for y to $y:[-2,2,1]$, we get a much better view of the x-intercepts as shown below.

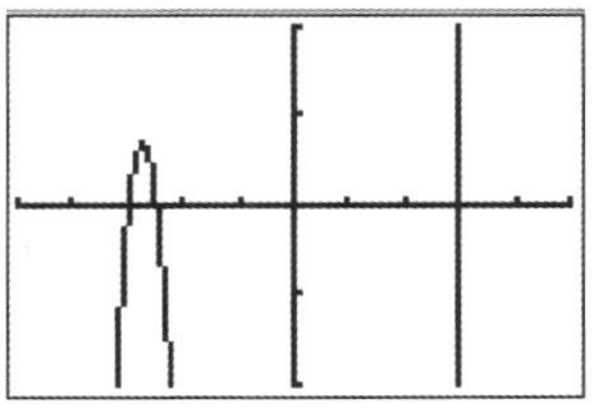

PRACTICE QUESTIONS

25. Technology can be used to determine the roots of the equation $2x^3-3x^2-5x+6=0$. The smallest root of this equation is

A. -1.5 **B.** -1.25

C. 1 **D.** 2

Use the following information to answer the next question.

The graph of $y=f(x)$ is shown below

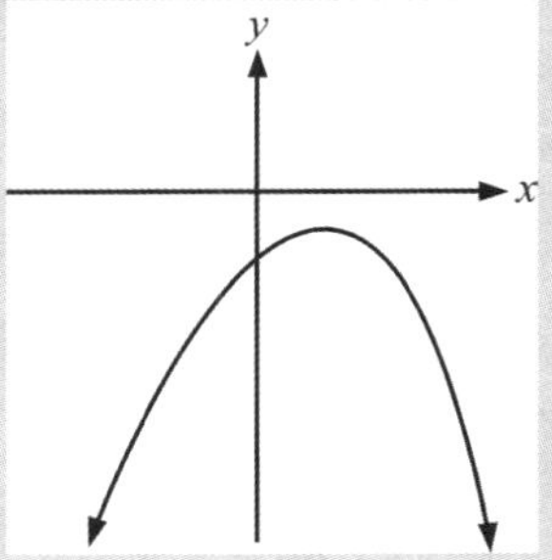

26. Which of the statements about the graph of $y=f(x)$ is **true**?

A. The graph has no x-intercepts, therefore the corresponding polynomial equation $f(x)=0$ will have no real roots.

B. The graph has one x-intercept, therefore the corresponding polynomial $f(x)=0$ equation will have one real root.

C. The graph has no y-intercepts, therefore the corresponding polynomial equation $f(x)=0$ will have no real roots.

D. The graph has one y-intercept, therefore the corresponding polynomial equation will have one real root.

27. The solution to the polynomial equation $6x^3+5x^2-2x-1=0$ is

A. $x=1$ or $x=\pm\frac{1}{2}$

B. $x=-1$ or $x=\pm\frac{1}{2}$

C. $x=1$, $x=\frac{1}{3}$, or $x=-\frac{1}{2}$

D. $x=-1$, $x=-\frac{1}{3}$, or $x=\frac{1}{2}$

28. Which of the following equations represents a polynomial equation where the x-intercepts of the graph of the corresponding polynomial function are 2 and 3?

A. $x^2-x-6=0$ **B.** $x^2+x-6=0$

C. $x^2-5x+6=0$ **D.** $x^2+5x+6=0$

Numerical Response

NR3. A potential rational root of the polynomial equation $2x^4-x^2+3x-6=0$, $1<x<2$, correct to one decimal place, is __________.

NR4. The sum of the roots of the polynomial equation $(x^2-9)(x^2-13x-30)=0$ is ____________.

3.5 *determine, through investigation using technology, the connection between the real roots of a rational equation and the x-intercepts of the graph of the corresponding rational function, and describe this connection*

3.6 *solve simple rational equations in one variable algebraically, and verify solutions using technology*

SOLVING RATIONAL EQUATIONS

Example

Solve the rational equation $\frac{x^2-5x-36}{x+3}=0$, algebraically and verify the roots graphically.

Solution

We can solve the equation by first multiplying both sides of the equation by $x+3$:

$$(x+3)\left(\frac{x^2-5x-36}{x+3}\right)=0\times(x+3)$$

which gives

$$x^2-5x-36=0$$
$$(x-9)(x+4)=0$$
$$x-9=0 \quad \text{and } x+4=0$$
$$x=9 \qquad\qquad x=-4$$

These two solutions should be the x-intercepts of the graph of the function

$$f(x)=\frac{x^2-5x-36}{x+3}.$$

Graphing $\backslash Y_1=(X^2-5X-36)/(X+3)$ on a viewing window $x:[-10,10,1]\quad y:[-10,10,1]$

Gives us the graph below.

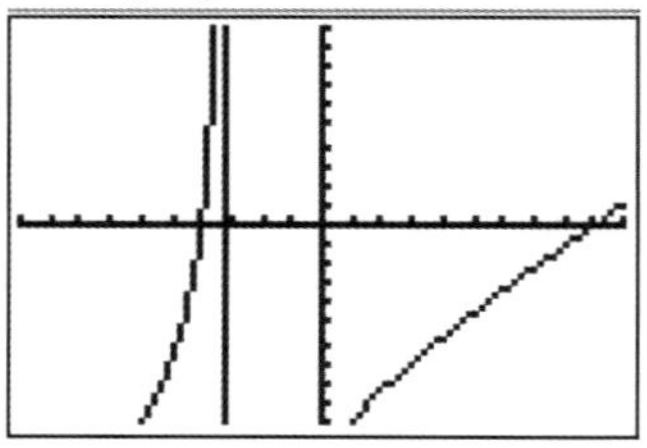

Note: $x\pm-3$

Using the zero feature will verify that the two x-intercepts are indeed -4 and 9.

PRACTICE QUESTIONS

29. Which of the following statements about the graph of the rational function $F(x)=\frac{x^2-4}{x^2-9}$ is **true**?

A. The graph does not intersect the x-axis.

B. The horizontal asymptote of the graph is at $y=1$

C. The y-intercept of the graph is at the ordered pair $\left(0,-\frac{4}{9}\right)$

D. The vertical asymptotes of the graph are at $x=2$ and $x=-2$.

Use the following information to answer the next question.

The graph of a particular rational function is shown below.

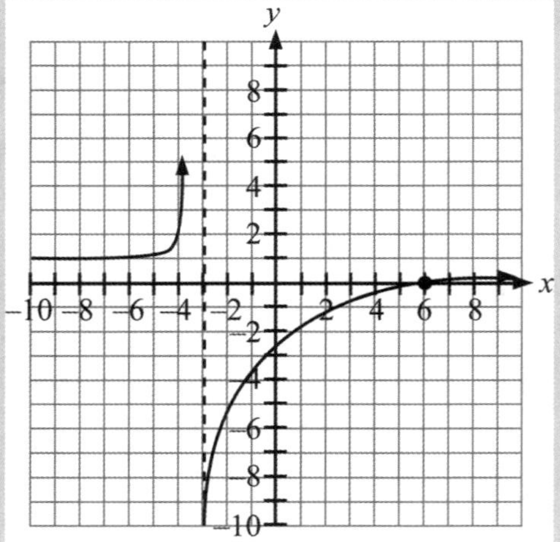

30. The real root of the corresponding rational equation is

A. –3

B. –2

C. 6

D. Undefined

31. The solution to the rational equation $\frac{3-2x}{6}=\frac{5-x}{8}$ is x equals

A. $-\frac{3}{5}$ **B.** $-\frac{11}{2}$

C. $\frac{3}{5}$ **D.** $\frac{4}{11}$

32. Which of the following procedures could be used to verify the solution to the rational equation $\frac{3}{x+1}=\frac{-4}{2x-3}$?

A. Graph $y=\frac{4}{2x-3}-\frac{3}{x+1}$ and determine the y-intercept.

B. Graph $y=\frac{3}{x+1}-\frac{4}{2x-3}$ and determine the x-intercepts.

C. Graph $y=\frac{3}{x+1}$ and $y=-\frac{4}{2x-3}$ on the same grid and determine the x-coordinate of the point of intersection of the two curves.

D. Graph $y=\frac{3}{x+1}$ and $y=-\frac{4}{2x-3}$ on the same grid and determine the y-coordinate of the point of intersection of the two curves.

Numerical Response

NR5. The solution to the rational equation $\frac{3}{x}-\frac{2}{x-1}=-\frac{1}{x}$, to the nearest integer, is x equals ________.

3.7 solve problems involving applications of polynomial and simple rational functions and equations

APPLICATIONS OF POLYNOMIAL AND RATIONAL FUNCTIONS

Example

When the polynomial function $f(x)=mx^3+7x^2-18x+n$ is divided by $x+2$, the remainder is –15. If $x-3$ is also a factor of $f(x)$, what are the values of m and n?

Solution

The remainder theorem states that the remainder $R=f(a)$ when $f(x)$ is divided by $x-a$. Therefore, $f(-2)=-15$. Also, since $x-3$ is a factor of $f(x)$, $f(3)=0$. By making a system of two linear equations and solving the system you can determine the values of m and n.

$$f(-2)=-15$$
$$m(-2)^3+7(-2)^2-18(-2)+n=-15$$
$$-8m+28+36+n=-15$$
$$-8m+n=-79$$
$$f(3)=0$$
$$m(3)^3+7(3)^2-18(3)+n=0$$
$$27m+63-54+n=0$$
$$27m+n=-9$$

Thus, the system of equations is

$$\begin{cases}-8m+n=-79\\27m+n=-9\end{cases}$$

The system can be solved by the method of elimination.

$$-8m+n=-79$$
$$\underline{27m+n=-9}$$
$$-35m\quad=-70$$ Subtract the second equation from the first.
$$m\quad=2$$

Substituting $m=2$ into $-8m+n=-79$ gives $-8(2)+n=-79$, so $n=-79+16=-63$.

The function is
$f(x) = 2x^3 + 7x^2 - 18x - 63.$
This function could be graphed to verify that there is an x-intercept at 3, and the trace feature could be used to verify that $f(-2) = -15.$

Practice Questions

33. The rational function $f(x) = \dfrac{x^2 - 6x + 11}{x - 2}$ is equivalent to

A. $f(x) = x - 4 + \dfrac{3}{x-2}$

B. $f(x) = x + 4 + \dfrac{19}{x-2}$

C. $f(x) = x - 8 - \dfrac{5}{x-2}$

D. $f(x) = x + 8 - \dfrac{27}{x-2}$

34. For which value of b would the polynomial $p(x) = 2x^3 - bx^2 + 9x - 11$ have the same remainder when divided by either $(x + 3)$ or $(x - 2)$?

A. $-\dfrac{7}{5}$ **B.** $\dfrac{7}{5}$

C. 23 **D.** –23

4.1 *explain, for polynomial and simple rational functions, the difference between the solution to an equation in one variable and the solution to an inequality in one variable, and demonstrate that given solutions satisfy an inequality.*

4.2 *determine solutions to polynomial inequalities in one variable and to simple rational inequalities in one variable by graphing the corresponding functions, using graphing technology, and identifying intervals for which x satisfies the inequalities.*

Polynomial and Rational Inequalities

Example

Graphically determine the solutions of the equation $x^3 - 6x^2 - x + 30 = 0$ and the inequality $x^3 - 6x^2 - x + 30 > 0.$

Solution

When solving the equation
$f(x) = x^3 - 6x^2 - x + 30 = 0$,
we must find the values of x that make $y = f(x)$ equal to zero. These are the x-intercepts on the graph. The function intersects the x-axis at −2, 3 and 5, so the solutions to the equation are $x = -2, 3, 5.$

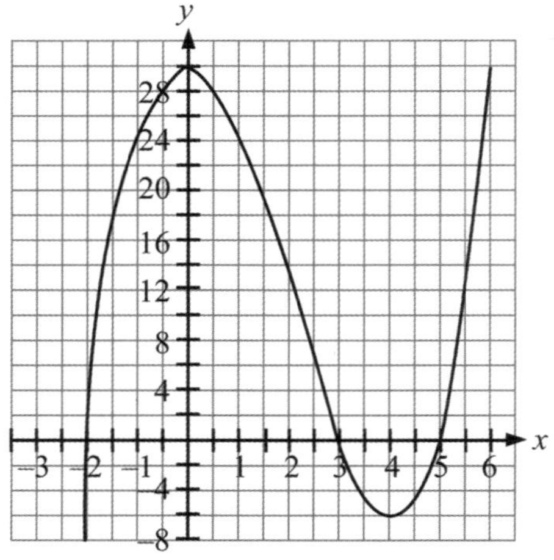

To solve the inequality $x^3 - 6x^2 - x + 30 > 0$, we need to identify where $f(x) > 0$.

Since the y-coordinates are positive above the x-axis, all intervals of x for which the graph is above the x-axis will be the solutions to the inequality. From the graph we see the function is positive between $x = -2$ and $x = 3$, and also for all x-coordinates larger than 5, so the solution to the inequality is $-2 < x < 3$ or $x > 5$.

The solution(s) to an equation or inequality will be specific values, while the solution to the corresponding inequality will be values between or outside these solutions.

PRACTICE QUESTIONS

35. The solution to the polynomial inequality $x^3 + 5x^2 - 4x - 20 > 0$ is

A. $x < -5$ or $-2 < x < 2$

B. $-5 < x < -2$ or $x > 2$

C. $x > 5$ or $-2 < x < 2$

D. $2 < x < 5$ or $x < -2$

Use the following information to answer the next question.

The graph of $y = f(x)$ is shown.

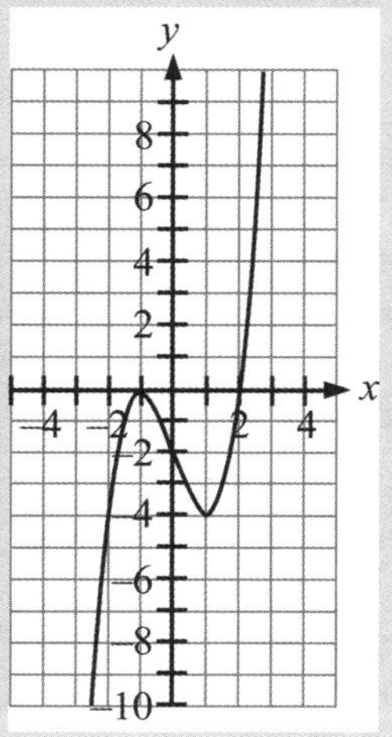

36. Which of the following number lines gives the solution for the inequality $f(x) > 0$?

A.

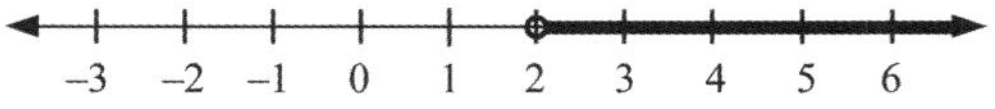

B.

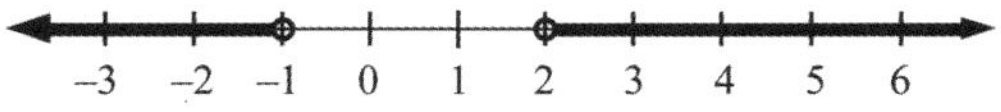

C.

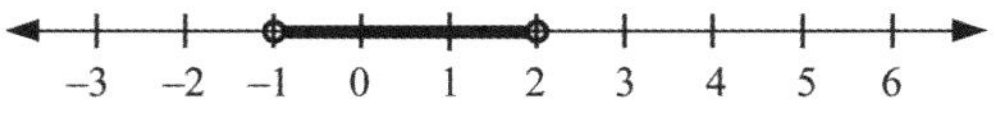

D.

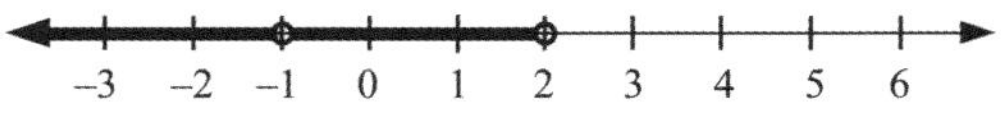

37. Joe was asked to solve the rational inequality $\frac{x^2-7x-8}{x+1} \geq 3$. He decided to simplify the inequality by first moving everything to one side. Which of the following represents Joe's initial step?

A. $\frac{x^2-7x-5}{x+4} \geq 0$

B. $\frac{x^2-7x-11}{x-2} > 0$

C. $\frac{x^2-10x-11}{x+1} \geq 0$

D. $\frac{x^2-7x-8}{x+1} + 3 \geq 0$

4.3 solve linear inequalities and factorable polynomial inequalities in one variable in a variety of ways, and represent the solutions on a number line or algebraically.

SOLVING POLYNOMIAL INEQUALITIES

If a polynomial function, $f(x)$, can be factored, the solution to any of the inequalities, $f(x)>0, f(x)<0, f(x)\geq 0,$ or $f(x)\leq 0,$ can be determined algebraically by examining the sign of the product of the factors of $f(x)$ in the intervals between the zeros of $f(x)$.

Example

Solve $(x+5)(x+1)(x-2)(x-6)\leq 0$ algebraically and graph the solution on a number line.

Solution

The four zeros of the polynomial function $f(x)=(x+5)(x+1)(x-2)(x-6)$ are -5, -1, 2, and 6. Since the inequality is of the form $\leq$, the equality is included in the solution and thus, $x=-5,-1,2,$ 6 are solution values.

There are five intervals of real numbers to examine: $x<-5$, $-5<x<-1$, $-1<x<2$, $2<x<6$, and $x>6$.

By evaluating each factor of the polynomial $f(x)$ for a single x-value within each interval, you can determine the sign $(+$ or $-)$ of each factor in that interval and thus the product of the signs of the factors in that interval.

Interval	Test value	$(x+5)$	$(x+1)$	$(x-2)$	$(x-6)$	$f(x)$
$x<-5$	-6	-1	-5	-8	-12	+
$-5<x<-1$	-3	2	-2	-5	-9	−
$-1<x<2$	0	5	1	-2	-6	+
$2<x<6$	4	9	5	2	-2	−
$x>6$	7	12	8	5	1	+

From the analysis, observe that $f(x)\leq 0$ for $-5<x<-1$ or $2<x<6$, so these two intervals are solutions to the inequality. Since equality is part of the solution, the complete solution is $-5\leq x\leq -1$ or $2\leq x\leq 6$. If you examined the graph of $f(x)=(x+5)(x+1)(x-2)(x-6)$, you would observe that the graph is below the x-axis in these two intervals.

The solution, $-5\leq x\leq -1$ or $2\leq x\leq 6$, is represented on a number line by graphing the solutions to the corresponding equality and shading the solution intervals as follows.

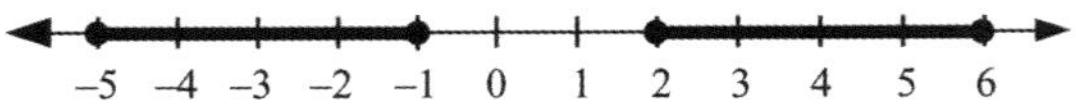

PRACTICE QUESTIONS

38. Which of the following expressions represents the solution to $x^2 - x - 6 \leq 0$?

A. $-2 \leq x \leq 3$

B. $-3 \leq x \leq 2$

C. $x \leq -2$, $x \geq 3$

D. $x \leq -3$, $x \geq 2$

39. When solving the inequality $x^3 - x^2 - 9x + 9 < 0$ algebraically, the number of test regions required would be

A. 3

B. 4

C. 5

D. 6

Use the following information to answer the next question.

A number line shown below.

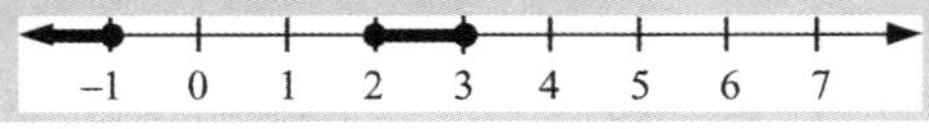

40. Which of the following polynomial inequality's solutions is represented on the given number line?

A. $(x-1)(x+2)(x+3) \geq 0$

B. $(x-1)(x+2)(x+3) \leq 0$

C. $(x+1)(x-2)(x-3) \geq 0$

D. $(x+1)(x-2)(x-3) \leq 0$

ANSWERS AND SOLUTIONS— POLYNOMIAL AND RATIONAL FUNCTIONS

1. C	**9. A**	**15. B**	**21. D**	**NR3. 1.5**	**34. D**
2. D	**10. C**	**16. C**	**22. A**	**NR4. 13**	**35. B**
3. B	**11. B**	**17. C**	**23. B**	**29. B**	**36. A**
4. B	**12. D**	**18. D**	**24. B**	**30. C**	**37. C**
5. D	**NR1. –36**	**19. D**	**25. A**	**31. A**	**38. A**
6. B	**OR1. See Solution**	**NR2. 2.5**	**26. A**	**32. C**	**39. B**
7. D	**13. B**	**OR2.See Solution**	**27. D**	**NR5. 2**	**40. D**
8. C	**14. C**	**20. A**	**28. C**	**33. A**	

1. **C**

The function $g(x) = 4x^{-4} - 3x^{-1} + 5x^2 + 67$ is not a polynomial function because the exponents –4 and –1 are not whole numbers.

2. **D**

The graph shown is tangent to the *x*-axis in two distinct locations, crosses the *x*-axis in a distinct third location and has a point of inflection on the *x*-axis in a distinct fourth location. Thus, there are two factors that each occur a minimum of two times, one factor that occurs at least once and one factor that occurs a minimum of three times. The minimum degree of the polynomial function illustrated by the given graph is $2 + 2 + 1 + 3 = 8$.

3. **B**

The function $P(x) = Ax^4 + Bx^2 + 7$ is of degree four. Therefore, the maximum number of *x*-intercepts for the graph of this function is 4.

4. **B**

The domain of all polynomial functions is $x \in R$. The minimum value of the graph of the given polynomial function is –4. Thus, the range of the polynomial function is $y \geq -4$.

5. **D**

If the range of a polynomial function is $y \leq 25$, then the polynomial function must be of even degree and have a leading coefficient that is negative. Alterative **D** is of even degree (4) and has a leading coefficient that is negative. **Note**: the function $S(x) = -Ax^4 + Bx^3 - Cx + 10$ has a maximum value since $y \to -\infty$ as $x \to \pm\infty$.

6. **B**

The range of a:

- polynomial function is either $y \in R$, $y \leq p$, where *p* is the maximum *y*-coordinate of the graph or $y \geq p$ where *p* is the minimum *y*-coordinate of the graph
- exponential function is $y > 0$, so this alternative is correct
- logarithmic function is $y \in R$
- sinusoidal function is restricted between two particular values

7. **D**

The x-intercepts (zeros) of the given graph are $x=-4, x=-1$, and $x=3$. The corresponding factors are $x+4$, $x+1$ and $x-3$. Thus, $x-4$ is not a factor of the function represented by the given graph.

8. **C**

The zeros of the polynomial function $p(x)=-4(x-2)(x+2)(x-1)$ are $x=2$, –2, and 1. Arranged in ascending order, the zeros are $x=-2$, 1, and 2. Thus, the test regions Sarah will need to use are: $x<-2$, $-2<x<1$, $1<x<2$, and $x>2$.

9. **A**

When the graph of the function $y=f(x)$ is transformed into the graph of $y=f(x-1)-3$, each ordered pair on the graph of $y=f(x)$ will be translated horizontally 1 unit to the right and vertically down 3 units. Thus, the ordered pair $(-3,7)$ that is on the graph of $y=f(x)$ will transform to the ordered pair $(-2,4)$ on the graph of $y=f(x-1)-3$.

10. **C**

If $k<1$, then the graph of $y=f(x)$ is stretched horizontally about the y-axis by a factor of $\frac{1}{k}$. As well, if $k<0$, there is a reflection in the y-axis. These two conditions are given in alternative **C**.

11. **B**

Since $P(-5)=P(-2)=P(6)=0$, $P(x)$ must have the factors $x+5$, $x+2$, and $x-6$. Thus, $P(x)$ can be expressed as $P(x)=(x+5)(x+2)(x-6)$ because the leading coefficient is 1. Solve for c in the equation $P(x)=x^3+bx^2+cx+d$ as shown below.

$P(x)=(x+5)(x+2)(x-6)$

Expanding $(x+5)(x+2)$ gives:

$P(x)=(x^2+7x+10)(x-6)$

Expanding $(x^2+7x+10)(x-6)$ gives:

$P(x)=x^3+x^2-32x-60$

Therefore,

$x^3+x^2-32x-60=x^3+bx^2+cx+d$

Hence, the value of c is –32.

12. **D**

Recall that when given the equation of a function, the x-intercepts of the graph of the function can be determined by substituting 0 for y in the given equation and then solving for x. Therefore, in the equation $y=2x^3+bx^2+7x-6$, the x-intercepts of the corresponding graph can be determined by solving the equation $2x^3+bx^2+7x-6=0$. Since –2 is one x-intercept, solve for b by substituting –2 for x, as shown below.

$$\begin{aligned}2(-2)^3+b(-2)^2+7(-2)-6&=0\\2(-8)+b(4)-14-6&=0\\-16+4b-14-6&=0\\4b-36&=0\\4b&=36\\b&=9\end{aligned}$$

NR1. –36

Since there are zeros at –2, 1, and 3, $f(x)$ must have the factors $x+2$, $x-1$, and $x-3$. Because the zero 3 occurs twice, the equation of $f(x)$ is $f(x)=a(x+2)(x-1)(x-3)^2$, where a is a real number. Next, solve for a.

It is given that $f(4)=36$; therefore, determine the value of a by substituting 4 for x and 36 for $f(x)$, as shown below.

$$f(x)=a(x+2)(x-1)(x-3)^2$$
$$36=a(4+2)(4-1)(4-3)^2$$
$$36=a(6)(3)(1)$$
$$36=18a$$
$$2=a$$

Thus, $f(x)=2(x+2)(x-1)(x-3)^2$.

To solve for e it is necessary to expand $f(x)$ as follows:

$$f(x)=2(x+2)(x-1)(x-3)^2$$
$$=2\left(x^2-x+2x-2\right)\left(x^2-3x-3x+9\right)$$
$$=2\left(x^2+x-2\right)\left(x^2-6x+9\right)$$
$$=2\left(x^4-6x^3+9x^2+x^3-6x^2+9x-2x^2+12x-18\right)$$
$$=2\left(x^4-5x^3+x^2+21x-18\right)$$
$$=2x^4-10x^3+2x^2+42x-36$$

It can now be observed that the value of e in the equation $f(x)=ax^4+bx^3+cx^2+dx+e$ is –36.

OR1.

a) From the given graph, it can be observed that the graph is tangent to the x-axis at –3 and that it passes through the x-axis at 2 and 4.
Thus, in factored form, $P(x)$ can be expressed as
$P(x)=a(x+3)^2(x-2)(x-4)$ where a is a non-zero real number. The value of a can be determined by making use of the ordered pair $(3, 9)$.
Substitute 3 for x and 9 for $P(x)$ and solve for a as shown below.

$$P(x) = a(x+3)^2(x-2)(x-4)$$
$$9 = a(3+3)^2(3-2)(3-4)$$
$$9 = a(36)(1)(-1)$$
$$9 = -36a$$
$$-\frac{1}{4} = a$$

Thus, the equation of $P(x)$ in factored form is

$$P(x) = -\frac{1}{4}(x+3)^2(x-2)(x-4).$$

b) The y-intercept of the graph of $y = P(x)$ can be determined by substituting 0 for x and solving for y as follows:

$$y = P(x) = -\frac{1}{4}(x+3)^2(x-2)(x-4)$$
$$y = -\frac{1}{4}(0+3)^2(0-2)(0-4)$$
$$y = -\frac{1}{4}(9)(-2)(-4)$$
$$y = -18$$

The y-intercept of the graph of $y = P(x)$ is –18.

13. **B**

Since there are zeros at –5 and 7, $f(x)$ must have the factors $x+5$ and $x-7$. Therefore, $f(x)=a(x+5)(x-7)$.

It is given that the graph of $f(x)$ has a y-intercept at 70, so solve for a by substituting 70 for $f(x)$ and 0 for x as shown below.

$$f(x)=a(x+5)(x-7)$$
$$70=a(0+5)(0-7)$$
$$70=a(5)(-7)$$
$$70=-35a$$
$$-2=a$$

Hence, $f(x)=-2(x+5)(x-7)$.

Now, expand $f(x)$.

$$\begin{aligned}f(x)&=-2(x+5)(x-7)\\&=-2\left(x^2-7x+5x-35\right)\\&=-2\left(x^2-2x-35\right)\\&=-2x^2+4x+70\end{aligned}$$

14. **C**

From the given diagram, it can be observed that the x-intercepts of the graph are at –1, 1, and 3. Thus, the zeros of the polynomial function are –1, 1, and 3. The function can now be written as

$f(x)=y=K(x-(-1))(x-1)(x-3)$ or

$f(x)=y=K(x+1)(x-1)(x-3)$.

Since the point (2, 9) is on the graph, the value of K can be determined by substituting 2 for x and 9 for y in the equation $y=K(x+1)(x-1)(x-3)$, as shown below.

$$9=K(2+1)(2-1)(2-3)$$
$$9=K(3)(1)(-1)$$
$$9=-3K$$
$$-3=K$$

15. **B**

If $f(-x)=-f(x)$, then $f(x)$ is an odd function and the graph of $y=f(x)$ is symmetrical about the origin. From the given graphs, the only graph that is symmetrical about the origin is graph **B**.

16. **C**

The functions $y=f(x)$ and $y=\dfrac{1}{f(x)}$ are reciprocal functions. Since the reciprocal of 1 is 1 and the reciprocal of –1 is –1, the lines $y=1$ and $y=-1$ are used to determine the location of the invariant points of the functions $y=f(x)$ and $y=\dfrac{1}{f(x)}$.

17. **C**

Using technology, you could graph $y=\dfrac{1}{x-3}$. From the graph, it can be determined that $y\neq 0$. The range can also be determined algebraically, as shown below.

$$y=\frac{1}{x-3}$$
$$y(x-3)=1$$
$$x-3=\frac{1}{y}$$
$$x=\frac{1}{y}+3$$

Since division by zero is undefined, the value of y cannot be zero $(y\neq 0)$.

18. **D**

All of Amanda's conclusions are correct except for conclusion IV. The range of the function is $y \neq 1$. This can be seen by graphing (using technology) $y = \frac{3x}{3x-5}$ or by determining algebraically as shown below.

$$y = \frac{3x}{3x-5}$$
$$y(3x-5) = 3x$$
$$3xy - 5y = 3x$$
$$3xy - 3x = 5y$$
$$x(3y-3) = 5y$$
$$x = \frac{5y}{3y-3}$$

Therefore, $3y - 3 \neq 0$ or $y \neq 1$.

19. **D**

The given graph has a vertical asymptote at $x = -3$ since the graph does not have a value when $x = -3$ (the graph does not intersect the line $x = -3$). For the left end of the graph, as $x \to -\infty$, $y \to -2$, and for the right end of the graph, as $x \to +\infty$, $y \to -2$. Thus, the line $y = -2$ is a horizontal asymptote.

NR2. **2.5**

The x-intercept of the graph of the function $y = \frac{2x-5}{x}$ can be found by substituting 0 for y in the equation $y = \frac{2x-5}{x}$ and then solving for x as shown below.

$$0 = \frac{2x-5}{x} = 2x - 5$$
$$5 = 2x$$
$$\frac{5}{2} = x$$

The x-intercept of the graph of the function $y = \frac{2x-5}{x}$ is $\frac{5}{2}$ or 2.5.

OR2.

a) Begin by factoring $x^3 + x^2 - 9x - 9$ by grouping as shown below

$$x^3 + x^2 - 9x - 9 = x^2(x+1) - 9(x+1)$$
$$= (x+1)(x^2 - 9)$$
$$= (x+1)(x+3)(x-3)$$

Therefore, $(x+1)(x+3)(x-3) > 0$.

A possible procedure is to now let $f(x) = (x+1)(x+3)(x-3)$ and determine the zeros of $f(x)$.

Use these zeros to set up an interval chart. The zeros of $f(x)$ are –1, –3, and 3. Arranged in ascending order the zeros are –3, –1, and 3.

Interval	$x+1$	$x+3$	$x-3$	$f(x)$
$x < -3$	–	–	–	–
$-3 < x < -1$	–	+	–	+
$-1 < x < 3$	+	+	–	–
$x > 3$	+	+	+	+

Thus $f(x)$ is positive (greater than zero) in the intervals $-3 < x < -1$ and $x > 3$. Hence, the solution to the inequality $x^3 + x^2 - 9x - 9 > 0$ is $-3 < x < -1$ or $x > 3$.

b) Let $y = x^3 + x^2 - 9x - 9$.

Using technology graph $y = x^3 + x^2 - 9x - 9$. Next determine the x-intercepts of the resulting graph. Use these x-intercepts as a reference and observe where the given graph is above the x-axis (where $y > 0$). The applicable intervals will be the solution to the inequality $x^3 + 9x^2 - 9x - 9 > 0$.

20. **A**

When the graph of a function rises from left to right, the function is increasing over that particular interval. When the graph of a function falls from left to right, the function is decreasing over that particular interval. The graph given in alternative **A** increases when $x<-2$ and $-2<x<0$ and decreases when $0<x<2$ and $x>2$. Thus, the correct alternative is **A**.

21. **D**

Each of the three given statements is true.

22. **A**

The factors of $p(x)$ are, $x-3$, $x-2$, and $x+4$. It follows that $p(3)=0$, $p(2)=0$, and $p(-4)=0$. Thus, the true statement is given in alternative **A**.

23. **B**

The zeros of $p(x)$ can be determined by using technology and graphing $p(x)$. The zeros of $p(x)$ are $\frac{1}{5}$, $\frac{1}{2}$ and $\frac{-2}{3}$.

Thus, the factors of $p(x)$ are $5x-1$, $2x-1$, and $3x+2$.

Only alternative **B** contains one of these factors. An alternate means of solving this problem would be to determine which one of the following equations is correct: $p\left(\frac{2}{3}\right)=0$, $p\left(\frac{1}{2}\right)=0$, $p\left(\frac{-1}{5}\right)=0$, or $p(-2)=0$.

24. **B**

Begin by factoring, $2x^3+3x^2-2x-3$ by grouping as shown below.

$$\begin{aligned}2x^3+3x^2-2x-3&=x^2(2x+3)-1(2x+3)\\&=(2x+3)\left(x^2-1\right)\end{aligned}$$

Next, x^2-1 can be factored by difference of squares.

Hence, $x^2-1=(x+1)(x-1)$.

Therefore,

$$2x^3+3x^2-2x-3=(2x+3)(x+1)(x-1)$$

25. **A**

Using technology, graph $y=2x^3-3x^2-5x+6$. The x-intercepts of this function correspond to the real roots of the equation $2x^3-3x^2-5x+6=0$. Therefore, the smallest root of the equation $2x^3-3x^2-5x+6=0$ is -1.5.

26. **A**

The x-intercepts of a graph of a polynomial function $f(x)$ are the real number solutions to the equation $f(x)=0$. Since the graph of $f(x)$ does not intersect the x-axis, there are no x-intercepts, and the corresponding polynomial equation $f(x)=0$ will have no real roots.

27. **D**

The factors of -1 are ± 1. The factors of 6 are ± 1, ± 2, ± 3, and ± 6. Thus, the potential rational zeros of the function $P(x)=6x^3+5x^2-2x-1$ are ± 1, $\pm\frac{1}{2}$, $\pm\frac{1}{3}$, and $\pm\frac{1}{6}$. By substitution, it can be determined that $p(-1)=0$. Using the factor theorem, $x+1$ is a factor of $p(x)$. Now, apply synthetic division to find the second-degree factor of $p(x)$, as shown below.

$$\begin{array}{r|rrrr} 1 & 6 & 5 & -2 & -1 \\ & & 6 & -1 & -1 \\ \hline & 6 & -1 & -1 & 0 \end{array}$$

The second-degree factor of $p(x)$ is $6x^2-x-1$.
It follows that
$p(x)=(x+1)\left(6x^2-x-1\right)$.

Factoring $6x^2-x-1$ gives
$p(x)=(x+1)(3x+1)(2x-1)$.

The zeros of $p(x)$ are -1, $\frac{-1}{3}$, and $\frac{1}{2}$.

Hence, the solution to the equation $6x^3+5x^2-2x-1=0$ is $x=-1$, $x=\frac{-1}{3}$, or $x=\frac{1}{2}$.

28. **C**

The x-intercepts of the graph of the polynomial function are 2 and 3. Thus, the zeros of the polynomial function are 2 and 3. The polynomial function can be written as $y=a(x-2)(x-3)$ or, by expanding as $y=a\left(x^2-5x+6\right)$, where a is a real number. It follows that the corresponding polynomial equation is $0=a\left(x^2-5x+6\right)$. The only alternative that can satisfy this equation is alternative **C** when $a=1$.

NR3. **1.5**

The factors of -6 are ± 1, ± 2, ± 3, and ± 6. The factors of 2 are ± 1 and ± 2. Therefore, the potential rational roots of the equation $2x^4-x^2+3x-6=0$ are ± 1, $\pm\frac{1}{2}$, ± 2, ± 3, $\pm\frac{3}{2}$, and ± 6.

The only potential rational zero between 1 and 2 is $\frac{3}{2}$. Therefore, the correct answer is 1.5.

NR4. **13**

The binomial x^2-9 can be expressed in factored form as $(x+3)(x-3)$, and the trinomial $x^2-13x-30$ can be expressed in factored form as $(x-15)(x+2)$. Therefore, the equation $\left(x^2-9\right)\left(x^2-13x-30\right)=0$ can be written as $(x+3)(x-3)(x-15)(x+2)=0$.

The roots of the equation $(x+3)(x-3)(x-15)(x+2)=0$ can now easily be determined. They are -3, 3, 15 and -2. The sum of these roots is $(-3)+(3)+(15)+(-2)=13$.

29. **B**

The statement in alternative:

i) **A** is false because the given graph intersects the x-axis at (2, 0) and (−2, 0)

ii) **C** is false because the y-intercept of the given graph is at the ordered pair $\left(0, \frac{4}{9}\right)$

iii) **D** is false because the vertical asymptotes of the given graph are at $x = 3$ and $x = -3$.

Statement **B** is true.

30. **C**

The real root of the corresponding rational equation has the same value as the x-intercept of the graph of the rational function. Since the x-intercept of the graph of the given rational function is 6, the real root of the corresponding rational equation is 6.

31. **A**

To solve the given equation, first multiply each side by 24 (the lowest common denominator).

$$(24)\times\frac{3-2x}{6} = (24)\times\frac{5-x}{8}$$

This equation can now be expressed as $4(3-2x) = 3(5-x)$. The equation can now be solved as shown below.

$$\begin{aligned} 4(3-2x) &= 3(5-x) \\ 12-8x &= 15-3x \\ -5x &= 3 \\ x &= -\frac{3}{5} \end{aligned}$$

32. **C**

In order to determine the solution to the rational equation $\frac{3}{x+1} = \frac{-4}{2x-3}$, you need to determine the value of x that satisfies the equation. Thus, it is necessary to state the x-coordinate of the point of intersection of the curves $y = \frac{3}{x+1}$ and $y = \frac{-4}{2x-3}$.

NR5. **2**

First, multiply each side of the given equation by the lowest common denominator $x(x-1)$.

$$x(x-1)\left(\frac{3}{x} - \frac{2}{x-1}\right) = x(x-1)\left(\frac{-1}{x}\right)$$

Simplifying results in $3(x-1) - 2x = (x-1)(-1)$.

This equation can now be solved as shown below.

$$\begin{aligned} 3(x-1)-2x &= (x-1)(-1) \\ 3x-3-2x &= -x+1 \\ x-3 &= -x+1 \\ 2x &= 4 \\ x &= 2 \end{aligned}$$

33. **A**

Using either long division or synthetic division, the given rational function can be expressed as the sum of a polynomial function and a rational function as follows:

Long Division

$$\begin{array}{r} x-4 \\ x-2\overline{)x^2-6x+11} \\ \underline{x^2-2x} \\ -4x+11 \\ \underline{-4x+8} \\ 3 \end{array}$$

Synthetic Division

$$\begin{array}{r|rrr} -2 & 1 & -6 & 11 \\ & & -2 & 8 \\ \hline & 1 & -4 & 3 \end{array}$$

Thus, an equivalent form of the given function is $f(x) = x - 4 + \frac{3}{x-2}$

34. **D**

The remainder when the given polynomial is divided by $x+3$ can be determined by applying the remainder theorem as shown below.

$$p(x)=2x^3-bx^2+9x-11$$
$$p(-3)=2(-3)^3-b(-3)^2+9(-3)-11$$
$$p(-3)=-54-9b-27-11$$
$$p(-3)=-9b-92$$

Similarly, the remainder when the given polynomial is divided by $x-2$ can be determined as follows:

$$p(x)=2x^3-bx^2+9x-11$$
$$p(2)=2(2)^3-b(2)^2+9(2)-11$$
$$p(2)=16-4b+18-11$$
$$p(2)=-4b+23$$

The remainders are equal:
$-9b-92=-4b+23$, which gives $-5b=115$. Therefore, $b=-23$.

35. **B**

First, using technology, graph $y=x^3+5x-4x-20$. A sketch of this graph is shown below.

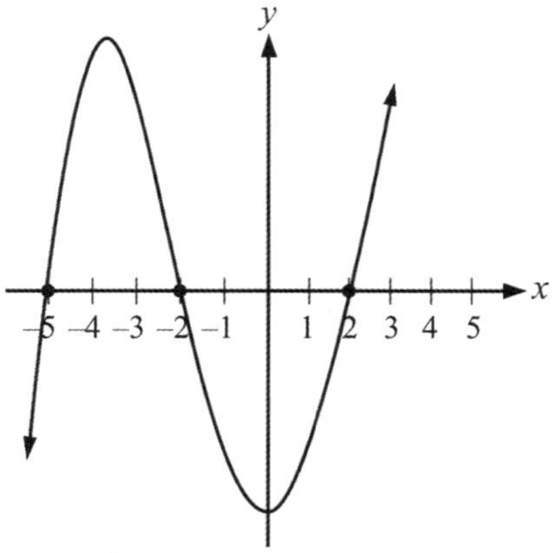

The x-intercepts of the graph are –5, –2, and 2. In order to solve the inequality $x^3+5x^2-4x-20>0$, determine the portion of the graph of $y=x^3+5x^2-4x-20$ that is above the x-axis. Thus, the solution to the inequality $x^3+5x^2-4x-20>0$ is $-5<x<-2$ or $x>2$.

36. **A**

The graph of $f(x)$ is greater than zero occurs when any part of the graph (y-values) is above, but not touching, the x-axis. The right part of the graph intercepts the x-axis at 2 and continues to increase there after. Therefore $f(x)$ is greater that zero when $x>2$.
The correct number line depicting this inequality is **A**.

37. **C**

To simplify the inequality Joe needs to subtract 3 from both sides.

$\frac{x^2-7x-8}{x+1}-3\geq 3-3$. Now find the common denominator in order to simplify the rational expression.

$$\frac{x^2-7x-8}{x+1}\frac{-3(x+1)}{(x+1)}\geq 0$$
$$\frac{x^2-7x-8-3x-3}{x+1}\geq 0$$
$$\frac{x^2-10x-11}{x+1}\geq 0$$

The correct answer is **C.**

38. **A**

Graph the function $y=x^2-x-6$, on the TI-83 Plus graphing calculator.
The graph generated is illustrated below.

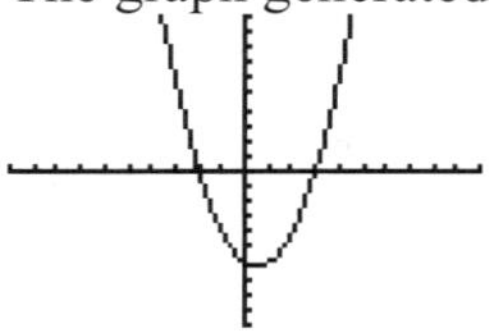

Notice that the x intercepts occur at –2 and 3, the interval of the graph that is less than or equal to 0 occurs when any part of the graph is below or touching the x-axis.
Therefore the solution is $-2\leq x\leq 3$.
The correct answer is **A**.

39. **B**

Begin by solving the equation $x^3 - x^2 - 9x + 9 = 0$ as follows:

$$x^2(x-1) - 9(x-1) = 0$$

$$(x-1)(x^2-9) = 0$$

$$(x-1)(x+3)(x-3) = 0$$

$x - 1 = 0$ or $x + 3 = 0$ or $x - 3 = 0$

$x = 1$ $\quad x = -3$ $\quad x = 3$

Since the equation $x^3 - x^2 - 9x + 9 = 0$ has 3 distinct roots the graph of the function $y = x^3 - x^2 - 9x + 9$ will cross the x-axis 3 times. This will split the x-axis into four regions, so there are 4 sample test regions required in order to solve the inequality $x^3 - x^2 - 9x + 9 < 0$. The correct answer is **B**.

40. **D**

From the number line it is given that the x-intercepts of the graph of the polynomial occur at –1, 2, 3, therefore the factors of the polynomial are $(x+1), (x-2)$, and $(x-3)$. So A or B cannot be the answer.

The graph of $y = (x+1)(x-2)(x-3)$ is shown:

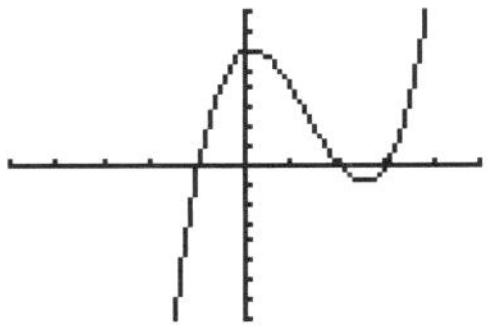

The number line represents the solution $x \le -1,\ 2 \le x \le 3$, and in the graph this interval represents values of y that are equal to or less than 0. Therefore the polynomial inequality represented by the number line is $(x+1)(x-2)(x-3) \le 0$.

The correct answer is **D**.

UNIT TEST — POLYNOMIAL AND RATIONAL FUNCTIONS

1. Which of the following functions is **not** a polynomial function?

A. $f(x) = 2x - \frac{3}{4}$

B. $h(x) = (x-5)^2$

C. $p(x) = (2x-1)(x-3)(x+4)$

D. $r(x) = \frac{x+3}{(x-9)^2}$

Use the following information to answer the next question.

A student made the following statements about the graphs of polynomial functions.

I. The range will always be $y \in R$.

II. The domain will always be $x \in R$.

III. The polynomial function will either have an absolute maximum or an absolute minimum value.

IV. The graph of a polynomial function of degree 3 will always begin in the third quadrant and end in the first quadrant.

V. The graph of a polynomial function of degree 4 with a positive leading coefficient will always begin in the second quadrant and end in the first quadrant.

2. Which of the given statements are always **true**?

A. I and IV only

B. II and V only

C. I, III, and IV only

D. II, III, and V only

Use the following information to answer the next question.

A partial table of values for a particular polynomial function is given below.

x	$f(x)$
–4	–20
–2	16
0	–6
2	–4
4	0
6	–4
8	–4
10	0
12	6

3. The minimum possible degree of this polynomial function is

A. 2

B. 3

C. 4

D. 5

Use the following information to answer the next question.

The graph of a particular polynomial function is shown below.

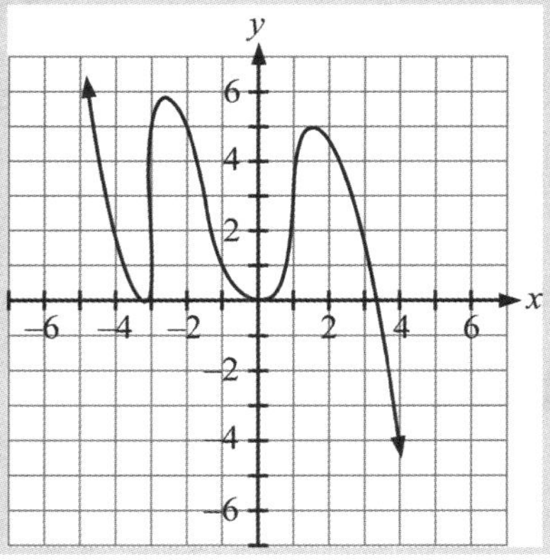

4. The domain and range of the polynomial function are, respectively,

A. $x \in R$ and $y \in R$

B. $x \in R$ and $y \geq 0$

C. $-5 \leq x \leq 4$ and $y \in R$

D. $-5 \leq x \leq 4$ and $y \geq 0$

Use the following information to answer the next question.

The graph of a particular function is shown below.

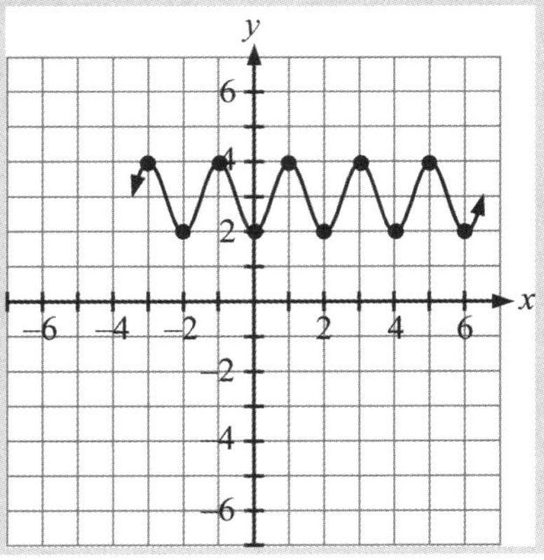

5. The graph shown illustrates a

A. polynomial function

B. exponential function

C. logarithmic function

D. sinusoidal function

6. The y-intercept of the graph of the polynomial function $p(x) = y = -5(x-3)(x-1)(x+4)^2$ is

A. 12 **B.** 60

C. −60 **D.** −240

7. Which of the following graphs represent a third-degree polynomial function with a negative leading coefficient and factors of $x - 3$ and $x^2 + 4x + 4$?

A.

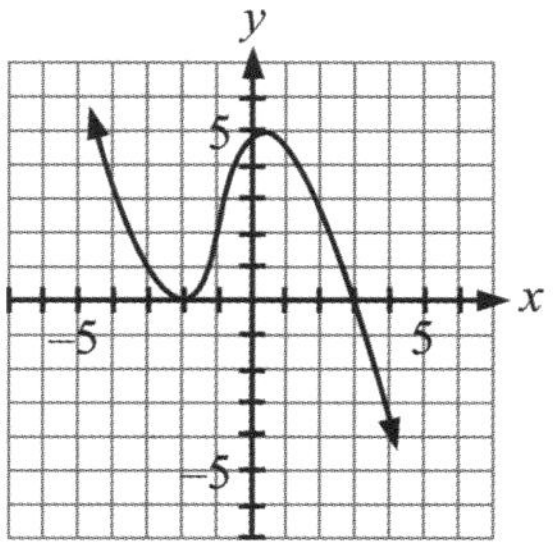

B.

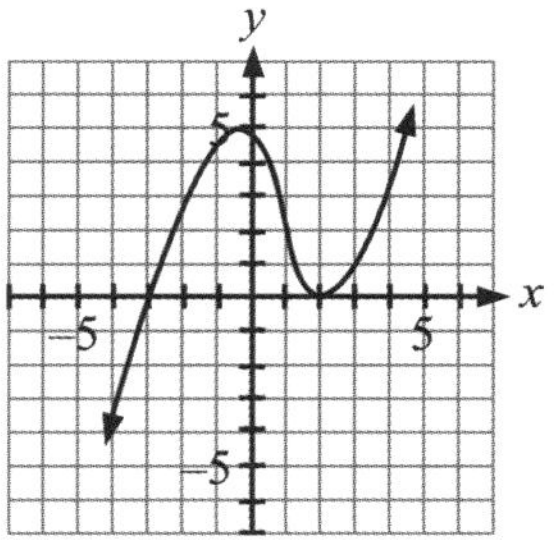

C.

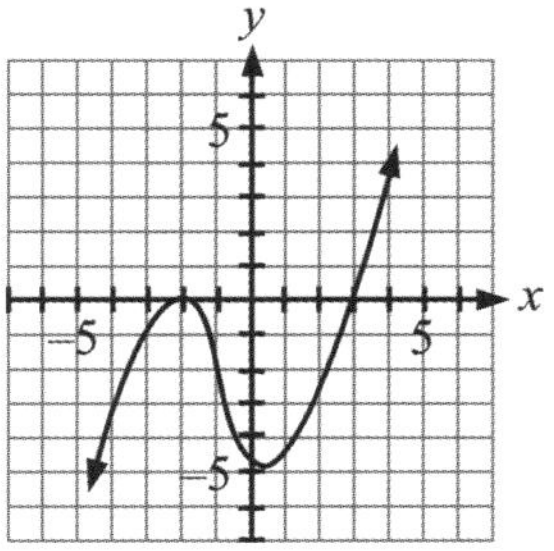

D.

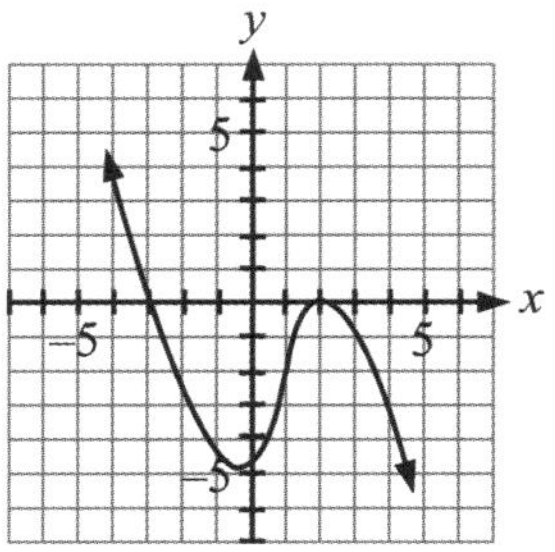

8. If the graph of $f(x) = x^3$ is stretched vertically about the x-axis by a factor of $\frac{1}{4}$ and then translated horizontally 3 units right to produce the function $g(x)$, then the equation of $g(x)$ is

A. $g(x) = \frac{1}{4}x^3 + 3$ **B.** $g(x) = 4x^3 - 3$

C. $g(x) = \frac{1}{4}(x-3)^3$ **D.** $g(x) = 4(x+3)^3$

9. The graph of a third-degree polynomial function has x-intercepts of −2, 2, and 4. The polynomial function could be

A. $p(x) = 5(x+2)(x-2)(x-4)$

B. $p(x) = 6(x-2)(x+2)(x+4)$

C. $p(x) = -7(x-2)(x+2)(x+4)^3$

D. $p(x) = -3(x+2)(x-2)(x-4)^2$

Use the following information to answer the next question.

The graph of a polynomial function $y = f(x)$ with x-intercepts −2, 1, and 3 is shown below.

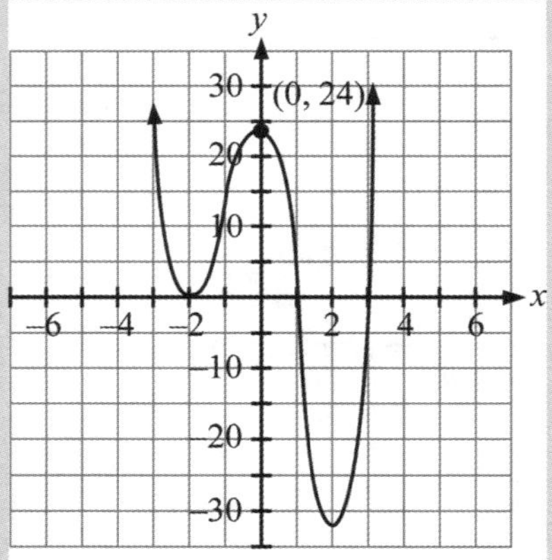

Not to scale

10. The equation of the polynomial function is

A. $f(x) = 2(x+2)^2(x-1)(x-3)$

B. $f(x) = 2(x-2)^2(x+1)(x+3)$

C. $f(x) = 4(x+2)(x-1)(x-3)$

D. $f(x) = 4(x-2)(x+1)(x+3)$

11. Determine the equation of the fourth degree polynomial function, in factored form, whose graph has x-intercepts at $x = -3$, −2, 1, and 2 and a y-intercept of −48.

A. $p(x) = (x+3)(x+2)(x-1)(x-2)$

B. $p(x) = (x-3)(x-2)(x+1)(x+2)$

C. $p(x) = 4(x+3)(x+2)(x-1)(x-2)$

D. $p(x) = -4(x+3)(x+2)(x-1)(x-2)$

Numerical Response

Use the following information to answer the next question.

The graph of $f(x) = \sin x$ over the interval $0 \le x \le 2\pi$ is shown below.

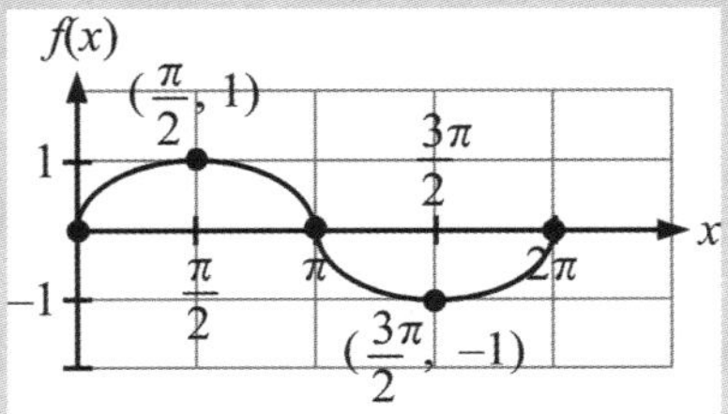

NR1. The x-intercept between 2 and 4, to the nearest hundredth, of the third-degree polynomial function that approximates the graph of $y = \sin x$ is __________.

12. Which of the following equations is an odd polynomial function?

A. $y = (x-5)^3$

B. $y = x^2$

C. $y = 2x^3 + 4x$

D. $y = x^3 \bullet x^5$

13. Which of the following statements about the functions $y = f(x)$ and $y = \dfrac{1}{f(x)}$ is true?

A. If the value of $f(x)$ is 1, then the value of $\dfrac{1}{f(x)}$ is -1.

B. If the value of $f(x)$ is 0, then the value of $\dfrac{1}{f(x)}$ is undefined.

C. Where $f(x) = 0$, the graph of $y = \dfrac{1}{f(x)}$ will have a horizontal asymptote.

D. Where the value of $f(x)$ increases over a given interval, the value of $\dfrac{1}{f(x)}$ will also increase.

14. If $f(x) = x^2 + 3x - 4$, then the domain of $y = \dfrac{1}{f(x)}$ is

A. $x \in R$

B. $-4 < x < 1$

C. $x > 1 \quad \text{or} \quad x < -4$

D. $x \neq -4, x \neq 1$

Numerical Response

NR2. The graph of $y = f(x) = x - 7$ passes through the point (9, 2). If this ordered pair becomes (a, b) on the graph of $y = \dfrac{1}{f(x)}$, then the value of b, to the nearest tenth, is ___________.

15. The equation of the horizontal asymptote of the graph of the function $f(x) = \dfrac{3x}{x+5}$ is

A. $y = -5$

B. $y = 3$

C. $x = -5$

D. $x = 3$

Use the following information to answer the next question.

The graph of a rational function is shown below.

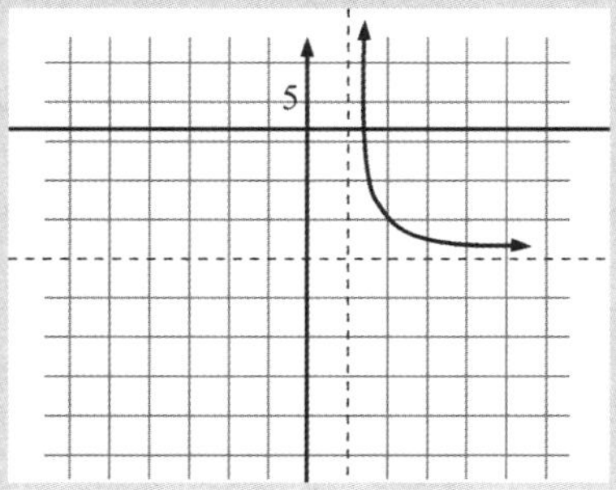

16. The equation of the rational function could be

A. $y = \dfrac{x-b}{x-a}$

B. $y = \dfrac{x+b}{x-a}$

C. $y = \dfrac{x-b}{x+a}$

D. $y = \dfrac{x+b}{x+a}$

Open Response

OR1.

a) On the grid given below, sketch the graph of a rational function that has:

1. a x-intercept of 3 and a y-intercept of -3
2. a vertical asymptote at $x = -2$ and a horizontal asymptote at $y = 2$
3. a domain of $x^1 - 2$, $x \in R$, and a range of $y^1 2$, $y \in R$.

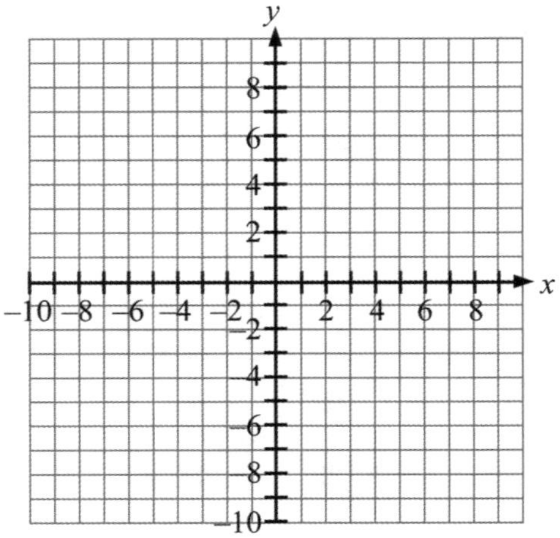

b) Write a possible equation of a rational function whose graph satisfies the condition outlined in part a).

17. Which of the following graphs illustrates the graph of the function $y = \dfrac{1}{2x-3}$?

A.

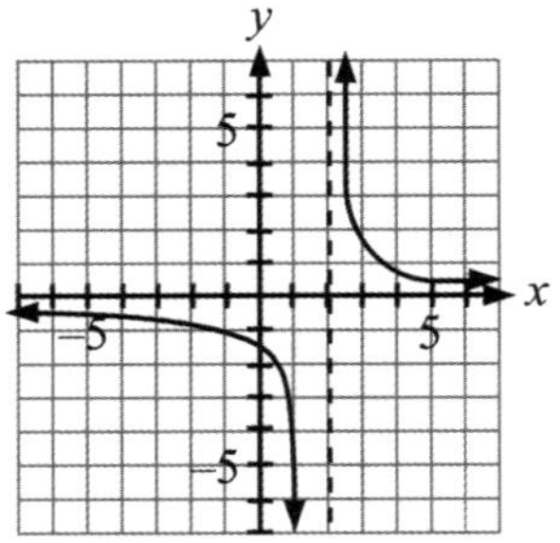

B.

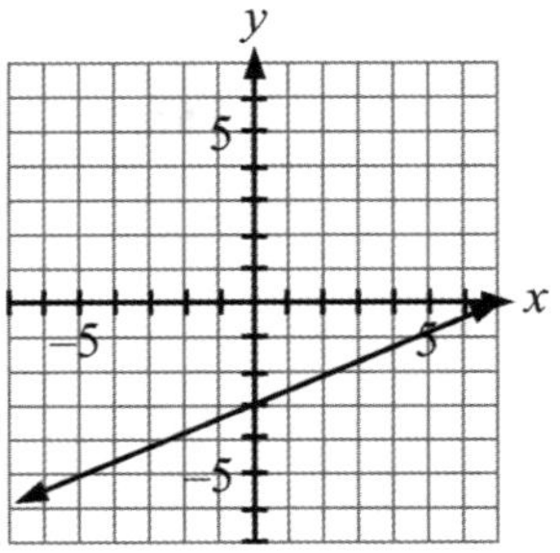

C.

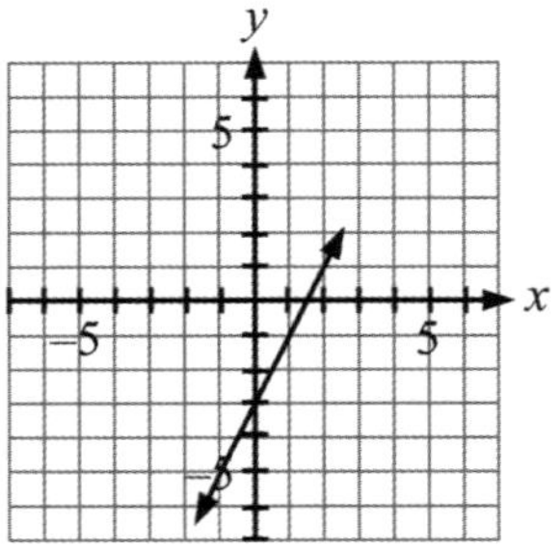

D.

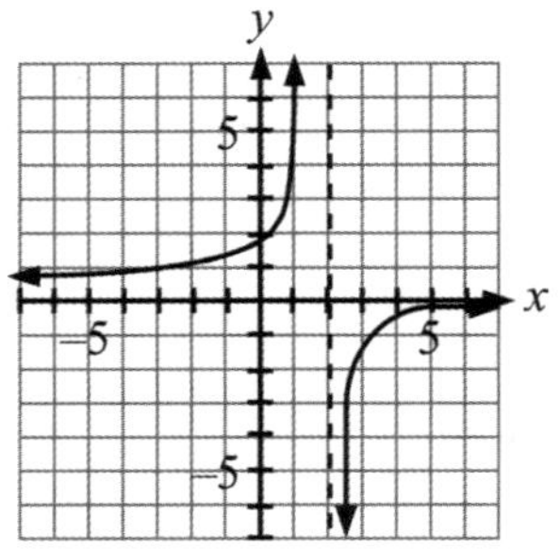

18. If $P(x)=3x^3-22x^2+43x-12$, then which of the following statements is **false**?

A. The expression $P(5)$ is equal to 28.

B. The expression $(x-4)$ is a factor of $P(x)$.

C. If $(3x-1)$ is a factor of $P(x)$, then $P\left(\frac{1}{3}\right)=0$.

D. The remainder from the division $P(x)\div(x-2)$ can be determined by evaluating $P(-2)$.

19. When $f(x)=2x^3-11x^2-4x+a$ is divided by $x+2$, the remainder is -4. What is the value of a?

A. 48 **B.** –48

C. 56 **D.** –56

20. The potential factors of the polynomial $P(x)=x^4-x^3-37x^2-47x+84$ include

A. $(x\pm1), (x\pm7), (x\pm8)$

B. $(x\pm2), (x\pm3), (x\pm14)$

C. $(x\pm3), (x\pm4), (x\pm5)$

D. $(x\pm6), (x\pm9), (x\pm12)$

21. A factor of the polynomial function $p(x)=-x^4-2x^3+x^2-7x-3$ is

A. $(x-3)$

B. $(x-1)$

C. $(x+1)$

D. $(x+3)$

Numerical Response

NR3. If $(x+4)$ is a factor of $P(x)=x^4+3x^3-ax^2+7x-4$, then the value of a is _____.

22. Which of the following statements regarding polynomial functions is **false**?

A. The real roots of the equation $x^4-29x^2+100=0$ are the x-intercepts of the graph of the polynomial function $f(x)=x^4-29x^2+100$.

B. The zeros of the graph of the polynomial function $f(x)=x^3+2x^2-x-2$ are equal to the real roots of the equation $x^3+2x^2-x-2-0$.

C. The graph of a linear relation has a maximum of one x-intercept, and the graph of a quadratic function has a maximum of two x-intercepts.

D. If the graph of a particular polynomial function has exactly two x-intercepts, then the function must be quadratic.

23. The solution to the equation $x^3-x^2-9x+9=0$ is

A. $x=1$ or $x=\pm3$

B. $x=1$ or $x=\pm9$

C. $x=-1$ or $x=\pm3$

D. $x=-1$ or $x=\pm9$

24. If two potential roots of the quadratic equation $ax^2+bx+c=0, a\neq0$, where a, b and c are real numbers, are $x=\frac{2}{3}$ and $x=\frac{3}{4}$, then the values of a and c could be

A. $a=3,\ c=4$

B. $a=4,\ c=6$

C. $a=8,\ c=12$

D. $a=12,\ c=6$

25. The graph of the rational function $f(x)=\dfrac{2}{x+4}$ does not intersect the x-axis.

Therefore, the equation $\dfrac{2}{x+4}=0$ has

A. a real root of –4

B. a real root of 0

C. a real root of 2

D. no real roots

26. If $\dfrac{1}{1+x}=3,$ then x equals

A. –2

B. $\dfrac{3}{2}$

C. 2

D. $-\dfrac{2}{3}$

Numerical Response

NR4. If $x-\dfrac{2x-4}{5}=2,$ then the value of x, to the nearest integer, is _______.

Open Response

OR2.

a) Using technology, graph the rational function $F(x)=y=\dfrac{x+3}{x-1}$ and sketch the resulting graph on the grid given below.

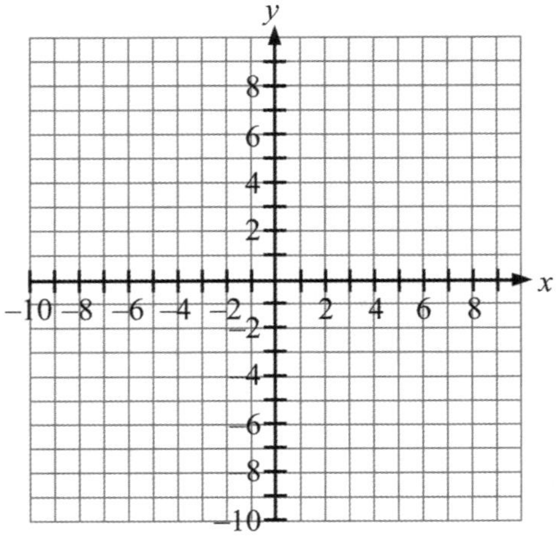

b) What are the x- and y- intercepts of the graph of $F(x)$?

c) What are the equations of the vertical and horizontal asymptotes of the graph of $F(x)$?

d) If the graph of the rational function $G(x)=\dfrac{4}{x}+2$ is drawn on the same grid as the graph of the rational function $F(x)=\dfrac{x+2}{x-1}$, determine the points of intersection of the graph of $G(x)$ and the graph of $F(x)$ by using an algebraic procedure.

27. For what value of a would $(x-2)$ be a factor of the polynomial $p(x)=2x^4-2x^3+14x^2+ax-78$?

A. 3 **B.** −3

C. 6 **D.** −6

Use the following information to answer the next question.

Shannon analyzed the graph of the rational function $y=\dfrac{x^2}{2x^2+3x-5}$ and came to the following conclusions.

I. The graph of the function has vertical asymptotes $x=-\dfrac{5}{2}$ and $x=1$.

II. $y=\dfrac{1}{2}$ is the equation of the only horizontal asymptote of the graph of the function.

III. $y\neq\dfrac{1}{2},\ y\in R$, is the range of the function.

IV. $x=0$ is one of two distinct x-intercepts of the graph of the function.

V. $x\in R$ is the domain of the function.

28. Which of Shannon's conclusions are correct?

A. I and II only

B. I, II, and III only

C. III, IV, and V only

D. II, III, IV, and V only

29. The solution to the inequality $(x^2-9)(x^2-1)<0$ is

A. $x<-3$ or $-1<x<1$ or $x>3$

B. $-3<x<-1$ or $1<x<3$

C. $x<-3$ or $-3<x<-1$

D. $x>3$ or $1<x<3$

Use the following information to answer the next question.

The graph of $y=f(x)$ is shown below.

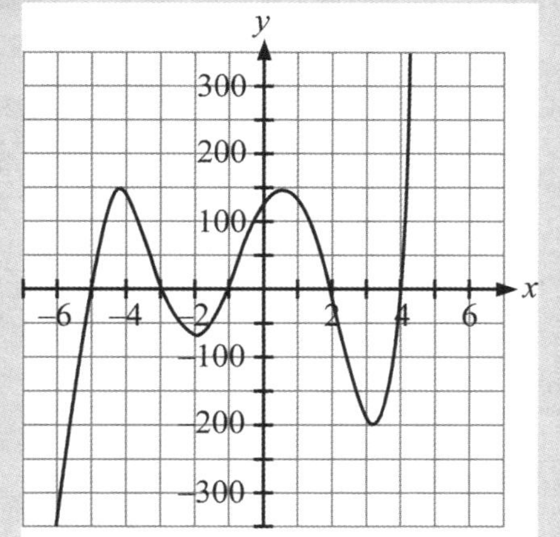

Not to scale

30. Which of the following represents a partial solution to the inequality $f(x)>0$ if $f(x)=x^5+3x^4-23x-51x^2+94x+120$?

A. $x<-5$ **B.** $-5<x<-3$

C. $-1\leq x\leq 2$ **D.** $2<x<4$

31. Which of the following polynomial inequalities has a solution of $x>4$?

A. $x+4>0$ **B.** $2x-4>0$

C. $\dfrac{1}{2}x-2>0$ **D.** $2x-2>0$

32. Which of the following graphs represents the solution of the inequality $(x-2)(x+1)(x+2)<0$?

A.

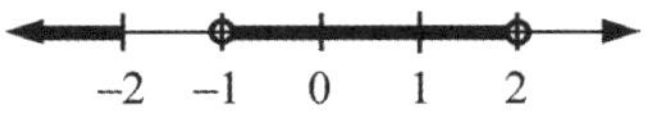

B.

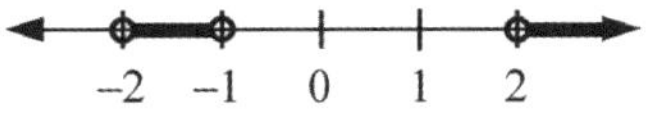

C.

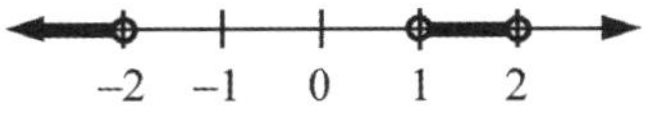

D.

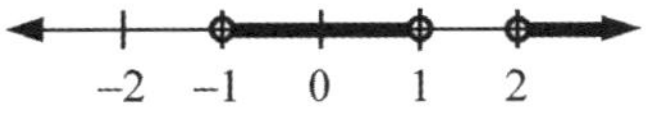

ANSWERS AND SOLUTIONS—UNIT TEST POLYNOMIAL AND RATIONAL FUNCTIONS

1. D	**9. A**	**15. B**	**NR3. 2**	**27. A**
2. B	**10. A**	**16. B**	**22. D**	**28. A**
3. A	**11. D**	**OR1. See Solution**	**23. A**	**29. B**
4. A	**NR1. 3.14**	**17. A**	**24. D**	**30. B**
5. D	**12. C**	**18. D**	**25. D**	**31. C**
6. D	**13. B**	**19. A**	**26. D**	**32. A**
7. A	**14. D**	**20. B**	**NR4. 2**	
8. C	**NR2. 0.5**	**21. D**	**OR2. See Solution**	

1. **D**

The function $r(x)=\dfrac{x+3}{(x-9)^2}$ can be rewritten as $r(x)=(x+3)(x-9)^{-2}$. Since the exponent -2 is not a whole number, the function $r(x)=\dfrac{x+3}{(x-9)^2}$ is not a polynomial function. The function $r(x)=\dfrac{x+3}{(x-9)^2}$ is referred to as a rational function.

2. **B**

Statement I is not always true.
The following graph illustrates the graph of a polynomial function whose range is not $y\in R$.

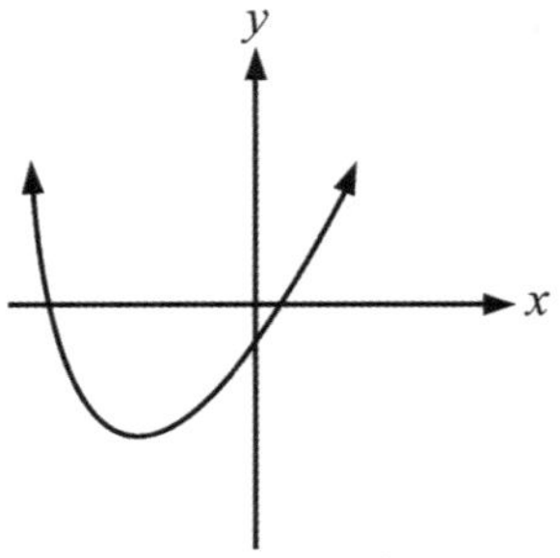

Statement II is always true.
Statement III is not always true.
The following graph illustrates the graph of a polynomial function that has neither an absolute maximum nor an absolute minimum value.

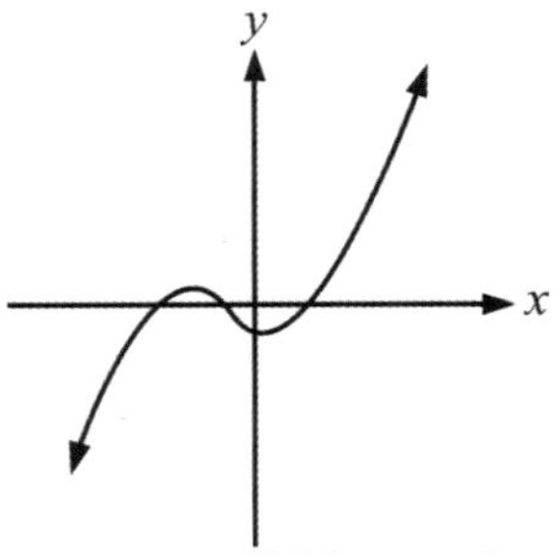

Statement IV is not always true.
The following graph illustrates the graph of a polynomial function of degree 3 that does not begin in the third quadrant and end in the first quadrant.

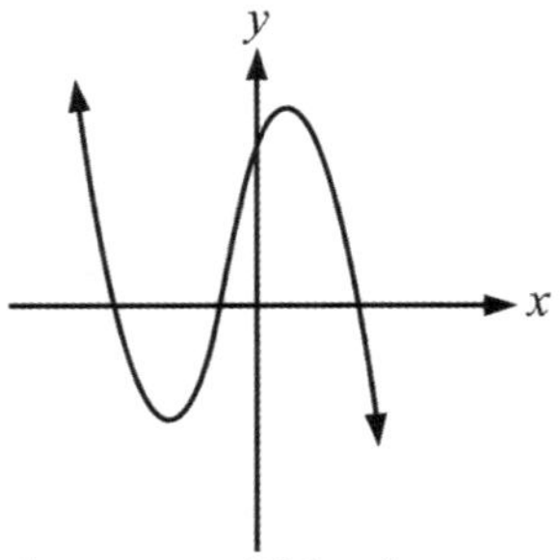

Statement V is always true.

3. **A**

From the given partial table of values, it can be observed that (4, 0) and (10, 0) are two x-intercepts of the polynomial function. Since the function has at least two x-intercepts, the minimum degree of the polynomial function is two.

4. **A**

The domain of all polynomial functions is $x \in R$. From the given graph, it can be observed that as $x \to -\infty$, $y \to +\infty$ and as $x \to +\infty$, $y \to -\infty$; therefore, the range of the polynomial function is $y \in R$.

5. **D**

The given graph is periodic and has a wave-shaped pattern. Furthermore, the range is restricted between two values $(2 \le y \le 4)$.

6. **D**

The y-intercept of the graph of the polynomial function $p(x) = y = -5(x-3)(x-1)(x+4)^2$ can be determined by substituting 0 for x and solving for y, as shown below.

$$y = -5(x-3)(x-1)(x+4)^2$$
$$y = -5(0-3)(0-1)(0+4)^2$$
$$y = -5(-3)(-1)(4)^2$$
$$y = -240$$

7. **A**

Since the polynomial function is of degree three and has a negative leading coefficient, the left end of the graph of the function must be in quadrant II and the right end of the graph must be in quadrant IV. Also, since $x-3$ is a factor, the graph must intersect the x-axis at $x = 3$. The factored form of $x^2 + 4x + 4$ is $(x+2)^2$; therefore, the graph must be tangent to the x-axis at $x = -2$. The graph that satisfies these conditions is illustrated in alternative **A**.

8. **C**

Recall the roles of the parameters a, k, d, and c when the function $y = f(x)$ is transformed into a function of the form $y = a\,f(k(x-d)) + c$.

In order to perform a vertical stretch about the x-axis by a factor of $\frac{1}{4}$, parameter $a = \frac{1}{4}$. For a horizontal translation of 3 units right, parameter $d = 3$.

Thus, $g(x) = \frac{1}{4}f(x-3) = \frac{1}{4}(x-3)^3$.

9. **A**

Since the stated polynomial function is of degree 3, consider only the functions given in alternatives **A** and B.

The x-intercepts of the graph of the function are –2, 2, and 4; therefore, the polynomial function must have the factors $x+2$, $x-2$ and $x-4$.

These factors are present in the function defined by the equation in alternative **A**.

10. **A**

The x-intercepts of the graph are –2, 1, and 3, therefore $x+2$, $x-1$, and $x-3$ must be factors of the function.

However, the factor $x+2$ must occur twice since the graph is tangent to the x-axis at –2. Thus, the general form of the equation can be written as $f(x) = a(x+2)^2(x-1)(x-3)$, where a is a real number. The y-intercept of the graph is (0, 24), so solve for a by substituting 24 for $f(x)$ and 0 for x, as shown below.

$$f(x) = a(x+2)^2(x-1)(x-3)$$
$$24 = a(0+2)^2(0-1)(0-3)$$
$$24 = a(4)(-1)(-3)$$
$$24 = 12a$$
$$2 = a$$

The equation of the polynomial function is $f(x) = 2(x+2)^2(x-1)(x-3)$.

11. **D**

Since the graph of the function has x-intercepts at –3, –2, 1, and 2, the given function must have factors of $x+3$, $x+2$, $x-1$, and $x-2$. Thus, the function can be written as $f(x) = k(x+3)(x+2)(x-1)(x-2)$, where k is a non-zero constant. It is given that the graph of the function has a y-intercept of –48; therefore, the value of k can be determined by substituting –48 for y and 0 for x in the equation $f(x) = k(x+3)(x+2)(x-1)(x-2)$, as shown below.

$$-48 = k(0+3)(0+2)(0-1)(0-2)$$
$$-48 = k(3)(2)(-1)(-2)$$
$$-48 = 12k$$
$$-4 = k$$

Thus, the equation of the given function is $f(x) = -4(x+3)(x+2)(x-1)(x-2)$.

NR1. **3.14**

To solve this problem use the ordered pairs $(0, 0)$, $\left(\frac{\pi}{2}, 1\right)$, $(\pi, 0)$, $\left(\frac{3\pi}{2}, -1\right)$, and $(2\pi, 0)$

Using a TI 83 calculator, select the stats menu and input the x-coordinates into L1 and the y-coordinates into L2. Next, ensure the calculator is in the radian mode and choose a window setting such as $x:[-1,7,1]$ and $y:[-1.5,1.5,1]$

To determine the equation input [STAT] scroll right to CALC and press 6 to access CubicReg. Now input [2nd] [1] [,] [2nd] [2] [,] [VARS] scroll right toY-Vars and press [ENTER] twice, so the display shows CubicReg L_1, L_2, Y_1. Now do the regression by pressing [ENTER] one more time.

The display will show
a = .0860040918
b = –.8105694691
c = 1.697652726
d = 0.

With coefficients rounded to the nearest thousandth the cubic function is

$$y = 0.086\,x^3 - 0.811\,x^2 + 1.698x.$$

Press [GRAPH] and the calculator will graph the polynomial function

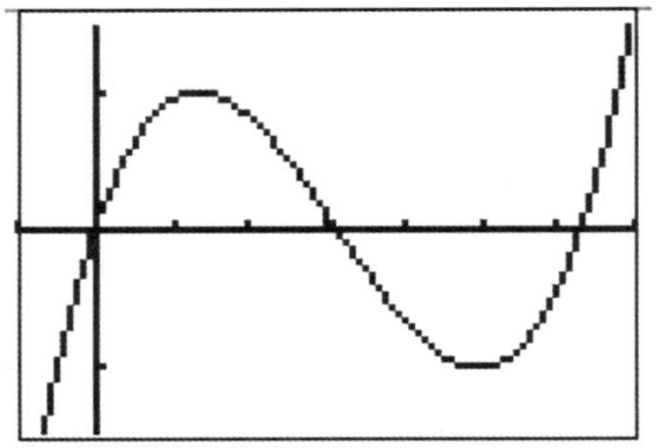

Using the zero feature by pressing [2nd] [TRACE] [2] the x-intercept between 2 and 4, can be determined to the nearest hundredth as 3.14.

12. **C**

A polynomial function whose terms consist of only odd-degree monomials is an odd function. The only function that satisfies this condition is given in alternative **C**.

Note:

$y=(x-5)^3=x^3-15x^2+75x-125$ and

$y=x^3\bullet x^5=x^8$

13. **B**

The functions $y=f(x)$ and $y=\dfrac{1}{f(x)}$ are reciprocal functions. Since the reciprocal of 0 is undefined, the value of $y=\dfrac{1}{f(x)}$ is undefined when $y=f(x)=0$. Thus, the statement in alternative **B** is true. The statements in the remaining alternatives are all false.

14. **D**

The reciprocal function $y=\dfrac{1}{f(x)}$ is undefined when $f(x)=0$. Therefore, $x^2+3x-4\neq 0$. In factored form, x^2+3x-4 is $(x+4)(x-1)$. Thus, $(x+4)(x-1)\neq 0$. The domain of $y=\dfrac{1}{f(x)}$ is $x\neq -4$ (since $x+4\neq 0$) and $x\neq 1$ (since $x-1\neq 0$).

NR2. **0.5**

The reciprocal function, $\dfrac{1}{f(x)}$, pairs the original *x*-coordinate with the reciprocal of the original *y*-coordinate. The new point would be $\left(9,\dfrac{1}{2}\right)$, so the value of *b* to the nearest tenth is 0.5.

15. **B**

Begin by graphing (using technology) the function $f(x)=y=\dfrac{3x-5}{x+5}$.

Observe that as $x\to-\infty$, $y\to 3$, and as $x\to+\infty$, $y\to 3$. Thus, $y=3$ is the equation of the horizontal asymptote.

16. **B**

By examining the given graph, it can be determined that the line $x=a$ is a vertical asymptote. This means that the domain is $x\neq a$, so the denominator of the rational function must be $x-a$. There is an *x*-intercept of $-b$, so the function must satisfy the condition $f(-b)=0$. The functions must have $x+b$ in the numerator to satisfy this condition. The correct function is $y=\dfrac{x+b}{x-a}$..

OR1.

a) The graph of a rational function that satisfies the given conditions is shown below.

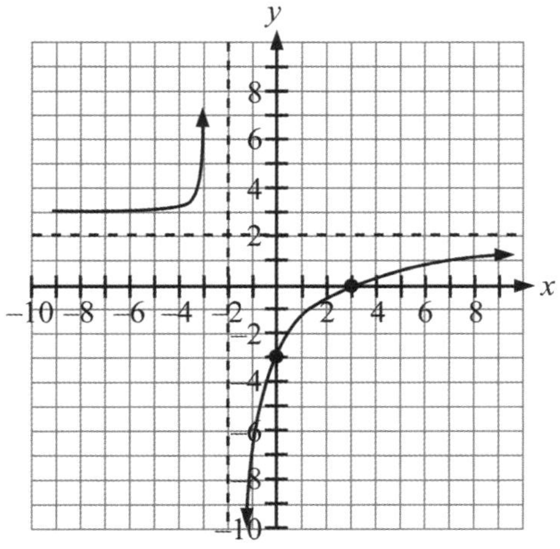

b) One possible equation of the rational function is $y=\dfrac{2x-6}{x+2}$.

However, other equations are possible.

17. **A**

The graph of the function $y=\dfrac{1}{2x-3}$ will have a vertical asymptote at $x=\dfrac{3}{2}$ since $2x-3\neq 0$. When the function $y=\dfrac{1}{2x-3}$ is graphed (using technology), it can be observed that as $x\to -\infty,\ y\to 0$, and as $x\to +\infty,\ y\to 0$. Thus, $y=0$ is a horizontal asymptote. Furthermore, the graph of the function is decreasing when $x<\dfrac{3}{2}$ and $x>\dfrac{3}{2}$. The only graph that satisfies these conditions is given in alternative **A**.

18. **D**

The statements given in alternatives A, B, and C are all true. However, alternative **D** is false because the remainder from the division $p(x)\div(x-2)$ can be determined by evaluating $P(2)$, not $P(-2)$.

19. **A**

Applying the remainder theorem $f(-2)=-4$ since the remainder is –4 when $f(x)$ is divided by $x+2$.
The value of a can be determined as shown below.

$$f(x)=2x^3-11x^2-4x+a$$
$$f(-2)=2(-2)^3-11(-2)^2-4(-2)+a$$
$$f(-2)=-16-44+8+a$$
$$f(-2)=-52+a$$

Therefore:

$$-52+a=-4$$
$$a=48$$

20. **B**

Any integral zero of $P(x)$ must be a factor of the constant term, which in this case is 84. The factors of 84 are ±1, ±2, ±3, ±4, ±6, ±7, ±12, ±14, ±21, ±28, ±42 and ±84. Thus, the potential factors of $P(x)$ are
$x\pm 1, x\pm 2, x\pm 3, x\pm 4, x\pm 6, x\pm 7,$
$x\pm 12, x\pm 14, x\pm 21, x\pm 28, x\pm 42$ and
$x\pm 84$. The only alternative that contains only factors from the preceding set of a factors is alternative **B**.

21. **D**

Any integral zero of $p(x)$ must be a factor of the constant term, which is –3. The factors of –3 are ±1 and ±3.
Thus, potential factors of $p(x)$ are $x+1,\ x-1,\ x+3,$ and $x-3$. Since all four of these factors are given in the respective alternatives, determine which one of the following equations is correct:
$p(-1)=0,\ p(1)=0,\ p(-3)=0,$ or $p(3)=0$.
The correct equation is $p(-3)=0$; therefore, $x+3$ is a factor of $p(x)$.
Another way to solve this problem would be to use technology to graph $p(x)$ and state the zeros of $p(x)$.

NR3. **2**

If $x+4$ is a factor of $P(x)$, then $P(-4)=0$. The value of a can be determined as shown below.

$$P(x)=x^4+3x^3-ax^2+7x-4$$
$$P(-4)=(-4)^4+3(-4)^3-a(-4)^2+7(-4)-4$$
$$P(-4)=256-192-16a-28-4$$
$$P(-4)=-16a+32$$

Therefore,

$$-16a+32=0$$
$$-16a=-32$$
$$a=2$$

22. D

The statements in alternatives A, B, and C are true. However, the statement in alternative **D** is not necessarily true. Two possible exceptions would be the graph of the third-degree function and the graph of the fourth-degree function, as shown below.

Third Degree

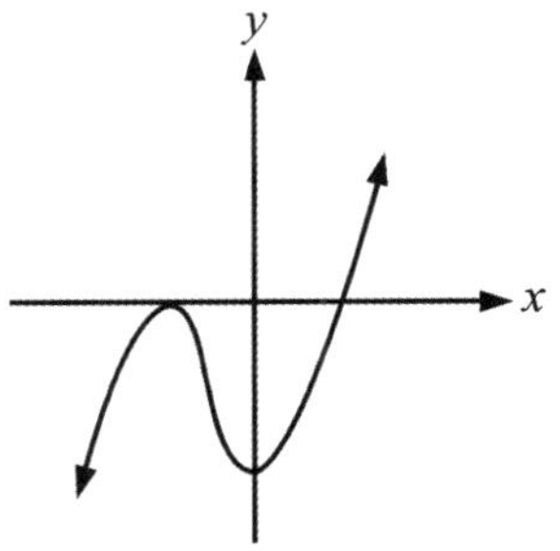

Fourth Degree

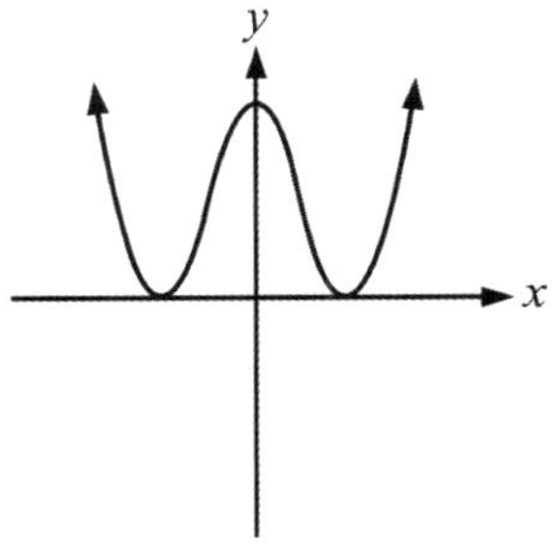

23. A

To begin, factor $x^3 - x^2 - 9x + 9 = 0$ by grouping:

$$x^3 - x^2 - 9x + 9 = x^2(x-1) - 9(x-1)$$
$$= (x-1)(x^2 - 9)$$

Next, factor $x^2 - 9$ by applying the difference of squares procedure:

$$x^2 - 9 = (x+3)(x-3)$$

Thus,

$x^3 - x^2 - 9x + 9 = (x-1)(x+3)(x-3)$.

The solution to the equation $x^3 - x^2 - 9x + 9 = 0$ is $x = 1, x = -3,$ or $x = 3$.

24. D

The potential roots of the quadratic equation $ax^2 + 5x + c = 0$ are of the form $\frac{m}{n}$ where m is a factor of c and n is a factor of a. Therefore, both 2 and 3 must be factors of c and both 3 and 4 must be factors of a. The only alternative where a and c satisfy these conditions is alternative **D**.

25. D

Since the graph of $f(x) = \frac{2}{x+4}$ does not interest the x-axis, the corresponding equation $\frac{2}{x+4} = 0$ has no real roots.

26. D

To solve the given equation, first multiply each side by $1 + x$.

$$\frac{1}{1+x}(1+x) = 3(1+x)$$

Simplify: $1 = 3 + 3x$

$$-2 = 3x$$
$$-\frac{2}{3} = x$$

NR4. 2

First, multiply each side of the given equation by 5.

$$5\left(x - \frac{2x-4}{5}\right) = 5 \times 2$$

Simplifying gives $5x - (2x - 4) = 10$.

This equation can now be solved as shown below.

$$5x - (2x-4) = 10$$
$$5x - 2x + 4 = 10$$
$$3x + 4 = 10$$
$$3x = 6$$
$$x = 2$$

OR2.

a) The sketch of the graph of $F(x) = y = \dfrac{x+3}{x-1}$ is shown below

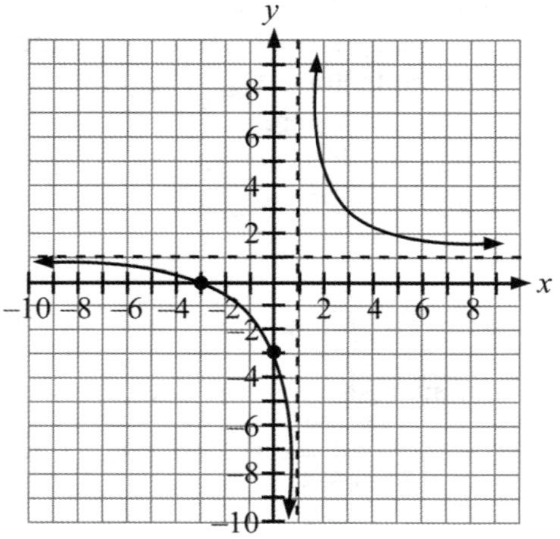

b) From the graph of $F(x)$, it can be observed that the x-intercept is −3 and the y-intercept is −3. The x- and y-intercepts can be verified algebraically, as shown below.

***x*-intercept**	***y*-intercept**
Substitute 0 for y and solve for x	Substitute 0 for x and solve for y
$0 = \dfrac{x+3}{x-1}$ $0 = x+3$ $-3 = x$	$y = \dfrac{0+3}{0-1}$ $y = -3$

c) From the graph of $F(x)$ it can be observed that the equation of the vertical asymptote is $x = 1$ and the equation of the horizontal asymptote is $y = 1$.

d) The graphs of $F(x)$ and $G(x)$ will intersect where $F(x) = G(x)$.
These points of intersection can be determined as follows:

$$F(x) = G(x)$$
$$\frac{x+2}{x-1} = \frac{4}{x} + 2$$

Multiply each side of the equation by the lowest common denominator: $x(x-1)$.

$$x(x-1)\left(\frac{x+2}{x-1}\right) = x(x-1)\left(\frac{4}{x} + 2\right)$$

Now, simplify and solve for x.

$$x(x+2) = 4(x-1) + 2x(x-1)$$
$$x^2 + 2x = 4x - 4 + 2x^2 - 2x$$
$$x^2 + 2x = 2x^2 + 2x - 4$$
$$0 = x^2 - 4$$
$$0 = (x+2)(x-2)$$
$$x + 2 = 0 \quad \text{or} \quad x - 2 = 0$$
$$x = -2 \quad \text{or} \quad x = 2$$

Substitute −2 for x in either $F(x)$ or $G(x)$; the result is $y = 0$.
Substitute 2 for x in either $F(x)$ or $G(x)$; the result is $y = 4$.
Thus, the graphs of $F(x)$ and $G(x)$ will intersect at the points $(-2,0)$ and $(2,4)$.

27. **A**

If $x - 2$ is a factor of the given polynomial, then $P(2) = 0$. The value of a can be determined as follows:

$$P(x) = 2x^4 - 2x^3 + 14x^2 + ax - 78$$
$$P(2) = 2(2)^4 - 2(2)^3 + 14(2)^2 + a(2) - 78$$
$$P(2) = 32 - 16 + 56 + 2a - 78$$
$$P(2) = 2a - 6$$

Thus, $2a - 6 = 0$
$$2a = 6$$
$$a = 3$$

28. **A**

Conclusions I and II are correct.
However, conclusion:

i) III is incorrect because the range is $y \in R$

ii) IV is incorrect because $x = 0$ is the only x-intercept of the graph of the function

iii) V is incorrect because the domain is $x \neq \frac{-5}{2}$, $x \neq 1$, $x \in R$

Thus, the correct alternative is **A**.

29. **B**

First, express $(x^2 - 9)(x^2 - 1) < 0$ in factored form as $(x+3)(x-3)(x+1)(x-1) < 0$.
Next, let $f(x) = (x+3)(x-3)(x+1)(x-1)$.
The zeros of $f(x)$ are –3, 3, –1, and 1.
An interval chart is one possible method that can be used to solve the given inequality.

Interval	$x+3$	$x-3$	$x+1$	$x-1$	$f(x)$
$x < -3$	–	–	–	–	+
$-3 < x < -1$	+	–	–	–	–
$-1 < x < 1$	+	–	+	–	+
$1 < x < 3$	+	–	+	+	–
$x > 3$	+	+	+	+	+

The solution to the inequality $(x^2 - 9)(x^2 - 1) < 0$ can be determined by analyzing where $f(x)$ is negative in the interval chart. Thus, the solution is $-3 < x < -1$ or $1 < x < 3$.

30. **B**

The solution to $f(x) > 0$ occurs when the graph is above the x-axis.
This occurs on the intervals $-5 < x < -3$, $-1 < x < 2$, and $x > 1$.
Of these, only $-5 < x < -3$ is a choice.
Option C, $-1 \leq x \leq 2$ is not correct, as it includes –1 and 2 for which $f(-1) = f(2) = 0$.

31. **C**

Solve for x in alternative **C** as follows:

$$\frac{1}{2}x - 2 > 0$$

$$\frac{1}{2}x > 2$$

$$2\left(\frac{1}{2}x\right) > 2(2)$$

$$x > 4$$

The solution for alternative A is $x > -4$.
The solution for alternative B is $x > 2$.
The solution for alternative D is $x > 1$.

32. **A**

The graph of $f(x) = (x-2)(x+1)(x+2)$ is shown.

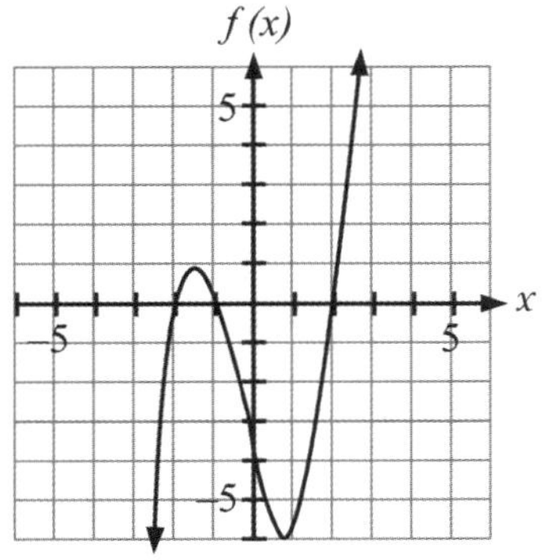

We can see that $f(x)$ is negative for $x < -2$ and $-1 < x < 2$. This illustrated by the number line in A.

NOTES

Characteristics of Functions

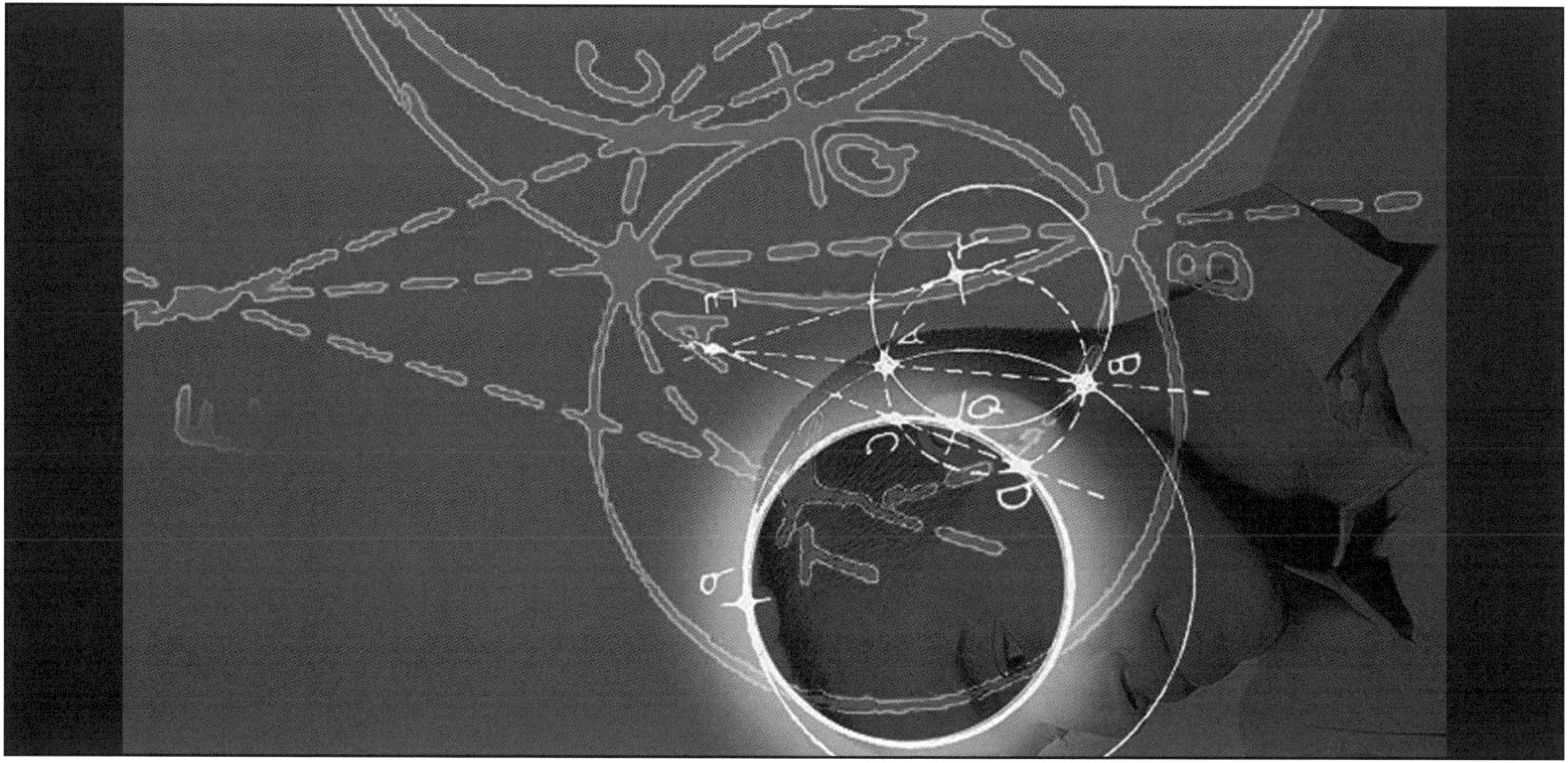

CHARACTERISTICS OF FUNCTIONS

Table of Correlations

Specific Expectation		Practice Questions	Unit Test Questions
1.1	*gather, interpret, and describe information about real-world applications of rates of change, and recognize different ways of representing rates of change*		
1.2	*recognize that the rate of change for a function is a comparison of changes in the dependent variable to changes in the independent variable, and distinguish situations in which the rate of change is zero, constant, or changing by examining applications, including those arising from real-world situations*	1, 2	1, 2
1.3	*sketch a graph that represents a relationship involving rate of change, as described in words, and verify with technology when possible*	3, 4	3
1.4	*calculate and interpret average rates of change of functions arising from real-world applications, given various representations of the functions*	5	4
1.5	*recognize examples of instantaneous rates of change arising from real-world situations, and make connections between instantaneous rates of change and average rates of change*	6	5
1.6	*determine, through investigation using various representations of relationships, approximate instantaneous rates of change arising from real-world applications by using average rates of change and reducing the interval over which the average rate of change is determined*	7, NR1	6, OR1
1.7	*make connections, through investigation, between the slope of a secant on the graph of a function and the average rate of change of the function over an interval, and between the slope of the tangent to a point on the graph of a function and the instantaneous rate of change of the function at that point*	8	7
1.8	*determine, through investigation using a variety of tools and strategies, the approximate slope of the tangent to a given point on the graph of a function by using the slopes of secants through the given point, and make connections to average and instantaneous rates of change*	9, 10, OR1	8
1.9	*solve problems involving average and instantaneous rates of change, including problems arising from real-world applications, by using numerical and graphical methods*		9

2.1 *determine, through investigation using graphing technology, key features of the graphs of functions created by adding, subtracting, multiplying, or dividing functions, and describe factors that affect these properties* *Sample Problem: Investigate the effect of the behaviours of* $f(x)=\sin x$, $f(x)=\sin 2x$, *and* $f(x)=\sin 4x$ *on the shape of* $f(x)=\sin x+\sin 2x+\sin 4x$		
2.2 *recognize real-world applications of combinations of functions, and solve related problems graphically*		
2.3 *determine, through investigation, and explain some properties (i.e., odd, even, or neither; increasing/decreasing behaviours) of functions formed by adding, subtracting, multiplying, and dividing general functions*	11	10
2.4 *determine the composition of two functions [i.e., f(g(x))] numerically (i.e., by using a table of values) and graphically, with technology, for functions represented in a variety of ways, and interpret the composition of two functions in real-world applications*	12, 13	11, NR1
2.5 *determine algebraically the composition of two functions [i.e., f(g(x))], verify that f(g(x)) is not always equal to g(f(x)), and state the domain [i.e., by defining f(g(x)) for those x-values for which g(x) is defined and for which it is included in the domain of f(x)] and the range of the composition of two functions*	14, 15, NR2	12, 13
2.6 *solve problems involving the composition of two functions, including problems arising from real-world applications*	16	14
2.7 *demonstrate, by giving examples for functions represented in a variety of ways, the property that the composition of a function and its inverse function maps a number onto itself [i.e., f (f(x)) = x and f(f (x)) = x demonstrate that the inverse function is the reverse process of the original function and that it undoes what the function does]*	17	15
2.8 *make connections, through investigation using technology, between transformations (i.e., vertical and horizontal translations; reflections in the axes; vertical and horizontal stretches and compressions to and from the x- and y-axes) of simple functions f(x) [e.g., f(x) = x + 20, f(x) = sin x, f(x) = log x] and the composition of these functions with a linear function of the form g(x) = A(x + B)*	18, 19	16
3.1 *compare, through investigation using a variety of tools and strategies the characteristics of various functions (i.e., polynomial, rational, trigonometric, exponential, logarithmic)*	20	17
3.2 *solve graphically and numerically equations and inequalities whose solutions are not accessible by standard algebraic techniques*	21	18, NR2
3.3 *solve problems, using a variety of tools and strategies, including problems arising from real-world applications, by reasoning with functions and by applying concepts and procedures involving functions*	22, 23, OR 2	19

NOTES

CHARACTERISTICS OF FUNCTIONS

1.1 *gather, interpret, and describe information about real-world applications of rates of change and recognize different ways of representing rates of change.*

1.2 *recognize that the rate of change for a function is a comparison of changes in the dependent variable to changes in the independent variable, and distinguish situations in which the rate of change is zero, constant, or changing by examining applications, including those arising from real-world situations.*

THE RATE OF CHANGE FOR A FUNCTION

The speed of an object is an example of a rate of change. Speed is defined as the rate of change of distance with respect to time. If an object travelled at a constant speed of 5 m/s, we can interpret this as the distance changes by 5 m for every 1 s change in time. If we let v represent the speed, we could write this as $v = 5$ m/s.

If we draw a graph of speed versus time for this constant speed of 5 m/s, the graph would be a horizontal line, since the speed is not changing. We would say that the rate of change of speed, or the acceleration, is zero. Whenever the rate of change of a quantity is zero, the corresponding graph is a horizontal line.

Speed versus Time

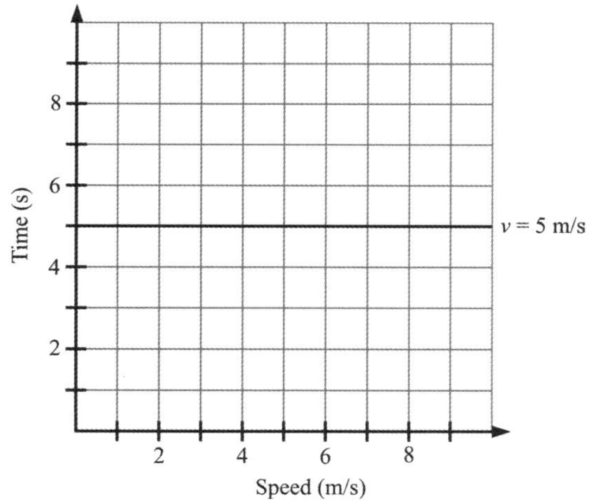

However if we draw a graph of distance versus time, the graph is an oblique line with a slope of 5 m/s, equal to the speed. Whenever the rate of change of a quantity is constant, or uniform, the graph will be an oblique line. If we let d represent the distance travelled, and t the amount of time passed, we could write the equation $d = 5t$ to represent the situation algebraically.

Distance versus Time

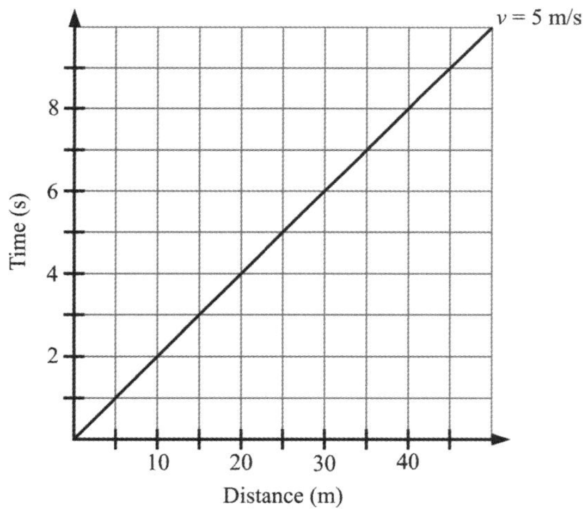

For functions of the form $y = f(x)$, the average rate of change of $f(x)$ with respect to x, between two values x_1 and x_2, is given by $\dfrac{f(x_2) - f(x_1)}{x_2 - x_1}$.

This ratio also represents the slope of the line joining these points on the graph of $y = f(x)$.

Example

A balloon is being inflated mechanically in such a way that the volume is increasing at a constant rate of $15\ \text{cm}^3/\text{s}$. If the volume of the balloon was originally $30\ \text{cm}^3$, determine the average rate of change of the volume of the balloon with respect to the radius of the balloon, to the nearest centimetre cubed per centimetre, between 0 s and 10 s, and between 10 s and 20 s.
Is the rate of change of volume with respect to radius constant?

Solution

We are told that the rate of change of volume with respect to time is a constant $15\ \text{cm}^3/\text{s}$. For every 10 s, the volume will increase by
$10\ \text{s} \times 15\ \text{cm}^3/\text{s} = 150\ \text{cm}^3$.
Then after 10 s the volume would be $30\ \text{cm}^3 + 150\ \text{cm}^3 = 180\ \text{cm}^3$, and after 20 s it would be
$180\ \text{cm}^3 + 150\ \text{cm}^3 = 330\ \text{cm}^3$.
Now we need to find the radius at 0 s, 10 s, and 20 s. Using the formula for the volume of a sphere, $V = \frac{4}{3}\pi r^3$, we need to solve for r, which gives $r = \sqrt[3]{\frac{3V}{4\pi}}$.
Substituting the three values for V, gives a radius of 1.92 cm initially, 3.50 cm after 10 s, and 4.29 cm after 20 s.
The average rate of change of volume with respect to radius is calculated by
$\dfrac{V_2 - V_1}{r_2 - r_1}$.

Therefore, between 0 s and 10 s, the average rate of change of volume with respect to volume is
$\dfrac{180 - 30}{3.50 - 1.92} = 95\ \text{cm}^3/\text{cm}$, and between
10 s and 20 s, it is
$\dfrac{330 - 180}{4.29 - 3.50} = 190\ \text{cm}^3/\text{cm}$.
These two values illustrate that the rate of change of volume with respect to radius is not constant but is decreasing as time passes. This is because the rate of change of the radius with respect to time is decreasing when the volume increases at a constant rate with respect to time.

PRACTICE QUESTIONS

Use the following information to answer the next question.

The graph below illustrates the changes in population for a particular town.

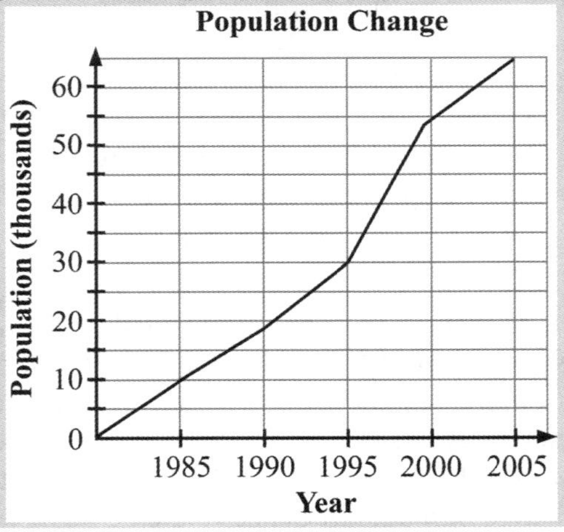

1. The rate of change of the population was the greatest from

A. 1985 to 1990

B. 1990 to 1995

C. 1995 to 2000

D. 2000 to 2005

2. A cylindrical hot tub is being filled by a hose that pours out water at a constant rate of 0.25 m^3/min. At 8:00 A.M., the volume of water in the pool was 8 m^3. If the radius of the hot tub is 2 m, the average rate of change of the volume of water in the hot tub, with respect to its height, between 9:00 A.M. and 10:00 A.M. is

A. 1.8 m^3/m

B. 12.6 m^3/m

C. 15.0 m^3/m

D. 23.0 m^3/m

1.3 *sketch a graph that represents a relationship involving rate of change, as described in words, and verify with technology (e.g., motion sensor) when possible*
Sample problem: John rides his bicycle at a constant cruising speed along a flat road. He then decelerates (i.e., decreases speed) as he climbs a hill. At the top, he accelerates (i.e., increases speed) on a flat road back to his constant cruising speed, and he then accelerates down a hill. Finally, he comes to another hill and glides to a stop as he starts to climb. Sketch a graph of John's speed versus time and a graph of his distance travelled versus time.

GRAPHING A RATE OF CHANGE

Example:

Sketch a speed versus time graph for the sample problem above.

Solution:

Since he is travelling initially at a constant speed the graph would start from the vertical axis as a horizontal line. As his speed decreases the graph would curve downwards and continue down until he reaches the top of the hill. At this point the graph would begin to curve upward as his speed begins to increase until it reaches the same height (speed) as the original horizontal line. The horizontal line continues until he reaches the hill at which point it will curve downwards until it reaches the horizontal axis as his speed is zero when he comes to a stop.

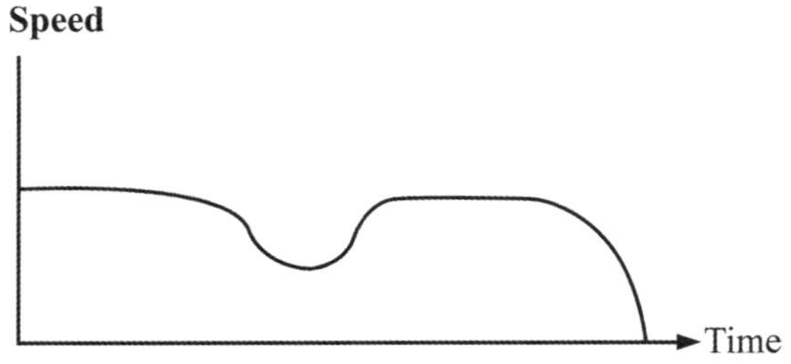

Example:

Sketch a distance versus time graph for the sample problem above.

Solution:

The graph could start from the origin if we start measuring distance travelled from the instant we started the speed versus time graph. Since he is travelling initially at a constant speed the graph would begin as an oblique line rising to the right from the origin. As his speed decreases the graph would curve downwards while still increasing in height, but would never reach horizontal. At the instant he accelerates again, the graph will begin to curve upwards and does so until he reaches his constant speed where the graph will once again become an oblique line with the same slope as the original line. As he accelerates down the hill, the graph curves upward again until the point at which he reaches the last hill where the graph will curve downwards until it reaches horizontal indicating that he has come to stop.

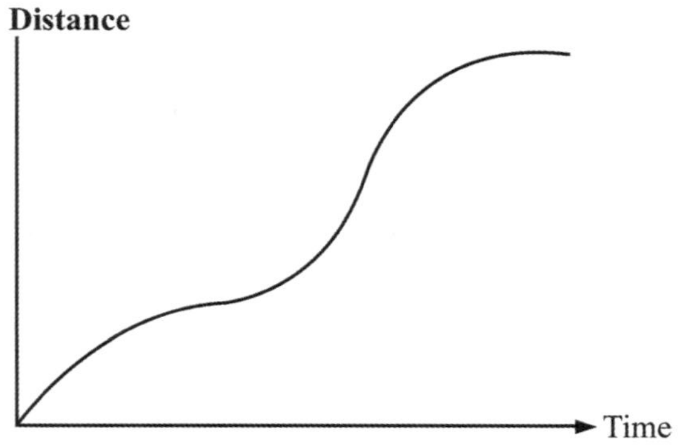

PRACTICE QUESTIONS

Use the following graph to answer the next question.

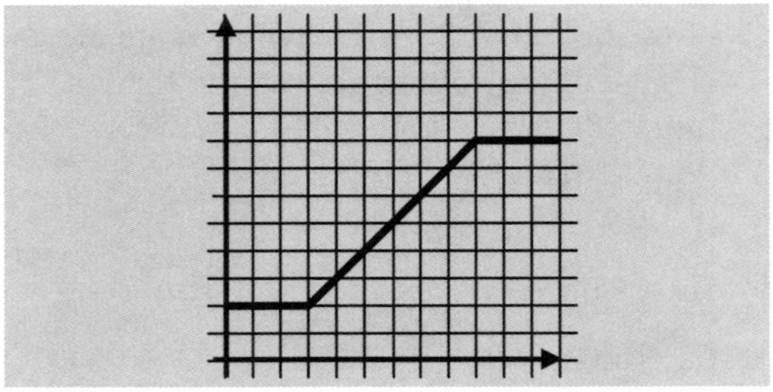

3. Which of the following practical situations could the graph shown above represent?

A. A horse slowing down for the corners on a horse race track

B. A block of ice being melted and then heated to boiling point

C. A balloon increasing in size when it is exposed to constant heat

D. A car driving slowly on a side street, then accelerating onto a freeway where it can go faster

4. While the cars of a train are being loaded, the train moves forward quickly, then backs up slowly just a little, and finally rolls forward to a stop. Which of the following "total distance travelled vs. time" graphs **best** illustrates the situation described?

A.

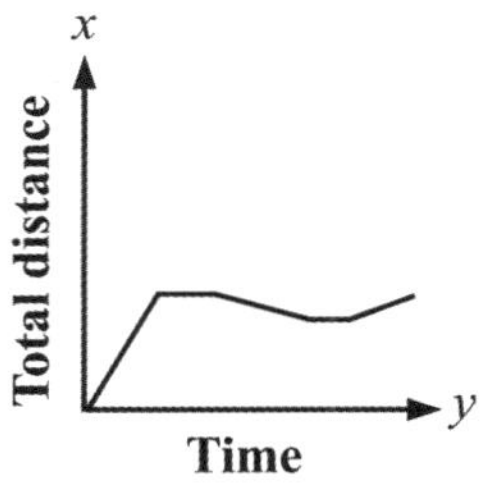

B.

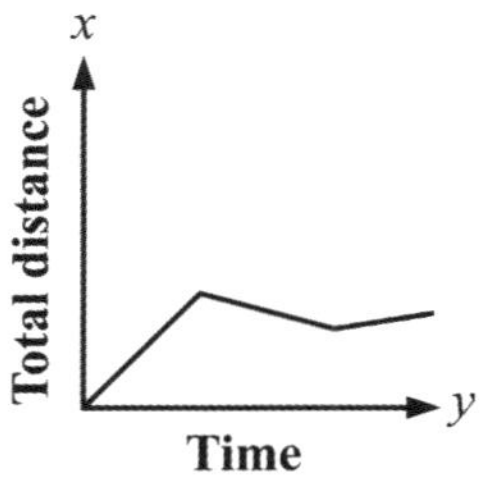

C.

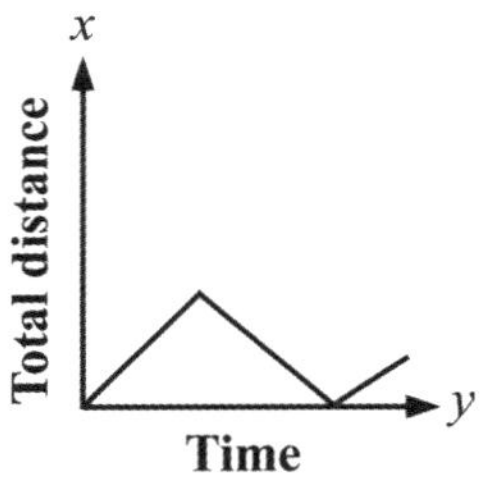

D.

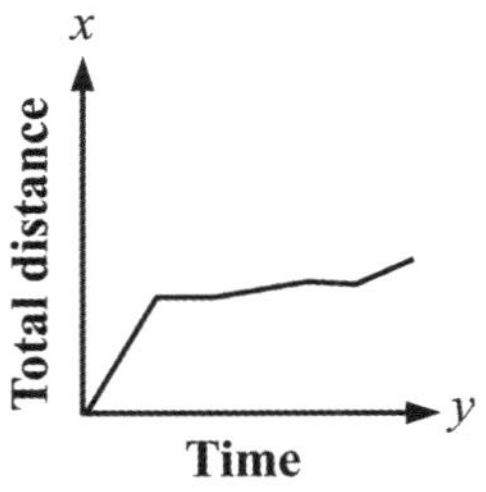

1.4 calculate and interpret average rates of change of functions arising from real-world applications, given various representations of the functions

APPLICATIONS OF AVERAGE RATES OF CHANGE

Example

The population of bacteria in a culture grows such that it can be modelled to the equation $N(t)=260(2)^{\frac{t}{6.5}}$, where t is the time in hours and $N(t)$ is the number of bacteria after t hours have passed. Calculate and interpret the average rate of change of the bacteria population between 0 h and 20 h. Also calculate the average rate of change of the bacteria population between 0 h and 10 h and between 10 h and 20 h and then compare these rates to the rate of change over the 20 h interval.

Solution

Calculating gives

$N(0)=260(2)^{\frac{0}{6.5}}=260,$

$N(10)=260(2)^{\frac{10}{6.5}}=755$, and

$N(20)=260(2)^{\frac{20}{6.5}}=2194.$

The average rate of change between 0 h and 20 h is

$\frac{N(20)-N(0)}{20-0}=\frac{2194-260}{20}$

$=96.7$ bacteria/h.

This means that if the population increased uniformly by 96.7 bacteria every hour over the 20 h interval it would reach the same population of 2194 bacteria, as previously calculated.

Between 0 h and 10 h, the average rate of change is

$\frac{N(10)-N(0)}{10-0}=\frac{755-260}{10}$

$=49.5$ bacteria/h,

and between 10 h and 20 h it is

$$\frac{N(20)-N(10)}{20-10}=\frac{2194-755}{10}$$

$=143.9$ bacteria/h.

The average rate of change or the growth rate of the population is increasing as time passes since it changes from 96.7 bacteria/h over the first ten hours to 143.9 bacteria/h over the second ten hours. The average of these two rates equals the growth rate over the twenty hour interval.

Practice Question

5. The height, h, in metres, of a seat on a Ferris wheel is defined by the function $h(t)=6\sin(t+5)+6.5$, where t represents time in seconds. The average rate of change of the seat's height over the first two seconds of the ride is

   A. 2.81 m/s

   B. 4.85 m/s

   C. 5.62 m/s

   D. 9.70 m/s

1.5 *recognize examples of instantaneous rates of change arising from real-world situations, and make connections between instantaneous rates of change and average rates of change*

1.6 *determine, through investigation using various representations of relationships, approximate instantaneous rates of change arising from real-world applications by using average rates of change and reducing the interval over which the average rate of change is determined*

Instantaneous Rates of Change

The instantaneous rate of change of one quantity with respect to another is the rate of change at an instant in time. Recall that the average rate of change is measured over a specified interval.

For example, if Ben drives a distance of 300 km in 3 h, then Ben's average speed over that entire 3 h time interval is

$$V_{\text{ave}}=\frac{d}{t}=\frac{300\text{km}}{3\text{h}}=100\text{km/h}$$

This means that if Ben had been able to drive at a constant speed of 100 km/h for the entire 3 h, he would also have travelled 300 km. However this would be impossible to do, since the car must start from rest and speed up and slow down many times during a 3 h journey. When a person driving a car looks at the speedometer, he or she sees the speed at that instant which is the instantaneous speed. The instantaneous speed is likely to be changing from second to second and at many points in the journey, the instantaneous speed would be more or less than 100 km/h.

Example

The isotope fluorine-20 has a half-life of 11.4 s. The equation that relates the mass of fluorine remaining, $A(t)$ in grams, after a time of t seconds, from an original sample of 200 grams, is given by the equation $A(t)=200(0.5)^{\frac{t}{11.4}}$.

Approximate the instantaneous rate of change of the isotope at a time of 20 s, by finding the average rate of change in smaller and smaller intervals approaching 20 s.

Solution

Start by finding the average rate of change between 19 s and 20 s from the calculation $\frac{A(21)-A(19)}{21-19}$

$$=\frac{200(0.5)^{\frac{21}{11.4}}-200(0.5)^{\frac{19}{11.4}}}{2}$$

$$=\frac{55.78-63.00}{2}=-3.61\text{ g/s}.$$

This means that over the time interval from 19 s to 21 s there was an average decrease of 3.61 g/s of the sample of fluorine-20.

Shortening the interval to 0.1 s approaching the time of 20 s gives

$$\frac{A(20.1)-A(19.9)}{20.1-19.9}$$

$$=\frac{200(0.5)^{\frac{20.1}{11.4}}-200(0.5)^{\frac{19.9}{11.4}}}{0.2}$$

$$=\frac{58.92-59.64}{0.2}=-3.60\text{ g/s}.$$

Further shortening the time interval to between 19.99 s and 20.01 s gives

$$\frac{A(20.01)-A(19.99)}{20.01-19.99}=\frac{59.24-59.32}{0.02}$$

$$=-3.60\text{ g/s}$$

which is the same as the previous calculation when expressed to the nearest hundredth.

Using a very short time interval from 19.999 9 s to 20.000 1, which is only 0.000 2 second in duration gives

$$\frac{A(20.000\,1)-A(19.999\,9)}{20.000\,1-19.999\,9}=\frac{59.279\,5-59.280\,2}{0.000\,2}$$

$$=-3.60\text{ g/s},$$

to the nearest hundredth.

Even this last time interval which is extremely short in duration gives the same value as the previous two calculations so it appears that the instantaneous rate of change of the mass of the isotope fluorine-20 after 20 s is decreasing by 3.60 g/s.

PRACTICE QUESTIONS

6. A thermometer, stored at room temperature, is placed in a pot of boiling water. If the thermometer measures the water temperature to be 100°C after 10 s, at which of the following times would the instantaneous rate of change of the thermometer's mercury be the lowest?

A. 1 s **B.** 2 s

C. 5 s **D.** 10 s

7. To find an accurate approximation to an instantaneous rate of change at a given point *P*, one must calculate the average rate of change between

A. point *P* and the origin

B. the two known points farthest from *P*

C. the two known points directly on either side of *P*

D. the two known points closest to and farthest from *P*

Numerical Response

NR1. A ball is dropped from a 10 m high balcony. The height, *h*, in metres, of the ball at time *t*, in seconds, is defined by $h(t)=-4.9t^2+10$. At $t = 2$ s, the instantaneous rate of change of the ball's height with respect to time, accurate to the nearest tenth, is ____________.

1.7 *make connections, through investigation, between the slope of a secant on the graph of a function and the average rate of change of the function over an interval, and between the slope of the tangent to a point on the graph of a function and the instantaneous rate of change of the function at that point*

1.8 *determine, through investigation using a variety of tools and strategies, the approximate slope of the tangent to a given point on the graph of a function by using the slopes of secants through the given point, and make connections to average and instantaneous rates of change.*

SLOPE OF THE TANGENT AND INSTANTANEOUS RATES OF CHANGE

Example

Approximate the instantaneous rate change of y with respect to x for the quadratic function $f(x)=x^2-4x$ at the point (4, 0).

Solution

Tables can be used to help find the slopes of secant lines through the point (4,0) and points that are near (4,0), as the second point gets closer and closer to (4,0). The average rate of change can be calculated by the slope formula

$$m=\frac{y_2-y_1}{x_2-x_1}=\frac{f(x_2)-0}{x_2-4}=\frac{f(x_2)}{x-4},$$

where $(x_2, f(x_2))$ is the second point.

The first table starts with points where $x_2<4$.

x_2	$f(x_2)$	Slope of secant line $\frac{f(x_2)}{x-4}$
3	$f(3)=3^2-4(3)$ $=-3$	$\frac{-3}{3-4}=3$
3.5	-1.75	$\frac{-1.75}{3.5-4}=3.5$
3.8	−0.76	$\frac{-0,76}{3.8-4}=3.8$
3.9	−0.39	$\frac{-0.39}{3.9-4}=3.9$
3.99	−0.0399	$\frac{-0.0399}{3.99-4}=3.99$
3.999	−0.003 999	$\frac{-0.003999}{3.999-4}=3.999$
3.99 99	−0.0003999	$\frac{-0.0003999}{3.9999-4}=3.9999$

From this table it appears that as the value of x_2 gets closer and closer to 4, the slope of the secant line also gets closer and closer to 4.

The second table starts with points where $x_2 > 4$

x_2	$f(x_2)$	Slope of secant line $\frac{f(x_2)}{x-4}$
5	$f(5)=5^2-4(5)$	$\frac{5}{5-4}=5$
4.5	2.25	$\frac{2.25}{4.5-4}=4.5$
4.2	0.84	$\frac{0.84}{4.2-4}=4.2$
4.1	0.41	$\frac{0.41}{4.1-4}=4.1$
4.01	0.0401	$\frac{0.0401}{4.01-4}=4.01$
4.001	0.004001	$\frac{0.004001}{4.001-4}=4.001$
4.0001	0.00040001	$\frac{0.000\,400\,01}{4.000\,1-4}=4.000\,1$

Again it appears that as the value of x_2 gets closer and closer to 4, the slope of the secant line also gets closer and closer to 4. A logical conclusion is that the slope of the tangent line to the graph of the function $f(x)=x^2-4x$ at the point (4, 0) is 4.

Using graphing technology, such as the TI-83 we can verify this by inputting $Y_1 = X^2 - 4X$ and graphing on the viewing window, $x:[-10,10,1]$ $y:[-10,10,1]$.
The calculator will draw the tangent line if we access the Draw Tangent feature by pressing [2nd][PRGM][5] with the calculator screen showing the graph. Inputting 4 for x and pressing enter will cause the calculator to draw the tangent at $x = 4$, and give the equation $y=4x+-16$, which can be written as $y=4x-16$, verifying the slope of 4.

In order to determine the instantaneous rate of change of y with respect to x for a function at a particular point, we can find the average rate of change (slopes of secant lines) using the requested point and points that are near that point.

PRACTICE QUESTIONS

8. The average rate of change over a given interval of a function is zero. Which of the following statements about the graph of the function is **false**?

A. The graph is a horizontal line.

B. The graph is a parabola with the given interval being between the two x-intercepts.

C. The graph is a sinusoidal curve with the given interval being between two maximas.

D. The graph represents a degree four polynomial with the given interval being between two local maximas.

9. For which of the following partial graphs would finding the average rate of change between points **A** and **B** be a poor approximation for the instantaneous rate of change at **C**?

A.

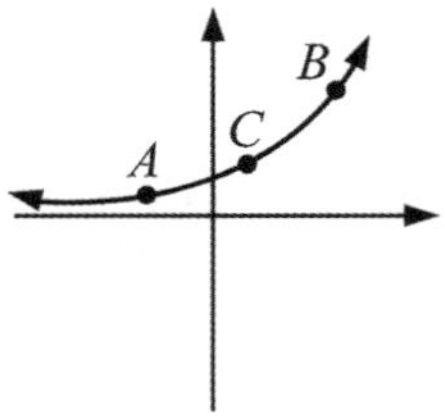

B.

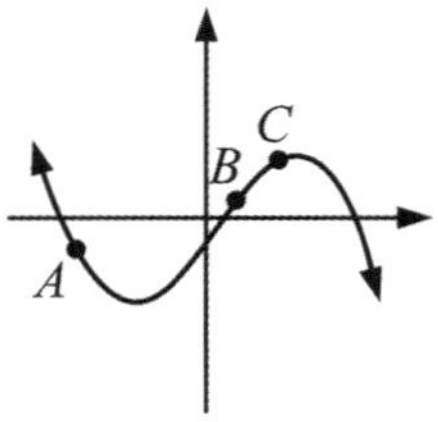

C.

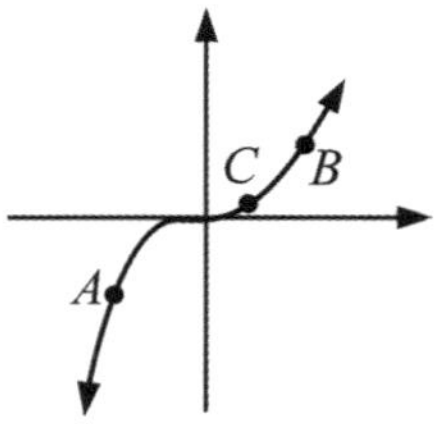

D.

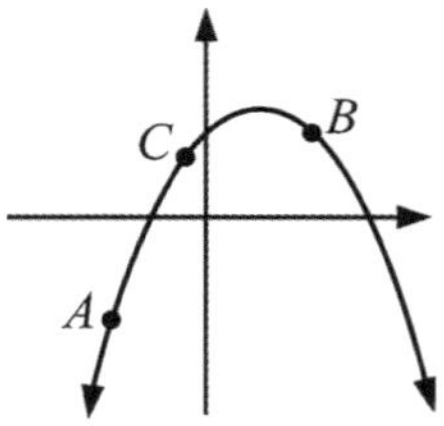

Use the following information to answer the next question.

A partial table of values for a particular function is shown below.

x	y
–0.5	–7.5
0	–5
0.5	–4
1	–6
1.5	–12.5
2	–74

10. Given that the function is a continuous curve on $x \in R$, the **best** approximation of the slope of the tangent at the point $(0.75, \ -4.53125)$ is

A. –26.6

B. –5.875

C. –2.125

D. 2

Open Response

OR1. The partial graph of a polynomial, $f(x)$, with x-intercepts –3 and 1 and a y-intercept of 2, is shown below.

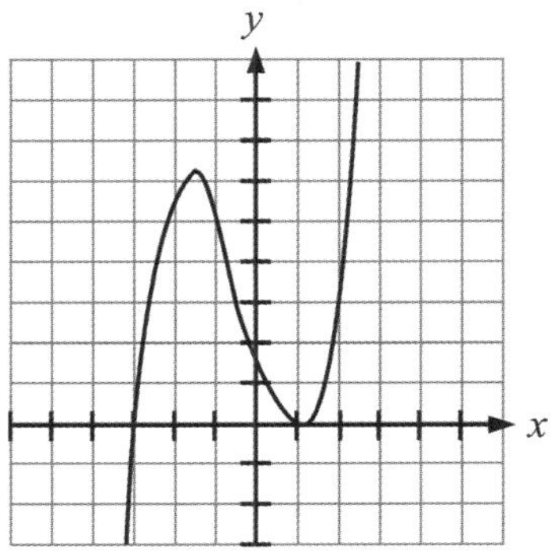

a) Determine the equation of the polynomial function *f(x)* in factored form.

b) Approximate the instantaneous rate of change, y, with respect to x for the function shown above at the point $(-2, 6)$.

c) Determine the equation of the line tangent to the curve at the point (4, 3).

1.9 solve problems involving average and instantaneous rates of change, including problems arising from real-world applications, by using numerical and graphical methods

AVERAGE AND INSTANTANEOUS RATES OF CHANGE PROBLEMS

Example

The speed of a dragster is modeled by the equation $v(t) = 12t^2 - 5t$, where t is the time in seconds and $v(t)$ is the speed in metres per second, for $0 \le t \le 5$ s.
The graph is shown below.

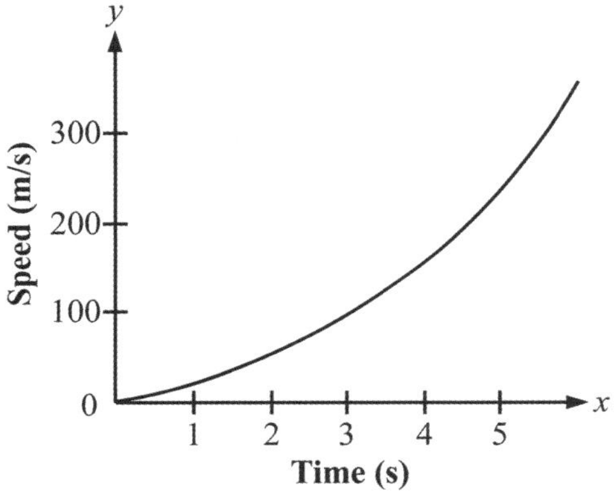

Determine the instantaneous acceleration of the dragster at $t = 1$ s.

Solution

Find the slope of a secant line anywhere on the graph. Since slope is given by $\frac{\text{rise}}{\text{run}}$, the units of this slope would be $\frac{\text{m}}{\text{m/s}}$ or m/s^2, the units of acceleration.
Recall that the instantaneous value is given by the slope of the tangent line and the instantaneous value can be approximated by using a secant line with one point $t = 1$ s, and another at a point very close to $t = 1$ s. Trying one point slightly less than 1 s and one slightly greater than 1 s should provide a good estimate of the slope of the tangent line at 1 s, which would be the instantaneous acceleration.

Using $t = 0.999\,9$ s,

$$\frac{v(1)-v(0.999\,9)}{1-0.999\,9}$$

$$=\frac{\left[12(1)^2-5(1)\right]-\left[12(0.999\,9)^2-5(0.999\,9)\right]}{0.000\,1}$$

$$=19.0\text{ m / s}^2.$$

Using $t = 1.000\,1$ s,

$$\frac{v(1)-v(1.0001)}{1-1.0001}$$

$$=\frac{\left[12(1)^2-5(1)\right]-\left[12(1.0001)^2-5(1.0001)\right]}{-0.0001}$$

$$=19.0\text{m / s}^2.$$

Thus to three significant digits, the instantaneous acceleration at $t = 1$ s must be 19.0 m/s^2.

This answer can be checked graphically using a TI-83 calculator by having the calculator draw the tangent line at $t = 1$ as shown below.

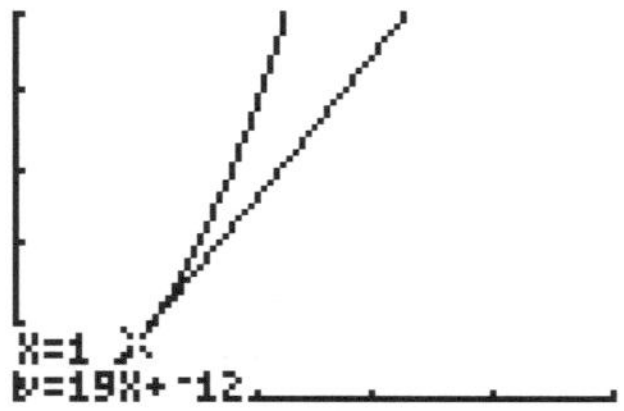

The calculator shows an equation of $y = 19x + -12$ which can be written as $y = 19x - 12,$ thus verifying the slope of 19 m/s^2.

2.1 determine, through investigation using graphing technology, key features of the graphs of functions created by adding, subtracting, multiplying, or dividing functions, and describe factors that affect these properties.

Sample Problem: Investigate the effect of the behaviours of $f(x) = \sin x$, $f(x) = \sin 2x$, and $f(x) = \sin 4x$ on the shape of $f(x) = \sin x + \sin 2x + \sin 4x$

THE GRAPHS OF COMBINED FUNCTIONS

Functions can be combined using any of the four basic operations of addition, subtraction, multiplication and division. Many functions that have been considered in this unit can be interpreted as actually being a combination of functions. For example, the quadratic function $f(x) = x^2 + 4x$ can be considered as the sum of the quadratic function $y = x^2$ and the linear function $y = 4x$. Also, the rational function $f(x) = \frac{2x}{x-3}$ can be interpreted as the quotient of two linear functions, $y = 2x$ and $y = x - 3$.

Since function values are the y-values, the function values of any combination of functions are a combination of the y-coordinates of the individual functions.

In the sample problem outlined in outcome 2.1 the maximum value of each of $\sin x$, $\sin 2x$, and $\sin 4x$ is 1, and the minimum value is –1.

The maximum value of the sum of these three functions could be $1 + 1 + 1 = 3$ if they all had their maximum values at the same x-coordinate. Likewise, the minimum value of the sum could be –3 if they all had their minimum values at the same x-coordinate. However, this does not happen, so the range is not $-3 \le y \le 3$, but rather it is approximately $-2.23 \le y \le 2.23$.

The period of $\sin x$ is 2π, of $\sin 2x$ it is π, and of $\sin 4x$ it is $\frac{\pi}{2}$. Therefore, the period of the sum of these functions is 2π, because in this case the period is the smallest multiple of the individual periods.

As another example, consider the function $f(x)=\cos x+\cos 2x+\cos 4x$. Here, each individual function has its maximum of 1 at $x=0$, so the function does have a maximum of 3 at $x=0$. However, the minimums never all occur at the same x-coordinate. The minimum value of $f(x)$ is approximately –1.76, so the range is approximately $-1.76\le y\le 3$.

The graph of $f(x)=\cos x+\cos 2x+\cos 4x$ produced by a TI-83 calculator is shown below.

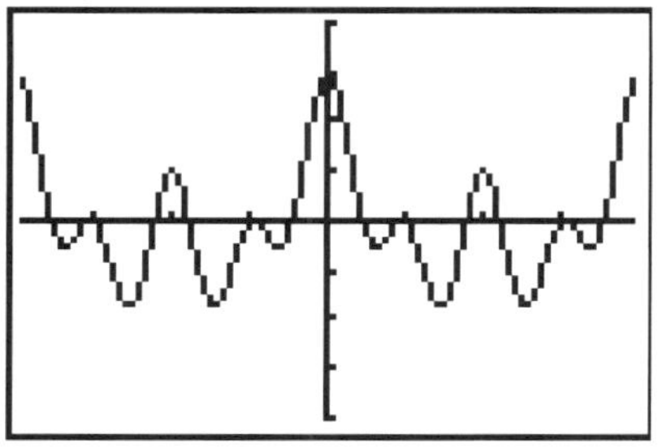

2.2 recognize real-world applications of combinations of functions, and solve related problems graphically.

Applications of the Combinations of Functions

Example

The amplitude of the motion of a damped pendulum is given by the product of the functions $f(t)=4\times 1.2^{-t}$ and $g(t)=\sin(4t)$, where the amplitude is measured in metres and time in seconds. Use a graphical approach with technology to determine the period of the pendulum, which is the minimum time it takes for the pendulum to swing from left to right and back again.

Also determine the length of the fifth swing. Give the answers to the nearest thousandth.

Solution

The product of the two functions is $f(t)g(t)=4\times 1.2^{-x}\sin(4t)$.

Using a TI-83 calculator, input $Y_1=4*1.2\wedge -x\sin(4x)$ into the [Y=] menu, using an appropriate viewing window such as $x:[0,10,1]$ $y:[-4,4,1]$, to obtain the graph below.

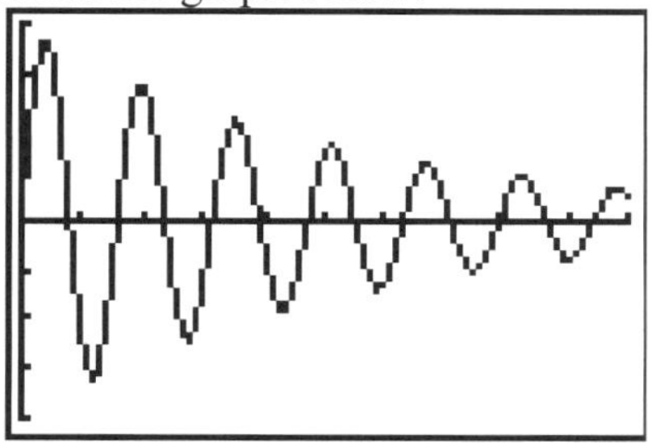

Using the zero feature, find the period by inputting [2nd] [TRACE] [2]. To the right of $x=0$, the next x-intercept required is between 1 and 2 s and finding its value gives approximately 1.571 s. This can be verified algebraically since it must match the period of $y=\sin 4x$ which is $\frac{2\pi}{4}\approx 1.571$.

To determine the distance travelled on the fifth swing determine the maximum and minimum displacements of that swing by using the CALC feature of the calculator. Inputting [2nd] [TRACE] [4], and scrolling to the 5th maximum gives a value of approximately1.1855, and using [2nd] [TRACE] [3] shows that the 5th minimum is approximately -1.0273. Subtracting these values gives the length of the 5th swing as $1.1855-(-1.0273)\approx 2.213$ m.

2.3 *determine, through investigation, and explain some properties (i.e., odd, even, or neither; increasing/decreasing behaviours) of functions formed by adding, subtracting, multiplying, and dividing general functions*

PROPERTIES OF COMBINED FUNCTIONS

A function is odd if it satisfies the condition $f(-x)=-f(x)$ for all x in its domain.
This causes the function to be symmetric with respect to the origin.
A function is even if it satisfies the condition $f(-x)=-f(x)$ for all x in its domain, which causes symmetry with respect to the y-axis.
The sum of two odd functions must also be odd since if $f(x)$ and $g(x)$ are both odd, and if you let their sum be $F(x)=f(x)+g(x)$, then

$$\begin{aligned}F(-x)&=f(-x)+g(-x)\\&=-f(x)+-g(x)\\&=-[f(x)+g(x)]\\&=-F(x)\end{aligned}$$

Likewise the sum of two even functions is even.
The product of two odd functions will however be even, since if $G(x)=f(x)g(x)$, where $f(x)$ and $g(x)$ are both odd, then

$G(-x)=f(-x)g(-x)$

$=-f(x)\times-g(x)$

$=f(x)g(x)$

$=G(x)$, which makes it even.

For example, consider $f(x)=x$ and $g(x)=x^3$, two odd functions. Their sum is $F(x)=x+x^3$, which is odd, and their product is $G(x)=x\times x^3=x^4$, which is even.

The product of two even functions can be shown to be even as well.

Where a function increases or decreases is determined on an interval by interval basis.
For example, the parabola $y=x^2$ $\boldsymbol{y=x^2}$, shown below, decreases on $x<0$ and increases on $x>0$. Note on the partial graph that the intervals of decrease and increase are separated by a minimum. Similarly, for a function with a maximum, the intervals of increase and decrease would be separated by that maximum.

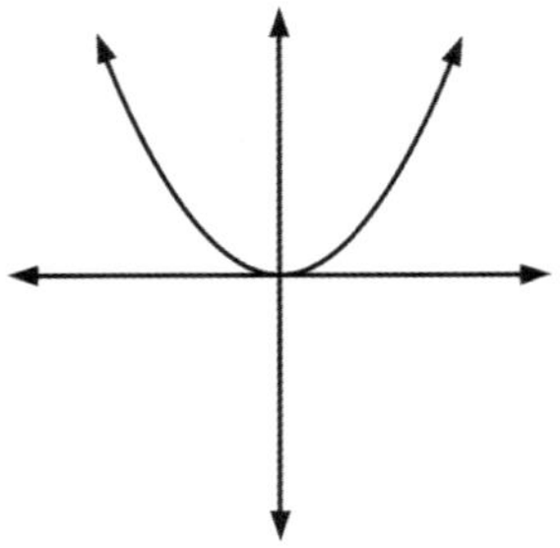

Vertical asymptotes and other breaks in a graph serve as natural breaks in its increasing and decreasing behaviour as well as corresponding intervals.
When two functions are combined by addition, the increasing and decreasing behaviour of the resulting function can also be determined.
A few general rules apply to determining such behaviour.
On a particular interval, if $f(x)$ and $f(x)g(x)$ are increasing, then so too would the function $h(x) = f(x) + g(x)$.
Similarly, if both are decreasing, the resulting function $h(x)=f(x) + g(x)$ would be decreasing.
However, when one function is increasing and the other is decreasing over a particular interval, you must establish which function is increasing or decreasing fastest. In other words, over the given interval, whose slope is the steepest? The function that has the steepest slope will determine the behaviour of the combined function's behaviour.
For example, if, on the interval $-1 < x < 3$, $f(x)$ has a slope of 5 (increasing) and $g(x)$ has a slope of –7 (decreasing) you can conclude that $g(x)$ is steepest over that interval and thus the behaviour of $g(x)$ prevails and the resulting

function $h(x)=f(x)+g(x)$ will be decreasing.

When trying to establish the behaviour of functions such as $h(x)=f(x)-g(x)$, $h(x)=f(x)g(x)$, and $h(x)=\frac{f(x)}{g(x)}$, an effective strategy is to create a table of values from the given partial graphs of $f(x)$ and $g(x)$ as the ones shown below. (Of course, it is essential to include in the table any values that would make $f(x)$ and $g(x)$ undefined as this would create breaks in the resulting function $h(x)$.

Consider the following two functions, $h(x)$ and $g(x)$.

$f(x)$

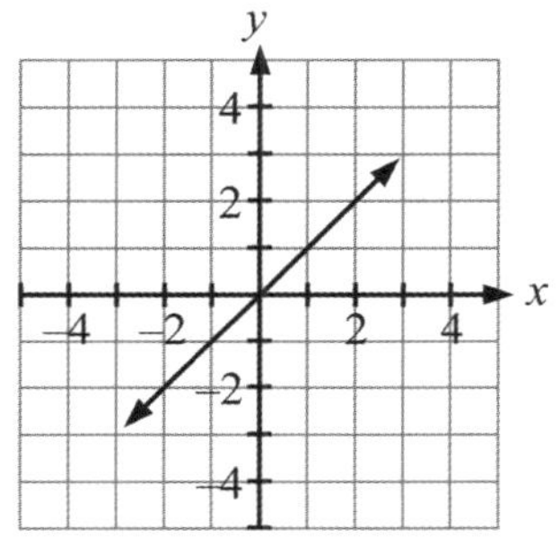

$g(x)$

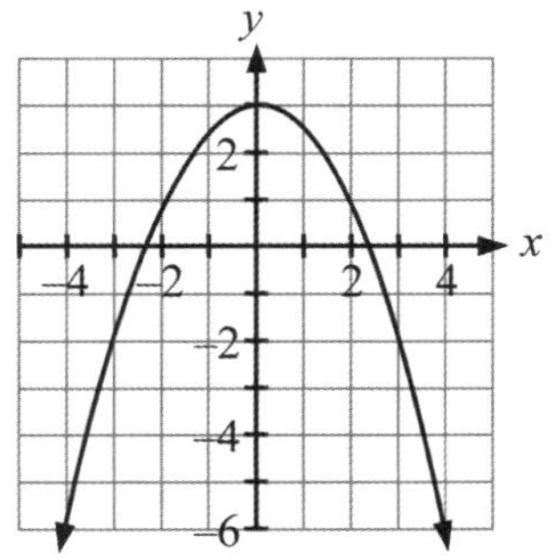

x	$f(x)$	$g(x)$	$h(x)=f(x)-g(x)$	Behaviour
–4	–4	–6	2	Decreasing
–3	–3	–3	0	
–2	–2	0	–2	
–1	–1	2	–3	
0	0	3	–3	Increasing
1	1	2	–1	
2	2	0	2	
3	3	–3	6	
4	4	–6	10	

x	$f(x)$	$g(x)$	$h(x)=f(x)\,g(x)$	Behaviour
–4	–4	–6	24	Decreasing
–3	–3	–3	9	
–2	–2	0	0	
–1	–1	2	–2	Increasing
0	0	3	0	
1	1	2	2	
2	2	0	0	Decreasing
3	3	–3	–9	
4	4	–6	–24	

x	$f(x)$	$g(x)$	$h(x)=\frac{f(x)}{g(x)}$	Behaviour
–4	–4	–6	$\frac{2}{3}$	Increasing
–3	–3	–3	1	
–2	–2	0	Undefined	
–1	–1	2	$\frac{1}{2}$	Increasing
0	0	3	0	
1	1	2	$\frac{1}{2}$	
2	2	0	Undefined	
3	3	–3	–1	Increasing
4	4	–6	$-\frac{2}{3}$	

Note that these tables give a broad picture of the behaviour of the resulting function $h(x)$. To obtain more precise information, $f(x)$ and $g(x)$ would need to be evaluated for far more values of x, with far less distance between successive values.

PRACTICE QUESTION

11. Which of the following equations is an odd function?

A. $y = x^2 + x^3$

B. $y = \frac{1}{x} + \frac{1}{x^2}$

C. $y = x^2 + \frac{1}{x^2}$

D. $y = \frac{1}{x} + x^3$

2.4 *determine the composition of two functions numerically and graphically, with technology, for functions represented in a variety of ways, and interpret the composition of two functions in real-world applications.*

2.5 *determine algebraically the composition of two functions, verify that $f(g(x))$ is not always equal to $g(f(x))$, and state the domain and the range of the composition of two functions.*

THE COMPOSITIONS OF FUNCTIONS

The composition of function $f(x)$ with function $g(x)$ is given by the expression $f(g(x))$. To perform the composition you must substitute the function $g(x)$ for every x in the function $f(x)$

Example

Given $f(x) = x^2$ and $g(x) = \sqrt{x+2}$ determine $f(g(x))$ and $g(f(x))$ and state their domain and range.
Verify the results by using graphing technology.

Solution

$$f(g(x)) = f\left(\sqrt{x+2}\right) = \left(\sqrt{x+2}\right)^2 = x+2,\ x \geq -2$$

$$g(f(x)) = g\left(x^2\right) = \sqrt{x^2+2}$$

For $f(g(x))$, the domain is $x \geq -2$ because the domain is restricted by the domain of $g(x)$, which is $x \geq -2$. Because of this restriction on the domain, the range of $f(g(x))$ is restricted to $y \geq 0$.

For $g(f(x))$, the domain is $x \in R$ and the range is $y \geq \sqrt{2}$.

When using technology to graph composite functions, enter them in their non-simplified form. This will ensure that the required restrictions on the domain remain in place.

Using a TI-83 calculator, enter $f(g(x)) = f\left(\sqrt{x+2}\right) = \left(\sqrt{x+2}\right)^2$ as $Y_1 = (\sqrt{(X+2)})^2$ and $g(f(x)) = g\left(x^2\right) = \sqrt{x^2+2}$ as $Y_2 = \sqrt{(X^2+2)}$. The graphs are shown below, drawn with a ZOOM 4:ZDecimal window, and with the second function, $g(f(x))$, as a thick line.

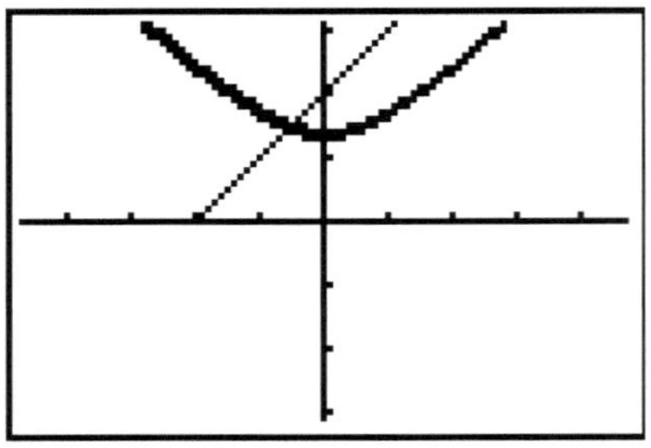

Note: When giving the domain and range of composite functions you must check for all restrictions in the function that is inside the parentheses and in the final composition.
A composed function such as $f(g(x))$ cannot be defined for values that were not allowed in $g(x)$.

Example

Given $p(x)=\sin x$ and $q(x)=x-2$ determine $p(q(x))$ and $q(p(x))$ and state their domain and range.

Solution

$$p(q(x))=p(x-2) \qquad q(p(x))=q(\sin x)$$
$$=\sin(x-2) \qquad =\sin x-2$$

You can interpret the graph of $p(q(x))=\sin(x-2)$ as the graph of $y=\sin x$ with a horizontal phase shift of 2 units right. Its domain is $x\in R$, and its range is $-1\le y\le 1$.

The graph of $q(p(x))=\sin x-2$ is the graph of $y=\sin x$ with a vertical translation of 2 units down. Its domain is $x\in R$, and its range is $-3\le y\le -1$.

The previous two examples illustrate that it is very common that $f(g(x))\ne g(f(x))$.

Example

For a particular car travelling at a constant speed, the distance driven, d in kilometres, is represented by $d(t)=80t$, where t is the time in hours. The cost of gasoline, in dollars, is represented by $C(d)=0.09d$.

Determine and interpret $C(d(5))$, and describe the relationship represented by $C(d(t))$.

Solution

Since $d(t)$ represents the distance traveled, $d(5)$ is the distance travelled in 5 h, which is $d(5)=80(5)=400$ km.

$C(d)$ represents the cost of driving d kilometres, so $C(d(5))=C(400)$ represents the cost of driving 400 km, which is the cost of driving for 5 h.

Thus, the composite function $C(d(t))$ represents the cost of driving for t hours.

PRACTICE QUESTIONS

12. A drycleaner's use of chemicals depends on the number of items being cleaned.
For dress shirts, the number of litres of chemical required is represented by $V(s) = 0.03$ s, where V is the number of litres and s is the number of shirts.
The cost, C, in dollars, to dry clean shirts is defined by $C(V) = 7.5V$. Given this information, $C(V(25))$ represents

A. \$5.63, the cost of cleaning 25 shirts

B. \$187.50, the cost of cleaning 25 shirts

C. \$5.63, the cost of 25 litres of chemical

D. \$187.50, the cost of 25 litres of chemical

13. The function $f(g(x))=\sin^2+10\sin x+21$ the composition of the two functions $f(x)$ and $g(x)$. If $f(x)=x^2-4$, then the equation of $g(x)$ is

A. $g(x)=\sin x-4$

B. $g(x)=\sin x-1$

C. $g(x)=\sin x+5$

D. $g(x)=\sin^2 x+10\sin x+4$

14. Two functions are given as $f(x)=\dfrac{1}{x-5}$ and $g(x)=2^2$. What are the domains of the functions $f(g(x))$ and $g(f(x))$?

A. Domain of $f(g(x)):\{x \mid x\neq 5, x\in R\}$
Domain of $g(f(x)):\{x \mid x\neq 5, x\in R\}$

B. Domain of $f(g(x)):\{x \mid x\neq 5, x\in R\}$;
Domain of $g(f(x)):\{x \mid x\neq \pm\sqrt{5}, x\in R\}$

C. Domain of $f(g(x)):\{x \mid x\neq \pm\sqrt{5}, x\in R\}$
Domain of $g(f(x)):\{x \mid x\neq 5, x\in R\}$

D. Domain of $f(g(x)):\{x \mid x\neq +\sqrt{5}, x\in R\}$
Domain of $g(f(x)):\{x \mid x\neq \pm\sqrt{5}, x\in R\}$

15. For which of the following pairs of functions is $f(x)=g(f(x))$?

A. $f(x)=2x,\quad g(x)=3x-1$

B. $f(x)=x+5,\quad g(x)=x-9$

C. $f(x)=3x+5,\ g(x)=x+5$

D. $f(x)=x-2,\ g(x)=5x+3$

Numerical Response

NR2. Two functions are defined as $f(x)=\sin x$ and $g(x)=x^2+\cos^2 x+5$.
The value of $g(f(0))$ is _________.

2.6 solve problems involving the composition of two functions, including problems arising from real-world applications

APPLICATIONS OF THE COMPOSITION OF FUNCTIONS

Example

The monthly amount of electrical energy, $E(t)$ measured in kilowatt hours (Kwh) consumed in a particular household is given by the equation $E(t)=300\cos\left(\dfrac{\pi}{6}t\right)+600$, where t is the number of the month, $1\le t\le 12$, $t\in N$, with $t=1$ for January, $t=2$ for February, etc. The cost of electricity, $C(E)$ in dollars, is represented by $C(E)=0.06E$. Express the cost of electricity as a function of the number of the month, and then determine the maximum and minimum monthly costs of electricity and in which months they occur.

Solution

The composite function $C(E(t))$ will express the cost as a function of the month number.

$$\begin{aligned} C(E(t)) &= C\left(300\cos\left(\frac{\pi}{6}t\right)+600\right)\\ &= 0.06\left(300\cos\left(\frac{\pi}{6}t\right)+600\right)\\ &= 18\cos\left(\frac{\pi}{6}t\right)+36 \end{aligned}$$

This is a cosine function with a period of 12 months. There is no phase shift of the function, so the maximum would occur at $t=0$, which is not in the domain, and again at $t=12$, making January the most expensive month.

This cost is:

$$C(12) = 18\cos\left(\frac{\pi}{6}(12)\right) + 36$$
$$= 18\cos(2\pi) + 36$$
$$= 18(1) + 36$$
$$= \$54$$

The minimum cost would occur at $t = 6$ and is:

$$C(6) = 18\cos\left(\frac{\pi}{6}(6)\right) + 36$$
$$= 18\cos(\pi) + 36$$
$$= 18(-1) + 36$$
$$= \$18$$

Example:

The speed of a car, v, in kilometres per hour, at a time of t hours after passing the city limits is represented by $v(t) = 80 - 3t + t^2$, $0 \le t \le 4$. The rate of gasoline consumption of the car, c, in litres per kilometre, at a speed of v kilometres per hour is represented by $c(v) = \left(\frac{v}{500} - 0.1\right)^2 + 0.15$. Determine an algebraic form of $c(v(t))$, the rate of gasoline consumption as a function of time. Determine, using technology, the time when the car is running most economically during a four-hour trip.

Solution

$$c(v(t)) = c(80 - 3t + t^2)$$
$$= \left(\frac{80 - 3t + t^2}{500} - 0.1\right)^2 + 0.15$$

Using a TI-83 calculator, input $Y_1 = ((80-3X+X^2)/500 - 0.1)^2+0.15$, on an appropriate viewing window such as $x:[0,5,1]$ $y:[0.15,0.16,0.01]$.

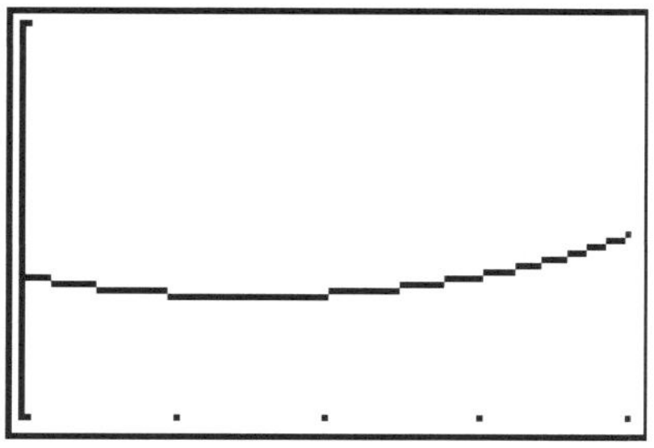

The function decreases slightly and then increases. Use the minimum feature by inputting 2nd TRACE 3, to find that the minimum is located at $t = 1.499955$, which can be rounded to 1.5 h. Thus, the car is running most economically at approximately 1.5 h into the trip. At this time the rate of fuel consumption is approximately 0.153 litres per kilometre.

Practice Question

16. A tank that holds 4 000 gallons of water will drain completely into a reservoir in 32 minutes from the bottom of the tank. The volume of water remaining in the tank after t minutes is given by the function $V(t) = 4\,000\left(1 - \frac{t}{32}\right)^2$, $0 \le t \le 32$. The amount of water in the reservoir depends on how much water has drained out of the tank and is defined by $A(V) = 14000 - V$. After how many minutes will the amount of water in the reservoir reach 12 000 gallons?

A. 2 min

B. 3.75 min

C. 9.37 min

D. 16 min

2.7 *demonstrate, by giving examples for functions represented in a variety of ways, the property that the composition of a function and its inverse function maps a number onto itself.*

THE INVERSE OF A COMPOSITE FUNCTION

The inverse of a function $f(x)$ is formed by interchanging the variables x and y in the equation defining the function. If the inverse is a function it can be represented in function notation as $f^{-1}(x)$.

Example

Given the linear function $f(x)=3x-4$, find:

a) $f^{-1}(x)$, which is the *inverse* of $f(x)$.

b) $f^{-1}(f(x))$.

c) $f(f^{-1}(x))$.

Solution

a) To form the inverse, rewrite $f(x)=3x-4$ as $y=3x-4$, and then interchange x and y to get $x=3y-4$. Solving for y by adding 4 to each side and dividing each side by 3 gives the inverse as $\frac{x+4}{3}=y$.

$$f^{-1}(x)=\frac{x+4}{3}$$

b)
$$\begin{aligned} f^{-1}(f(x)) &= f^{-1}(3x-4) \\ &= \frac{(3x-4)+4}{3} \\ &= \frac{3x}{3} \\ &= x \end{aligned}$$

c)
$$\begin{aligned} f(f^{-1}(x)) &= f\left(\frac{x+4}{3}\right) \\ &= 3\left(\frac{x+4}{3}\right)-4 \\ &= x+4-4 \\ &= x \end{aligned}$$

Notice that both $f^{-1}(f(x))$ and $f(f^{-1}(x))$. give a result of x. This is because the inverse undoes the operations that the original function performed, and vice versa.

As a further example of this relationship, consider the exponential function $f(x)=2^x$ and its inverse, $f^{-1}(x)=\log_2 x$. Composing these functions in either order gives the same result of x as shown below:

$f^{-1}(f(x))=f^{-1}(2^x)=\log_2(2^x)=x$ and

$f(f^{-1}(x))=f(\log_2 x)=2^{\log_2 x}=x$.

The relationship of $f^{-1}(f(x))=f(f^{-1}(x))=x$ will hold true as long as $f(x)$ and $f^{-1}(x)$ are both functions. In some situations, such as trigonometric functions, a restriction must be placed on the domain of $f(x)$ in order for $f^{-1}(x)$ to be a function.

For example, you would expect that $\sin^{-1}(\sin 750°)=750°$, but a TI-83 calculator will return a value of 30°. This is because $\sin 750°=\frac{1}{2}$, but $\sin^{-1}\left(\frac{1}{2}\right)$ has an infinite number of values with the calculator programmed to give only one answer, 30°.

If $f(x)$ is one-to-one, that is, for every x value there is only one y value and for every y value there is only one x value, then the inverse will be a function and both $f^{-1}(f(x))=x$ and $f(f^{-1}(x))=x$.

PRACTICE QUESTION

17. The point P(3, –5) lies on the graph of a continuous one-to-one function, $f(x)$.

The value of $f^{-1}(f(x))$ is

A. –5

B. –3

C. 3

D. 5

2.8 make connections, through investigation using technology, between transformations of simple functions $f(x)$ and the composition of these functions with a linear function of the form $g(x)=A(x+B)$

COMPOSITIONS AND TRANSFORMATIONS OF FUNCTIONS

Consider the compositions of the functions $f(x)=\log x$ and $g(x)=\frac{1}{2}(x-d)$, where $d=-4$ and also where $d=3$.
The two compositions of these functions are:

$f(g(x))=f\left(\frac{1}{2}(x-d)\right)=\log\left(\frac{1}{2}(x-d)\right)$ and

$g(f(x))=g(\log x)=\frac{1}{2}(\log x-d)=\frac{1}{2}\log x-\frac{d}{2}$

From knowledge you have already gained about transformations and considering $f(g(x))=f\left(\frac{1}{2}(x-d)\right)$, recall that the coefficient $\frac{1}{2}$ causes a horizontal stretch of the graph of $y=f(x)$ by a factor of 2 from the y-axis. Also, recall that replacing x by $x-d$ would cause a horizontal translation of d units left if d is negative and of d units right if d is positive. This is true for any function $y=f(x)$. Thus, the graph of $f(x)=\log x$ will undergo a horizontal stretch by a factor of 2 from the y-axis and will be translated horizontally left 4 units when d = –4, and 3 units right when $d=3$.

If you consider $g(f(x))$ from the perspective of substituting $f(x)$ for every x in function $g(x)$, you get

$g(f(x))=\frac{1}{2}(f(x)-d)=\frac{1}{2}f(x)-\frac{d}{2}$.

In this form the coefficient $\frac{1}{2}$ causes a vertical compression of the graph of $f(x)$ by a factor of $\frac{1}{2}$ to the x-axis. Furthermore subtracting $\frac{d}{2}$ causes a vertical translation of $\frac{d}{2}$ units up if $d<0$, and of $\frac{d}{2}$ units down if $d>0$. When $d=-4$, $g(f(x))=\frac{1}{2}\log x+2$, and the graph of $\log x$ will be vertically compressed by a factor of $\frac{1}{2}$ to the x-axis, then translated vertically up 2 units. When $d=3$, $g(f(x))=\frac{1}{2}\log x-\frac{3}{2}$, and the graph of $\log x$ will be vertically compressed by a factor of $\frac{1}{2}$ to the x-axis, then translated vertically down $\frac{3}{2}$ units. The two possible compositions of any function $f(x)$ and a linear function $g(x)=A(x+B)$ can be summarized as:

Composition	Stretch or Compression	Translation
$f(g(x))$ $=f(A(x+B))$	Horizontal by factor $\frac{1}{A}$	Horizontal B units left if $B>0$, right if $B<0$
$g(f(x))$ $=Af(x)+AB$	Vertical by factor A	Vertical AB units up if $AB>0$, down if $AB<0$

Composing a function $f(x)$ with a linear function will produce horizontal effects on the graph of $f(x)$, while composing a linear function with $f(x)$ produces vertical effects.

PRACTICE QUESTIONS

18. The point $P(-1, 7)$ lies on the graph of $h(x)=2x+9$. The y-coordinate of the image point P' for the function $h(g(x))$, where $g(x)=x^2$ is

A. 1

B. 7

C. 11

D. 13

19. Given $f(x)=x^2$ and $g(x)=-3(x+4)$, if $f(x)$ is transformed to $f(g(x))$, the graph of $f(x)$ would have a

A. vertical expansion by a factor of 9, followed by a horizontal translation of 4 units left

B. vertical compression by a factor of $\frac{1}{9}$, followed by a horizontal translation 16 units left

C. vertical expansion by a factor of 9, followed by a reflection in the x-axis, followed by a horizontal translation 16 units to the left

D. vertical compression by a factor of $\frac{1}{9}$, followed by a reflection in the x-axis, followed by a horizontal translation 4 units to the left

3.1 compare, through investigation using a variety of tools and strategies the characteristics of various functions.

THE CHARACTERISTICS OF FUNCTIONS

A summary of the key features of the various types of functions is presented below.

POLYNOMIAL FUNCTIONS:

The equation of a polynomial function has the form

$f(x)=a_nx^n+a_{n-1}x^{n-1}+a_{n-2}x^{n-2}+\ldots+a_1x+a_0$

where $n\in W$, $a_0,a_1,a_2,\ldots,a_n\in R$.

Two examples are: $y=3x^4-2x^2+4x-7$ and $f(x)=6x^3+8x^2-5x+3$. The domain is $x\in R$ and if the degree is odd, then the function will have a range of $y\in R$. If the degree is even (>0) and $a_n<0$ the graph will reach an absolute maximum, so $y\le M$, where M is the maximum, or if and $a_n<0$ the graph of the function will reach an absolute minimum, so $y\ge M$, where M is the minimum.

There are no asymptotes. The end behaviour of the graph can be determined by the term a_nx^n

RATIONAL FUNCTIONS:

The equation of a rational function has the form

$f(x)=\dfrac{P(x)}{Q(x)}$,

where $P(x)$ and $Q(x)$ are polynomial functions, $Q(x)\neq 0$. There are often horizontal and/or vertical asymptotes, and thus the domain and range are not always all real numbers.

TRIGONOMETRIC FUNCTIONS:

The equations of trigonometric functions involve any of the six trigonometric expressions

$\sin x$, $\cos x$, $\tan x$, $\sec x$, $\csc x$, or $\cot x$.

All basic functions, such as $y=\sin x$, are periodic, with a period of π for $y=\tan x$ and $y=\cot x$, and a period of 2π for all the others. The period is changed if the function has undergone a horizontal stretch or compression. Both $y=\sin x$ and $y=\cos x$ have a domain of $x\in R$, a range of $-1\le y\le 1$, and an amplitude of 1. All the other basic trig functions have vertical asymptotes and restrictions on their domains. Both $y=\tan x$ and $y=\cot x$ have a range of $y\in R$, while $y=\sec x$ and $y=\csc x$ have a range of $|y|\ge 1$.

EXPONENTIAL FUNCTIONS:

The equation of a basic exponential function has the form $f(x)=b^x$, $b>0$, $b\neq 1$.

The domain is $x\in R$, and the range is $y>0$. There is a horizontal asymptote of $y=0$. The function can be applied to representing growth if $b>1$, and to representing decay if $0<b<1$.

LOGARITHMIC FUNCTIONS:

The equation of a basic function logarithmic function has the form

$f(x)=\log_b x$, $b>0$ $b\neq 1$.

The domain is $x>0$, and the range is $y\in R$.

There is a vertical asymptote of $x=0$.

Logarithmic functions are inverses of exponential function that have the same base.

PRACTICE QUESTION

20. The graph of $y = \log_5 x$ is translated 2 units down. A student writes the equation of the transformed image in the form $y = \log_5 kx$, where k is a real number. The value of k, to the nearest hundredth, is

A. 0.04 **B.** 0.10

C. 0.25 **D.** 0.50

3.2 solve graphically and numerically equations and inequalities whose solutions are not accessible by standard algebraic techniques

SOLVING EQUATIONS AND INEQUALITIES GRAPHICALLY

Example

a) Graphically solve the equation $2\sin x = \frac{1}{4}x^2 + x$ to the nearest hundredth.

b) Use the solution(s) from part a) to write the solution to the inequalities $2\sin x \le \frac{1}{4}x^2 + x$ and $2\sin x > \frac{1}{4}x^2 + x$ correct to the nearest hundredth.

Solution

The equation $2\sin x = \frac{1}{4}x^2 + x$ involves both a trigonometric and a polynomial expression. One method of solving this problem is to rewrite the equation as $2\sin x - \frac{1}{4}x^2 - x = 0$ and then input $Y_1 = 2\sin(X) - X^2/4 - X$ into the graphing menu of a TI-83 calculator.

The calculator must be in radian mode since no degree units are indicated in the trig expression. Choose an appropriate viewing window such as $x:[-2\pi, 2\pi, 1]$ $y:[-5, 5, 0]$.

The graph is shown below.

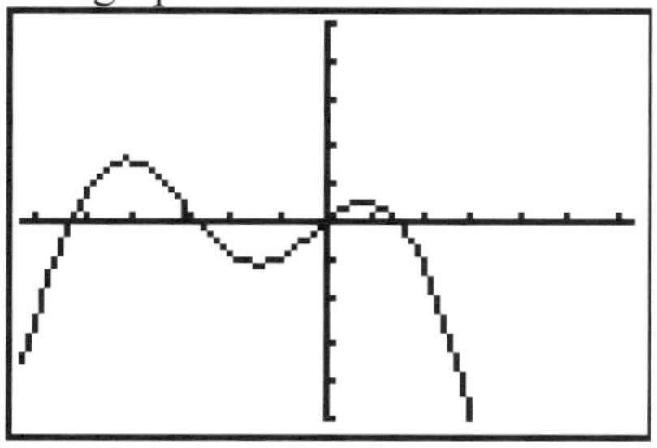

a) Because the equation is equated to 0, the solutions are the x-intercepts of $y = 2\sin x - \frac{1}{4}x^2 - x$. If you are not certain that all the x-intercepts are showing you can adjust the viewing window. However, notice that $-\frac{1}{4}x^2$ is the dominant turn so you know that for extreme positive or negative x-values the graph will be in quadrants III and IV. Observe that there are 4 solutions since there are 4 x-intercepts. Using the ZERO feature by inputting [2nd] [CALC] [2], you get $x = -5.28, \ -2.68, \ 0$, and 1.46, correct to the nearest hundredth.

b) If you rewrite $2\sin x \le \frac{1}{4}x^2 + x$ as $2\sin x - \frac{1}{4}x^2 - x \le 0$, then the solution to the inequality $2\sin x \le \frac{1}{4}x^2 + x$ is all intervals of x for which the graph is below or on the x-axis. From the graph you can see that this occurs for $x \le -5.28$ or $-2.68 \le x \le 0$ or $x \ge 1.46$.

The solution to $2\sin x > \frac{1}{4}x^2 + x$,
can be found by identifying the intervals of x that cause the function $y = 2\sin x - \frac{1}{4}x^2 - x$ to be positive (above the x-axis). The solution is $-5.28 < x < -2.68$ or $0 < x < 1.46$.

PRACTICE QUESTION

21. The sum of the solutions to the equation $x^2 = \sin(6x) + 1$, where $0 \le x \le 2\pi$, to the nearest tenth, is

A. 1.7

B. 2.0

C. 3.1

D. 3.4

3.3 solve problems, using a variety of tools and strategies, including problems arising from real-world applications, by reasoning with functions and by applying concepts and procedures involving functions

APPLICATIONS OF FUNCTIONS

Example

The distance that a particular car travels after the brakes are applied is measured for several different speeds. The data is given in the following table.

Speed (km/h)	5	10	15	20	25	30	35
Stopping distance (m)	0.82	3.3	7.3	13.1	20.4	29.4	39.8

Use technology to investigate linear, quadratic, and exponential models for the relationship of speed and stopping distance, and describe how well each model fits the data. Use each model to predict the stopping distance for a speed of 50 km/h. Determine which model gives the most realistic answer?

Solution

Using a TI-83 calculator, graph the data by carrying out the following procedure. First, clear the lists by pressing [2nd] [MEM] [4] [ENTER]. Press [Y =] and clear any functions that were previously graphed. Then press [STAT] [ENTER]. Input the speeds in L1 and the stopping distances in L2. Next, set the viewing window to $x:[0,60,5]$ $y:[0,100,10]$.

Now, press [2nd] [Y =] [ENTER] and turn Plot 1 on by pressing [ENTER] again. The type of graph should be a scatter plot, the Xlist is L1, and the Ylist is L2. Pressing [GRAPH] will show you the following graph.

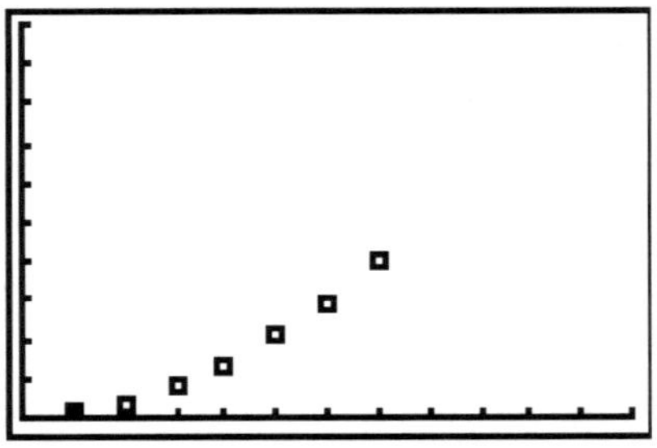

There is no need to do linear regression, since the graph is a curve. However, if you did need to, you would press [STAT], then scroll right to [CALC] and choose 4: LinReg($ax + b$). For quadratic regression press [STAT], then scroll right to [CALC] and choose 5. Then press [2nd] [L1], [2nd] [L2], [VARS], scroll right to [Y – Vars], and press [ENTER] twice. The screen should now display QuadReg L1, L2, Y1. Pressing [ENTER] will perform the regression and produce the following screen.

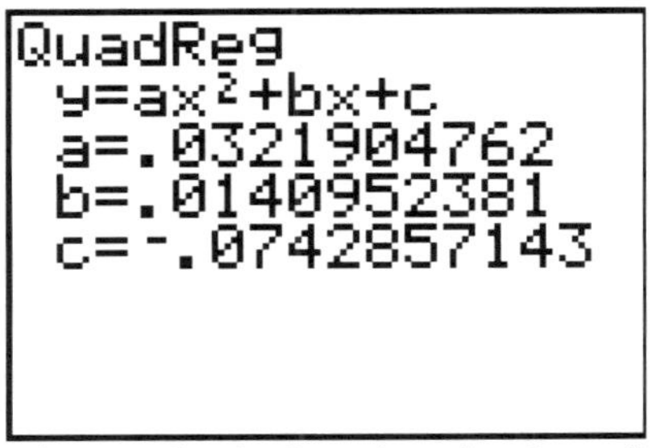

The quadratic function that best fits the data is approximately the equation

$$y = 0.032\,190\,5x^2 + 0.014\,095\,2x - 0.074\,285\,7.$$

If you press GRAPH, the calculator will draw the graph because you have stored the regression equation as Y_1.

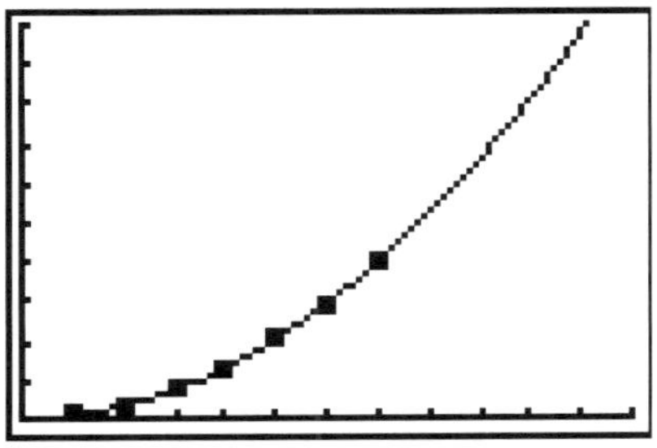

This function appears to be a fairly good fit to the given data.

To determine the predicted stopping distance for a speed of 50 km/h, press 2nd CALC ENTER and input 50.

The calculator gives a stopping distance of 81.1 m, to the nearest tenth, for the quadratic model.

To see how well an exponential function fits the data, repeat the steps or press 2nd ENTER while on the calculating window and change QuadReg to ExpReg by pressing STAT ; then scroll right to CALC and choose 0. The screen will now display ExpReg L1, L2, Y1.

Press ENTER to perform the regression. The result should be an equation with approximate values of $y = 0.8178(1.1295)^x$ Press GRAPH to see how well this function fits the data.

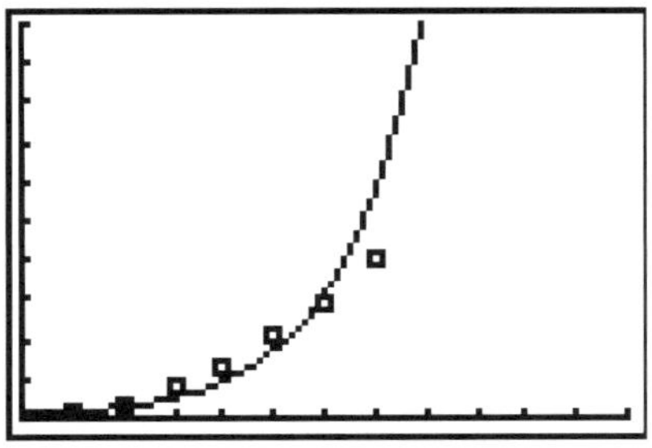

This function does not appear to fit the data as well as the quadratic function did since several points are above the curve and the graph rises rapidly to the right of the final point. To use this model to determine the predicted stopping distance for a speed of 50 km/h, again press 2nd CALC ENTER and input 50. The stopping distance for this model is approximately 360.3 m, which is unreasonably large.

The quadratic model is the more realistic relationship for this data.

PRACTICE QUESTIONS

22. A Ferris wheel has a diameter of 40 m. The maximum height of the wheel is 42 m. The wheel takes 4 minutes to complete one full rotation. The equation of the function, in the form $h(t) = a\sin b(t - c) + d$, where $a > 0$, that represents the height of a cart relative to time t, measured in seconds, if the cart is at its highest position $t = 0$, is

A. $h(t) = 20\sin\frac{\pi}{2}t + 22$

B. $h(t) = 40\sin\frac{\pi}{2}t + 20$

C. $h(t) = 20\sin\frac{\pi}{2}(t - 3) + 22$

D. $h(t) = 40\sin\frac{\pi}{2}(t - 3) + 22$

Use the following information to answer the next question

The Leaning Tower of Pisa's tilt has been increasing for years. The table below gives data of the tower's lean (the horizontal distance from the vertical to a fixed point on the tower) measured in metres, over an 11 year period.

Year	Lean (m)
1975	2.9642
1976	2.9644
1977	2.9656
1978	2.9667
1979	2.9673
1980	2.9688
1981	2.9696
1982	2.9698
1983	2.9713
1984	2.9717
1985	2.9725

23. If this trend continued, at the start of what year would the tower's lean exceed 2.98 m?

A. 1993 **B.** 1994

C. 1996 **D.** 1997

Open Response

OR2. From a height of 1 metre, a student tossed a ball into the air.
She recorded several data values of height and time as the ball ascended and then descended. Upon review of her data, the student concluded that a sinusoidal regression model of the data was most appropriate. Discuss the merit of this conclusion in relation to other regression models the student could have chosen.

ANSWERS AND SOLUTIONS—CHARACTERISTICS OF FUNCTIONS

1. C	**NR1. –19.6m/s**	**13. C**	**19. A**
2 B	**8. D**	**14. C**	**20. A**
3. B	**9. B**	**15. B**	**21. C**
4. C	**10. C**	**NR2. 6.**	**22. C**
5. B	**OR1. See Solution**	**16. C**	**23. B**
6. D	**11. D**	**17. C**	**OR2. See Solution**
7. C	**12. A**	**18. C**	

1. **C**

Recall that the average rate of change of a function is equal to the slope of line represented by the function. The steeper the slope, the greater the rate of change. By examining the graph, it is clear that the steepest slope is between the years 1995 and 2000.

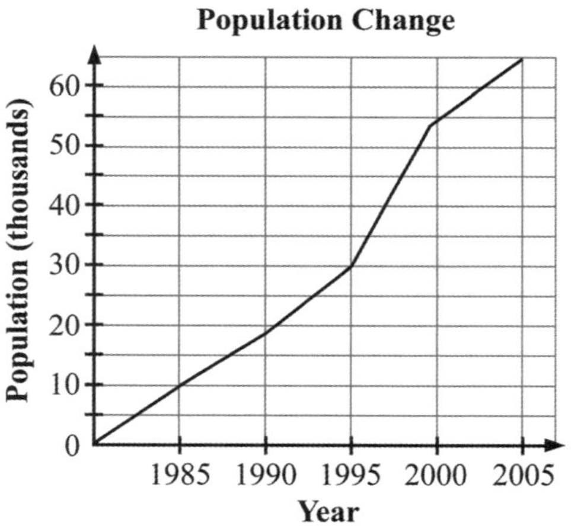

2. **B**

The rate of change of volume of the water in the hot tub with respect to time is a constant of 0.25 m^3/min.
Therefore, every 60 minutes, the volume increases by 15 m^3
($60\text{ min}\times 0.25\text{ m}^3/\text{min} = 15\text{ m}^3$).
At 8:00 A.M., the given volume is 8 m^3.
At 9:00 A.M., the volume will be
$8\text{ m}^3 + 15\text{ m}^3 = 23\text{ m}^3$.
At 10:00 A.M., the volume will be
$23\text{ m}^3 + 15\text{ m}^3 = 38\text{ m}^3$.

Now, determine the height at 9:00 A.M., and 10:00 A.M.
Using the formula for the volume of a cylinder, $V = \pi r^2 h$, solve for *h*, which gives $h = \frac{V}{\pi r^2}$.
Substituting the two values for *V*:
At 9:00 A.M., $h = \frac{23}{\pi(2)^2} = 1.83\text{ m}$ and at
10:00 A.M., $h = \frac{38}{\pi(2)^2} = 3.02\text{ m}$.
The average rate of volume with respect to height is calculated using the ratio $\frac{V_2 - V_1}{h_2 - h_1}$.
Between 9:00 A.M. and 10:00 A.M., the rate of change of the volume of water in the hot tub is calculated to be
$\frac{38-23}{3.02-1.83} = \frac{15}{1.19} = 12.6\text{ m}^3/\text{m}$.

3. **B**

Each situation and its corresponding graph, is shown below.

A block of ice being melted and then heated to boiling point

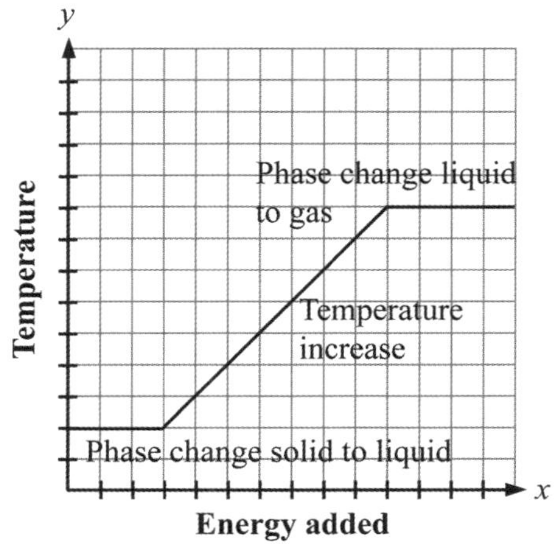

The graph represents a relationship between temperature and energy added. There is a horizontal line during phase changes (energy is being added but the temperature remains constant) and an oblique line during a temperature increase.

A balloon increasing in size when it is exposed to constant heat

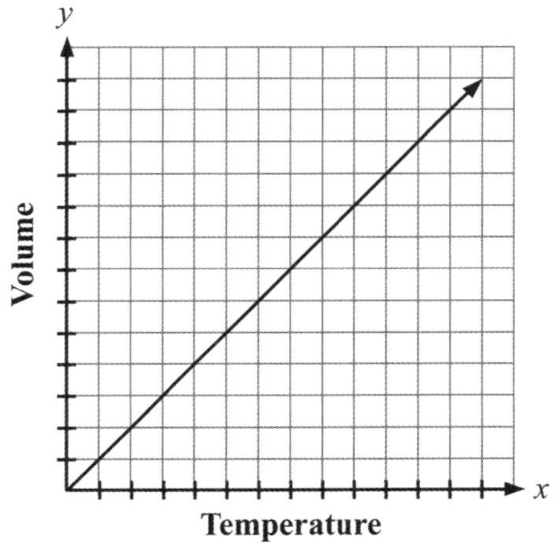

The graph represents a linear relationship between volume and temperature, since when temperature increases, volume increases.

A car driving slowly on a side street, then accelerating onto a freeway where it can go faster.

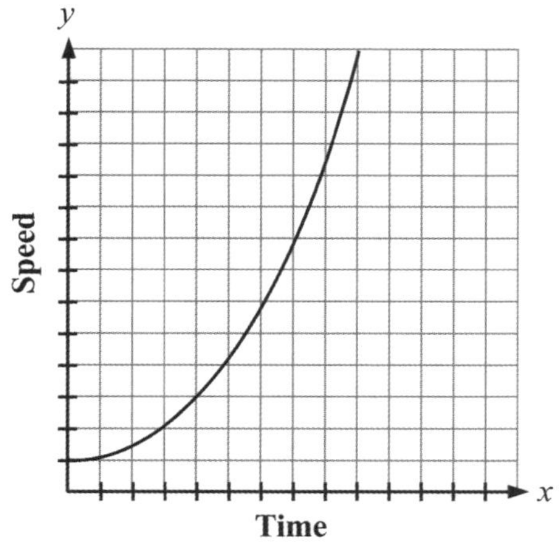

The graph represents an exponential relationship between speed and time (acceleration).

A horse slowing down for the corners on a horse race track

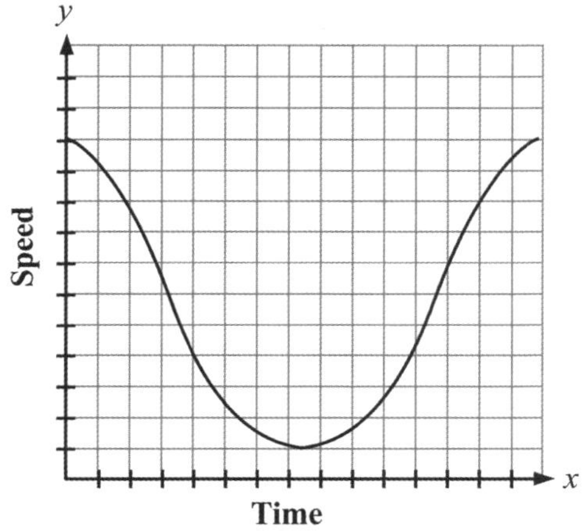

The graph of an object slowing down then speeding up is often represented with a sinusoidal curve as shown.

4. **C**

The graph starts at the origin because the distance travelled is measured from the instant the graph begins. Since the train is initially travelling at a constant speed, the graph would begin as an oblique line rising to the right from the origin. Since the train was moving forward, it must stop in order to move backward. This is indicated by a short horizontal line. Then, the train moves at a slower constant rate, which would be shown by an oblique line with a slight slope rising to the right from the horizontal line (the line is rising because the total distance covered increases despite the train's change in direction). After moving backward, the train must stop again in order to roll forward. The stop is indicted by another short horizontal line. As the train rolls forward, the graph will once again become an oblique line with a slight slope rising to the right from the previous horizontal line.
The explanation is illustrated below.

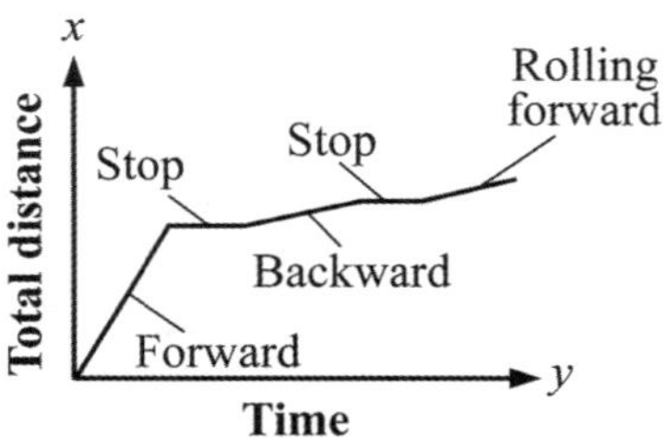

5. **B**

Begin by determining the height of the seat after 0 s and 2 s. (Be sure to use radian mode in your calculator).

$h(0) = 6\sin(0+5)+6.5$

$h(0) = 0.75$

$h(2) = 6\sin(2+5)+6.5$

$h(2) = 10.44$

The average rate of change over the first two seconds is calculated using the ratio: $\dfrac{h_2 - h_1}{t_2 - t_1}$

$$\frac{h(2)-h(0)}{2-0} = \frac{10.44-0.75}{2} = \frac{9.69}{2} = 4.85 \text{ m/s}$$

6. **D**

The instantaneous rate of change would be the lowest at the instant the change in temperature would decrease or stop. Since water boils at 100°C, it will no longer increase in temperature, but begin changing states (from liquid to gas). Therefore, since the temperature at 10 s is 100˚C, the instantaneous rate of change of the thermometer's mercury at that point will be the lowest.

7. **C**

Accurately approximating the instantaneous rate of change at a given point *P* involves reducing the interval over which the average rate of change is determined. The best approximations involve using interval points that are directly on either side of point *P* since the true instantaneous rate of change occurs at point *P*.

NR1. **–19.6**

To determine the instantaneous rate of change of the ball's height with respect to time, at $t = 2$ s $\mathbf{t = 2}$, use the average rate of change ratio: $\dfrac{h(t_2)-h(t_1)}{t_2-t_1}$

Begin by determining the average rate of change between 1.5 s and 2.5 s:

$$\frac{h(2.5)-h(1.5)}{2.5-1.5}$$

$$= \frac{\left(-4.9(2.5)^2+10\right)-\left(-4.9(1.5)^2+10\right)}{2.5-1.5}$$

$$\frac{-20.625-(-1.025)}{1} = -19.6 \text{ m/s}$$

Reducing the interval to 0.1 s about the time of 2 s gives:

$$\frac{h(2.1)-h(1.9)}{2.1-1.9}$$

$$=\frac{\left(-4.9(2.1)^2+10\right)-\left(-4.9(1.9)^2+10\right)}{2.1-1.9}$$

$$\frac{-11.609-(-7.689)}{0.2}=-19.6 \text{ m/s}$$

Using a very short time interval from 1.999 s to 2.001 s gives:

$$\frac{h(2.001)-h(1.999)}{2.001-1.999}$$

$$=\frac{\left(-4.9(2.001)^2+10\right)-\left(-4.9(1.999)^2+10\right)}{2.001-1.999}$$

$$\frac{-9.6196049-(-9.5804049)}{0.002}=-19.6 \text{ m/s}$$

Since each average rate of change calculation is the same value over decreasing intervals of time, the instantaneous rate of change of the ball's height with respect to time is decreasing by 19.6 m/s.

8. **D**

If the average rate of change over a given interval of a function is zero, then the slope of the secant on the graph over the interval is also zero.

A secant with a slope of zero is a horizontal line.

On the graph of a parabola, a secant drawn between the two x-intercepts is a horizontal line and has a slope of zero.

An example is shown below.

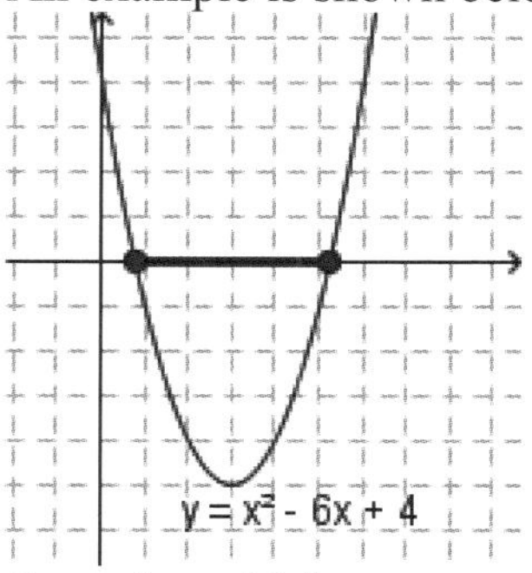

On a sinusoidal curve, a secant drawn between two maximas is a horizontal line and has a slope of zero.

An example is shown below.

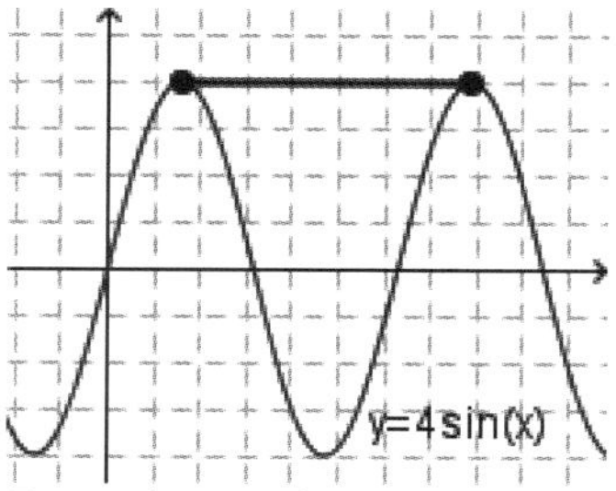

For a degree four polynomial, when a secant is drawn between the local maximas, it may or may not have a slope of zero. In the example shown, the slope of the secant does not have a slope of zero.

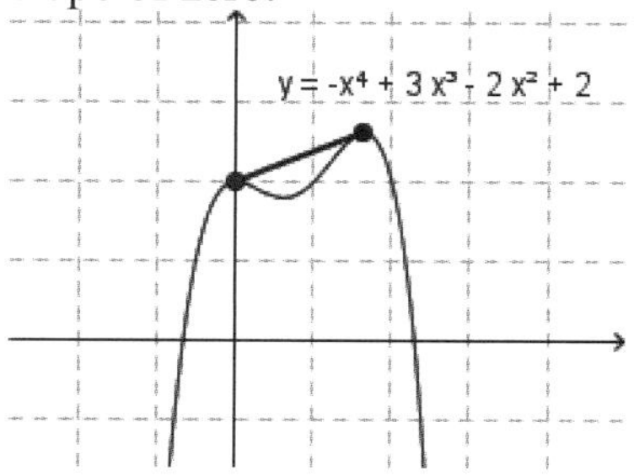

9. **B**

The instantaneous rate of change can be approximated using the slope of a secant through a given point. In graph B, point C is located outside of points A and B. When determining the slope of the secant of AB, the slope will not be parallel to the tangent at point C, which in this case, will be zero since C is a maximum point.

10. **C**

The best approximation is found by determining the slope of the secant using the points $(0.75, -4.53125)$ and $(0.5, -4)$ from the given table of values.

$$\frac{-4.53125-(-4)}{0.75-0.5}=-2.125$$

OR 1

a) From the given graph, it can be observed that the graph is tangent to the x-axis at 1 and that it passes through the x-axis at -3. Thus, in factored form, $f(x)$ can be expressed as $f(x)=a(x-1)^2(x+3)$, where a is a non-zero real number. The value of a can be determined by making use of the y-intercept (0, 2). Substitute 0 for x and 2 for $f(x)$ and solve for a as shown below.

$$f(x)=a(x-1)^2(x+3)$$
$$2=a(0-1)^2(0+3)$$
$$2=a(1)(3)$$
$$2=3a$$
$$\frac{2}{3}=a$$

Thus the equation of $f(x)$ in factored form is $f(x)=\frac{2}{3}(x-1)^2(x+3)$.

b) Use a table of values and find the slopes of secant lines through the point $(-2,6)$ and points that are near $(-2,6)$, as the second point, x^2, gets closer and closer to $(-2,6)$.

The average rate of change can be calculated by applying the slope formula

$$m=\frac{y_2-y_1}{x_2-x_1}=\frac{f(x_2)-6}{x_2-(-2)}.$$

Table One $(x_2<-2)$

x_2	$f(x_2)$	Slope of secant line $\frac{f(x_2)-6}{x_2-(-2)}$
–2.1	5.766	2.34
–2.01	5.97966	2.034
–2.001	5.9979967	2.0033

As x_2 approaches –2, the slope of the secant line approaches 2.

Table Two $(x_2>-2)$

x_2	$f(x_2)$	Slope of secant line $\frac{f(x_2)-6}{x_2-(-2)}$
–1.9	6.1673333	1.673333
–1.99	6.0196673	1.96673
–1.999	6.0019967	1.9967

As x_2 approaches –2, the slope of the secant line approaches 2.

From the preceding tables, determine that the approximate instantaneous rate of change of y with respect to x for the function shown at the point $(-2,6)$ is 2.

c) Determine the equation of the line tangent to the curve at the point $(-2,6)$

To determine the equation of the line tangent to the curve at point $(-2,6)$, use the slope of the tangent line and the point $(-2,6)$ in the point slope equation $y-y_1=m(x-x_1)$.

Substituting –2 for x_1, 6 for y_1, and 2 for m gives

$$y-6=2(x-(-2))$$
$$y=2(x+2)+6$$
$$y=2x+4+6$$
$$y=2x+10$$

The equation of the line tangent to the curve at the point $(-2,6)$ is $y=2x+10$.

11. **D**

Recall that the sum of two odd functions is also odd and that the sum of two even functions is even. Review the given alternatives based on this knowledge.

A. $y=x^2+x^3$

One even term and one odd term—further investigation is required.

B. $y = \frac{1}{x} + \frac{1}{x^2}$

One odd term and one even term – further investigation is required.

C. $y = x^2 + \frac{1}{x^2}$

Both terms of this function are even, therefore, the sum of the two results is an even function.

D. $y = \frac{1}{x} + x^3$

Both terms of this function are odd, therefore, the sum of the two results is an odd function. This answer is correct. Confirm that answers **A** and **B** cannot be odd as well.

A. Replacing x, with $1x$ gives $y = (-x)^2 + (-x)^3$, which simplifies to $y = x^2 - x^3$. This resulting function is neither odd nor even because it involves the sum of an even term and an odd term.

B. Similarly to **A**, the function in **B** is comprised of an odd term and an even term, which results in a function that is neither odd nor even.

12. **A**

Since $V(s)$ represents the number of litres of chemical required to clean s shirts, $V(25)$ represents the number of litres required to clean 25 shirts, which is $V(25) = 0.03(25) = 0.75$ L.

$C(V) = 7.5V$ represents the cost of cleaning using V litres of chemical. Consequently, the composite function $C(V(s))$ represents the cost of cleaning s shirts and

$C(V(25)) = 7.5 \times 0.75 = \$5.63$,

represents the cost of cleaning 25 shirts. Therefore, the correct answer is **A**.

13. **C**

The composition function $f(g(x))$ is determined by replacing all x values in the function $f(x)$ with the function $g(x)$. Since $f(x) = x^2 - 4$ and $f(g(x)) = \sin^2 x + 10\sin x + 21$, it is necessary to find something to replace x with in $f(x)$ so that the resulting function is

$f(g(x)) = \sin^2 x + 10\sin x + 21$

In other words,

$$\begin{aligned} f(g(x)) &= (g(x))^2 - 4 \\ &= \sin^2 x + 10\sin x + 21 \end{aligned}$$

The unknown function $g(x)$ can be determined by solving the equation below.

$(g(x))^2 - 4 = \sin^2 x + 10\sin x + 21$

Add 4 to both sides

$(g(x))^2 = \sin^2 x + 10\sin x + 21 + 4$

$(g(x))^2 = \sin^2 x + 10\sin x + 25$

Now, factor the right side of the equation:

$(g(x))^2 = (\sin x + 5)(\sin x + 5)$

or $(g(x))^2 = (\sin x + 5)^2$

Therefore, $g(x) = \sin x + 5$

14. **C**

First, find $f(g(x)) = f(x^2) = \frac{1}{x^2 - 5}$.

In finding the domain of this function, ensure that x is restricted to values that make $f(g(x))$ defined. Therefore, $x^2 - 5 \neq 0$, which means $x \neq \pm\sqrt{5}$. Since that is the only restriction on the function $f(g(x))$, the correct answer must either be **C** or **D**.

To determine the correct answer, find
$g(f(x)) = g\left(\frac{1}{x-5}\right) = \left(\frac{1}{x-5}\right)^2$.
The domain of this function is $x \neq 5$, since this is the only value of x that would make the composite function undefined.
Therefore, the correct answer is **C**.

15. **B**

Examples of functions satisfying the condition that $f(g(x)) = g(f(x))$ are rare. However, such relationships do exist when two linear functions, with coefficients on x equal to 1, are involved. Find $f(g(x))$ and $g(f(x))$ for each option to confirm.

A.
$f(g(x)) = f(3x-1) = 2(3x-1) = 6x-2$
$g(f(x)) = g(2x) = 3(2x-1) = 6x-1$
NOT EQUAL

B.
$f(g(x)) = f(x-9) = x-9+5 = x-4$
$g(f(x)) = g(x+5) = x+5-9 = x-4$
EQUAL

C.
$f(g(x)) = f(x+5) = 3(x+5)-5$
$= 3x+15-5 = 3x+10$
$g(f(x)) = g(3x-5) = 3x-5+5 = 3x$
NOT EQUAL

D.
$f(g(x)) = f(5x+3) = (5x+3)-2$
$= 5x+3-2 = 5x+1$
$g(f(x)) = g(x-2) = 5(x-2)+3$
$= 5x-10+3 = 5x-7$

NR2. **6**

To find $g(f(0))$ evaluate $f(0)$.
$f(0) = \sin 0$
$f(0) = 0$
Since $f(0) = 0$, it is necessary to evaluate $g(f(0)) = g(0)$.
$g(0) = 0^2 + (\cos 0)^2 + 5$
$g(0) = 0 + 1^2 + 5$
$g(0) = 6 = g(f(0))$
Therefore, the correct answer is 6.

16. **C**

To determine the time, t, at which the amount of water, A, in the reservoir will reach 12 000 gallons, determine the amount of water, V, remaining in the tank at that point in time.

Using the formula $A(V) = 14\ 000 - V$, solve for V.
$12\ 000 = 14\ 000 - V$
$-2\ 000 = -V$
$2\ 000 = V$

Therefore, you are looking for the time when 2 000 gallons of water remain in the tank. To find the time when 2 000 gallons of water remain in the tank, use the formula $V(t) = 4\ 000\left(1 - \frac{t}{32}\right)^2$ and solve for t.

$$2\ 000 = 4\ 000\left(1 - \frac{t}{32}\right)^2$$

$$\frac{2\ 000}{4\ 000} = \left(1 - \frac{t}{32}\right)^2$$

$$\frac{1}{2} = \left(1 - \frac{t}{32}\right)^2$$

$$\pm\sqrt{\frac{1}{2}} = 1 - \frac{t}{32}$$

$$\pm\sqrt{\frac{1}{2}} - 1 = -\frac{t}{32}$$

$$-32\left(\pm\sqrt{\frac{1}{2}} - 1\right) = t$$

$t = 9.37$ or 54.63 min.
Since $0 \le t \le 32$, the only acceptable solution is $t = 9.37$ min.

Note: This question could also be solved graphically by graphing the functions $y = 2\ 000$ and $y = 4\ 000\left(1 - \frac{x}{32}\right)^2$ then finding the x-coordinate of the point of intersection.

17. **C**

Think of some function $f(x)$ taking an x-value of 3 and transforming it to the value –5. Then, applying the inverse would involve taking the –5 and undoing the operations so that it goes back to a value of 3.

18. **C**

First find $h(g(x))$.

$h(g(x)) = h(x^2) = 2x^2 + 9$

Originally, when x was –1, $h(x)$ was 7. After the composition of functions is applied, $h(g(-1)) = 2(-1)^2 + 9 = 11$.

19. **A**

First, find $f(g(x))$. Since $g(x) = -3(x+4)$, $f(g(x))$

$$= f(-3(x+4))$$
$$= 9(x+4)^2$$

Thus, if the graph of $f(x) = x^2$ is transformed to the graph of $f(g(x)) = 9(x+4)^2$, then the graph of $f(x)$ would have a vertical expansion by a factor of 9 followed by a horizontal translation 4 units to the left.

20. **A**

The equation of the function $y = \log_5 x$, after a vertical translation 2 units down, would be $y = \log_5 x - 2$. However, it is necessary to express the function $y = \log_5 x - 2$ in the form $y = \log_5 kx$. To begin, express the number 2 as $\log_5 25$ since $5^2 = 25$. Therefore, the function $y = \log_5 x - 2$ can be rewritten as $y = \log_5 x - \log_5 25$. Using the laws of logarithms, the difference of two logarithms with common bases can be expressed as $y = \log_5\left(\frac{x}{25}\right)$ or as $y = \log_5\left(\frac{1}{25}x\right)$. Thus, $k = \frac{1}{25} = 0.04$.

21. **C**

To solve this equation, graph the functions $y = x^2$ and $y = \sin(6x) + 1$ using a graphing calculator and find all points of intersection that lie within the interval of $0 \le x \le 2\pi$, which can be accomplished by setting the window to include only the required interval such as $X: \left[0, 2\pi, \frac{\pi}{4}\right]$, $Y: [-5, 5, 1]$.

Looking at the graph, notice that the parabola intersects the sinusoidal curve at least 3 times in the interval. If it looks like there may be another point of intersection near $x = 0$, consider changing the window slightly to confirm. $X:\left[-\frac{\pi}{4}, 2\pi, \frac{\pi}{4}\right]$, $Y:[-5, 5, 1]$ would be appropriate here.

With this new window, it can be seen that there are only 3 points of intersection within the given interval. Using [2nd] [CALC] on your TI-83+, select option 5 and move the cursor until it lies on one of the points of intersection,
then press [ENTER]. Press [ENTER] 2 more times and the coordinates of the point are given. For the point farthest left,
the coordinates are (0.631, 0.398). Repeat these steps to find the other two points: (1.072, 1.150) and (1.381, 1.908). Since the question asks for the sum of the solutions to the equation, add up the three x-coordinates: $0.631 + 1.072 + 1.381 = 3.084$, which is 3.1 when rounded to the nearest tenth.

$X:\left[-\frac{\pi}{4}, 2\pi, \frac{\pi}{4}\right]$, $Y:[-5, 5, 1]$ would be appropriate here. With this new window, it can be seen that there are only 3 points of intersection within the given interval. Using [2nd] [CALC] on your TI-83+, select option 5 and move the cursor until it lies on one of the points of intersection, then press [ENTER]. Press [ENTER] 2 more times and the coordinates of the point are given.

For the point farthest left, the coordinates are (0.631, 0.398). Repeat these steps to find the other two points: (1.072, 1.150) and (1.381, 1.908). Since the question asks for the sum of the solutions to the equation, add up the three x-coordinates: $0.631 + 1.072 + 1.381 = 3.084$, which is 3.1 when rounded to the nearest tenth.

22. **C**

One of the easiest ways to determine the equation of a sinusoidal function, from a description of a particular situation, is to draw a graph as shown below.

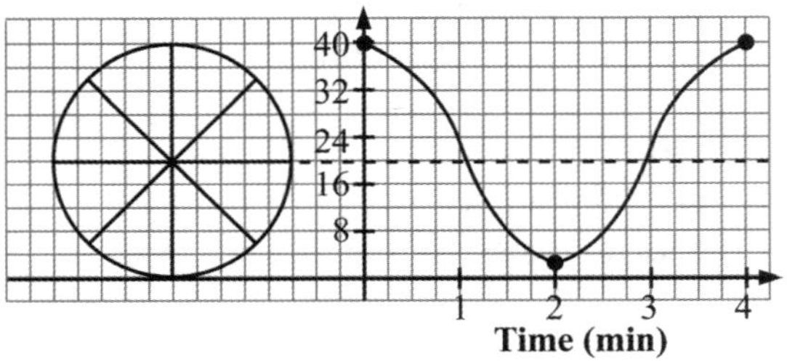

If the Ferris wheel reaches a maximum height of 42 m and has a diameter of 40 m, the base of the wheel must sit 2 m off the ground and then the centre of the Ferris wheel must be halfway between the minimum and maximum $\frac{2+42}{2} = 22$ m. Therefore, the vertical displacement of the curve is 22 m. The amplitude of the graph is 20 m since the diameter is 40 m. The period of the curve is 4 min; therefore, $b = \frac{2\pi}{4} = \frac{\pi}{2}$ and the phase shift is 3 minutes.
Thus, the equation of the sinusoidal function that satisfies this situation is $h(t) = 20\sin\frac{\pi}{2}(t-3) + 22$, where $h(t)$ is the height in metres and t is the time in minutes.

23. **B**

When given data and asked to determine a value that is not provided, finding a line/curve of best fit is often the place to start. You may need to perform more than one type of regression to assess which model gives the most accurate portrayal of the data. However, plotting the given points will help you decide which model(s) might be appropriate. This can be done by pressing STAT and then selecting option 1. Put the values for Year in L1 and the values for Lean in L2. Then, go to 2nd Y = and select option 1. Press ENTER to turn on Plot 1. Clear any equations from Y= and set an appropriate window (in this case $X:[1974, 2000, 1], Y:[2.96, 2.99, 0.1]$ would be appropriate). Then, press GRAPH and the points should appear. The points appear to almost be in a straight line, therefore start with a linear regression. However, it might be valuable to analyze the graph using an exponential regression.

Before you do the regression, however, make sure our Diagnostics are ON so that the value of the correlation coefficient is given. This will indicate the accuracy of the regression model (the closer the value is to 1 or –1, the better the equation fits the data). To do this, press 2nd and then 0 and then the x^{-1} key. Scroll down until you land on DiagnosticON. Press ENTER twice. When done correctly, your screen should say Done.

Now, perform the linear regression. Press STAT and then move over to CALC and select option 4. Your screen should show LinReg $(ax+b)$. Press the VARS key and shift to YVARS and select option 1 and then option 1 again. This will put the exponential regression equation into your Y= feature. Press ENTER and the equation and correlation coefficient should appear. Note that in this case, $r = 0.994\ 58$, which means that the data fits nearly perfectly to a linear model. Once this has been established, you can press graph and watch as the graph of the equation passes nearly through the centre of all points in the data.

(As an aside, you can perform an exponential regression by pressing STAT and then moving over to CALC and selecting option 0. Press the VARS key and shift to YVARS and select option 1 and then option 1 again. Press ENTER and a correlation coefficient should appear stating that $r = 0.994\ 57$. Comparing the two, linear regression is better, but only very slightly.)

To determine when the lean would have reached 2.98 m, it is necessary to graph $y = 2.98$ and find the point of intersection between that line and the curve you just graphed from the linear regression.

To find the point of intersection, press [2nd] [CALC] on your TI-83+, select option 5 and move the cursor until it lies on the point of intersection, then press [ENTER]. Press [ENTER] 2 more times and the coordinates of the point are given. The coordinates of the point are (1993.3, 2.98). Since in 1993.3, the tower's lean reached 2.98 m, it was not until the START of 1994 that the tower's lean exceeded 2.98 m and therefore alternative **B** is correct.

OR2.

If the ball's path is simply being measured as it rises and then falls to the ground, either a quadratic or sinusoidal curve might be appropriate. The student may have chosen a sinusoidal model because of the apparent similarities between a ball rising, hitting the ground, bouncing up again, falling, and so forth. However, it is important to note that the ball will never rise up to the height it previously reached and therefore it will not actually model a sinusoidal curve indefinitely. The problem does not exactly state why the student concluded that a sinusoidal regression model would be best, but certainly by performing quadratic and sinusoidal regressions on the data, it would become more clear which is the better choice.

UNIT TEST—CHARACTERISTICS OF FUNCTIONS

Use the following information to answer the next question.

A vehicle is driving down the highway.
The following table shows the vehicle's speed at five times throughout the journey.

Time (P.M.)	Speed (km/h)
2:00	100
3:00	120
4:00	0
5:00	110
6:00	110

1. The net acceleration of the vehicle was zero between

A. 2:00 P.M. and 3:00 P.M.

B. 3:00 P.M. and 4:00 P.M.

C. 4:00 P.M. and 5:00 P.M.

D. 5:00 P.M. and 6:00 P.M.

2. A cylindrical hot tub is being filled by a hose that gives out water at a constant rate of 0.25 m^3/min. At 8:00 P.M. , the volume of water in the pool was 8 m^3. If the length of the hot tub's radius is 2 m, the average rate of change of the radius of the hot tub with respect to its height between 9:00 P.M. and 10:00 P.M. is:

A. 0 m/min

B. 0.7 m/min

C. 2 m/min

D. 4 m/min

3. Which of the following graphs represents the number of daylight hours as a function of calendar date for Ottawa, Ontario?

A.

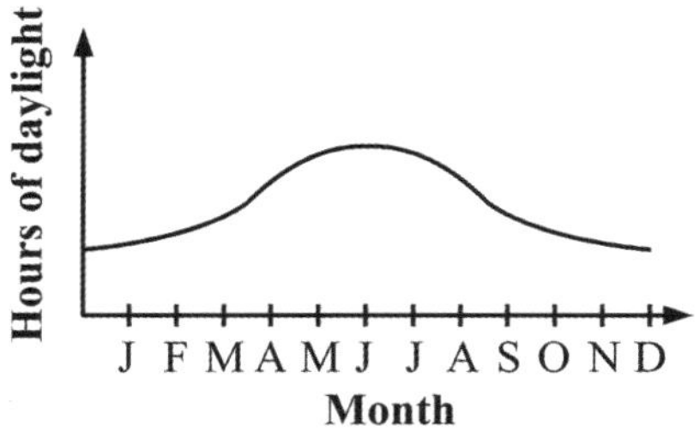

B.

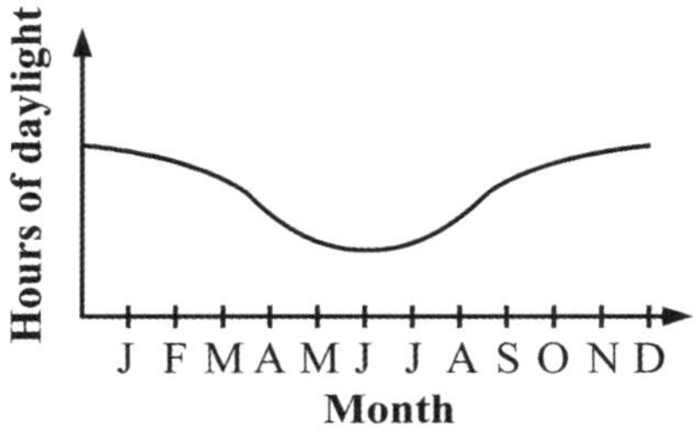

C.

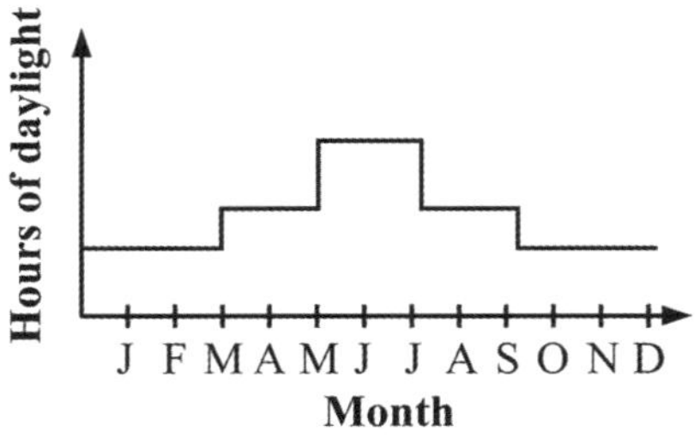

D.

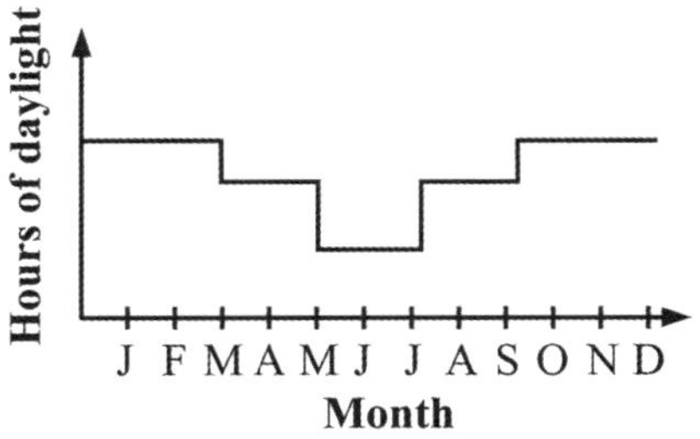

4. A ball is kicked off the roof of a 35 m tall building at a speed of 10 m/s. The height of the ball is defined by the function $h(t) = -4.9t^2 + 10t + 35$, where h is the height of the ball in metres and t is the time in seconds. During which of the following intervals of time is the average rate of change of the ball's height the greatest?

A. 0 to 0.5 s **B.** 0.5 to 1 s

C. 1 to 1.5 s **D.** 1.5 to 2 s

5. Which of the following situations describes an instantaneous rate of change?

A. When a baseball comes into contact with a bat, its speed is 36 m/s.

B. On July 16th, between 8 a.m. and 10 a.m., the ocean's tide caused the surf to recede by 2 m.

C. A meteorologist correctly predicts that the increase in temperature, over the course of an afternoon, will be 8 °C.

D. A runner in a marathon completes the race in 3.5 hours and determines his race pace to be 5 min/km.

Use the following graph to answer the next question.

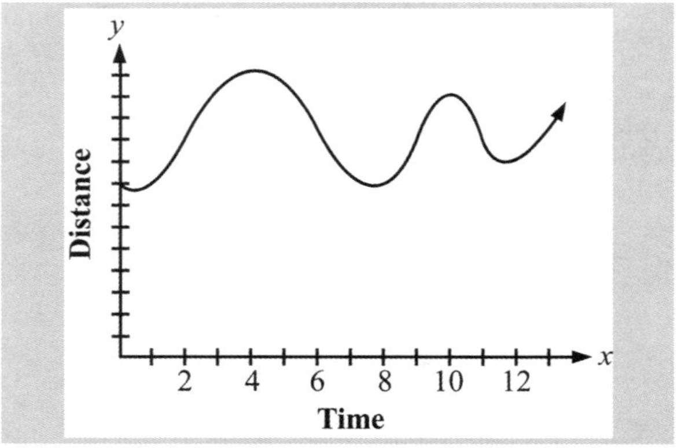

6. Which of the following intervals of time could be used to give the best approximation for the instantaneous rate of change of the function at $t = 4$ for this graph?

A. 0 – 2 **B.** 2 – 5

C. 7 – 9 **D.** 11 – 12

Open Response

OR1. The velocity of a child's toy car is defined by the function $v = 3t^2 = 2t$, where v is the velocity in metres per second and t is the time in seconds. Approximate the instantaneous rate of change of the car's velocity when $t = 3$.

Use the following information to answer the next question.

Jason, a math student, was told that the average rate of change between a continuous function's two minimum values is zero. He then concluded that the instantaneous rate of change of the function at any point between minimas must also be zero. Four of Jason's peers evaluated his conclusion and made the following remarks.

Jason has an insufficient amount of information to draw any type of conclusion.

The only place between the intervals that could yield an instantaneous rate of change of zero would be at the maximum that must exist between the two minimas.

Jason's conclusion is reasonable because average rates of change are accurate representations of instantaneous rates of change at any given point within the interval.

Jason's conclusion is impossible because between the two minimas, the function's value increases, thereby ensuring instantaneous rates of change greater than zero.

7. Which of Jason's peer's remarks are true?

A. I and II

B. I and III

C. II and III

D. II and IV

8. For which of the following graphs will the instantaneous rate of change equal the average rate of change for all values in the domain?

A.

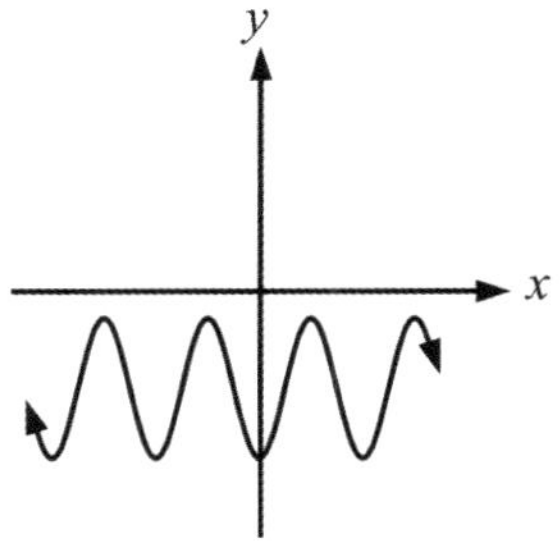

B.

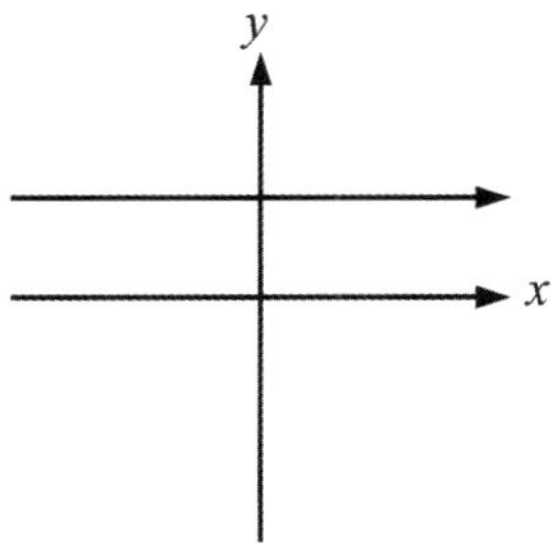

C.

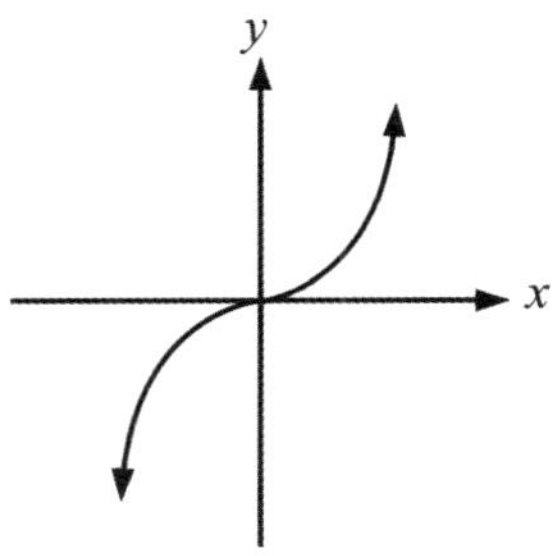

D.

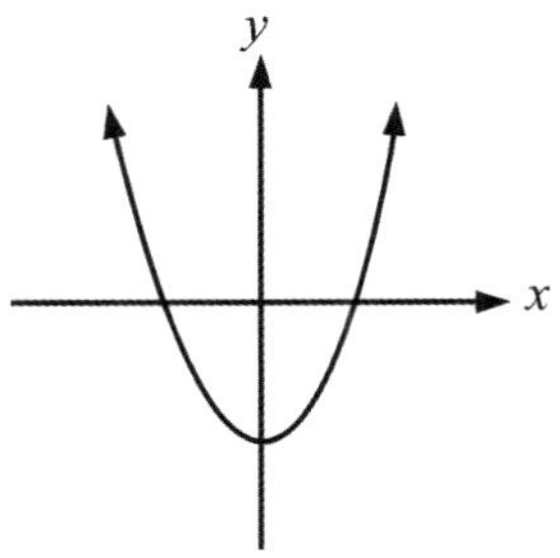

9. The volume of water in a water balloon can be calculated using the formula $V = \frac{4}{3}\pi r^3$ where r is the radius of the balloon in metres. To the nearest tenth, the approximate instantaneous rate of change of the balloon's volume with respect to its radius when the radius of the balloon is 0.6 m is:

A. 0.96 m^3/m

B. 3.7 m^3/m

C. 4.5 m^3/m

D. 5.3 m^3/m

10. The function $f(x) = x^2$ multiplied by which of the following functions will yield an even function?

A. $g(x) = \frac{1}{x^2}$

B. $g(x) = \frac{1}{x^3}$

C. $g(x) = x^5$

D. $g(x) = x - 4$

11. The graphs of the functions $h(x)$ and $m(x)$ are shown below.

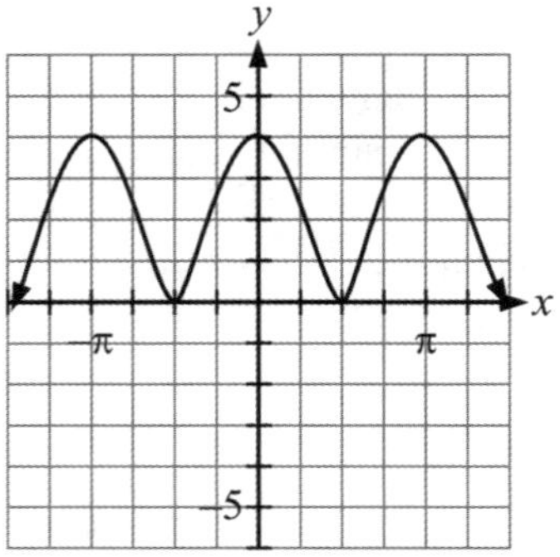

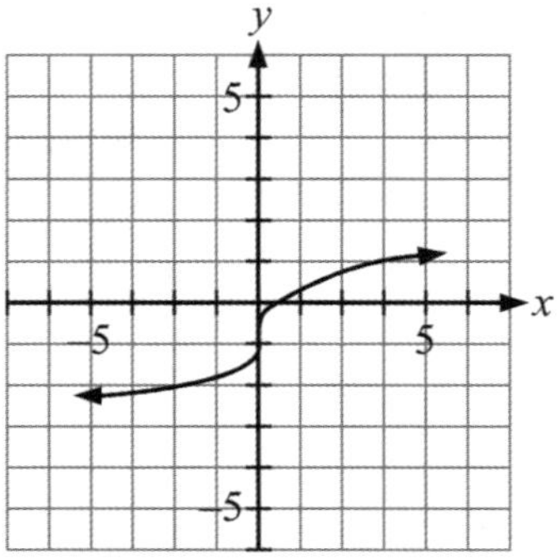

The value of is:

A. 0

B. 1

C. 2

D. 4

Numerical Response

NR1. A real estate investor recently purchased a home for $250,000. His plan is to rent out the house by charging enough to break even with the cost of interest and property taxes, which are $1 500 annually. The amount of annual interest charged is $I(r) = 250\,000r$ where r is the annual interest rate.
The monthly lease amount, L, is determined by $L(I) = \frac{I + 1\,500}{12}$. If the investor just accepted a lease offer of $1480 per month, the annual rate of interest, to the nearest tenth of a percentage is ______.

12. Two functions are given as $f(x) = \sqrt{x}$ and $g(x) = x - 7$. What are the ranges of the functions $f(g(x))$ and $g(f(x))$?

A. Range of $f(g(x)): \{y \mid y \geq 0,\ y \in R\}$

Range of $g(f(x)): \{y \mid y \geq 7,\ y \in R\}$

B. Range of $f(g(x)): \{y \mid y \geq 7,\ y \in R\}$

Range of $g(f(x)): \{y \mid y \geq 0,\ y \in R\}$

C. Range of $f(g(x)): \{y \mid y \geq D,\ y \in R$

Range of $g(f(x)): \{y \mid y \geq -7,\ y \in R\}$

D. Range of $f(g(x)): \{y \mid y \geq -7,\ y \in R\}$

Range of $g(f(x)): \{y \mid y \geq 0,\ y \in R\}$

13. Two functions are defined as $f(x) = 2x^2 - 3x - 1$ and $g(x) = x - 2$. The value of $f(g(-3))$ is

A. 24

B. 40

C. 52

D. 64

14. The percentage of the sun's ultraviolet light, l, that penetrates sunscreen with protection factor f is given by $l(f)=\frac{100}{f}$.

Some parents use the formula $f(a)=50(0.96)^a$, where a is the age of their child, to determine which sunscreen to purchase. Based on this method, what percentage of the sun's ultraviolet light will penetrate the sunscreen on the body of a 6-year-old?

A. 0.08%

B. 0.35%

C. 2.6%

D. 16.7%

15. For which of the following functions, f, would the statement $f\left(f^{-1}(x)\right)=x$ not hold true?

A. $f(x)=x^2$

B. $f(x)=\sqrt{x}$

C. $f(x)=5x-9$

D. $f(x) = 5x - 9$

16. The graph of $h(x) = \log x$ a vertical asymptote at $x=0$. The equation of the vertical asymptote for $h(f(x))$, where $f(x)=2x-3$, is

A. $x=-3$

B. $x=-\frac{3}{2}$

C. $x=\frac{3}{2}$

D. $x=3$

17. Three of the following four functions will have identical graphs in the domain $-\pi \le x \le \pi$. Which of the functions has a different graph?

A. $y=\sin(8x)$

B. $y=\cos(8x)\tan(8x)$

C. $y=2\sin(4x)\cos(4x)$

D. $y=4\sin(2x)\cos(2x)\left(\cos^2(2x)-\sin^2(2x)\right)$

18. The solution to the inequality $\log(2x - 1) \ge 2x - 5$ log is

A. $x>2.5$

B. $x\ge 2.5$

C. $0.5 < x \le 2.5$

D. $0.5 \le x \le 2.5$

Numerical Response

NR2. The solutions to the equation $\log(x^2)=\frac{1}{x-5}$ can be expressed as $x=a, x=b,$ and $x=c$, where a, b, and c are real numbers. The sum $a+b+c$, to the nearest hundredth, is ______.

Use the following information to answer the next question.

The table of values below gives data on a dog's distance from his water dish with respect to time.

Time (s)	Distance (m)
0	5
2	15
4	21
6	23

19. Which regression model would be most appropriate for finding the line/curve of best fit?

A. Linear

B. Quadratic

C. Sinusoidal

D. Exponential

ANSWERS AND SOLUTIONS—UNIT TEST CHARACTERISTICS OF FUNCTIONS

1. D	**OR1. See Solution**	**NR1. 6.5**	**17. B**
2 A	**7. D**	**12. C**	**18. C**
3. A	**8. B**	**13. A**	**NR2. 5.61**
4. A	**9. C**	**14. C**	**19. B**
5. A	**10. A**	**15. A**	
6. C	**11. B**	**16. C**	

1. **D**

Acceleration is defined as the rate of change of speed. Using the ratio $\frac{f(x_2)-f(x_1)}{x_2-x_1}$, calculate the acceleration for each interval of time.

Between 2:00 and 3:00:

$$\frac{120-100}{3-2}=\frac{20}{1}=20$$

Between 3:00 and 4:00:

$$\frac{0-120}{4-3}=\frac{-120}{1}=-120$$

Between 4:00 and 5:00:

$$\frac{110-0}{5-4}=\frac{110}{1}=110$$

Between 5:00 and 6:00:

$$\frac{110-110}{6-5}=\frac{0}{1}=0$$

The net acceleration of the vehicle was zero between 5:00 P.M. and 6:00 P.M.

2. **A**

Since the radius of the hot tub is fixed at 2 m, it will not change regardless of the height of the water. Since the radius is not changing the rate of change of the radius with respect to its height will be 0 m/m.

$$\frac{r_2-r_1}{h_2-h_1}=\frac{2-2}{h_2-h_1}=\frac{0}{h_2-h_1}=0\text{ m/m}.$$

3. **A**

The number of daylight hours as a function of calendar date is typically a sinusoidal function. The graph begins with a curve that increases as each month passes, which corresponds to increasing daylight from winter to spring months. This curve will increase until it reaches the longest day of the year, June 21. At this point, the graph will begin to curve downward as daylight hours begin decreasing during the months from summer to winter. Therefore, the graph that represents the number of daylight hours as a function of calendar date for Ottawa, Ontario, is graph **A**.

4. **A**

Calculate the average rate of change for each interval. For ease of calculation, begin by determining the heights at each given time:

$$h(0)=-4.9(0)^2+10(0)+35=35\text{ m}$$

$$h(0.5)=-4.9(0.5)^2+10(0.5)+35$$
$$=38.775\text{ m}$$

$$h(1)=-4.9(1)^2+10(1)+35=40.1\text{ m}$$

$$h(1.5)=-4.9(1.5)^2+10(1.5)+35$$
$$=38.975\text{ m}$$

$$h(2)=-4.9(2)^2+10(2)+35=35.4\text{ m}$$

Using the ratio $\frac{h_2-h_1}{t_2-t_1}$, calculate the average rate of change.

From 0 to 0.5 s:
$$\frac{h(0.5)-h(0)}{0.5-0}=\frac{38.775-35}{0.5}=\frac{3.775}{0.5}$$
$=7.55$ m/s
From 0.5 to 1 s:
$$\frac{h(1)-h(0.5)}{0.5-0}=\frac{40.1-38.775}{0.5}=\frac{1.325}{0.5}$$
$=2.65$ m/s
From 1 to 1.5 s:
$$\frac{h(1.5)-h(1)}{0.5-0}=\frac{38.975-40.1}{0.5}=\frac{-1.125}{0.5}$$
$=-2.25$ m/s
From 1.5 to 2 s:
$$\frac{h(2)-h(1.5)}{0.5-0}=\frac{35.4-38.975}{0.5}=\frac{-3.575}{0.5}$$
$=-7.15$ m/s
Therefore, the average rate of change of the ball's height is the greatest from 0 to 0.5 s.

5. **A**

The instantaneous rate of change of one quantity with respect to another is the rate of change at an instant in time. The correct situation must be describing the rate of change at a specific moment. When a baseball comes into contact with a bat, the speed is measured at that exact moment in time. The other situations each describe a rate of change over a given interval (average rate of change).

6. **C**

From the graph, the instantaneous rate of change at $t = 4$ is zero. Sketching the slopes for each of the given intervals, the best interval used for approximating the instantaneous rate of change at $t = 4$ is between 7 s and 9 s since the slope of the average rate of change is equal to zero.

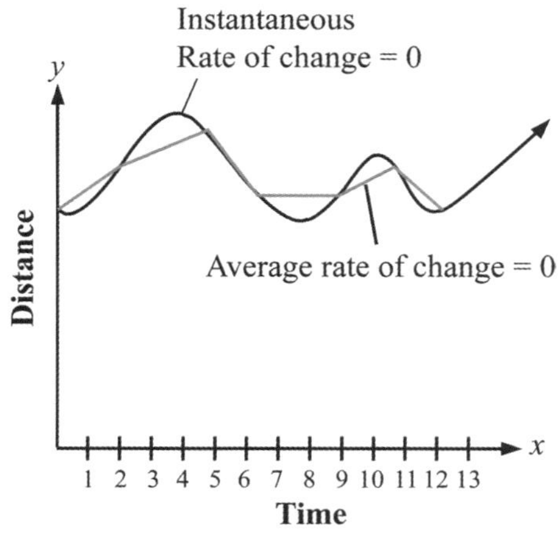

OR1.

To determine the instantaneous rate of change of the ball's height with respect to time at $t=3$ s, use the average rate of change ratio: $\dfrac{v(t_2)-v(t_1)}{t_2-t_1}$

Begin by determining the average rate of change between 2.5 seconds and 3.5 seconds:
$$\frac{v(3.5)-v(2.5)}{3.5-2.5}$$
$$=\frac{\left(3(3.5)^2-2(3.5)\right)-\left(3(2.5)^2-2(2.5)\right)}{3.5-2.5}$$
$$\frac{29.75-13.75}{1}=16\text{ m/s}^2$$
Reducing the interval to 0.1 s about the time of 3 s gives:
$$\frac{v(3.1)-v(2.9)}{3.1-2.9}$$
$$=\frac{\left(3(3.1)^2-2(3.1)\right)-\left(3(2.9)^2-2(2.9)\right)}{3.1-2.9}$$
$$\frac{22.63-19.43}{0.2}=16\text{ m/s}^2$$
Using a very short time interval from 2.999 s to 3.001 s gives:
$$\frac{v(3.001)-v(2.999)}{3.001-2.999}$$
$$=\frac{\left(3(3.001)^2-2(3.001)\right)-\left(3(2.999)^2-2(2.999)\right)}{3.001-2.999}$$
$$\frac{21.016003-20.984003}{0.002}=16\text{ m/s}^2$$

Since each average rate of change calculation is the same value over decreasing intervals of time, the instantaneous rate of change of the car's velocity is 16 m/s^2.

7. **D**

Jason is told that the average rate of change between a continuous function's two minimum values is zero.
An example sketch is shown below.

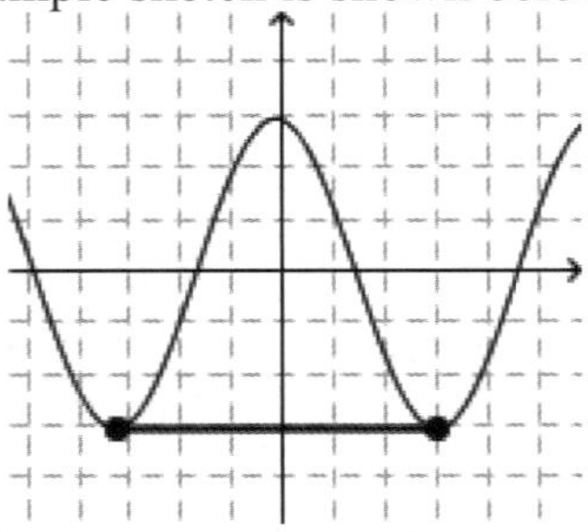

According to the sketch, Jason's conclusion is impossible because between the two minimas, the function's value increases and decreases, ensuring instantaneous rates of change greater than zero. The only place between the intervals that could yield an instantaneous rate of change of zero would be at the maximum that must exist between the two minimas.
Therefore, the answer is alternative **D**.

8. **B**

The instantaneous rate of change will equal the average rate of change for all values in the domain if the slope of the tangent and the slope of the secant are equal for all points in the domain.
In graph B, both the slope of the tangent and the slope of the secant are equal to zero since the function is a horizontal line.

9. **C**

To approximate the instantaneous rate of change (the slope of the tangent line), use a secant line with one point at $r = 0.6$ m and the other at a point very close to $r = 0.6$ m.
Using r = 0.5999 m, gives:

$$\frac{V(0.6)-V(0.5999)}{0.6-0.5999}$$

$$=\frac{\left(\frac{4}{3}\pi(0.6)^3\right)-\left(\frac{4}{3}\pi(0.5999)^3\right)}{0.0001}$$

$$=4.5231\text{m}^3/\text{m}$$

Using $r = 0.6001$ m, gives:

$$\frac{V(0.6001)-V(0.6)}{0.6001-0.6}$$

$$=\frac{\left(\frac{4}{3}\pi(0.6001)^3\right)-\left(\frac{4}{3}\pi(0.6)^3\right)}{0.0001}$$

$$=4.5247\text{m}^3/\text{m}$$

Thus, to the nearest tenth, the instantaneous rate of change of the balloon's volume with respect to its radius when the radius of the balloon is 0.6 is 4.5 m^3/m.

Verifying graphically using a TI-83 calculator by having the calculator draw the tangent line at $r = 0.6$ m.

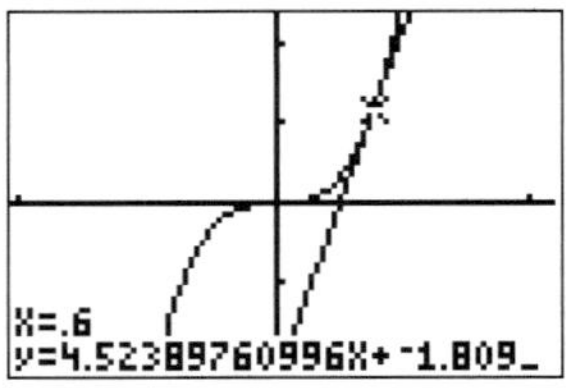

The calculator shows an equation of $y = 4.52x - 1.809$ verifying the slope of 4.5 m^3/m.

10. **A**

Recall that the product of two even functions is also even. Since $f(x)=x^2$ is even, it is necessary to look for another even function among the alternatives. Alternative **A** is the only even function among the given alternatives.

11. **B**

To evaluate $m(h(\pi))$, first find $h(\pi)=4$. Then, determine $m(4)=1$.

Since $m(h(\pi))=m(4)=1$, the correct answer is **B**.

NR1. **6.5**

In this question, you are given a composition of functions and are asked to work backward. Using the function $L(I)=\dfrac{I+1500}{12}$, where L is the monthly lease amount and I is the amount of interest charged annually, replace L with \$1480 (the recently accepted monthly lease offer) to calculate I.

$$1480=\frac{I+1500}{12}$$
$$12\times1480=I+1500$$
$$17760=I+1500$$
$$16260=I$$

The annual amount of interest, I, is \$16 260. For the annual interest amount to work out to \$16 260, the annual interest rate must be:

$$16260=250000r$$
$$\frac{16260}{250000}=r$$
$$0.065=r$$

Therefore the annual interest rate would be 6.5%.

12. **C**

First find $f(g)x))=f(x-7)=\sqrt{x-7}$.

Any function defined by a single square root is limited to values greater than or equal to zero. Therefore, the range of $f(g(x))$ is $y\geq0$.

Next, find $g(f)x))=g(\sqrt{x})=\sqrt{x}-7$.

In this case, the single square root is translated 7 units down, and thus the value of the function can be any value greater than or equal to –7.Therefore, the range of $g(f(x))$ is $y\geq-7$.

13. **D**

To find $f(g(-3))$, first evaluate $g(-3)$.

$$g(-3)=-3-2$$
$$g(-3)=-5$$

Since $g(-3)=-5$, it is necessary to evaluate $f(g(-3))=f(-5)$.

$$f(-5)=2(-5)^2-3(-5)-1$$
$$f(-5)=2(25)+15-1$$
$$f(-5)-50+14$$
$$f(-5)=64=f(g(-3))$$

14. **C**

To start, determine the protection factor, *f*, required for a 6-year-old according to the formula used by some parents.

$$f(6)=50(0.96)^6$$
$$f(6)=39.137$$

Assuming that sunscreen with a protection factor of 39.137 can be purchased, evaluate the percentage of the sun's ultra violetlight, *l*, that penetrates sunscreen with that particular protection factor.

$$l(39.137)=\frac{100}{39.137}$$
$$l(39.137)=2.555$$

Therefore, 2.6% of the sun's ultraviolet light would penetrate the sunscreen on the body of a 6-year-old.

15. **A**

Finding $f(f^{-1}(x))$ requires that $f(x)$ has an inverse to begin with. Therefore, all that is necessary is to determine which of the alternatives has no inverse.

Recall that a function must pass a vertical line test in order to be granted the name "function." Similarly, for a function to have an inverse, it must pass the horizontal line test, which states that if any horizontal line drawn through the given function passes through the graph of f more than once, *f* does NOT have an inverse. Similarly, if any horizontal line passes through the graph of *f* only once, it does have an inverse. Therefore, this problem can be solved by visualizing the graphs of all four alternatives and determining which function fails the horizontal line test.

A. $f(x)=x^2$ (Parabola, FAILS horizontal line test)

B. $f(x)=\sqrt{x}$ (curve, passes horizontal line test)

C. $f(x) - 5x - 9$, slanted, straight line, passes horizontal line test)

D. $f(x)=x^2$ (curve, passes horizontal line test)

Based on the results, observe that alternative A is the correct answer because as it is given (with no restriction on its domain), $f(x)=x^2$ has no inverse and therefore the statement $f\left(f^{-1}(x)\right)=x$ would not hold true.

Note: To eliminate the issue of a function not having an inverse, you can restrict the function's domain so that it passes the horizontal line test and thus has an inverse on the given domain of *f*.

16. **C**

The graph of $h(x)=\log x$ has a vertical asymptote at $x=0$ because $\log 0$ is undefined. If *x* is replaced by $2x-3$ in the composite function $h(f(x))$, where $f(x)=2x-3$, the result will be $h(2x-3)=\log(2x-3)$. Since $\log 0$ is undefined, the new location of the vertical asymptote will be defined by the value that makes $2x-3=0,\ x=\frac{3}{2}$.

17. **B**

In trigonometry, there are a number of identities that can be used to represent the same function, despite looking very different. In the question here, alternative A involves a double angle. Work with that throughout the remaining alternatives and compare the results by simplifying the functions in alternatives B, C, and D.

A. $y=\sin(8x)$ (Involves a double angle: $y=\sin(2g4x)$)

B. y = cos(8x)tan(8x) can be rewritten as $y=\cos(8x)\bullet\dfrac{\sin(8x)}{\cos(8x)}=\sin(8x)$.

However, in simplifying, keep in mind that the cos(8*x*) in the denominator cannot equal zero and thus the function's domain must be restricted accordingly. Therefore, this function will have holes wherever $\cos(8x)=0$, which is at $x=\frac{\pi}{16}\pm\frac{\pi n}{8}$.

C. $y=2\sin(4x)\cos(4x)$ can be simplified using the double- angle identity $\sin(2A)=2\sin(A)\cos(A)$. $y=\sin(2\bullet 4x)=\sin(8x)$, which is equivalent to A and has no restrictions on the domain.

D. $y = 4\sin(2x)\cos(2x)$
$\times (\cos^1(2x)) - \sin^1 2(2x))$
can be further simplified as follows:
$y = 2 (\sin(2x)\cos(2x))$
$\times (\cos 2(2x)(\cos^2(2x) - \sin^2(2x))$
Using the double-angle identities $\cos(2A) = \cos^2(A) - \sin^2(A)$ and $\sin(2A)$
$= 2\sin(A)\cos(A)$, y
$$= 2(2\sin(2x)\cos(2x))\begin{pmatrix}\cos^2(2x) \\ -\sin^2(2x)\end{pmatrix}$$
can be expressed as
$y = 2(\sin(4x))(\cos(4x))$,
which is the same equation as in alternative C. Therefore,
$y = \sin(2 \times 4x) = \sin(8x)$
and once again, there are no restrictions on the domain. Therefore, the only graph that would differ would be the graph of the function in alternative B because of the holes that would appear every time the function was undefined.

18. **C**

Graphically solving an inequality begins in the same way as solving an equation. Graph the functions $y = \log(2x-1)$ and $y = 2^x - 5$ using a graphing calculator. Select a window setting that shows any and all points of intersection between the two curves. In this example, a standard window setting of $X:[-10, 10, 1]$, $Y:[-10, 10, 1]$ would be appropriate (the shortcut for this window setting is Zoom 6).
Note that these curves have only one point of intersection at (2.485, 0.599), which can be found by pressing [2nd] [CALC] on your TI-83+, then selecting OPTION 5 and moving the cursor until it lies on the point of intersection, then press [ENTER]. Press [ENTER] two more times and the coordinates of the point are given. However, it is necessary to find the interval(s) that make $y = \log(2x - 1)$ greater than or equal to $y = 2^x - 5$.
In other words, it is necessary to find the region in which the logarithmic function lies above the exponential function. It can be observed that this happens to the left of the intersection point.
Thus, only for values $x \le 2.5$ can the inequality be true. However, there is a vertical asymptote at $x = 0.5$ that must also be considered because the logarithmic function $y = \log(2x - 1)$ does not exist on $x \le 0.5$. Therefore, the true solution to the inequality is $0.5 < x \le 2.5$.

NR2. **5.61**

To graphically solve this equation, graph the functions $y = \log(x^2)$ and $y = \frac{1}{x-5}$ and find all three points of intersection. Begin by selecting a window that makes all three points visible such as *X*:[–3, 8, 1], *Y*:[–5,5, 1]. Looking at the graph, observe that the logarithmic function intersects the rational function 3 times as was indicated in the question. Using [2nd] [CALC] on your TI-83+, select OPTION 5 and move the cursor until it lies on one of the points of intersection, then press [ENTER]. Press [ENTER] 2 more times and the coordinates of the point are given. For the point farthest left, the coordinates are $(-0.821, -0.172)$. Repeat these steps to find the other two points: $(0.762, -0.236)$ and $(5.664, 1.506)$. Since the question asks for the sum of the 3 solutions, add up the three *x*-coordinates:

$-0.821 + 0.762 + 5.664 = 5.61$,

rounded to the nearest hundredth.

19. **B**

When trying to establish the equation of a line/curve of best fit, a good start is to plot the data and observe the behaviour of the points in order to decide which model(s) might be appropriate. This can be done by pressing STAT and then selecting OPTION 1. Put the values for Time in L1 and the values for Distance in L2. Then, go to [2nd] [Y =] and select OPTION 1. Press [ENTER] to turn on Plot 1. Clear out any equations from Y= and set an appropriate window (in this case X:[0,12,1], Y: [0,25,5] would be appropriate). Then press [GRAPH] and the points should appear.

For the data given, a scatter plot of the data shows that linear and exponential regression models would not be appropriate. The graph appears to be a parabola. Therefore, start with a quadratic regression.

Before you do the regression, however, make sure the Diagnostics are ON so that the value of the correlation coefficient is given. This will indicate the accuracy of the regression model (the closer the value is to 1 or –1, the better the equation fits the data). To do this, press [2nd] and then 0 and then the x^{-1} key. Scroll down to DiagnosticON. Press [ENTER] twice. When done correctly, your screen should say Done. Now, perform the quadratic regression. Press [STAT] and then move over to [CALC] and select OPTION 5.

Press enter and the equation and correlation coefficient should appear. Note that in this case, $R^2 = 1$, which means that the data fits perfectly to a quadratic model and thus **B** is the correct answer.

Key Strategies for Success on Tests

NOTES

TEST PREPARATION AND TEST-TAKING SKILLS

Things to Consider When Taking a Test

- It is normal to feel anxious before you write a test. You can manage this anxiety by:
    - thinking positive thoughts. Visual imagery is a helpful technique to try.
    - making a conscious effort to relax by taking several slow, controlled, deep breaths. Concentrate on the air going in and out of your body.
- Before you begin the test, ask questions if you are unsure of anything.
- Jot down key words or phrases from any oral directions.
- Look over the entire test to assess the number and kinds of questions on the test.
- Read each question closely and reread if necessary.
- Pay close attention to key vocabulary words. Sometimes these are bolded or italicized, and they are usually important words in the question.
- Mark your answers on your answer sheet carefully. If you wish to change an answer, erase the mark completely and then ensure your final answer is darker than the one you have erased.
- On the test booklet, use highlighting to note directions, key words, and vocabulary that you find confusing or that are important to answering the question.
- Double-check to make sure you have answered everything before handing in your test.

When taking tests, the easy words are often overlooked. Failure to pay close attention to these words can result in an incorrect answer. One way to avoid this is to be aware of these words and to underline, circle, or highlight these words while you are taking the test.

Even though some words are easy to understand, they can change the meaning of the entire question, so it is important that you pay attention to them. Here are some examples.

all	**always**	**most likely**	**probably**	**best**	**not**
difference	**usually**	**except**	**most**	**unlikely**	**likely**

Example

1. Which of the following equations is **not** correct?

A. $3 + 2 = 5$

B. $4 - 3 = 1$

C. $5 \times 4 = 15$

D. $6 \times 3 = 18$

Helpful Strategies for Answering Multiple-Choice Questions

A multiple-choice question provides some information for you to consider and then asks you to select a response from four choices. Each question has one correct answer. The other answers are distractors, which are incorrect.

Below are some strategies to help you when answering multiple-choice questions.

- Quickly skim through the entire test. Find out how many questions there are and plan your time accordingly.
- Read and reread questions carefully. Underline key words and try to think of an answer before looking at the choices.
- If there is a graphic, look at the graphic, read the question, and go back to the graphic. Then, you may want to underline the important information from the question.
- Carefully read the choices. Read the question first and then each answer that goes with it.
- When choosing an answer, try to eliminate those choices that are clearly wrong or do not make sense.
- Some questions may ask you to select the best answer. These questions will always include words like **best**, **most appropriate**, or **most likely**. All of the answers will be correct to some degree, but one of the choices will be better than the others in some way. Carefully read all four choices before choosing the answer you think is the best.
- If you do not know the answer or if the question does not make sense to you, it is better to guess than to leave it blank.
- Do not spend too much time on any one question. Make a mark (*) beside a difficult question and come back to it. If you are leaving a question to come back to later, make sure you also leave the space on the answer sheet.
- Remember to go back to the difficult questions at the end of the test; sometimes clues are given throughout the test that will provide you with answers.
- Note any negative words like **no** or **not** and be sure your choice fits the question.
- Before changing an answer, *be sure* you have a very good reason to do so.
- Do not look for patterns on your answer sheet.

Helpful Strategies for Answering Open-Response Questions

A written response requires you to respond to a question or directive such as **explain**, **predict**, **list**, **describe**, **show your work**, **solve**, or **calculate.** In preparing for open-response tasks you may wish to:

- Read and reread the question carefully.
- Recognize and pay close attention to **directing words** such as **explain**, **show your work**, **and describe**.
- Underline key words and phrases that indicate what is required in your answer, such as explain, estimate, answer, calculate, or show your work.
- Write down rough, point-form notes regarding the information you want to include in your answer.
- Think about what you want to say and organize information and ideas in a coherent and concise manner within the time limit you have for the question.
- Be sure to answer every part of the question that is asked.
- Include as much information as you can when you are asked to explain your thinking.
- Include a picture or diagram if it will help to explain your thinking.
- Try to put your final answer to a problem in a complete sentence to be sure it is reasonable.
- Reread your response to ensure you have answered the question.
- **Think**: does your answer make sense
- **Listen**: does it sound right?
- Use appropriate subject vocabulary and terms in your response.

About Mathematics Tests

What You Need to Know about Mathematics Tests

To do well on a mathematics test, you need to understand and apply your knowledge of mathematical concepts. Reading skills can also make a difference in how well you perform. Reading skills can help you follow instructions and find key words, as well as read graphs, diagrams, and tables. They can also help you solve mathematics problems.

Mathematics tests usually have two types of questions: questions that ask for understanding of mathematics ideas and questions that test how well you can solve mathematics problems.

How You Can Prepare for the Mathematics Test

Below are some strategies that are particular to preparing for and writing mathematics tests.

- Know how to use your calculator and, if it is allowed, use your own for the test.
- Note-taking is a good way to review and study important information from your class notes and textbook.
- Sketch a picture of the problem, procedure, or term. Drawing is helpful for learning and remembering concepts.
- Check your answer to practice questions by working backward to the beginning. You can find the beginning by going step-by-step in reverse order.
- When answering questions with graphics (pictures, diagrams, tables, or graphs), read the test question carefully.
  - Read the title of the graphic and any key words.
  - Read the test question carefully to figure out what information you need to find in the graphic.
  - Go back to the graphic to find the information you need.
- Decide which operation is needed.
- Always pay close attention when pressing the keys on your calculator. Repeat the procedure a second time to be sure you pressed the correct keys.

TEST PREPARATION COUNTDOWN

There is little doubt that if you develop a plan for studying and test preparation, you *will* perform well on tests.

Below is a general plan to follow seven days before you write a test.

Countdown: 7 Days before the Test

1. Use "Finding Out About the Test" to help you make your own personal test preparation plan.
2. Review the following information:
   - areas to be included on the test
   - types of test items
   - general and specific test tips
3. Start preparing for the test at least 7 days before the test. Develop your test preparation plan and set time aside to prepare and study.

Countdown: 6, 5, 4, 3, 2 Days before the Test

1. Review old homework assignments, quizzes, and tests.
2. Rework problems on quizzes and tests to make sure you still know how to solve them.
3. Correct any errors made on quizzes and tests.
4. Review key concepts, processes, formulas, and vocabulary.
5. Create practice test questions for yourself and then answer them. Work out many sample problems.

Countdown: The Night before the Test

1. The night before the test is for final preparation, which includes reviewing and gathering material needed for the test before going to bed.
2. Most important is getting a good night's rest and knowing you have done everything possible to do well on the test.

Test Day

1. Eat a healthy and nutritious breakfast.
2. Ensure you have all the necessary materials.
3. Think positive thoughts: "I can do this." "I am ready." "I know I can do well."
4. Arrive at your school early so you are not rushing, which can cause you anxiety and stress.

Summary of How to be Successful During the Test

The following are some strategies you may find useful for writing your test.

- Take two or three deep breaths to help you relax.
- Read the directions carefully and underline, circle, or highlight any important words.
- Survey the entire test to understand what you will need to do.
- Budget your time.
- Begin with an easy question or a question you know you can answer correctly rather than following the numerical question order of the test.
- If you cannot remember how to answer a question, try repeating the deep breathing and physical relaxation activities first. Then, move to visualization and positive self-talk to get you going.
- Write down anything you remember about the subject on the reverse side of your test paper. This activity sometimes helps you to remind yourself that you *do* know something and you *are* capable of writing the test.
- Look over your test when you have finished and double-check your answers to be sure you did not forget anything.

Practice Tests

PRACTICE TESTS

Table of Correlations		
Specific Expectation	**Practice Test 1**	**Practice Test 2**
Exponential and Logarithmic Functions		
1.1 *recognize the logarithm of a number to a given base as the exponent to which the base must be raised to get the number, recognize the operation of finding the logarithm to be the inverse operation (i.e., the undoing or reversing) of exponentiation, and evaluate simple logarithmic expressions*	1	
1.4 *make connections between the laws of exponents and the laws of logarithms, verify the laws of logarithms with or without technology, and use the laws of logarithms to simplify and evaluate numerical expressions*		1
2.1 *determine, through investigation with technology and without technology, key features (i.e., vertical and horizontal asymptotes, domain and range, intercepts, increasing/decreasing behaviour) of the graphs of logarithmic functions of the form f(x) = log x, and make connections between the algebraic and graphical representations of these logarithmic functions*	2	2
2.3 *determine, through investigation using technology, the roles of the parameters d and c in functions of the form y = log (x – d) + c and the roles of the parameters a and k in functions of the form y = alog (kx), and describe these roles in terms of transformations on the graph of (x) = log10x (i.e., vertical and horizontal translations; reflections in the axes; vertical and horizontal stretches and compressions to and from the x- and y-axes)*	3	3
2.4 *pose problems based on real-world applications of exponential and logarithmic functions, and solve these and other such problems by using a given graph or a graph generated with technology from a table of values or from its equation*	4	4
3.2 *solve exponential equations in one variable by determining a common base and by using logarithms, recognizing that logarithms base 10 are commonly used*	5, NR1	5, NR1
3.3 *solve simple logarithmic equations in one variable algebraically*	6	6
3.4 *solve problems involving exponential and logarithmic equations algebraically, including problems arising from real-world applications*	7, OR1	7, OR1

Trigonometric Functions		
1.1 *recognize the radian as an alternative unit to the degree for angle measurement, define the radian measure of an angle as the length of the arc that subtends this angle at the centre of a unit circle, and develop and apply the relationship between radian and degree measure*	8	
1.2 *represent radian measure in terms of π and as a rational number*		NR2
1.3 *determine, with technology, the primary trigonometric ratios (i.e., sine, cosine, tangent) and the reciprocal trigonometric ratios (i.e., cosecant, secant, cotangent) of angles expressed in radian measure*	NR2	8
1.4 *determine, without technology, the exact values of the primary trigonometric ratios and the reciprocal trigonometric ratios for the special angles 0[fractions missing] and their multiples less than or equal to 2π*		9
2.1 *sketch the graphs of f(x) = sin x and f(x) = cos x for angle measures expressed in radians, and determine and describe some key properties in terms of radians*	9	10
2.3 *graph, with technology and using the primary trigonometric functions, the reciprocal trigonometric functions (i.e., cosecant, secant, cotangent) for angle measures expressed in radians, determine and describe key properties of the reciprocal functions, and recognize notations used to represent the reciprocal functions*	10	11
2.4 *determine the amplitude, period, and phase shift of sinusoidal functions whose equations are given in the form f(x) = a sin (k(x – d)) + c or f(x) = a cos(k(x – d)) + c, with angles expressed in radians*	11	12
2.5 *sketch graphs of y = a sin (k(x – d)) + c and y = a cos(k(x – d)) + c by applying transformations to the graphs of f(x) = sin x and f(x) = cos x with angles expressed in radians, and state the period, amplitude, and phase shift of the transformed functions*	12	
2.7 *pose problems based on applications involving a trigonometric function with domain expressed in radians, and solve these and other such problems by using a given graph or a graph generated with or without technology from a table of values or from its equation*	13	13
3.2 *explore the algebraic development of the compound angle formulas, and use the formulas to determine exact values of trigonometric ratios*	14	14
3.3 *recognize that trigonometric identities are equations that are true for every value in the domain (i.e., a counter-example can be used to show that an equation is not an identity), prove trigonometric identities through the application of reasoning skills, using a variety of relationships, and verify identities using technology*	15, OR2	15
3.4 *solve linear and quadratic trigonometric equations, with and without graphing technology, for the domain of real values from 0 to 2π, and solve related problems*	16	16, OR2

Polynomial and Rational Functions		
1.2 *compare, through investigation using graphing technology, the numeric, graphical, and algebraic representations of polynomial (i.e., linear, quadratic, cubic, quartic) functions (e.g., compare finite differences in tables of values; investigate the effect of the degree of a polynomial function on the shape of its graph and the maximum number of x-intercepts; investigate the effect of varying the sign of the leading coefficient on the end behaviour of the function for very large positive or negative x-values)*	17	
1.3 *describe key features of the graphs of polynomial functions*	18	17
1.5 *make connections, through investigation using graphing technology, between a polynomial function given in factored form and the x-intercepts of its graph, and sketch the graph of a polynomial function given in factored form using its key features*	19	18
1.6 *determine, through investigation using technology, the roles of the parameters a, k, d, and c in functions of the form y = a f (k(x – d)) + c, and describe these roles in terms of transformations on the graphs of f(x) = x and f(x) = x (i.e., vertical and horizontal translations; reflections in the axes; vertical and horizontal stretches and compressions to and from the x- and y-axes)*		19
1.7 *determine an equation of a polynomial function that satisfies a given set of conditions (e.g., degree of the polynomial, intercepts, points on the function), using methods appropriate to the situation, and recognize that there may be more than one polynomial function that can satisfy a given set of conditions*	20	20
2.1 *determine, through investigation with and without technology, key features (i.e., vertical and horizontal asymptotes, domain and range, intercepts, positive/negative intervals, increasing/decreasing intervals) of the graphs of rational functions that are the reciprocals of linear and quadratic functions, and make connections between the algebraic and graphical representations of these rational functions*		NR3
2.2 *determine, through investigation with and without technology, key features (i.e., vertical and horizontal asymptotes, domain and range, intercepts, positive/negative intervals, increasing/decreasing intervals) of the graphs of rational functions that have linear expressions in the numerator and denominator, and make connections between the algebraic and graphical representations of these rational functions*		21
3.1 *make connections, through investigation using technology, between the polynomial function f(x), the divisor x – a, the remainder from the division [fraction missing] and f(a) to verify the remainder theorem and the factor theorem*	21	22
3.2 *factor polynomial expressions in one variable, of degree no higher than four, by selecting and applying strategies (i.e., common factoring, difference of squares, trinomial factoring, factoring by grouping, remainder theorem, factor theorem)*	22	
3.3 *determine, through investigation using technology, the connection between the real roots of a polynomial equation and the x-intercepts of the graph of the corresponding polynomial function, and describe this connection*		23
3.4 *solve polynomial equations in one variable, of degree no higher than four, by selecting and applying strategies (i.e., common factoring, difference of squares, trinomial factoring, factoring by grouping, remainder theorem, factor theorem), and verify solutions using technology*	23, OR3	24

3.5 *determine, through investigation using technology (e.g., graphing calculator, computer algebra systems), the connection between the real roots of a rational equation and the x-intercepts of the graph of the corresponding rational function, and describe this connection*	24	
3.6 *solve simple rational equations in one variable algebraically, and verify solutions using technology*	NR3	25
3.7 *solve problems involving applications of polynomial and simple rational functions and equations*	25	OR3
4.2 *determine solutions to polynomial inequalities in one variable and to simple rational inequalities in one variable by graphing the corresponding functions, using graphing technology, and identifying intervals for which x satisfies the inequalities*	26	26
4.3 *solve linear inequalities and factorable polynomial inequalities in one variable in a variety of ways, and represent the solutions on a number line or algebraically*	27	27

Characteristics of Functions		
1.2 *recognize that the rate of change for a function is a comparison of changes in the dependent variable to changes in the independent variable, and distinguish situations in which the rate of change is zero, constant, or changing by examining applications, including those arising from real-world situations*	28	28
1.3 *sketch a graph that represents a relationship involving rate of change, as described in words, and verify with technology when possible*		29
1.6 *determine, through investigation using various representations of relationships, approximate instantaneous rates of change arising from real-world applications by using average rates of change and reducing the interval over which the average rate of change is determined*		30
1.8 *determine, through investigation using a variety of tools and strategies, the approximate slope of the tangent to a given point on the graph of a function by using the slopes of secants through the given point, and make connections to average and instantaneous rates of change*	29	31
1.9 *solve problems involving average and instantaneous rates of change, including problems arising from real-world applications, by using numerical and graphical methods*	30	

2.3 *determine, through investigation, and explain some properties (i.e., odd, even, or neither; increasing/decreasing behaviours) of functions formed by adding, subtracting, multiplying, and dividing general functions*	31	32
2.4 *determine the composition of two functions [i.e., f(g(x))] numerically (i.e., by using a table of values) and graphically, with technology, for functions represented in a variety of ways, and interpret the composition of two functions in real-world applications*		33
2.5 *determine algebraically the composition of two functions [i.e., f(g(x))], verify that f(g(x)) is not always equal to g(f(x)), and state the domain [i.e., by defining f(g(x)) for those x-values for which g(x) is defined and for which it is included in the domain of f(x)] and the range of the composition of two functions*	32	
2.6 *solve problems involving the composition of two functions, including problems arising from real-world applications*	33	
2.8 *make connections, through investigation using technology, between transformations (i.e., vertical and horizontal translations; reflections in the axes; vertical and horizontal stretches and compressions to and from the x- and y-axes) of simple functions f(x) [e.g., f(x) = x + 20, f(x) = sin x, f(x) = log x] and the composition of these functions with a linear function of the form g(x) = A(x + B)*		34
3.2 *solve graphically and numerically equations and inequalities whose solutions are not accessible by standard algebraic techniques*	NR4	NR4
3.3 *solve problems, using a variety of tools and strategies, including problems arising from real-world applications, by reasoning with functions and by applying concepts and procedures involving functions*	OR4	35

PRACTICE TEST 1

1. The expression $4\log_b 2b - \log_b(1.6b)$, where $b > 0$, $b \neq 1$, is equivalent to the expression

   A. $\log_b 14.4 + 3$

   B. $\log_b 3.75 + 3$

   C. $\log_b 10 + \log_b 3$

   D. $\log_b 10 + 3$

2. Which of the following statements about the graphs of $y = \log_2 x$ and $y = 2\log x$ is **true**?

   A. Both graphs are exactly the same.

   B. One of the graphs shows a greater domain.

   C. Both graphs have the same vertical asymptotes.

   D. Only one of the graphs comes into contact with the y-axis.

3. The graph of $y = \log_{\frac{1}{2}}(x - p) + q$ is translated 5 units to the right and 3 units up. The domain of the new function is

   A. $x > p + 5$ **B.** $x < p + 5$

   C. $x > p - 5$ **D.** $x < p - 5$

4. This year, Terry and Martha bought a property next to a lake in northern Ontario for \$48 000. The real estate agent who sold them the property told them they could expect the property to appreciate at a rate of 7.5% per year for the next 15 years. Use a graphical approach to determine the number of years, to the nearest year, until the property is worth at least \$96 000. The number of years is

   A. 5 **B.** 10

   C. 13 **D.** 14

5. The solution to $4^x \bullet 7^{x+1} = 2$ is

   A. $x = -\frac{1}{2}$

   B. $x = -\frac{\log 5}{\log 11}$

   C. $x = \frac{1}{2}\log 2 - \frac{1}{2}$

   D. $x = \frac{\log 2 - \log 7}{\log 4 + \log 7}$

Numerical Response

NR1. In the equation $2 = (1.045)^t$, t represents gives the number of years it takes for money to double when it is invested at 4.5% per year compounded annually. To the nearest year, $t =$ ____________.

6. The sum of the solution to $\log_2(6x - 8) = 4$ and the solution to $\log_3(12 - 3x) = 3$ is

   A. -1 **B.** 1

   C. 9 **D.** 12

7. Eric recently bought a new car for \$23 500. For the first 4 years, the car is expected to depreciate at a rate of 13% per year and for the following 5 years, the car is expected to depreciate at a rate of 9% per year. The expected value of the car, to the nearest dollar, exactly 7 years after purchase is

   A. \$8 067 **B.** \$8 401

   C. \$10 145 **D.** \$10 611

Open Response

OR1. In an orchestra two trumpets and a trombone all play the same note.
The two trumpets each play at a level of 60 decibels and the trombone plays at 55 decibels. What is the loudness in decibels of the total sound made by the three instruments? Give your answer to the nearest whole number.

8. A circle has a radius of 8 cm and an arc of this circle is 14 cm long. If this arc subtends angle θ, then the measure of angle θ, to the nearest tenth of a degree, is

A. 1.8°

B. 100.3°

C. 120.0°

D. 315.0°

Numerical Response

NR2. The value of $\cot\left(\frac{4}{\pi}\right)$, to the nearest tenth, is ____________.

9. The graph of $y = \cos x$ is equivalent to the graph of $y = \sin x$ translated

A. π radians left

B. π radians right

C. $\frac{\pi}{2}$ radians left

D. $\frac{\pi}{2}$ radians right

10. The range of the reciprocal of $y = \cos\theta$ is

A. $y \in R$

B. $-1 \le y \le 1$

C. $y \le -1$ or $y \ge 1$

D. $|y| \le 1$

11. If the function $y = a\sin(2\theta) - 3$ has a minimum value of -11, then the value of a is

A. 16 only

B. -11 or $+11$

C. -8 only

D. -8 or $+8$

12. Which of the following graphs is the graph of the function $y = -3\sin\left(x + \frac{\pi}{4}\right) - 3$?

A.

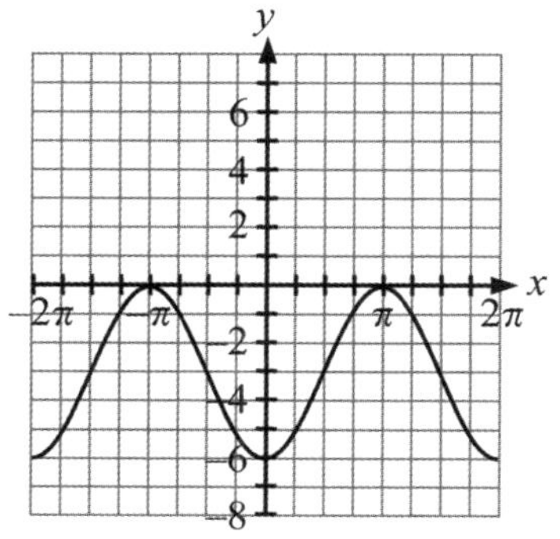

B.

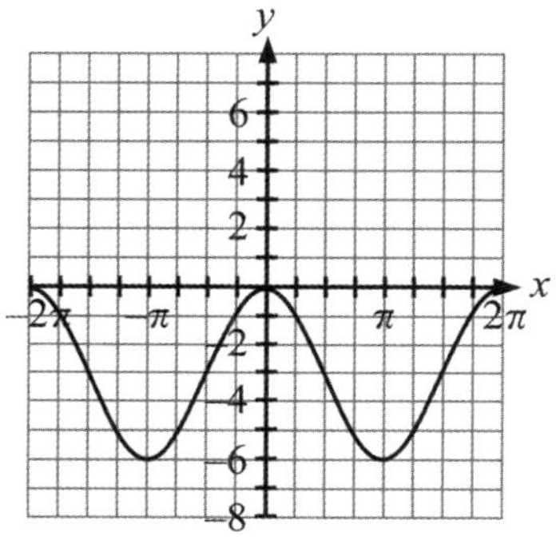

C.

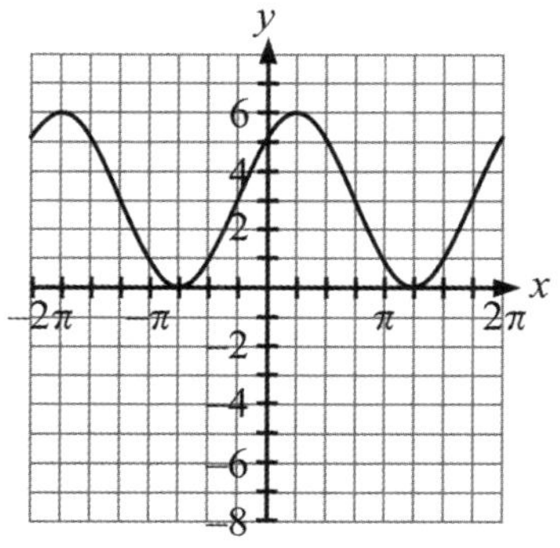

D.

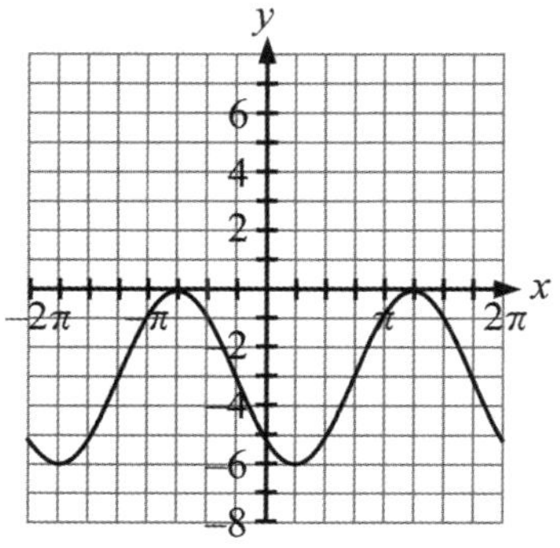

13. A piston in the engine of a particular car moves such that its height, $h(t)$, in centimetres, t seconds after the car is started is given by the function $h(t) = 12\sin\left(\frac{\pi t}{0.03}\right) + 15$. During the first 6 seconds after the car is started, the number of times that the piston is at a height of 20 cm is

A. 10

B. 11

C. 12

D. 13

14. When $\sin\left(\frac{\pi}{6} - x\right) + \cos\left(\frac{\pi}{3} - x\right)$ is simplified, it is equal to

A. $\cos x$

B. $\frac{1}{2}\cos x$

C. $\cos x + \sqrt{3}\sin x$

D. $\cos x - \sqrt{3}\sin x$

15. The expression $\frac{1 - \cos(2\theta)}{2}$ is equivalent to

A. $\frac{1}{2} - \cos\theta$

B. 0

C. $\sin^2\theta$

D. $\cos^2\theta$

Open Response

OR2. Given the identity $\frac{\cos(2x)+1}{\sin(2x)} = \cot x$,

a) verify the identity for $x = \frac{\pi}{6}$

b) verify the identity graphically over the interval by using technology

c) prove the identity algebraically

16. The complete solution set for the equation $2\cos\left(\frac{1}{2}x\right) - \cos\left(\frac{1}{2}x\right) = 0,\ 0 \le x \le 2\pi$, is

A. $\{0\}$

B. $\{0, \pi\}$

C. $\{0, \pi, 2\pi\}$

D. $\left\{0, \frac{\pi}{2}, \frac{3\pi}{2}, 2\pi\right\}$

17. Which of the following graphs represent the graph of a polynomial function of degree 4 with a negative leading coefficient?

A.

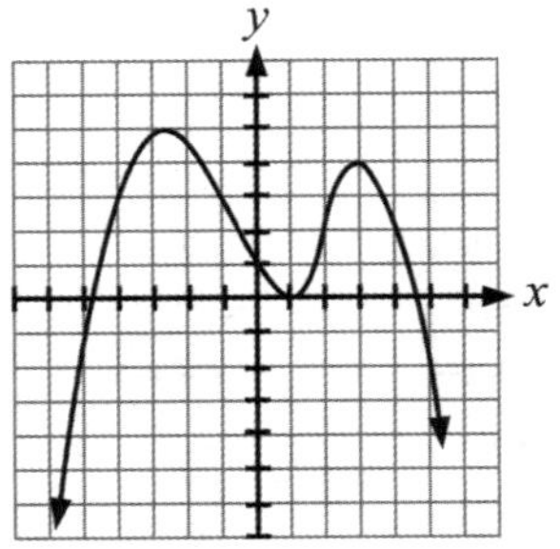

B.

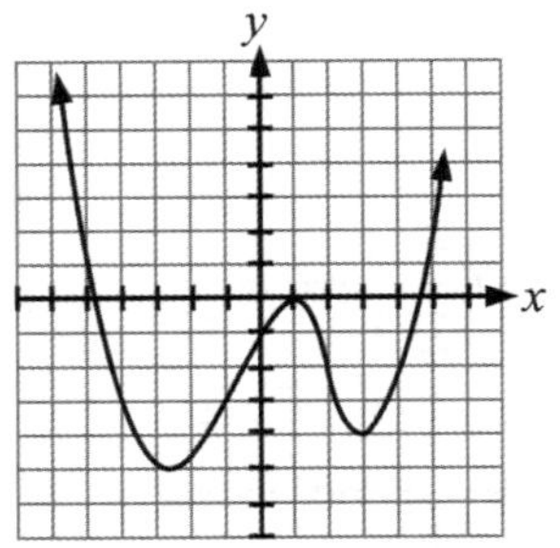

C.

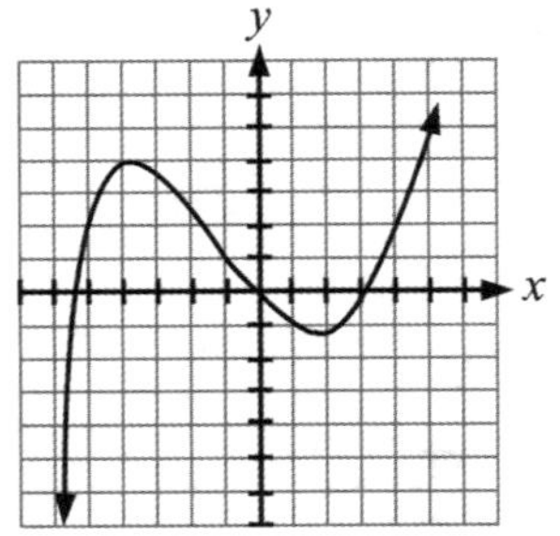

D.

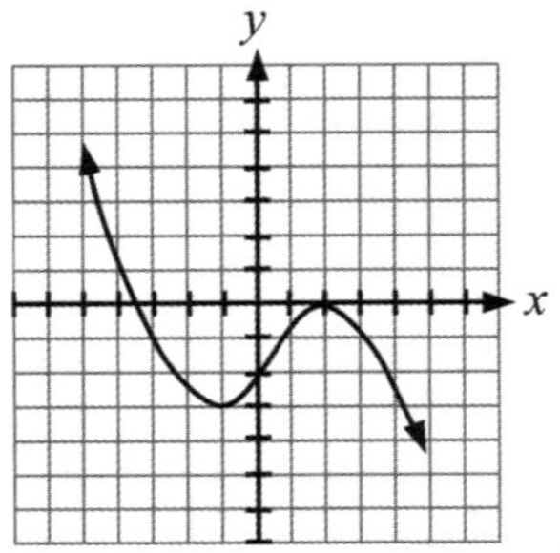

18. Which of the following graphs could represent the graph of a polynomial function whose domain is $x \in R$ and whose range is $y \geq -5$?

A.

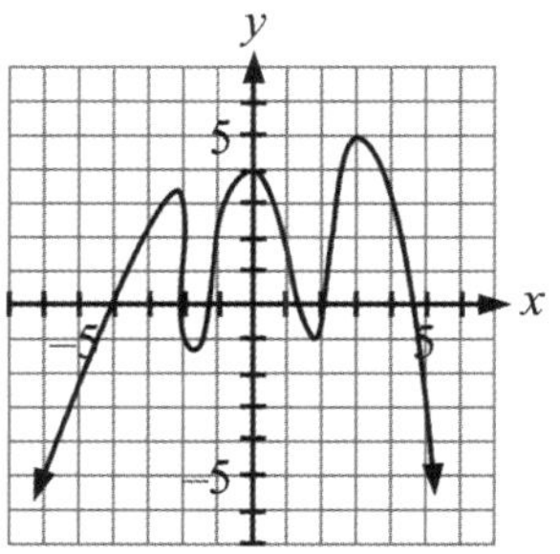

B.

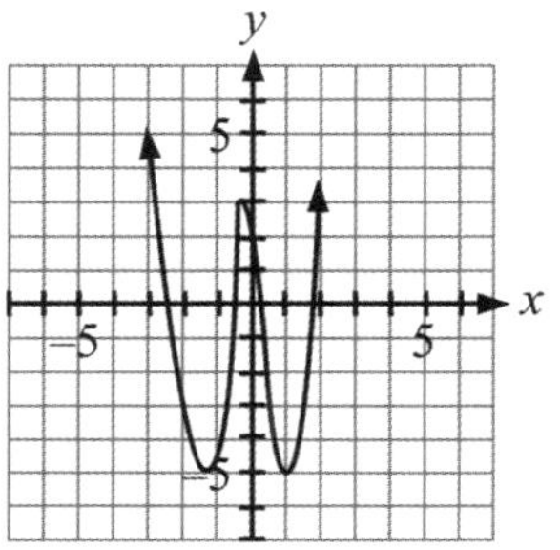

C.

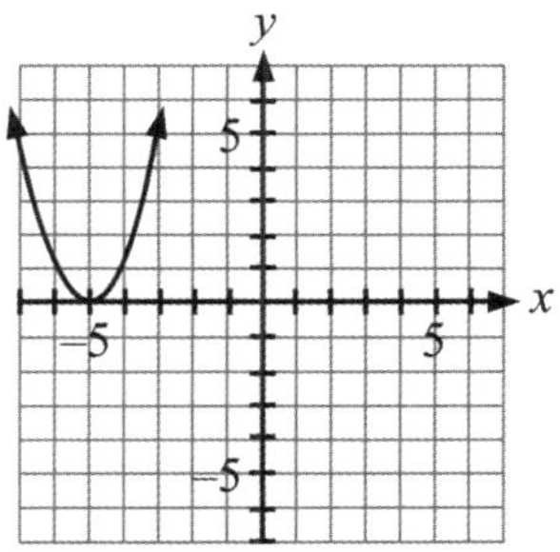

D.

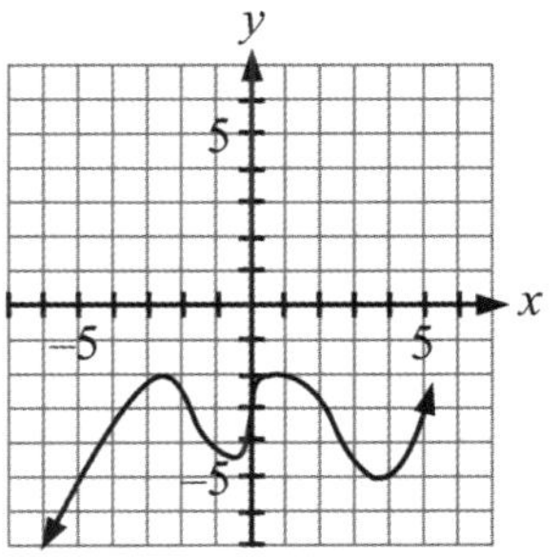

19. The x-intercepts of the graph of the polynomial function $p(x) = -5(x-3)(x-1)(x+4)^2$ are

A. –4, 1, 3 **B.** –3, –1, 4

C. –4, 1, 3, 4 **D.** –5, –3, –1, 4

20. The graph of a fourth-degree polynomial function has x-intercepts at –3, –1 and 2 only. Which of the following graphs is **not** a possible graph of this function?

A.

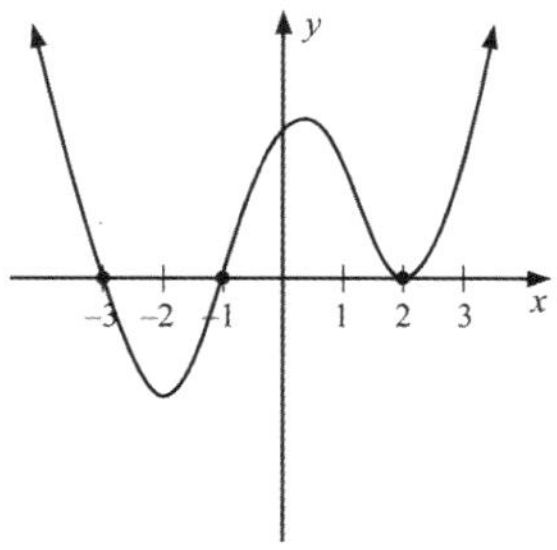

B.

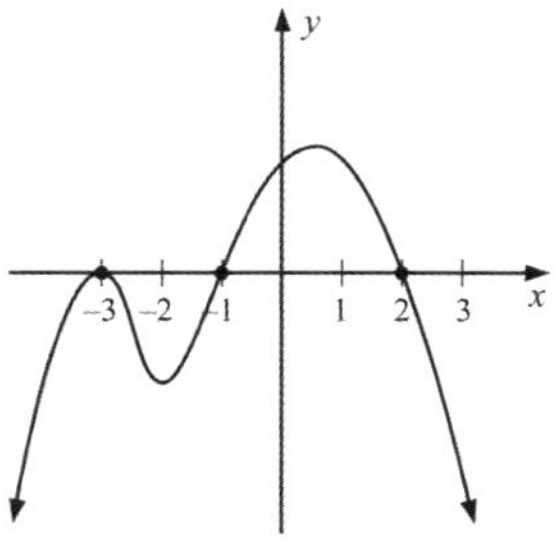

C.

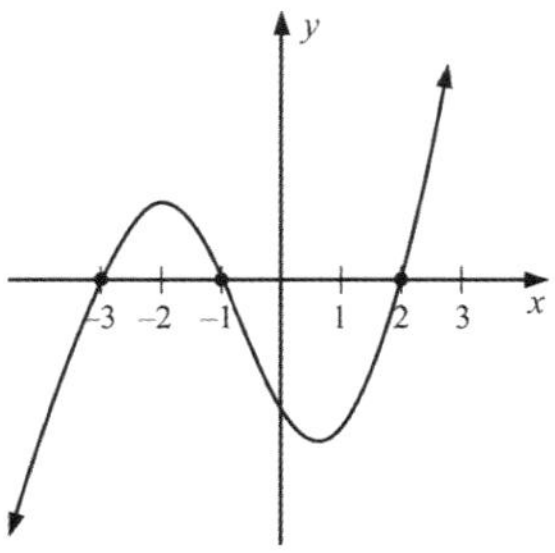

D.

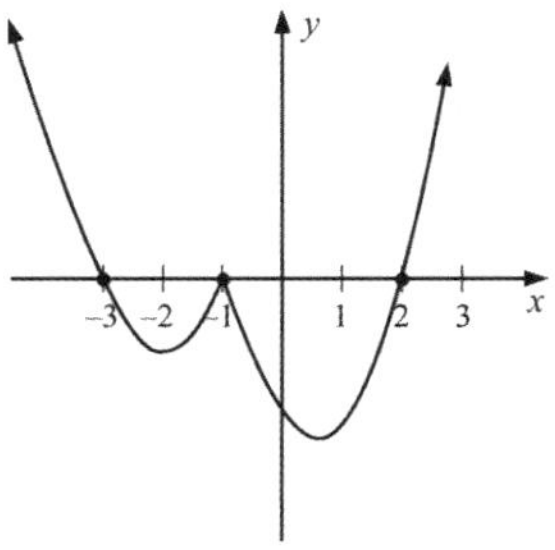

21. When the function $f(x) = -x^3 - 4x^2 + px + 1$ is divided by $x - 1$, the remainder is 3. What is the value of p?

A. -7 **B.** -1

C. 1 **D.** 7

22. Which of the following procedures would be **most appropriate** when factoring the polynomial $p(x) = x^3 + 2x^2 - 3x - 6$?

A. Common factoring

B. Trinomial factoring

C. Factoring by grouping

D. Factoring by difference of squares

23. Which of the following equations could **not** be a solution to the equation $0 = 5x^3 + ax^2 + bx - 12$, where a and b are real numbers?

A. $x = 2$

B. $x = 3$

C. $x = 4$

D. $x = 5$

Open Response

OR3.

a) Determine the possible integral zeros of the polynomial function
$P(x) = 2x^3 - 9x^2 - 2x + 24$

b) Algebraically solve the polynomial equation
$2x^3 - 9x^2 - 2x + 24 = 0$.

c) Explain how technology can be used to verify the solution to the equation
$2x^3 - 9x^2 - 2x + 24 = 0$.

24. The real root of the equation $\frac{x^2-1}{x-1}=0$ is 1.

Therefore, the graph of $f(x)=\frac{x^2-1}{x-1}$ has

A. x-intercepts of 1 and -1

B. only an x-intercept of 1

C. only an x-intercept of -1

D. no x-intercepts

Numerical Response

NR3. If $\frac{1}{3}(2-x)-\frac{1}{8}(5-x)=0,$ then, to the nearest tenth, x equals________________.

25. A polynomial function is defined by the equation $p(x)=3x^3+ax^2+bx+7,$ where $a,b\in I.$ If $p(-2)=5$ and $p(1)=14$, then the value of $a+b$ is

A. -6 **B.** -4

C. 4 **D.** 6

Use the following information to answer the next question.

The graph of $y=P(x)$ is shown.

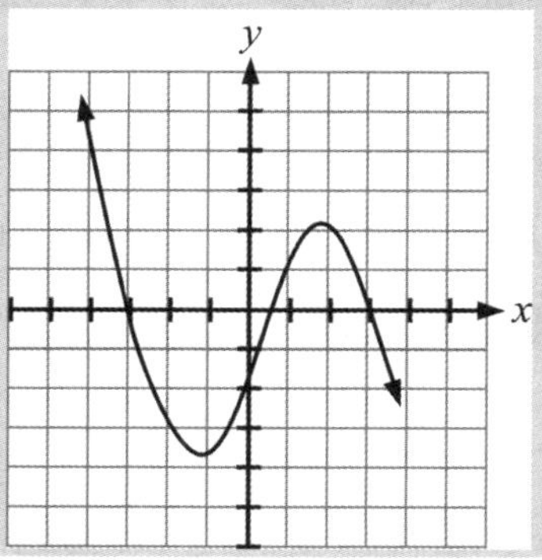

26. The solution to $y\le 0$ is

A. $0.5\le x\le 3$, $x\ge 3$

B. $-3.5\le x\le 0.5$, $x\ge 3$

C. $x\le -3.5$, $0.5\le x\le 3$

D. $x\le -3.5$, $-3.5\le x\le 0.5$

27. Which of the following graphs represents the solution for $x^2+10x+21\le 0$?

A.

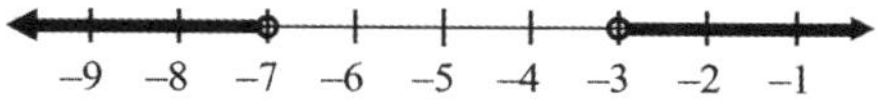

B.

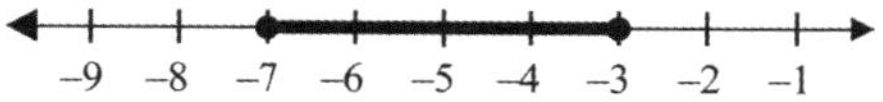

C.

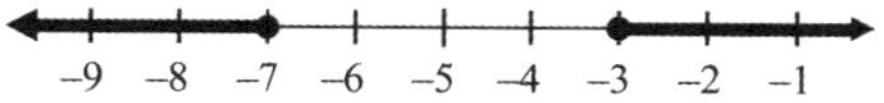

D.

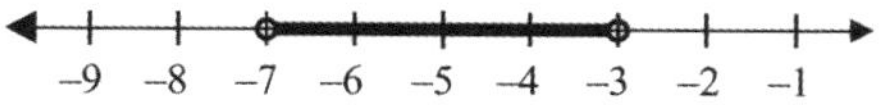

28. The rate of change of an object's position can also be called its

A. velocity **B.** momentum

C. acceleration **D.** displacement

Use the following information to answer the next question.

The population of rabbits in Rabbitville doubles every 6 months. The graph below represents past populations of rabbits from January 2003 to January 2006.

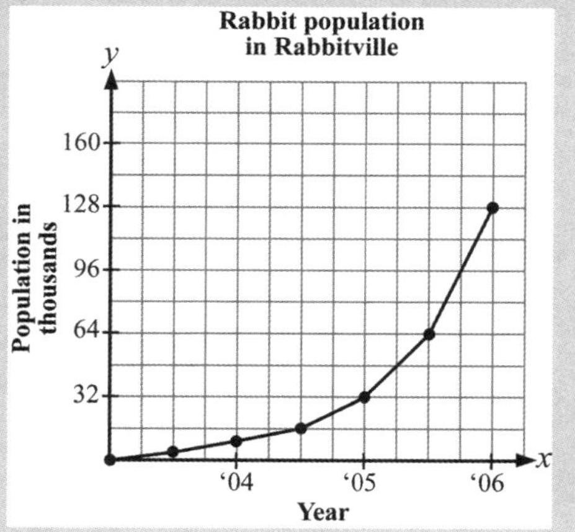

29. The instantaneous rate of change in the rabbit population in June of 2005 was

A. 8 000/year **B.** 24 000/year

C. 48 000/year **D.** 96 000/year

30. A rock is thrown vertically upward from ground level with an initial velocity of 30 m/s. At some point, the rock will hit the ground. The height *h,* in metres, of the rock is a function of time and is defined by $h(t) = -5t^2+30t$, where t represents the time, measured in seconds, and $t \geq 0$.
Which of the following statements about the rock is **true**?

A. At 3 s, the rock will hit the ground.

B. At 6 s, the rock will hit the ground.

C. At 3 s, the rock reaches its maximum height.

D. At 6 s, the rock reaches its maximum height.

Use the following graphs to answer the next question.

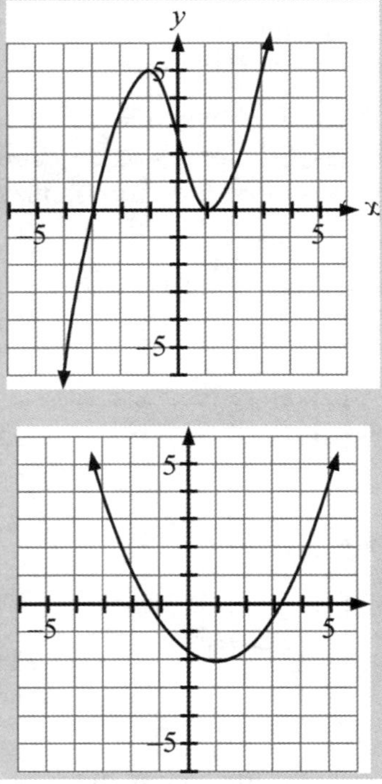

31. When the function $f(x)$, shown below (top), is added to the function $g(x)$, the resulting function $h(x)$ would be decreasing on which of the following intervals?

A. $x \in R$

B. $x > 1$

C. $x < -2$

D. $-1 < x < 1$

Use the following information to answer the next question.

Some students were given the functions shown in the table below and were asked to create compositions of functions.

Functions
$f(x) = \sqrt{x}$
$g(x) = x^2$
$h(x) = \frac{1}{x}$
$q(x) = x^3$
$k(x) = x - 5$

32. Which of the following compositions would be defined on $x \in R$?

A. $g(f(x))$

B. $g(x) = x^2$

C. $k(q(x))$

D. $q(f(x))$

33. A Sports Utility Vehicle (SUV) uses 0.13 litres of fuel for every highway kilometre. The fuel used, used in litres, can be expressed as a function of distance, *d*, in kilometres, by $f(d) = 0.13d$. If the vehicle travels at a constant rate of 110 km/h on the highway, what will be its rate of fuel consumption per hour?

A. 1.8 L/h

B. 8.5 L/h

C. 13 L/h

D. 14.3 L/h

Numerical Response

NR4. For the inequality $\sin(2x) < 3^x$, on the interval $\frac{-5\pi}{6} \leq x \leq 0$ the solution is $a < x \leq 0$, where a is a real number. The value of $a + 5$, to the nearest hundredth, is __________.

Open Response

OR4. A wheel with a dab of paint is used to repeatedly mark the pavement of a new road. The wheel has a radius of 70 cm and rotates at 6 revolutions per minute. The paint touches the ground for the first time after 7.5 s.

a) Sketch a graph of the height of the dab of paint as a function of time for the first 20 s.

b) Determine the equation for the dab of paint's height as a function of time in the form $h(t) = a\sin bt + d$, where $a > 0$.

ANSWER AND SOLUTIONS—PRACTICE TEST 1

1. D	7. C	12. D	18. B	24. B	30. C
2. C	OR1. **	13. C	19. A	NR3. 0.2	31. D
3. A	8. B	14. A	20. C	25. C	32. C
4. B	NR2. 0.3	15. C	21. D	26. B	33. D
5. D	9. C	OR2. **	22. C	27. B	NR4. 3.35
NR1. 16	10. C	16. B	23. D	28. A	OR4. **
6. A	11. D	17. A	OR3. **	29. D	

** See Solutions

1. **D**

$4\log_b 2b - \log_b(1.6b)$

Apply the power law for logarithms

$= \log_b (2b)^4 - \log_b(1.6b)$

Apply the quotient law for logarithms

$= \log_b \dfrac{(2b)^4}{1.6b}$

Apply power of a product law for exponents

$= \log_b \dfrac{16b^4}{1.6b}$

Divide

and apply the quotient law for exponents

$= \log_b \left(10b^3\right)$

Apply the product law for logarithms

$= \log_b 10 + \log_b b^3$

$= \log_b 10 + 3$ Simplify

2. **C**

The graphs of the two functions are shown below. Note that the function $y = \log_2 x$ is entered into the calculator as $\text{Y} = \dfrac{\log(x)}{\log(2)}$.

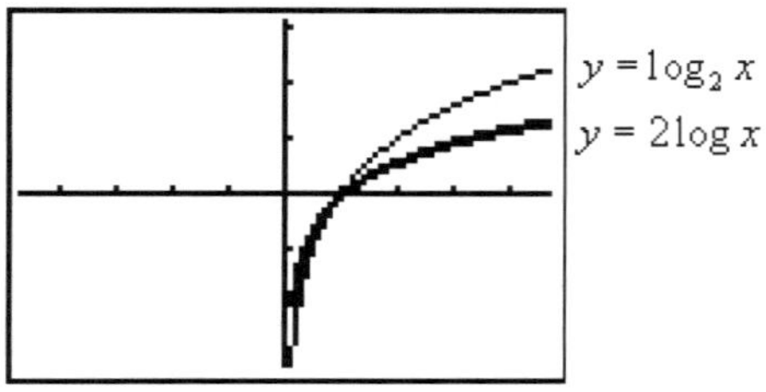

The graphs are not the same, both graphs show a domain of $x > 0$, and neither graph intersects the y-axis, but both graphs have the y-axis as a vertical asymptote.

3. **A**

The equation of the new function is $y = \log_{\frac{1}{2}}(x - p - 5) + (q + 3)$, which is

$y = \log_{\frac{1}{2}}(x - (p + 5)) + (q + 3)$.

The graph of this function is the graph of $y = \log_{\frac{1}{2}}(x) + (q + 3)$ translated $(p + 5)$ units to the right.

Thus, the domain is $x > p + 5$.

4. **B**

Graph $y = 48\,000(1.075)^x$ and $y = 96\,000$.
An appropriate window setting and the graphs are shown below.

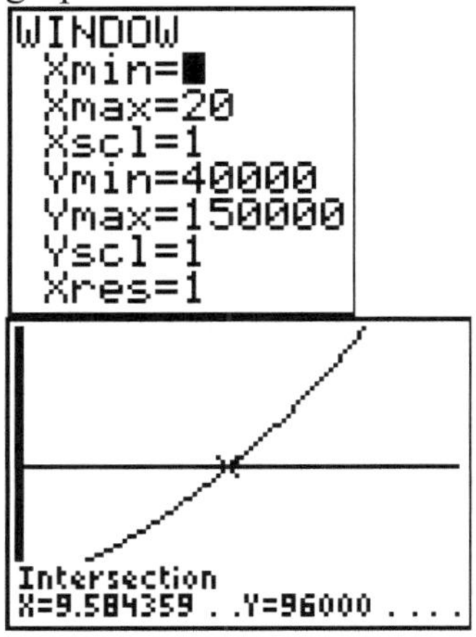

Using [2nd] [CALC] [5:interect] shows that the number of years, to the nearest year, is 10.

5. **D**

$$4^x \bullet 7^{x+1} = 2$$
$$\log\left(4^x \bullet 7^{x+1}\right) = \log 2$$
$$\log 4^x + \log 7^{x+1} = \log 2$$
$$x\log 4 + (x+1)\log 7 = \log 2$$
$$x\log 4 + x\log 7 + \log 7 = \log 2$$
$$x(\log 4 + \log 7) = \log 2 - \log 7$$
$$x = \frac{\log 2 - \log 7}{\log 4 + \log 7}$$

NR1. **16**

$$2 = (1.045)^t$$
$$\log 2 = \log(1.045)^t$$
$$\log 2 = t\log(1.045)$$
$$\frac{\log 2}{\log(1.045)} = t$$
$$15.75 \approx t$$

To the nearest year, the number of years is 16.

6. **A**

$$\log_2(6x-8) = 4$$
$$6x - 8 = 2^4$$
$$6x - 8 = 16$$
$$6x = 24$$
$$x = 4$$
$$\log_3(12-3x) = 3$$
$$12 - 3x = 3^3$$
$$12 - 3x = 27$$
$$-3x = 15$$
$$x = -5$$

The sum of the solutions is $4 + -5 = -1$.

7. **C**

For the first 4 years, depreciation at 13% means that at the end of each year, the car is worth 87% of its value at the start of the year.
Thus, the value at the end of 4 years is $V = 23500(0.87)^4$.
For the next 3 years, depreciation at 9% means that at the end of each year, the car is worth 91% of its value at the start of the year.
Thus, the value at the end of 7 years is $V = \left[23500(0.87)^4\right](0.91)^3 \approx \$10145$.

OR1.

The loudness of a sound in decibels (db) is defined by the equation $db = 10\log\left(\frac{I}{I_0}\right)$, where I is the intensity of the sound, and I_0 is the intensity of a reference sound of loudness 0 db.

If we let the intensity of each trumpet be I_1, then for each trumpet we have $60 = 10\log\left(\frac{I_1}{I_0}\right)$. Solving for I_1 by first dividing by 10 gives $6 = \log\left(\frac{I_1}{I_0}\right)$.

Rewriting in exponential form yields $10^6 = \frac{I_1}{I_0}$, and finally multiplying both sides by I_0 gives $I_1 = 10^6 I_0$.

Letting I_2 be the intensity of the trombone, we get $55 = 10\log\left(\frac{I_2}{I_0}\right)$, and repeating the same steps as for the trumpet equation gives $I_2 = 10^{5.5} I_0$.

For 2 trumpets and 1 trombone the total intensity is $I = 2I_1 + I_2$

$$= 2\times 10^6 I_0 + 10^{5.5} I_0$$
$$= \left(2\times 10^6 + 10^{5.5}\right) I_0.$$

The decibel level is given by:

$$db = 10\log\left[\frac{\left(2\times 10^6 + 10^{5.5}\right) I_0}{I_0}\right]$$
$$\approx 10(6.365)$$
$$\approx 64$$

The decibel level to the nearest whole number is 64.

8. **B**

The measure of angle θ in radians is $\frac{14}{8} = \frac{7}{4}$ rad. Since π radians $= 180°$, an angle of $\frac{7}{4}$ rad in degrees is

$$\frac{7}{4}\text{rad} = \frac{7}{4}\left(\frac{180}{\pi}\right) \approx 100.3°.$$

NR2. **0.3**

In radian mode, input $1/\tan(4/\pi)$ and press ENTER. The display shows .3066612592 so, to the nearest tenth, $\cot\left(\frac{4}{\pi}\right) = 0.3$.

9. **C**

When the graphs of $y = \sin x$ and $y = \cos x$ are graphed on the same set of axes, it is clear that translating the graph of $y = \sin x$ by $\frac{\pi}{2}$ rad to the left results in the same graph as $y = \cos x$.

10. **C**

The range of the reciprocal of $y = \cos\theta$, which is $y = \sec\theta$, is $y \le -1$ or $y \ge 1$.

Since the secant ratio is defined as $\frac{r}{x}$ for angles in standard position and since $|x| \le r$, the ratio is less than or equal to –1 or greater than or equal to +1.

11. **D**

Since $y = a\sin(2\theta) - 3$ indicates that a vertical translation of 3 units down has been applied to $y = a\sin(2\theta)$ and given that the minimum value is –11, then $|a| = -3 - (-11) = 8$. Since the function may be reflected in the horizontal axis and have the same maximum and minimum values, a could be +8 or –8.

12. **D**

The graph of $y=-3\sin\left(x+\frac{\pi}{4}\right)-3$ is the graph of $y=\sin x$ stretched by a factor of 3 about the x-axis, reflected in the x-axis, and then translated $\frac{\pi}{4}$ left and 3 units down.
These transformations are illustrated in graph **D**.

13. **C**
Using a TI-83 calculator with an appropriate viewing window such as $x:[0,6,1]$, $y:[0,30,1]$, input
$Y_1=12\sin(\pi X/0.030)+15$ and
$Y_2=20$ into the $\boxed{\text{Y=}}$ menu.
The resulting graphs are shown below.

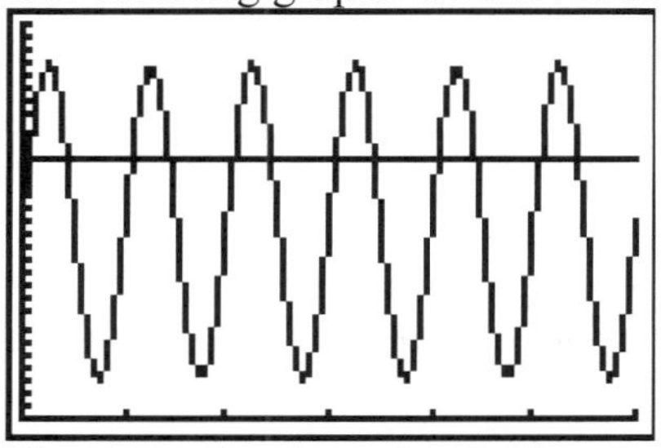

These graphs show that during the first 6, the graph of $Y_2=20$ intersects the graph of $Y_1=12\sin(\pi X/0.030)+15$ 12 times.

14. **A**
Use the formulas
$\sin(x-y)=\sin x\cos y-\cos x\sin y$ and
$\cos(x-y)=\cos x\cos y+\sin x\sin y$.

$$\sin\left(\frac{\pi}{6}-x\right)+\cos\left(\frac{\pi}{3}-x\right)$$
$$=\sin\left(\frac{\pi}{6}\right)\cos x-\cos\left(\frac{\pi}{6}\right)\sin x$$
$$+\cos\left(\frac{\pi}{3}\right)\cos x+\sin\left(\frac{\pi}{3}\right)\sin x$$
$$=\frac{1}{2}\cos x-\frac{\sqrt{3}}{2}\sin x+\frac{1}{2}\cos x+\frac{\sqrt{3}}{2}\sin x$$
$$=\cos x$$

15. **C**

Since $\cos(2\theta)=\cos^2\theta-\sin^2\theta$

$$\frac{1-\cos(2\theta)}{2}=\frac{1-\left(\cos^2\theta-\sin^2\theta\right)}{2}$$

Remove brackets

$$=\frac{1-\cos^2\theta+\sin^2\theta}{2}$$

Since $1-\cos^2\theta=\sin^2\theta$

$$=\frac{\sin^2\theta+\sin^2\theta}{2}$$

Addition

$$=\frac{2\sin^2\theta}{2}$$

Cancel (2)

$$=\sin^2\theta$$

OR2.

a) Substituting $x=\frac{\pi}{6}$ into both sides of the equation gives:

$$\text{L.S.}=\frac{\cos\left(2\left(\frac{\pi}{6}\right)\right)+1}{\sin\left(2\left(\frac{\pi}{6}\right)\right)}=\frac{\cos\left(\frac{\pi}{3}\right)+1}{\sin\left(\frac{\pi}{3}\right)}$$

$$=\frac{\frac{1}{2}+1}{\frac{\sqrt{3}}{2}}=\frac{\frac{3}{2}}{\frac{\sqrt{3}}{2}}=\frac{3}{\sqrt{3}}\times\frac{\sqrt{3}}{\sqrt{3}}=\frac{3\sqrt{3}}{3}=\sqrt{3}$$

$$\text{R.S.}=\cot\left(\frac{\pi}{6}\right)$$
$$=\sqrt{3}$$

Since L.S. = R.S., the identity is verified for $x=\frac{\pi}{6}$.

b) One method of verifying the identity graphically is to graph the two functions $y=\dfrac{\cos(2x)+1}{\sin(2x)}$ and $y=\cot x$. They should appear to be the same graph. Using a TI-83 calculator and appropriate window settings such as $x:[-2\pi,2\pi,\pi]$, $y:[-3,3,1]$, graph $Y_1=(\cos(2X)+1)/\sin(2X)$ and $Y_2=1/\tan(X)$. The graphs are shown below with the second function graphed with a thicker line in order to illustrate that the second function graphs on top of the first.

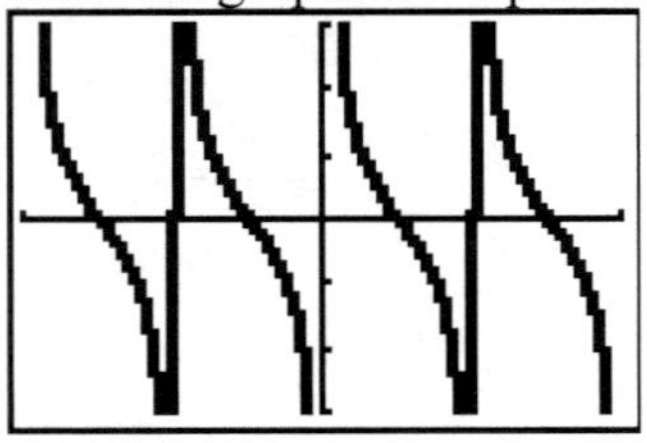

c)

$$\text{L.S.}=\frac{\cos(2x)+1}{\sin(2x)}$$

Using double-angle formulas

$$=\frac{\cos^2 x-\sin^2 x+1}{2\sin x\cos x}$$

Rearrange terms

$$=\frac{\cos^2 x+1-\sin^2 x}{2\sin x\cos x}$$

Since $1-\sin^2 x=\cos^2 x$

$$=\frac{\cos^2 x+\cos^2 x}{2\sin x\cos x}$$

Addition

$$=\frac{2\cos^2 x}{2\sin x\cos x}$$

Cancel $(2\cos x)$

$$=\frac{\cos x}{\sin x}$$

Since $\dfrac{\cos x}{\sin x}=\cot x$

$$=\cot x$$

$$\text{R.S.}=\cot x$$

Since L.S. = R.S., the identity is verified.

16. **B**

Since $0\le x\le 2\pi$, then $0\le \frac{1}{2}x\le \pi$.

First, solve for $\frac{1}{2}x$.

$$2\cos\left(\frac{1}{2}x\right)-\cos\left(\frac{1}{2}x\right)=0$$

$$\cos\left(\frac{1}{2}x\right)\left(\cos\left(\frac{1}{2}x\right)-1\right)=0$$

$$\cos\left(\frac{1}{2}x\right)=0 \text{ or } \cos\left(\frac{1}{2}x\right)=1$$

$$\frac{1}{2}x=\frac{\pi}{2} \quad\text{or}\quad \frac{1}{2}x=0 \qquad \text{Multiply by 2}$$

$$x=\pi \quad\text{or}\quad x=0$$

17. **A**

The graph of a function of degree four with a negative leading coefficient will have the left end of its graph in quadrant 3 and the right end of its graph in quadrant 4. The only alternative that illustrates a graph that satisfies these conditions is given in alternative **A**.

18. **B**

The domain of each of the four given graphs is $x\in R$. However, each of the graphs has a different range. The range of the polynomial function illustrated by the graphs in alternatives A, B, C, and D are $y\le 5$, $y\ge -5$, $y\ge 0$, and $y\in R$ respectively. Thus, the correct alternative is **B**.

19. **A**

The x-intercepts (zeros) of the graph of the polynomial function $p(x) = -5(x-3)(x-1)(x+4)^2$ can be determined by substituting 0 for $p(x)$ and solving for x as shown below.

$$p(x) = -5(x-3)(x-1)(x+4)^2$$
$$0 = -5(x-3)(x-1)(x+4)^2$$

Hence:

$x-3=0$ or $x-1=0$ or $x+4=0$

$x=3$ $\quad x=1$ $\quad x=-4$

The x-intercepts of the graph of $p(x) = -5(x-3)(x-1)(x+4)^2$ are 3, 1 and –4.

20. **C**

Although the graph given in alterative **C** has x-intercepts of –3, –1, and 2, the graph is of a third-degree rather than a fourth-degree function. The graphs given in alternatives A, B, and D are all possible graphs of the stated function.

21. **D**

Since the remainder is 3 when $f(x)$ is divided by $x - 1$ then $f(1) = 3$.

The value of p can be determined as shown below.

$$f(x) = -x^3 - 4x^2 + px + 1$$
$$f(1) = -(1)^3 - 4(1)^2 + p(1) + 1$$
$$f(1) = -1 - 4 + p + 1$$
$$f(1) = p - 4$$

Therefore, $p - 4 = 3$

$$p = 7$$

22. **C**

Factoring by grouping would be the most appropriate procedure to use when factoring $p(x)$. This factoring procedure is shown below.

$$x^3 + 2x^2 - 3x - 6 = x^2(x+2) - 3(x+2)$$
$$= (x+2)(x^2 - 3)$$

23. **D**

An integral root of a polynomial equation must be a factor of the constant term, which in this case is –12.

The factors of –12 are ±1, ±2, ±3, ±4, ±6, and ±12. Thus, the potential roots (solutions) of the equation $5x^3 + ax^2 + bx - 12 = 0$ are $x = \pm 1, \pm 2, \pm 3, \pm 4, \pm 6,$ or ± 12.

Since $x = 5$ is not one of the preceding roots, the correct alternative is **D**.

OR **3**

a) The possible integral zeros of the polynomial function $P(x) = 2x^3 - 9x^2 - 2x + 24$ are the factors of 24. Thus, the possible integral zeros of $P(x)$ are

$\pm 1, \pm 2, \pm 3, \pm 4, \pm 6, \pm 8, \pm 12,$ and ± 24

b) Let $P(x)=2x^3-9x^2-2x+24$.
Now, determine an integral zero that satisfies the equation $P(x)=0$.
One such integral zero is 2, as verified below.

$$P(x)=2x^3-9x^2-2x+24$$
$$P(2)=2(2)^3-9(2)^2-2(2)+24$$
$$P(2)=16-36-4+24$$
$$P(2)=0$$

Therefore, one factor of $P(x)$ is $x-2$. The second-degree factor of $P(x)$ can be determined by using synthetic division as shown below.

$\underline{-2}\rvert$	2	−9	−2	24
		−4	10	24
	2	−5	−12	0

The second-degree factor of $P(x)$ is $2x^2-5x-12$. In factored form, $2x^2-5x-12=(2x+3)(x-4)$.
$P(x)$ can now be expressed in factored form as
$P(x)=(x-2)(2x+3)(x-4)$.
Setting $P(x)=0$, you get
$(x-2)(2x+3)(x-4)=0$.
Thus, $x-2=0$ or $2x+3=0$

$$x=2 \qquad 2x=-3$$
$$x=-\frac{3}{2}$$

or $x-4=0$

$$x=4$$

The solution to the equation $2x^3-9x^2-2x+24=0$ is
$x=-\frac{3}{2}$, 2, or 4.

c) Use technology to graph the polynomial function
$P(x)=2x^3-9x^2-2x+24$.
Next, determine the x-intercepts of $P(x)$. The x-intercepts of $P(x)$ must correspond to the roots (the solution) of the polynomial equation
$2x^3-9x^2-2x+24=0$.

24. **B**

Since the real root of the equation $\frac{x^2-1}{x-1}=0$ is 1, the graph of the corresponding function $f(x)=\frac{x^2-1}{x^2-1}$ will have only an x-intercept of 1.

NR3. **0.2**

To solve the given equation, first multiply each side by 24 (the lowest common denominator).

$$24\left(\frac{1}{3}(2-x)-\frac{1}{8}(5-x)\right)=24\times 0$$

Simplify: $8(2-x)-3(5-x)=0$.
This equation can now be solved as shown below.

$$8(2-x)-3(5-x)=0$$
$$16-8x-15+3x=0$$
$$-5x+1=0$$
$$-5x=-1$$
$$x=\frac{1}{5}=0.2$$

25. **C**

It is necessary to set up a system of two linear equations in two variables to solve for a and b.

Since $p(x)=3x^3+ax^2+bx+7$ and $p(-2)=5$, one equation is:

$$3(-2)^3+a(-2)^2+b(-2)+7=5$$
$$-24+4a-2b+7=5$$
$$4a-2b=22$$

Given $p(1)=14$, the second equation is:

$$3(1)^3+a(1)^2+b(1)+7=14$$
$$3+a+b+7=14$$
$$a+b=4$$

Next, it is necessary to solve the following system of equations:

(1) $4a-2b=22$

(2) $a+b=4$

This system can be solving using the method of elimination:

$$\begin{array}{rl} (1) & 4a-2b=22 \\ 2\times(2) & \underline{2a+2b=8} \\ & 6a=30 \\ & a=5 \end{array}$$

The value of b can be determined by substituting 5 for a in either equation (1) or (2).

$$(2)\quad a+b=4$$
$$5+b=4$$
$$b=-1$$

The value of $a+b=5+(-1)=4$.

26. **B**

The solution to $y\le 0$ occurs whenever the graph is on or below the x-axis. This occurs on $-3.5\le x\le 0.5$ or $x\ge 3$.

27. **B**

The graph of $f(x)=x^2+10x+21$ is shown.

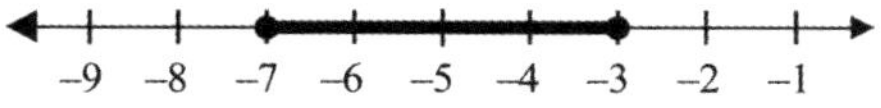

The function is equal to zero at both -3 and -7, and is less than zero between these values.

$\therefore$ the solution is $-7\le x\le -3$ illustrated by the number line in B.

28. **A**

By definition, velocity is the rate of change of an object's position.

29. **D**

In order to determine the instantaneous rate of change in the rabbit population in June of 2005, find the slope of the secant line using the two nearest points to June of 2005: January 2006 and January 2005.

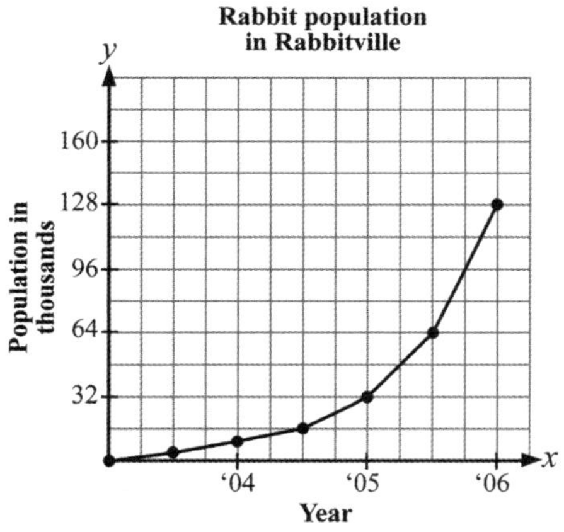

$$m=\frac{y_2-y_1}{x_2-x_1}$$
$$=\frac{128000-32000}{06-05}$$
$$=\frac{96000}{1}=96000\text{ / year}$$

30. C

Using the TI-83 graphing calculator, graph the function.

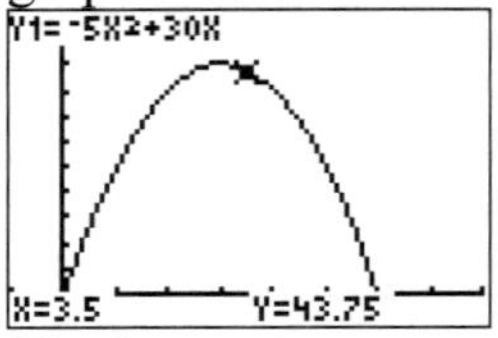

The instantaneous rate of change of the rock's height with respect to time is zero when the rock reaches its maximum height.

Using the maximum feature on the graphing calculator:

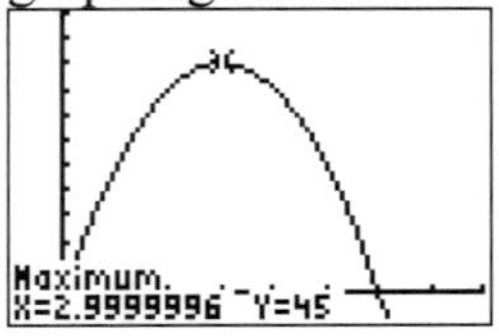

The maximum occurs after 3 s.

To verify that the slope of the tangent line is zero at 3 s, use the tangent feature on the graphing calculator:

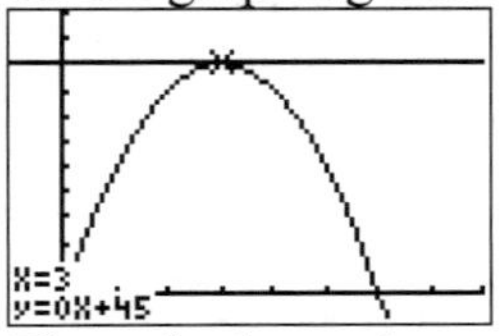

The calculator shows an equation of $y = 0x + 45$, verifying the slope of 0.

31. D

Functions $f(x)$ and $g(x)$ are being added together. The behaviour of the combined function $h(x) = f(x) + g(x)$ can be determined by combining the behaviour of each of the individual functions. In order to find when $h(x)$ is decreasing, it is necessary to analyze each individual function for intervals of increase and decrease. Use the intervals provided in the alternatives. This can be done using a table.

Interval	$f(x)$	$g(x)$	$h(x)$
$x < -1$	Increasing	Decreasing	By calculating the average slopesof $f(x)$ and $g(x)$ on the interval $x < -1$ to be $\text{slope}_{f(x)} = \frac{9}{3} = 3$ and $\text{slope}_{g(x)} = \frac{-5}{2}$, $= -2.5$ you can see that $f(x)$ is increasing at a faster rate than $g(x)$ is decreasing, therefore the net effect will have $h(x)$ increasing.
$-1 < x < 1$	Decreasing	Decreasing	Since both functions are decreasing, $h(x)$ will be decreasing
$x > 1$	Increasing	Increasing	Since both functions are increasing, $h(x)$ will be increasing

Therefore, the interval on which $h(x)$ is decreasing is $-1 < x < 1$.

32. **C**

The correct answer is **C** because $k(p(x))$ is the only composite function involving only polynomials, which have no restrictions on their domains.
We can confirm this by determining each of the compositions of functions.

A. $g(f(x)) - g(\sqrt{x}) - (\sqrt{x})^2 - x$

(Although it might appear as though $g(f(x))$ has no domain restrictions, you must always keep in mind the original functions from which the composition was created. In this case, a radical was involved and therefore affects the overall domain of the function, $x \geq 0$.)

B. $g(h(x)) = g\left(\frac{1}{x}\right) = \left(\frac{1}{x}\right)^2 = \frac{1}{x^2}$

(Clearly here, $x \neq 0$)

C. $k(q(x) = k(x^3) = x^3 - 5$ (No restrictions on x, $x \in R$)

D. $q(f(x)) = q(\sqrt{x}) = (\sqrt{x})^3 = x^{\frac{3}{2}}$

(Again, a radical is involved and therefore, $x \geq 0$)

33. **D**

In one hour, a vehicle would travel 110 km if travelling at a speed of 110 km/h. Therefore, the fuel used in one hour would amount to $f(110) = 0.13 \times 110 = 143$. The fuel consumption per hour would be 14.3 L/hour.

NR4 **3.35**

Graphically solving an inequality begins in the same way as solving an equation. Graph the functions $y = \sin 2x$ and $y = 3^x$ using a graphing calculator. Select a window setting that shows any and all points of intersection between the two curves. In this example, an appropriate window setting would include the interval given in the problem. $X:\left[-\frac{5\pi}{6,0},\frac{\pi}{6}\right]$, $Y:[-3,3,1]$.

Note that these curves have only one point of intersection at $(-1.653, 0.163)$, which can be found by pressing 2nd CALC on your TI-83+, then selecting option 5 and moving the cursor until it lies on the point of intersection, and then pressing ENTER. Press ENTER two more times and the coordinates of the point are given. However, you are required to find the interval that makes $y = \sin(2x)$ less than $y = 3^x$. In other words, it is necessary find the region in which the sinusoidal function lies below the exponential function. Observe that this happens to the right of the intersection point all the way to where the given interval ends at $x = 0$. Thus, for values $-1.653 < x \leq 0$ inequality holds true. And, $a = -1.653$; therefore, $a + 5 = -1.653 + 5 = 3.35$ when rounded to the nearest hundredth.

OR 4

a) Before sketching the curve, identify some key points on the graph.

i. The maximum height of the dab of paint will be 140 cm (the diameter of the wheel).

ii. Since the wheel touches the ground, the centre line of the graph will be at 70 cm.

iii. The wheel rotates at 6 revolutions per minute, which is equivalent to $\frac{6 \text{ revolutions}}{60 \text{ seconds}} = 1/10$ revolutions per second. Therefore, the period of the curve is 10 s. Since the question asks for a graph of the first 20 s, 2 cycles of the graph are required.

iv. If the dab of paint touches the ground at 7.5 s, it will also touch the ground 10 s later at 17.5 s. Since the maximum and minimum points on the curve are equidistant apart, the maximas must occur at 2.5 s and 12.5 s.

v. The curve should be at the midline height at 0 s, 5 s, 10 s, 15 s, and 20 s.

Using this information, plot the points and connect them to form a smooth curve as shown below.

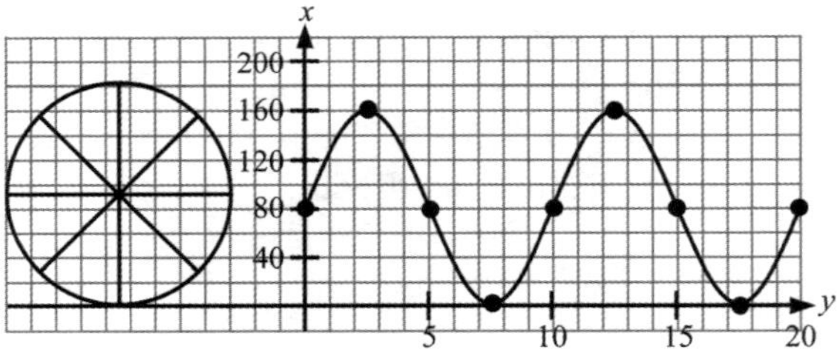

b) Next, determine the equation of this curve. Note that the amplitude is 70 cm (halfway between the maximum and the minimum heights) and the vertical displacement is 70 cm (equal to the height of the middle of the wheel). Since the period is 10 s, $b = \frac{2\pi}{10} = \frac{\pi}{5}$.

Since you are required to find a sine function that models the curve and the curve starts at the midline height when time is zero, there is no phase shift. Therefore, the equation of the function is $h(t) = 70\sin\left(\frac{\pi}{5}t\right) + 70$.

PRACTICE TEST 2

1. The value of $\log_2 6 + 2\log_2 3 - \log_2 10$ to the nearest hundredth is

A. 0.58

B. 1.07

C. 1.25

D. 2.43

2. When considering the graphs of the functions $f(x) = \log_a x$ and $g(x) = \log_{\frac{1}{a}} x$, where $a > 0$, one would notice that the graphs of $f(x)$ and $g(x)$

A. are identical.

B. have the x-axis as an axis of symmetry.

C. have the y-axis as an axis of symmetry.

D. have different asymptotes.

3. The graph of $y = \log_{10} x$ undergoes a vertical stretch by a factor of 2 from the x-axis and a horizontal compression by a factor of $\frac{1}{3}$ towards the y-axis.
The equation that represents the graph of this transformed function is

A. $y = 2\log_{10}(3x)$

B. $y = 2\log_{10}\left(\frac{1}{3}x\right)$

C. $y = \frac{1}{2}\log_{10}(3x)$

D. $y = \frac{1}{2}\log_{10}\left(\frac{1}{3}x\right)$

4. The population of a city in Ontario has grown exponentially from 62 000 in 2003 to 85 250 in 2008. If the population continues to grow at the same rate, then which of the following functions could be graphed in order to model the population growth where x is the number of years since 2003?

A. $y = 62\,000(1.066)^x$

B. $y = 85\,250(1.066)^x$

C. $y = 62\,000(1.075)^x$

D. $y = 85\,250(1.075)^x$

5. Which of the following equations represents a likely and correct step in the solution of $\left(4^3\right)^{x-2} = \log_2 8$?

A. $3x - 6 = 3 - \log 4$

B. $3x - 6 = \dfrac{\log 3}{\log 4}$

C. $x - 2 = \dfrac{\log 8}{\log 64}$

D. $2^{6x-12} = 2^3$

Numerical Response

NR1. If $5^{2x-1} = (25)\left(\sqrt{5}\right)^{6x-7}$, then $x =$ ____________.

6. The solution to $\log_{\frac{1}{6}} 36 = \log_5\left(\frac{x-2}{5}\right)$ is

A. $x = -8$

B. $x = 12$

C. $x = \frac{11}{5}$

D. $x = \frac{127}{5}$

Use the following information to answer the next question.

The loudness of a sound in decibels (db) is defined by the equation $db = 10\log\left(\frac{I}{I_0}\right)$, where I is the intensity of the sound, and I_0 is the intensity of a reference sound of loudness 0 db.

7. If a particular motorcycle creates a noise of approximately 90 decibels while a second motorcycle creates a noise of approximately 80 decibels, then the loudness of both motorcycles together is approximately

A. 17 dB

B. 90 dB

C. 98 dB

D. 170 dB

Open Response

OR1. The pH of the acid in a new battery is 0.8. An old battery has an acidity that is one-fifth as acidic as the acid in a new battery. Determine the pH of the acid in the old battery to the nearest tenth.

Numerical Response

NR2. When 234° is converted to radian measure, the result, to the nearest tenth, is ____________ rad.

8. The value of $\csc(3.14)$, to the nearest thousandth, is

A. 0.313 **B.** 18.247

C. 627.883 **D.** undefined

9. Which of the following procedures would be **most appropriate** to determine the exact value of $\sec\left(\frac{11\pi}{6}\right)$?

A. Sketch an angle with a reference angle of $\frac{\pi}{6}$ in quadrant III.

B. Sketch an angle with a reference angle of $\frac{\pi}{3}$ in quadrant III.

C. Sketch an angle with a reference angle of $\frac{\pi}{4}$ in quadrant IV.

D. Sketch an angle with a reference angle of $\frac{\pi}{6}$ in quadrant IV.

10. Which of the following statements about the domain of $y = \cos x$ is **true**?

A. The domain of $y = \cos x$ is $\frac{\pi}{2}$ less than the domain of $y = \sin x$.

B. The domain of $y = \cos x$ is the same as the domain of $y = \sin x$.

C. The domain of $y = \cos x$ is $-1 \leq x \leq 1$.

D. The domain of $y = \cos x$ is $x \geq 0$.

11. The domain of the reciprocal of $y = \tan\theta$ is

A. $\theta \neq n\pi,\ n \in I$ **B.** $\theta \neq n\frac{\pi}{2},\ n \in I$

C. $\theta \neq \frac{\pi}{2} + n\pi, n \in I$ **D.** $\theta \neq n\pi + n\frac{\pi}{2}, n \in I$

12. If $y = \cos x$ is transformed to $y = -6\cos(2x + 3\pi)$, the amplitude and phase shift are respectively,

A. 6 and 3π to the right

B. –6 and 3π to the left

C. 6 and $\frac{3\pi}{2}$ to the right

D. 6 and $\frac{3\pi}{2}$ to the left

Use the following information to answer the next question.

A stone is stuck in the tire of a bicycle wheel. The height of the stone, in centimetres, t seconds after it gets stuck in the tire is represented by the following graph.

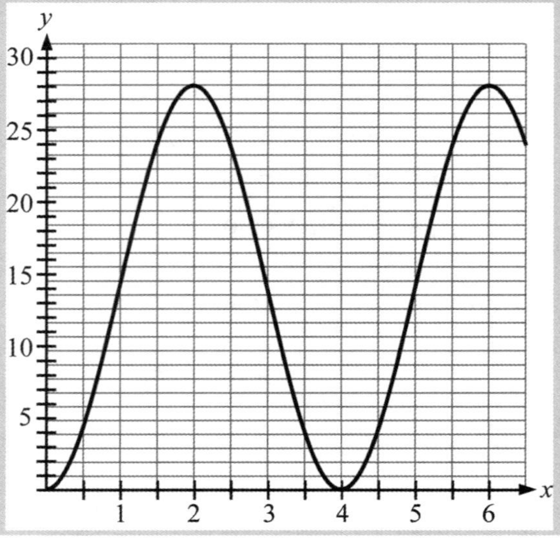

13. An equation that represents the height of the stone, $h(t)$, at any time, t, is

A. $h(t)=-14\sin\left(\frac{\pi t}{2}\right)+14$

B. $h(t)=14\cos\left(\frac{-\pi t}{2}\right)+14$

C. $h(t)=-14\cos\left(\frac{t}{2}\right)+14$

D. $h(t)=-14\cos\left(\frac{\pi t}{2}\right)+14$

14. The expression $\sin(7a)\cos(6a)-\sin(6a)\cos(7a)$ is equal to

A. $\sin(13a)$

B. $\cos(13a)$

C. $\sin(a)$

D. $\cos(a)$

15. Which of the following sets lists **all** undefined values for the expression $\frac{\sin x}{\sin^2 x-\cos^2 x}$ in the interval $0\le x\le 2\pi$?

A. $\{0,\pi,2\pi\}$

B. $\left\{\frac{\pi}{4},\frac{3\pi}{4}\right\}$

C. $\left\{\frac{\pi}{4},\frac{3\pi}{4},\frac{5\pi}{4},\frac{7\pi}{4}\right\}$

D. $\left\{\frac{\pi}{2},\frac{3\pi}{2}\right\}$

16. If $\sin 2x=\cos x$, then part of the solution is derived from

A. $\cos x=0$

B. $\sin x=0$

C. $\sin x=1$

D. $\sin x=-\frac{1}{2}$

Open Response

OR2. Given the equation
$2\sin^2 2x - \sin 2x = 0,\ 0 \le x \le 2\pi,$

a) determine the exact solutions

b) verify that the number of solutions is correct by graphing $y = 2\sin^2 2x - \sin 2x$ on the domain $0 \le x \le 2\pi$. Sketch the graph on the grid provided.

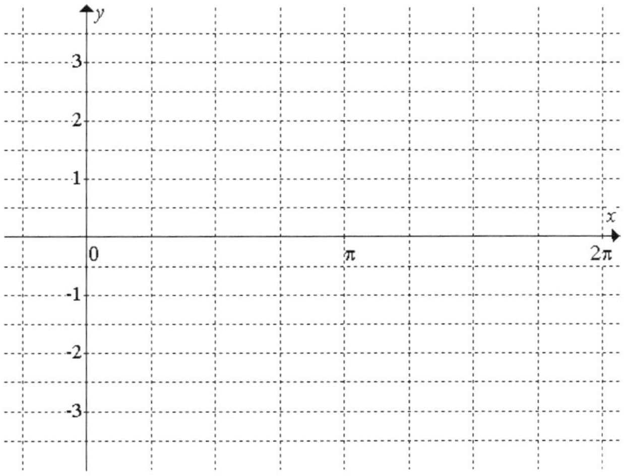

17. Which of the following graphs could represent the graph of a polynomial function whose domain is $x \in R$ and whose range is $y \le 3$?

A.

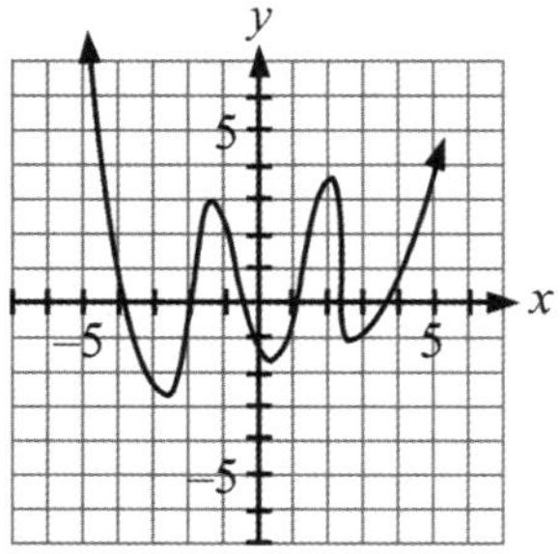

B.

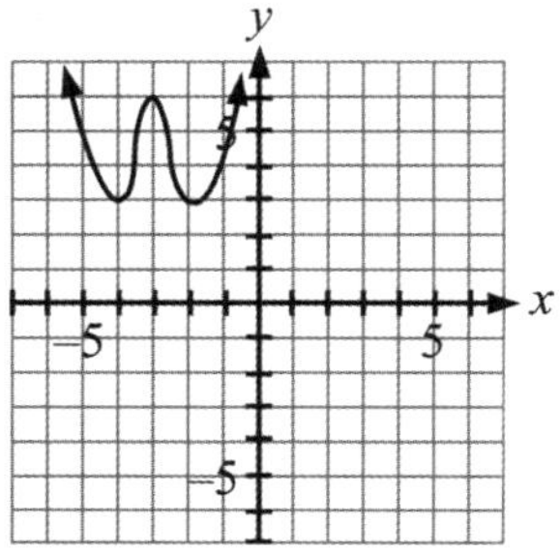

C.

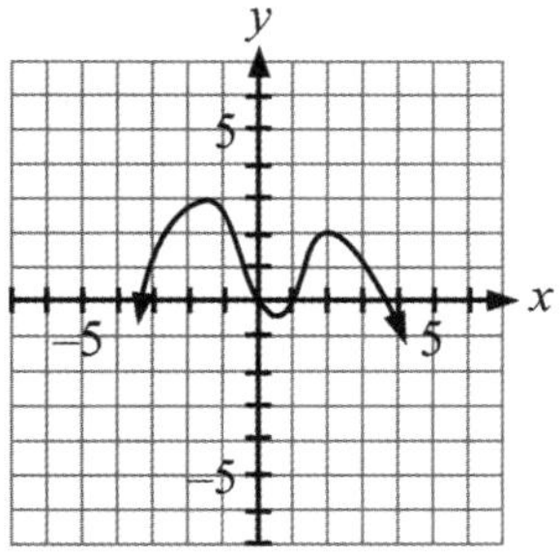

D.

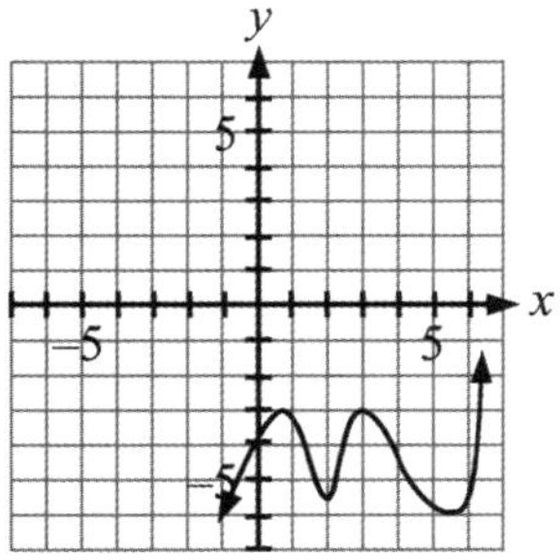

18. Which of the following statements about the graph of the polynomial function $p(x) = -5(x+3)(x+4)^2$ **is true**

A. The x-intercepts of the graph are 3 and 4.

B. The graph is tangent to the x-axis at $x = 4$.

C. The range of the graph is $y \leq p$, where p is the maximum y-value of the graph.

D. The left end of the graph is in quadrant 2 and the right end of the graph is in quadrant 4.

19. If the graph of $y = f(x)$ is reflected in the x-axis and then translated 4 units vertically up, the equation of the transformed function is

A. $y = f(-x) + 4$

B. $y = -f(x) + 4$

C. $y = f(-x+4)$

D. $y = -f(x+4)$

20. The graph of a sixth-degree polynomial function intersects the x-axis at 3, 2, and –2 only. A possible equation of this function is

A. $p(x) = -2(x-3)(x-2)(x+2)$

B. $p(x) = 5(x+3)(x-2)(x+2)$

C. $p(x) = 4(x+3)(x-2)^4(x+2)$

D. $p(x) = -3(x-3)^3(x-2)^2(x+2)$

Numerical Response

NR3. The graph of the rational function $f(x) = \dfrac{1}{2x^2 - 7x + 3}$ has vertical asymptotes at $x = a$ and $x = b$ and a horizontal asymptote at $y = c$, where a, b, and c are real numbers. The value of $a + b + c$, to the nearest tenth, is __________.

Use the following information to answer the next question.

The graph of a particular function is shown below.

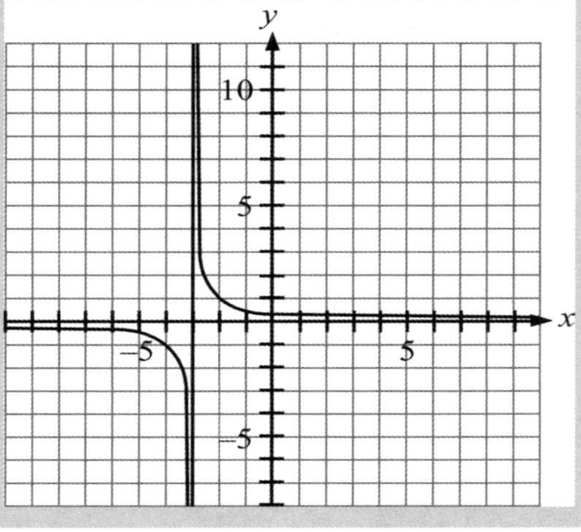

21. The function is

A. $y = \dfrac{1}{x-3}$

B. $y = \dfrac{1}{x+3}$

C. $x = \dfrac{1}{y+3}$

D. $x = \dfrac{1}{y-3}$

22. Which of the following binomials is **not** a factor of the polynomial $p(x) = x^4 - x^3 - 7x^2 + x + 6$?

A. $(x-1)$

B. $(x+1)$

C. $(x-3)$

D. $(x+3)$

23. Which of the following statements about the graph of $y = 2x^3 - 3x^2 - 5x + 6$ is true?

A. It has 3 x-intercepts; therefore, the equation $2x^3 - 3x^2 - 5x + 6 = 0$ has 3 real roots.

B. It has 3 x-intercepts; therefore, the equation $2x^3 - 3x^2 - 5x + 6 = 0$ has 2 real roots.

C. It has 2 x-intercepts; therefore, the equation $2x^3 - 3x^2 - 5x + 6 = 0$ has 2 real roots.

D. It has 2 x-intercepts; therefore, the equation $2x^3 - 3x^2 - 5x + 6 = 0$ has 3 real roots.

24. The polynomial equation $0 = x^3 + 5x^2 + 3x - 9$ can be expressed in factored form as $0 = (x - m)(x - n)^2$ where m and n are real numbers. The value of $m + n$ is

A. –4

B. –2

C. 2

D. 4

25. The solution to the rational equation $\dfrac{x^2 - 5x - 6}{x - 4} = 0$ is

A. $x = -3$ or $x = -2$

B. $x = 3$ or $x = 2$

C. $x = -6$ or $x = 1$

D. $x = 6$ or $x = -1$

Open Response

OR3.

a) When the polynomial function $P(x) = -2x^3 - Ax^2 + Bx - 6$, where A and B are real numbers, is divided by $x + 1$, the remainder is -12. If $P(2) = 12$, what are the values of A and B?

b) Is $x - 3$ a factor of $P(x)$?

26. The solution to the inequality $\frac{3x}{x-5} \geq 0$ is

A. $0 \leq x < 5$

B. $x \leq 0$ or $x > 5$

C. $x < 0$ or $x > 5$

D. $x > 5$

27. The solution(s) to the inequality $x^2 - 5x - 6 < 0$ $\mathbf{x^2 - 5x - 6 < 0}$is

A. $-1 < x < 6$

B. $x < -1, \; x > 6$ $\mathbf{x < -1, x > 6}$

C. $2 < x < 3$

D. $x < 2, \; x > 3$

28. Which of the following tables **best** represents a situation in which the rate of change of the variables is constant?

A.

x	y
3	10
5	20
7	30
9	40

B.

x	y
3	10
5	10
7	10
9	10

C.

x	y
3	9
5	25
7	49
9	81

D.

x	y
3	1
5	4
7	9
9	16

29. Markus took his skateboard to the top of a hill and rode it down the hill and then up another hill. Which of the following graphs **best** illustrates his speed as a function of time?

A.

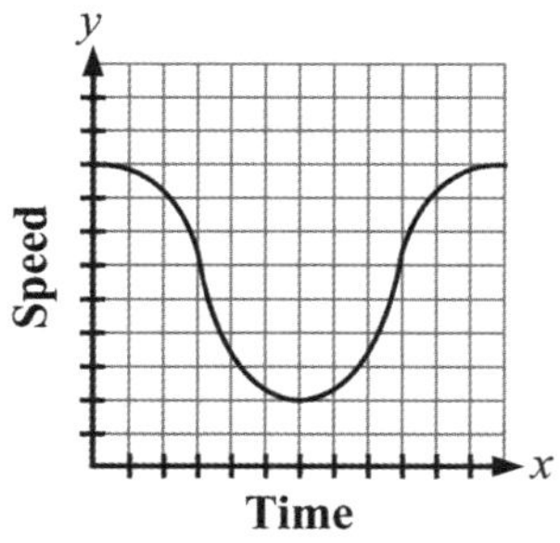

B.

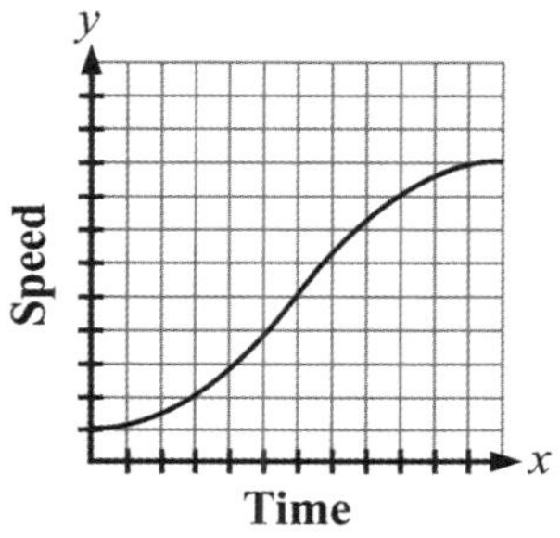

C.

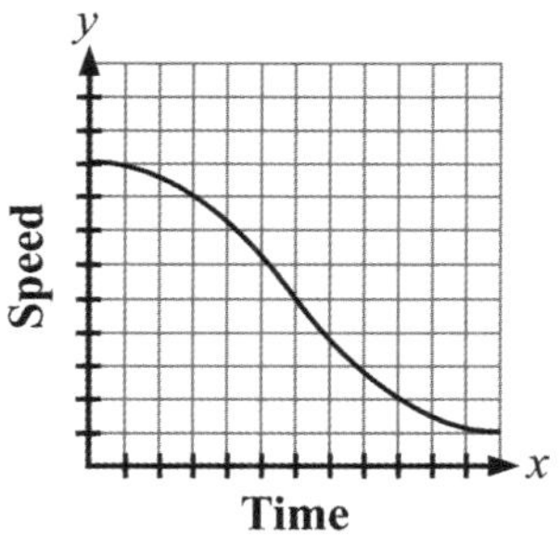

D.

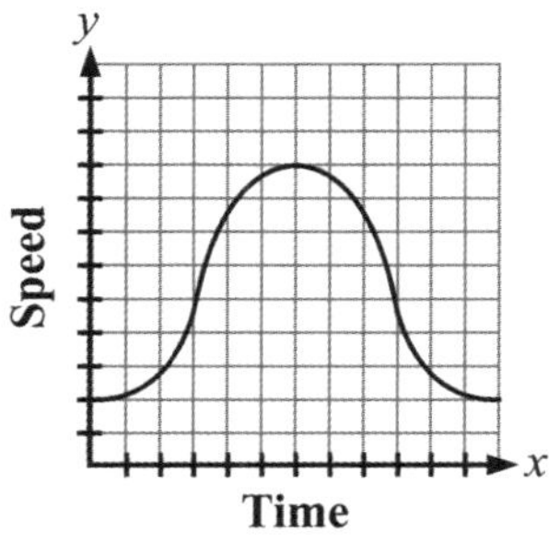

Use the following table to answer the next question.

Time (s)	Temperature (°C)
5.1	23
5.5	21
5.9	16
6.3	12
6.7	8

30. Given the data in the table, what is the **best** approximation for the instantaneous rate of change of temperature with respect to time at $t = 5.9$ s?

A. –9.4 C/s

B. –10.0 C/s

C. –11.25 C/s

D. –12.5 C/s

31. A student is asked to approximate the instantaneous rate of change of y with respect to x for the function $f(x) = x^2 + 3x$ at the point (2, 10). The answer that the student should arrive at is

A. 6

B. 6.5

C. 7

D. 7.5

32. Two functions, $f(x) = x^3 - x^2 + 4x$ and $g(x) = x - 1$, are divided and expressed as the new function $h(x) = \frac{f(x)}{g(x)}$. On which of the following interval(s) is $h(x)$ increasing?

A. $x > 2$

B. $x < 0, x > 2$

C. $x < 1, 1 < x < 2$

D. $x < 1, 1 < x\ 2$

Use the following graphs to answer the next question.

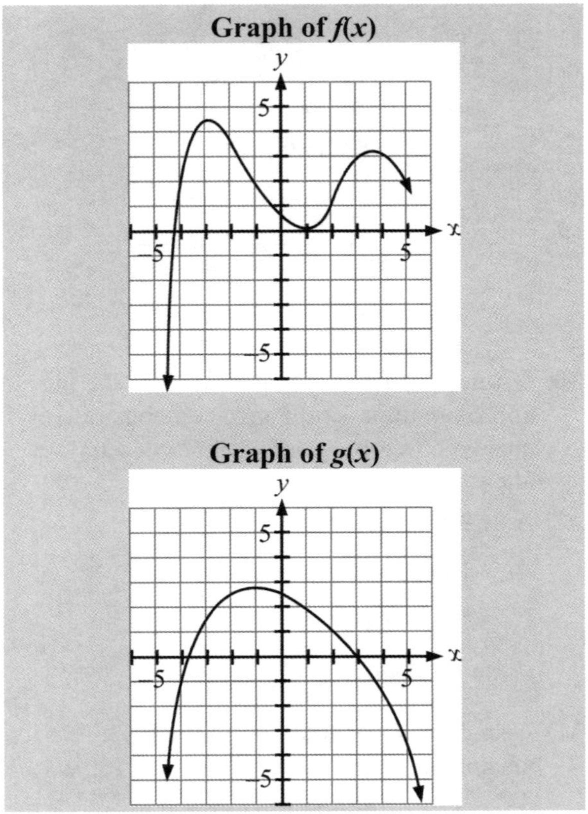

33. The value of $g(f(-4))$ is:

A. -1

B. 0

C. 1

D. 2

34. After the function $f(x)=\cos x$ is transformed to $f(g(x))$, where $g(x)=-3x-4$, how many more intersection points would it have with the line $y=-1$ on $0\le x\le 2\pi$?

A. 0

B. 1

C. 2

D. 3

Numerical Response

NR4. For the inequality $\cos x > x^2 - 4x + 3$, the solution is $a < x < b$, where a and b are real numbers. The value of $b - a$, to the nearest hundredth is _________.

Use the following information to answer the next question.

Data showing the growth of a population of bacteria is given below.

Time (minutes)	Population
1	6
5	35
8	259
12	4 095
17	131 076

35. Determine, to the nearest tenth of a minute, when the population will reach 237 500.

A. 18.3 min

B. 19.0 min

C. 21.0 min

D. 37.5 min

ANSWERS AND SOLUTIONS—PRACTICE TEST 2

1. D	7. B	12. D	18. D	24. B	30. C
2. B	OR1. **	13. D	19. B	25. D	31. C
3. A	NR2. 4.1	14. C	20. D	OR3. **	32. A
4. A	8. C	15. C	NR3. 3.5	26. B	33. D
5. B	9. D	16. A	21. B	27. A	34. B
NR1. 0.5	10. B	OR2. **	22. D	28. A	NR4. 1.81
6. C	11. A	17. C	23. A	29. D	35. A

****See Solutions**

1. **D**

$\log_2 6 + 2\log_2 3 - \log_2 10$

Apply the power law for logarithms

$= \log_2 6 + \log_2 3^2 - \log_2 10$

Apply the product & quotient laws for logarithms

$= \log_2\left(\dfrac{6\times 3^2}{10}\right)$

Simplify

$= \log_2(5.4)$

Apply the change of base formula

$= \dfrac{\log 5.4}{\log 2}$

Evaluate with calculator

≈ 2.43

2. **B**

As an example, the graphs of $y = \log_2 x$ and $y = \log_{\frac{1}{2}} x$ are shown below.

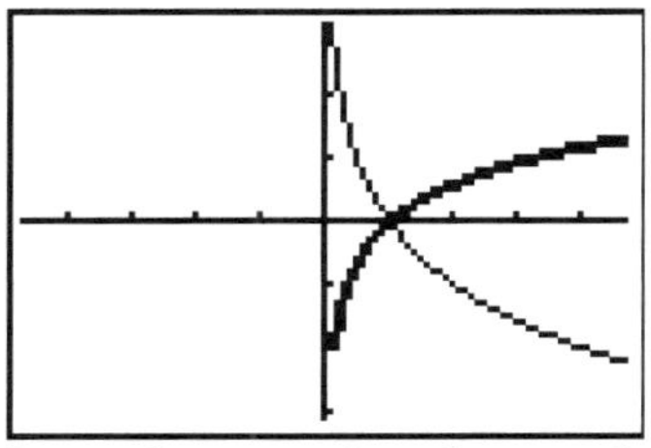

It can be seen that the graph is reflected in the x-axis.

3. **A**

Stretches and/or compressions are performed on the function $y = \log_{10}(x)$ when it is changed to the form $y = a\log_{10}(kx)$.

The vertical stretch factor is a, when $a > 1$ and the horizontal compression is by a factor of $\frac{1}{k}$, when $k > 1$.

Thus $a = 2$ and $k = 3$, so $y = 2\log_{10}(3x)$ is the correct function.

4. **A**

Using the equation $A = P(1+i)^n$, we need to solve the equation $85250 = 62000(1+i)^5$ for $1+i$.

Dividing both sides by 62 000 gives $1.375 = (1+i)^5$. Raising both sides to the $\frac{1}{5}$ power yields $1.0657 \approx 1+i$.

Since the population in 2003 is 62 000, the growth function has the form $y = 62000(1.066)^x$, where y represents the population x years after 2003.

5. B

The steps in solving $\left(4^3\right)^{x-2} = \log_2 8$ would most likely be:

$$\left(4^3\right)^{x-2} = \log_2 8$$
$$\left(4^3\right)^{x-2} = 3$$
$$4^{3x-6} = 3$$
$$\log 4^{3x-6} = \log 3$$
$$(3x-6)\log 4 = \log 3$$
$$3x-6 = \frac{\log 3}{\log 4}$$

NR1. 0.5

$$5^{2x-1} = (25)\left(\sqrt{5}\right)^{6x-7}$$
$$5^{2x-1} = \left(5^2\right)\left(5^{\frac{1}{2}}\right)^{6x-7}$$
$$5^{2x-1} = \left(5^2\right)\left(5^{3x-\frac{7}{2}}\right)$$
$$5^{2x-1} = 5^{3x-\frac{3}{2}}$$
$$2x-1 = 3x-\frac{3}{2}$$
$$\frac{1}{2} = x$$
$$x = \frac{1}{2} = 0.5$$

6. C

$$\log_{\frac{1}{6}} 36 = \log_5\left(\frac{x-2}{5}\right)$$
$$-2 = \log_5\left(\frac{x-2}{5}\right)$$
$$\frac{x-2}{5} = 5^{-2}$$
$$\frac{x-2}{5} = \frac{1}{25}$$
$$5(x-2) = 1$$
$$5x-10 = 1$$
$$5x = 11$$
$$x = \frac{11}{5}$$

7. B

Let I_1 be the intensity of the sound of the first motorcycle and I_2 be the intensity of the sound of the second motorcycle. For the first motorcycle:

$10\log\left(\frac{I_1}{I_0}\right) = 90$ and thus, $I_1 = 10^9 I_0$

For the second motorcycle:

$10\log\left(\frac{I_2}{I_0}\right) = 80$ and thus, $I_2 = 10^8 I_0$

The two motorcycles together create noise with an intensity of:

$$I_1 + I_2 = 10^9 I_0 + 10^8 I_0$$
$$= \left(10^9 + 10^8\right) I_0$$

The dB measure of the loudness is

$$\text{dB} = 10\log\left[\frac{\left(10^9 + 10^8\right) I_0}{I_0}\right]$$
$$= 10\log\left(10^9 + 10^8\right)$$
$$\approx 90$$

OR **1**

$\text{pH} = -\log\left[\text{H}^+\right]$, where $\left[\text{H}^+\right]$ is the hydrogen ion concentration in mol/L.
For the new battery, $-\log\left[\text{H}^+\right] = 0.8$ and thus, $[\text{H}^+] = 10^{-0.8}$.
Since the old battery is one-fifth as acidic, then its concentration is $\left[\text{H}^+\right] = \dfrac{10^{-0.8}}{5}$.
The pH of this acid is:

$$\begin{aligned}\text{pH} &= -\log\left(\frac{10^{-0.8}}{5}\right)\\ &\approx -\log(0.0317)\\ &\approx 1.5\end{aligned}$$

Thus, to the nearest tenth, the pH of the acid in the old battery is 1.5.

NR2. **4.1**

Since $180° = \pi$ radians, an angle of $234°$ in radians is

$$234° = 234\left(\frac{\pi}{180}\right) \approx 4.1 \text{ rad}.$$

8. **C**

In radian mode, input $1/\sin(3.14)$ and press ENTER. The display shows 627.8831939 so, to the nearest thousandth, $\csc(3.14) = 627.883$.
Note that $3.14 \neq \pi$ exactly, so alternative **D** is incorrect.

9. **D**

An angle of $\dfrac{11\pi}{6}$ rad terminates in quadrant IV and has a reference angle of $\dfrac{\pi}{6}$.

10. **B**

The domain of either $y = \sin x$ or $y = \cos x$ is $x \in R$. The domains are the same.

11. **A**

The reciprocal of the tangent ratio is the cotangent ratio, which is defined as $\dfrac{x}{y}$ for angles in standard position.
This ratio is undefined when $y = 0$, which is when $\theta = n\pi,\ n \in I$. The graph of $y = \cot\theta$ indicates that the graph is not defined when θ is a multiple of π and that there are asymptotes at these values of the domain.
Thus, $\theta \neq n\pi,\ n \in I$.

12. **D**

First, factor the 2 out of the part in parentheses so that the function fits the form $y = a\cos(k(x-d)) + c$.

$$y = -6\cos(2x + 3\pi), \rightarrow y = -6\cos\left(2\left(x + \frac{3\pi}{2}\right)\right)$$

To further fit the form, the function can be written as $y = -6\cos\left(2\left(x - \dfrac{-3\pi}{2}\right)\right)$.

The amplitude is $|a| = |-6| = 6$.

The phase shift is $\dfrac{3\pi}{2}$ left.

13. **D**

Since none of the alternative shows a phase shift, the graph has the form of a cosine function that is reflected in the horizontal axis with $a < 0$. Since the stone is back on the ground after 4 s, the period of the function is 4 s.

Thus, $\frac{2\pi}{k} = 4$ and then $k = \frac{\pi}{2}$.

Parameter c is 14 in all alternatives. The cosine function with $a < 0$ and $k = \frac{\pi}{2}$ so alternative **D** is correct.

14. **C**

Changing the order of the last two terms in the expression gives

$\sin(7a)\cos(6a) - \cos(7a)\sin(6a)$,

which fits the form

$\sin x \cos y - \cos x \sin y$.

Since

$\sin x \cos y - \cos x \sin y = \sin(x - y)$,

then

$\sin(7a)\cos(6a) - \cos(7a)\sin(6a)$

$= \sin(7a - 6a)$

$= \sin(a)$.

15. **C**

The expression $\frac{\sin^2 x}{\sin^2 x - \cos^2 x}$ is undefined when $\sin^2 x - \cos^2 x = 0$. Rearranging the terms of this equation gives:

$\sin^2 x = \cos^2 x$

$\frac{\sin^2 x}{\cos^2 x} = 1$

$\tan^2 x = 1$

$\tan x = \pm 1$

In the interval $0 \le x \le 2\pi$, $\tan x = 1$ when $x = \frac{\pi}{4}$ or $\frac{5\pi}{4}$ and $\tan x = -1$ when $x = \frac{3\pi}{4}$ or $\frac{7\pi}{4}$.

16. **A**

Solving $\sin 2x = \cos x$ gives:

Replace $\sin 2x$ with $2\sin x \cos x$

$$2\sin x \cos x - \cos x = 0$$

Factor

$$\cos x(2\sin x - 1) = 0$$

$$\cos x = 0 \text{ or } 2\sin x - 1 = 0$$

$$\text{or } \sin x = \frac{1}{2}$$

OR2.

a) Since $0 \le x \le 2\pi$, then $0 \le 2x \le 4\pi$.

$$2\sin^2 2x - \sin 2x = 0$$

$$\sin 2x(2\sin 2x - 1) = 0$$

$$\sin 2x = 0 \text{ or } 2\sin 2x = 1$$

$$\sin 2x = \frac{1}{2}$$

$$2x = 0, \pi, 2\pi, 3\pi, 4\pi, \frac{\pi}{6}, \frac{5\pi}{6}, \frac{13\pi}{6}, \frac{17\pi}{6}$$

$$x = 0, \frac{\pi}{2}, \pi, \frac{3\pi}{2}, 2\pi, \frac{\pi}{12}, \frac{5\pi}{12}, \frac{13\pi}{12}, \frac{17\pi}{12}$$

b)

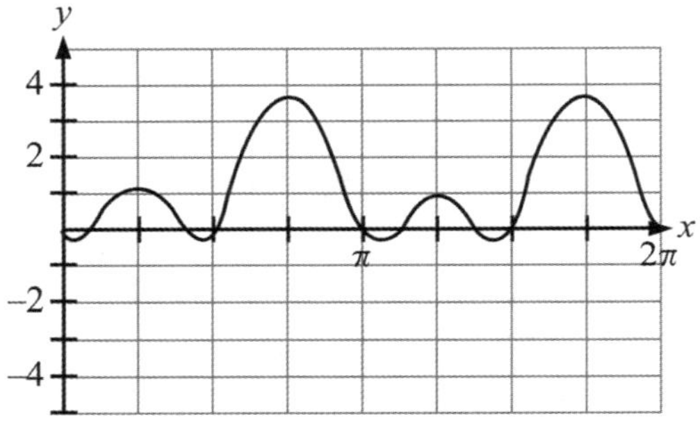

The graph shows 9 solutions, which is consistent with the algebraic solutions.

17. **C**

The domain of each of the four given graphs is $x \in R$. However, each of the graphs has a different range. The range of the polynomial function illustrated by the graphs in alternatives A, B, C, and D are $y \ge -3$, $y \ge 3$, $y \le 3$, and $y \in R$ respectively.

Thus, the correct alterative is **C**.

18. **D**

The statements given in alternatives A, B, and C are false for the following reasons respectively:

B the graph is tangent to the x-axis at $x = -4$

A the x-intercepts of the graph are -3 and -4

C the range of the graph is $y \in R$

19. **B**

Recall the roles of the parameters a, k, d, and c when the function $y = f(x)$ is transformed into a function of the form $y = a\,f(k(x-d)) + c$. When the graph of $y = f(x)$ is reflected in the x-axis, the equation of the transformed function is $y = -f(x)$ (parameter $a = -1$).

If this function is now translated 4 units vertically up, the resulting transformed function is $y = -f(x) + 4$ (parameter $c = 4$).

20. **D**

Since the stated polynomial function is of degree 6, consider only the functions given in alternatives C and D.

The graph of the function intersects the x-axis at 3, 2, and -2; therefore, the polynomial function must have the factors $x-3$, $x-2$, and $x+2$. These factors are present in the function defined by the equation in alternative **D**.

NR3. **3.5**

The graph of $y = \dfrac{1}{2x^2 - 7x + 3}$ does not exist for $2x^2 - 7x + 3 = 0$. The factored form of $2x^2 - 7x + 3$ is $(2x-1)(x-3)$.

Thus, the graph of $y = \dfrac{1}{2x^2 - 7x + 3}$ has vertical asymptotes at

$x = \dfrac{1}{2} = 0.5\left(2x - 1 = 0 \Rightarrow x = \dfrac{1}{2}\right)$ and $x = 3(x - 3 = 0 \Rightarrow x = 3)$.

Using technology, graph $y = \dfrac{1}{2x^2 - 7x + 3}$. It can be observed from the graph that as $x \to -\infty$, $y \to 0$, and as $x \to +\infty$, $y \to 0$.

Therefore, $y = 0$ is a horizontal asymptote. It follows that $a = 0.5$, $b = 3$ (the values of a and b could be reversed), and $c = 0$. The value of $a + b + c = 0.5 + 3 + 0 = 3.5$.

21. **B**

Observe from the graph that the equation of the vertical asymptote is $x = -3$ and that as $x \to -\infty$, $y \to 0$, and as $x \to +\infty$, $y \to 0$. Thus, the equation of the horizontal asymptote is $y = 0$.

The only function that satisfies the preceding conditions is given in alternative **B**.

Note: If $y = \dfrac{1}{x+3}$, then $x + 3 \neq 0$ or $x \neq -3$. Thus, $x = -3$ is a vertical asymptote.

22. **D**

If $x - a$ is a factor of $P(x)$, then $P(a) = 0$. In alternatives A, B, and C, $P(1) = 0$, $P(-1) = 0$, and $P(3) = 0$ respectively. However, in alternative **D**, $P(-3) \neq 0$, rather $P(-3) = 48$.

23. **A**

Using technology, graph $y = 2x^3 - 3x^2 - 5x + 6$. Observe that the given graph has exactly 3 x-intercepts.
Since the graph of $y = 2x^3 - 3x^2 - 5x + 6$ has 3 x-intercepts, the equation $2x^3 - 3x^2 - 5x + 6 = 0$ will have 3 real roots.

24. **B**

The factors of –9 are ±1, ±3, and ±9. Thus, the potential integral zeros of the function $f(x) = x^3 + 5x^2 + 3x - 9$ are ±1, ±3, and ±9. By substitution, it can be determined that $f(1) = 0$.
Applying the factor theorem, $x - 1$ is a factor of $f(x)$. Now, applying synthetic division, the second-degree factor of $f(x)$ can be determined as follows:

–1	1	5	3	–9
		–1	–6	–9
	1	6	9	0

The second-degree factor of $f(x)$ is $x^2 + 6x + 9$.
It follows that:

$f(x) = (x - 1)(x^2 + 6x + 9)$

$f(x) = (x - 1)(x + 3)^2$

Thus, the polynomial equation $x^3 + 5x^2 + 3x - 9 = 0$ can be written in factored form as $(x - 1)(x + 3)^2 = 0$.
Comparing the equation $(x - 1)(x + 3)^2 = 0$ with the equation $(x - m)(x - n)^2 = 0$ shows that $m = 1$ and $n = -3$. The value of $m + n = 1 + (-3) = -2$.

25. **D**

First, multiply each side of the given equation by $x - 4$.

$$(x-4)\times\frac{x^2 - 5x - 6}{x - 4} = (x-4)\times 0$$

Simplify: $x^2 - 5x - 6 = 0$.
This equation can now be solved as shown below.

$x^2 - 5x - 6 = 0$

$(x - 6)(x + 1) = 0$

$x - 6 = 0$ or $x + 1 = 0$

$x = 6$ or $x = -1$

OR **3.**

a) The Remainder Theorem states that if a polynomial function $P(x)$ is divided by $x-a$, then the remainder $R=P(a)$. When dividing by $x+1=x--1$, the value of $a=-1$. By the Remainder theorem $-12=P(-1)$. We can form and solve a system of two equations in two unknowns.

$$-12=P(-1)$$
$$-12=-2(-1)^3-A(-1)^2+B(-1)-6$$
$$-12=2-A-B-6$$
$$A+B=8$$

$$P(2)=12$$
$$-2(2)^3-A(2)^2+B(2)-6=12$$
$$-16-4A+2B-6=12$$
$$-4A+2B=34$$
$$-2A+B=17$$

If we multiply the first equation $A+B=8$ by 2 and add it to the second equation, we get

$$-2A+B=17$$
$$\underline{2A+2B=16}$$
$$0+3B=33$$
$$B=11$$

Substituting back into $A+B=8$ given $A+11=8$
$A=-3$
The values are $A=-3$ and $B=11$.

b) By the factor theorem if $x-3$ is a factor of $P(x)$ then $P(3)=0$.

$$P(x)=-2x^3+3x+11x-6$$
$$P(3)=-2(3)^3+3(3)^2+11(3)-6$$
$$=-54+27+33-6$$
$$=0$$

$\therefore\ x-3$ is a factor of $P(x)$

26. **B**

The graph of the rational function $f(x)=\dfrac{3x}{x-5}$ is shown.

<image> see solution hard copy

The solution to $\dfrac{3x}{x-5}\geq 0$ occurs whenever the graph intersects the x-axis or is above the x-axis.
This occurs for $x\leq 0$ or $x>5$.

27. **A**

From the graph of $f(x)=x^2-5x-6$, we can see that $f(x)<0$ occurs in the interval $-1<x<6$, where the graph is below the x-axis.

28. **A**

To determine which table represents a constant rate of change we use the ratio $\dfrac{y_2-y_1}{x_2-x_1}$, for each table.

For table A:

$$\frac{20-10}{5-3}=\frac{10}{2}=5$$
$$\frac{30-20}{7-5}=\frac{10}{2}=5$$
$$\frac{40-30}{9-7}=\frac{10}{2}=5$$

Since each ratio is equal, there is a constant rate of change.

For table B:

$$\frac{10-10}{5-3}=\frac{0}{2}=0$$
$$\frac{10-10}{7-5}=\frac{0}{2}=0$$

Whenever the rate of change of a quantity is zero, the corresponding graph is a horizontal line and there is no rate of change.

For table C:

$$\frac{25-9}{5-3}=\frac{16}{2}=8$$

$$\frac{49-25}{7-5}=\frac{24}{2}=12$$

For table D:

$$\frac{4-1}{5-3}=\frac{3}{2}=1.5$$

$$\frac{9-4}{7-5}=\frac{5}{2}=2.5$$

Since all tables were verified, the answer is alternative **A**.

29. **D**

Since Markus starts at the top of a hill, the graph begins above the origin on the vertical axis. As his speed increases, the graph curves upward until he reaches the bottom of the hill. At this point, the graph would begin to curve downward as his speed begins to decrease as he travels up the other hill.

30. **C**

The best approximation can be determined using the interval from 5.5 seconds to 6.3 seconds, which gives:

$$\frac{T_2-T_1}{t_2-t_1}=\frac{12-21}{6.3-5.5}=-11.25°\text{C/s}$$

Therefore, the answer is choice **C**.

31. **C**

The student could use a table of values and find the slopes of secant lines through the point $(2,10)$ and points that are near $(2,10)$, as the second point, x_2, gets closer and closer to $(2,10)$.

The average rate of change can be calculated by the slope formula,

$$m=\frac{y_2-y_1}{x_2-x_1}=\frac{f(x_2)-10}{x_2-2}.$$

Table One $(x_2<2)$		
x_2	$f(x_2)$	Slope of secant line $\frac{f(x_2)-10}{x_2-2}$
1.9	9.31	6.9
1.99	9.9301	6.99
1.999	9.993001	6.999

As x_2 approaches 2, the slope of the secant line approaches 7.

Table Two $(x_2>2)$		
x_2	$f(x_2)$	Slope of secant line $\frac{f(x_2)-10}{x_2-2}$
2.1	10.71	7.1
2.01	10.0701	7.01
2.001	10.007001	7.001

As x_2 approaches 2, the slope of the secant line approaches 7.

From the preceding tables, the student should determine that the approximate instantaneous rate of change of y with respect to x for the function $f(x)=x^2+3x$ at the point (2, 10) is 7.

32. **A**

This problem can be solved graphically, using technology, by graphing the function $h(x) = \dfrac{x^2 - x^2 + 4x}{x-1}$ and noting the interval(s) of increase. A general window to set as an initial guide is X:[–10, 10, 1] and Y:[–10,10,1].

Upon review, however, it is necessary to adjust the window to show any maximum and minimum points.

Do this by increasing the vertical range to Y:[–50, 50,10]. This window change is very important because upon inspection of the graph now, it is evident that the function is decreasing all the way to the vertical asymptote (at $x = 1$) on the interval $x < 1$. To the right of the vertical asymptote, the function decreases and then increases.

To determine the location of this behaviour change, determine the location of the minimum. This can also be done using technology. On a TI-83+, press [2nd] [CALC] 3 and then move the cursor to a point just left of the minimum, press [ENTER], move the cursor to a point just right of the minimum and then press [ENTER] twice. The location of the minimum is (2, 12). Therefore, the function is decreasing on $1 < x < 2$ and increasing on $x > 2$. Hence, alternative **A** is correct.

33. **D**

To evaluate $g(f(-4))$, first find $f(-4) = 1$. Then, determine $g(1) = 2$. Since $g(f(-4)) = g(1) = 2$, the correct answer is **D**.

34. **B**

Using technology, graph $y = \cos x$ and $y = -1$ on the same set of axes.

Note that the two graphs have one point of intersection in the domain $0 \le x \le 2\pi$.

Next, find $f(g(x))$. Since $g(x) = -3x - 4$, $f(g(x)) = f(-3x - 4) = \cos(-3x - 4)$.

Now, using technology, graph $y = \cos(-3x - 4)$ and $y = -1$ on the same set of axes. Note that these two graphs have three points of intersection in the domain $0 \le x \le 2\pi$.

Thus, the graphs of $y = \cos(-3x - 4)$ and $y = -1$ have two more points of intersection than the graphs of $y = \cos x$ and $y = -1$ in the domain $0 \le x \le 2\pi$.

NR4. **1.81**

Graphically solving an inequality begins in the same way as solving an equation. Graph the functions $y = \cos x$ and $y = x^2 - 4x + 3$ using a graphing calculator. Select a window setting that shows any and all points of intersection between the two curves. In this example, an appropriate window setting would be $X:[-5, 5, 1]$, $Y:[-5, 5, 1]$.

Note that these curves have two points of intersection at (0.663, 0.788) and (2.468, –0.781), which can be found by pressing [2nd] [CALC] on your TI-83+, then selecting option 5 and moving the cursor until it lies on one of the points of intersection, then press [ENTER].

Press [ENTER] two more times and the coordinates of the point are given. Repeat this procedure to find the second point of intersection.

However, you are required to find the interval that makes $y \cos x$ greater than $y = x^2 - 4x + 3$. In other words, it is necessary find the region in which the sinusoidal curve lies above the polynomial.

Observe that this happens between the two points of intersection. Thus, for values $0.663 < x < 2.468$, the inequality holds true. Since the solution is in the form $a < x < b$, the values of $b - a = 2.468 - 0.663 = 1.81$, to the nearest hundredth.

35. **A**

When given data and asked to determine a value that is not provided, finding a curve of best fit is often the place to start. You may need to perform more than one type of regression to assess which model gives the most accurate portrayal of the data. However, plotting the given points will help you decide which model(s) might be appropriate. This can be done by pressing [STAT] and then selecting option 1. Put the values for time in L1 and the values for Population in L2. Then, go to [2nd] [Y =] and select option 1. Press [ENTER] to turn on Plot 1. Clear out any equations from Y= and set an appropriate window (in this case $X:[0,20,2]$, $Y:[0,135000,10000]$ would be appropriate).

Then press [GRAPH] and the points should appear. In this graph, you should be able to clearly see 2 points, while the other 3 look very close to the x-axis and are therefore half missing. Looking at the path of the points, however, it is clear that the best regression model to begin with is an exponential one.

Before you do the regression, however, make sure the Diagnostics are ON so that the value of the correlation coefficient is given. This will indicate the accuracy of the regression model (the closer the value is to 1 or –1, the better the equation fits the data).

To do this, press [2nd] and then 0 and then the x^{-1} key. Scroll down to DiagnosticON. Press [ENTER] twice. When done correctly, your screen should say Done. Now, perform the exponential regression. Press [STAT] and move over to [CALC] and select option 0. Your screen should show ExpReg. Press the [VARS] key and shift to YVARS and select option 1 and then option 1 again. This will put the exponential regression equation into your Y= feature. Press [ENTER] and the equation and correlation coefficient should appear. Note that in this case, $r = 0.996\ 5$ which means that the data fits nearly perfectly to an exponential model. Now that this has been established, you can press graph and watch as the graph of the equation passes nearly through the centre of all 5 points in the data.

To determine when the population will reach 237 500, it is necessary to [GRAPH] $y = 237\ 500$ and find the point of intersection between that line and the curve you just graphed from the regression. At this point, it is important to change the window settings to include a y-value of 237 500. Change the window to

$X:[0,\ 20,\ 2]$, $Y:[0,\ 260000,\ 20000]$.

To find the point of intersection, press [2nd] [CALC] on your TI-83+, select option 5 and move the cursor until it lies on the point of intersection, then press [ENTER]. Press [ENTER] 2 more times and the coordinates of the point are given.

The coordinates of the point are (18.3, 237500). Therefore, the population will reach 237 500 after 18.3 min.

NOTES

NOTES

Data Tables

NOTES

DATA TABLES

The following information may be useful in writing an examination.

Graphing Calculator Window Format

$x:[x_{\min}, x_{\max}, x_{scl}]$

$y:[y_{\min}, y_{\max}, y_{scl}]$

Exponents, Logarithms, and Geometric Series

$A = P(1+i)^n$

$\log_a(m \times n) = \log_a m + \log_a n$

$\log_a\left(\frac{m}{n}\right) = \log_a m - \log_a n$

$\log_a m^n = n\log_a m$

$\log_b c = \frac{\log_a c}{\log_a b}$

Trigonometry

arc length $a = r\theta$

$\csc x = \frac{1}{\sin x}$

$\sec x = \frac{1}{\cos x}$

$\cot x = \frac{1}{\tan x}$

$\cot x = \frac{\cos x}{\tan x}$

$\tan x = \frac{\sin x}{\cos x}$

$\sin^2 x + \cos^2 x = 1$

$1 + \tan^2 x = \sec^2 x$

$1 + \cot^2 x = \csc^2 x$

$\sin(A+B) = \sin A\cos B + \cos A\sin B$

$\sin(A-B) = \sin A\cos B - \cos A\sin B$

$\cos(A+B) = \cos A\cos B - \sin A\sin B$

$\cos(A-B) = \cos A\cos B + \sin A\sin B$

$\sin(24) = 2\sin A\cos A$

$\cos(24) = \cos^2 A - \sin^2 A$

NOTES

RESOURCE INFORMATION *Order online at www.castlerockresearch.com*

SCHOOL ORDERS

Schools are eligible for an education discount. Contact Castle Rock Research Ontario for more information.

THE KEY Study Guides assist in preparing students for course assignments, unit tests, and final or provincial assessments.

THE KEY **Study Guides** – $29.95 each plus G.S.T.

SECONDARY	ELEMENTARY
Biology 12, University Prep (SBI4U)	Science 8
Canadian and World Politics 12, University Prep (CPW4U)	Math 7
Chemistry 12, University Prep (SCH4U)	Science 7
English 12, University Prep (ENG4U)	Language 6 Reading & Writing
English 12, College Prep (ENG4C)	Math 6
Math 12 Advanced Functions, University Prep (MHF4U)	Science 6
Math 12 Calculus and Vectors, University Prep (MCV4U)	Math 5
Math 12 Data Management, University Prep (MDM4U)	Science 5
Physics 12, University Prep (SPH4U)	Math 4
World History 12, University Prep (CHY4U)	Science 4
Biology 11, University Prep (SBI3U)	Language 3 Reading & Writing
Chemistry 11, University Prep (SCH3U)	Math 3
English 11, University Prep (ENG3U)	Science 3
Math 11, Foundations for College Mathematics (MBF3C)	
Math 11, Functions and Applications, U/C Prep (MCF3M)	
Math 11, Functions, University Prep (MCR3U)	
World History 11, University/College Prep (CHW3M)	
Canadian History 10, Academic (CHC2D)	
Canadian History 10, Applied (CHC2P)	
Civics 10, (CHV2O)	
English 10, Academic (ENG2D)	
Math 10, Academic, Principles of Mathematics (MPM2D)	
Math 10, Applied, Foundations of Mathematics (MFM2P)	
OSSLT, Ontario Secondary School Literacy Test	
Science 10, Academic (SNC2D)	
English 9, Academic (ENG1D)	
Geography of Canada 9, Academic (CGC1D)	
Math 9, Academic, Principles of Mathematics (MPM1D)	
Math 9, Applied, Foundations of Mathematics (MFM1P)	
Science 9, Academic (SNC1D)	

The **Student Notes and Problems (SNAP)** workbooks provide complete lessons for course expectations, detailed explanations of concepts, and exercises with complete solutions.

SNAP Workbooks – $29.95 each plus G.S.T.

SECONDARY
Physics 12, University Preparation (SPH4U)
Physics 11, University Preparation (SPH3U)
Math 10, Academic, Principles of Mathematics (MPM2D)
Math 9, Academic, Principles of Mathematics (MPM1D)
Math 9, Applied, Foundations of Mathematics (MFM1P)

Visit our website for a tour of resource content and features or order online at
www.castlerockresearch.com

5250 Satellite Drive, Unit 11
Mississauga, ON L4W 5G5
E-mail: Ontario@castlerockresearch.com

Phone: 905.625.3332
Fax: 905.625.3390

CASTLE ROCK
RESEARCH CORP